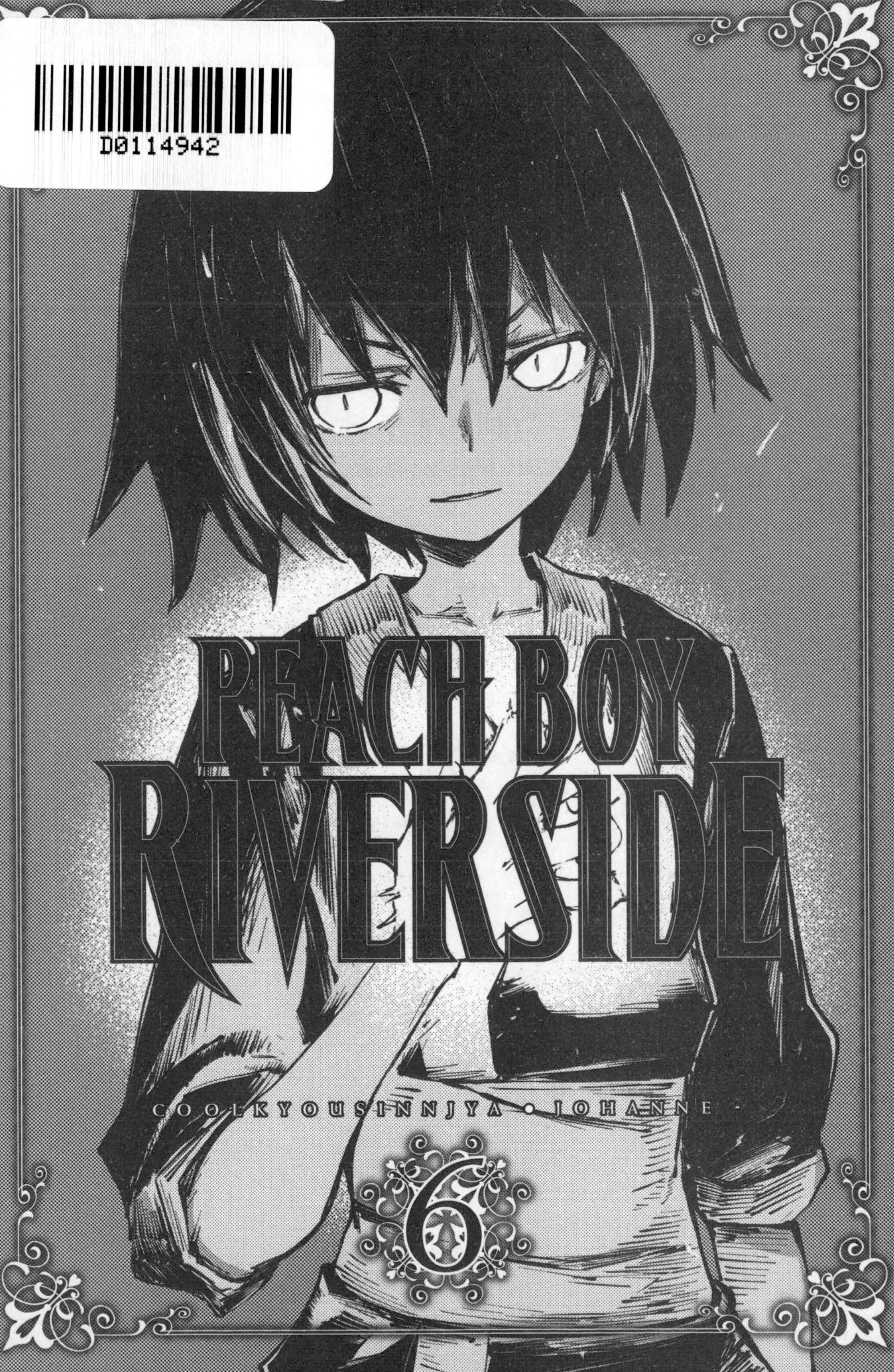
PEACH BOY
RIVERSIDE
COOLKYOUSINNJYA • JOHANNE
6

CONTENTS

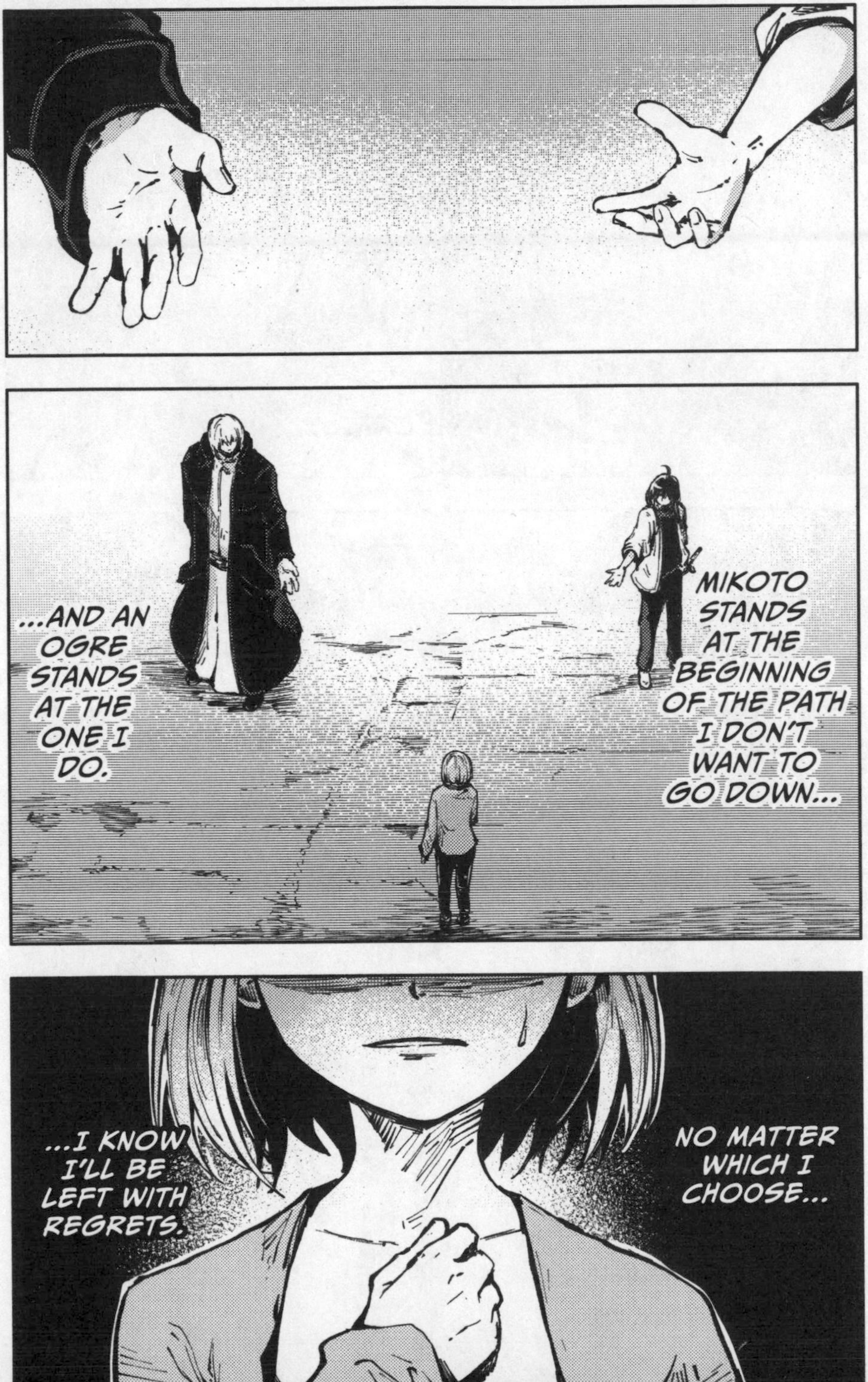
MIKOTO STANDS AT THE BEGINNING OF THE PATH I DON'T WANT TO GO DOWN...
...AND AN OGRE STANDS AT THE ONE I DO.
NO MATTER WHICH I CHOOSE...
...I KNOW I'LL BE LEFT WITH REGRETS.

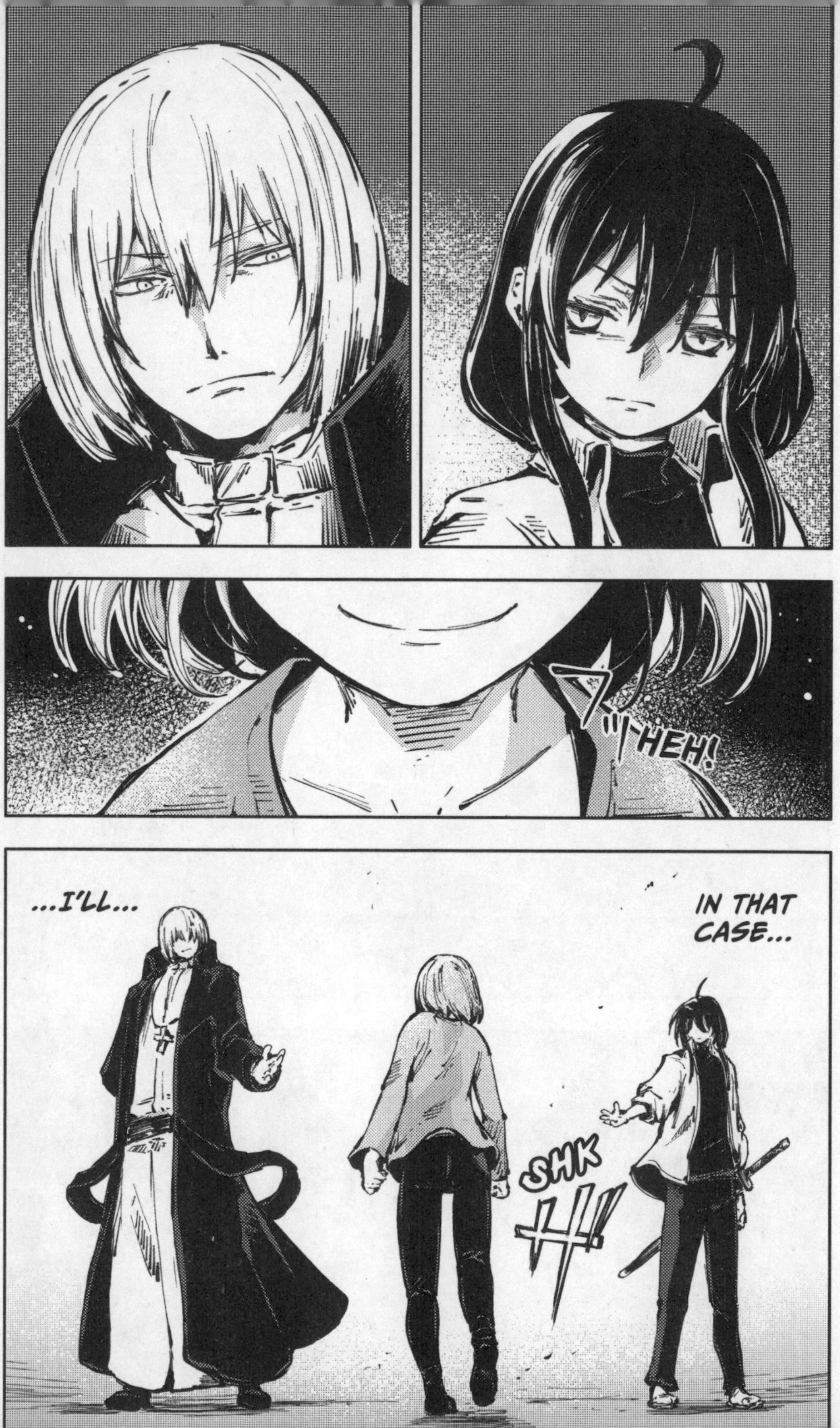
HEH!
IN THAT CASE...
...I'LL...
SHK

CHAPTER 20: THE HAND TAKEN AND THE ONE NOT TAKEN

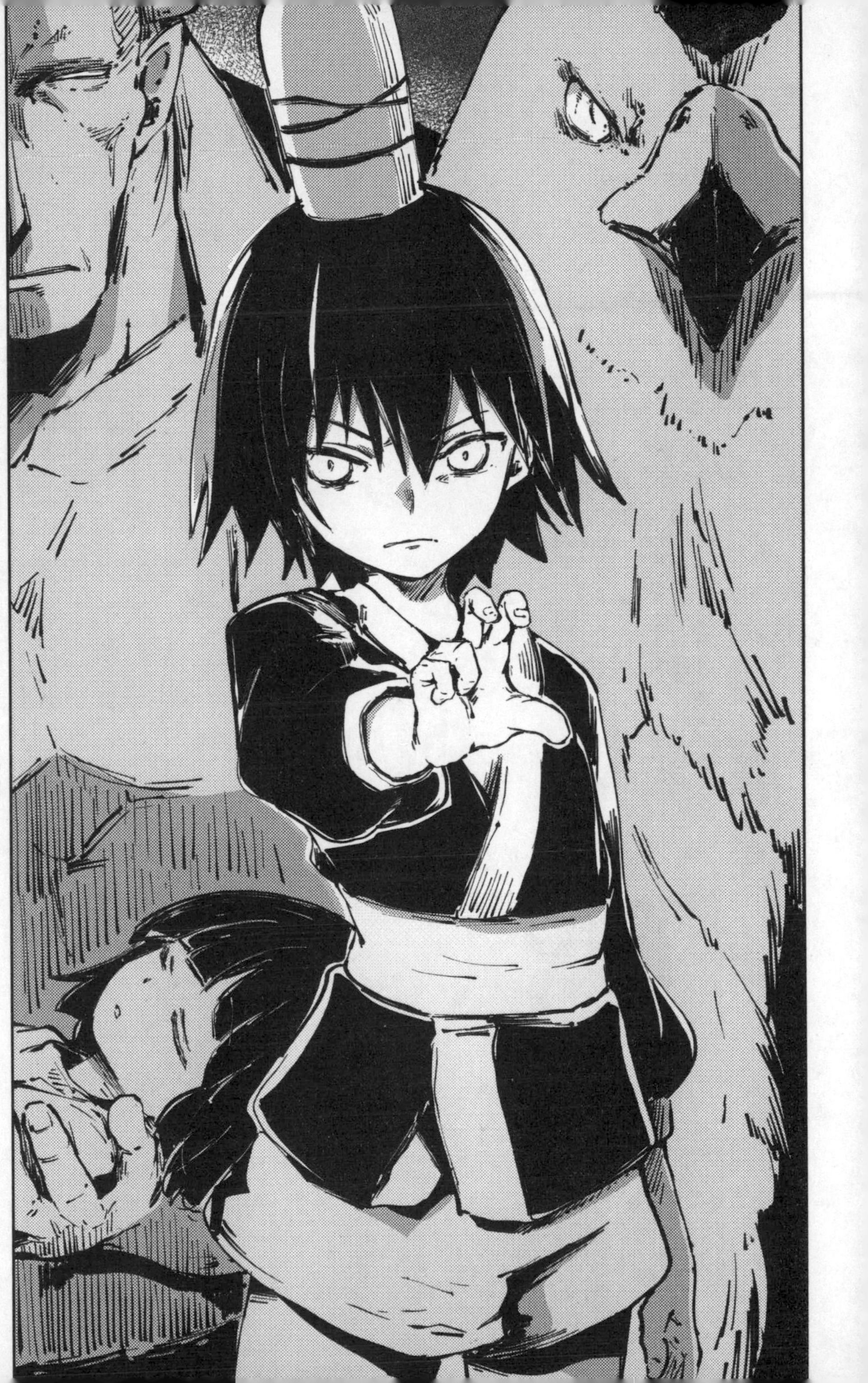

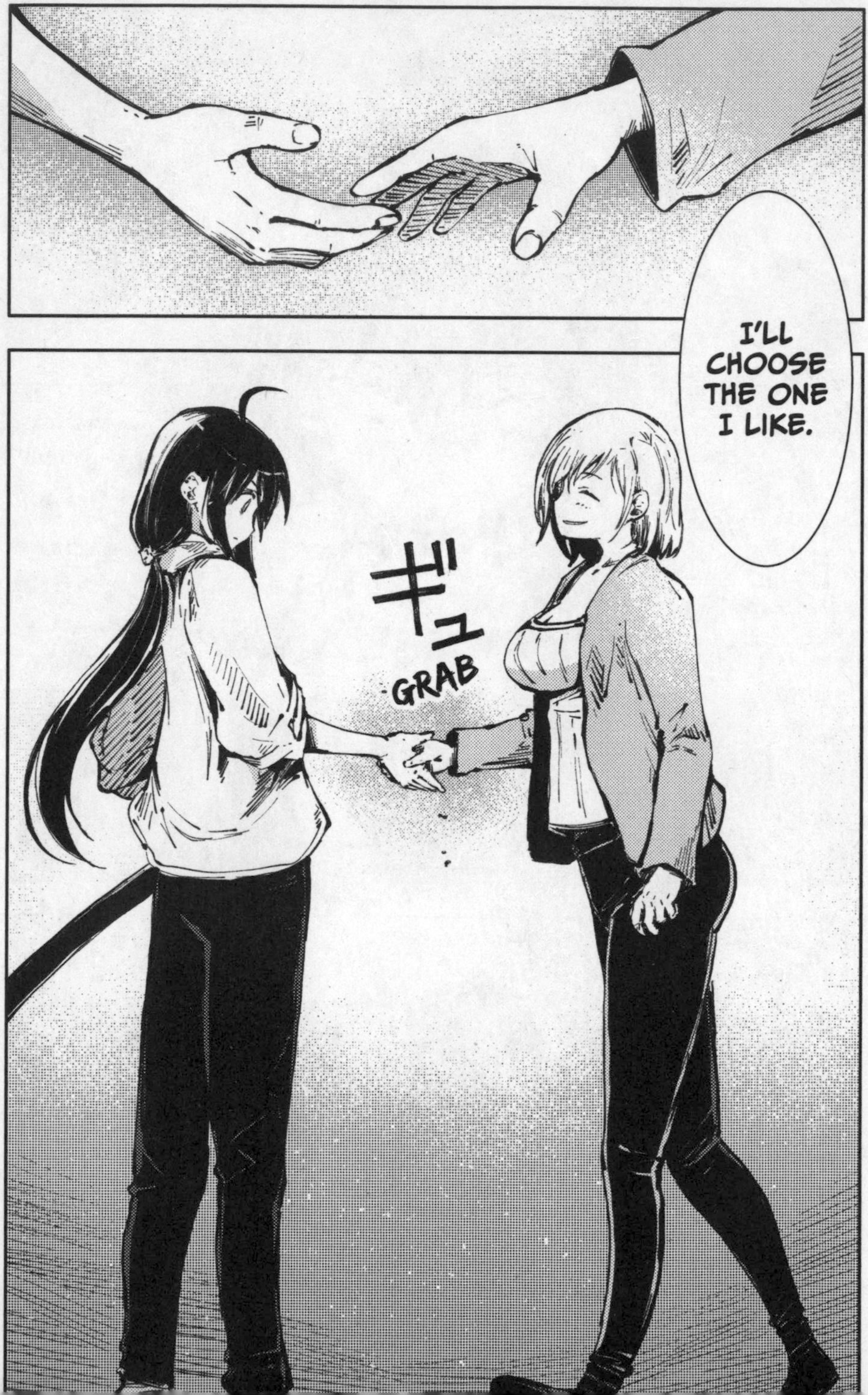
I'LL CHOOSE THE ONE I LIKE.
ギュ
GRAB

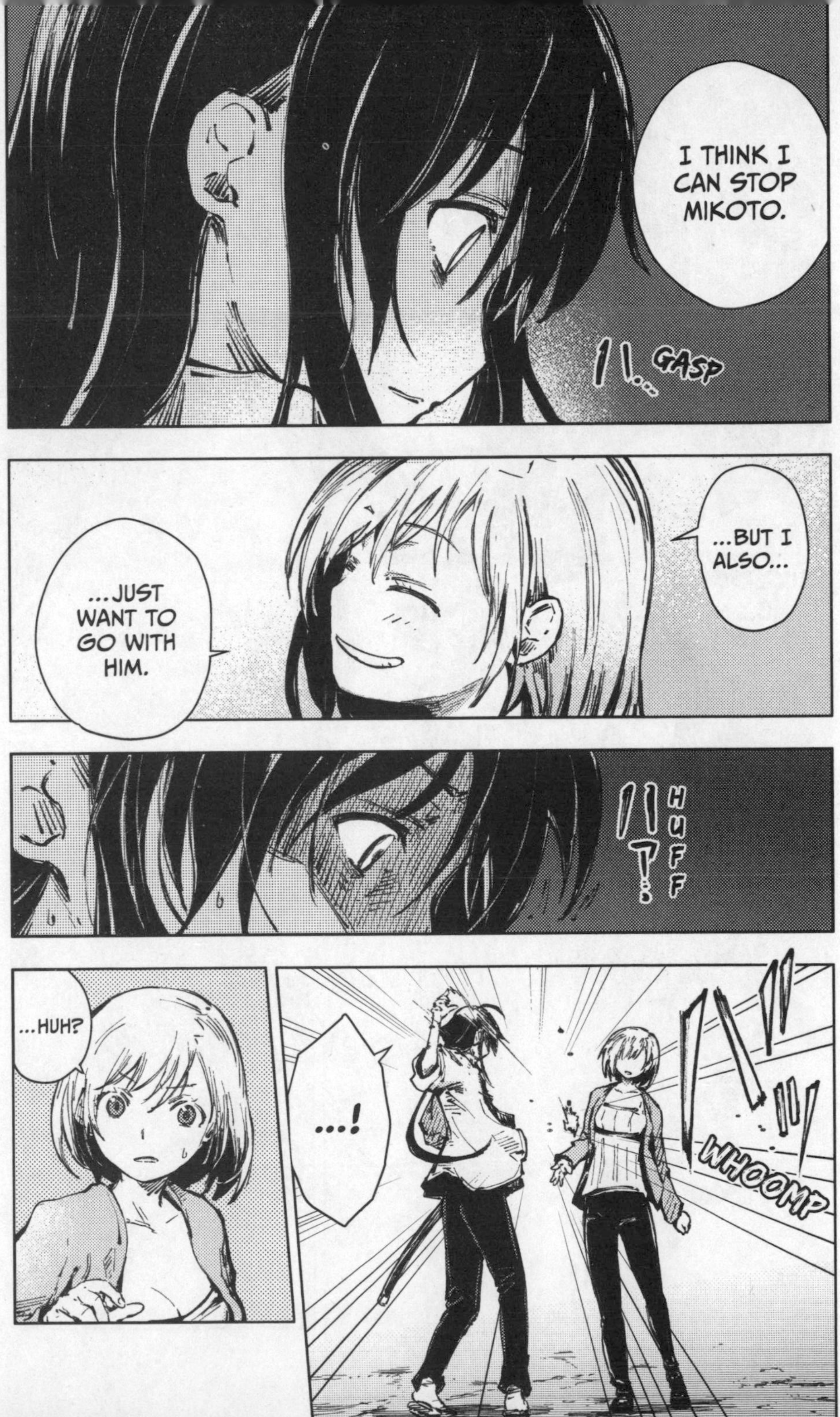
I THINK I CAN STOP MIKOTO.
GASP
...BUT I ALSO...
...JUST WANT TO GO WITH HIM.
HUFF
WHOOMP
...!
...HUH?

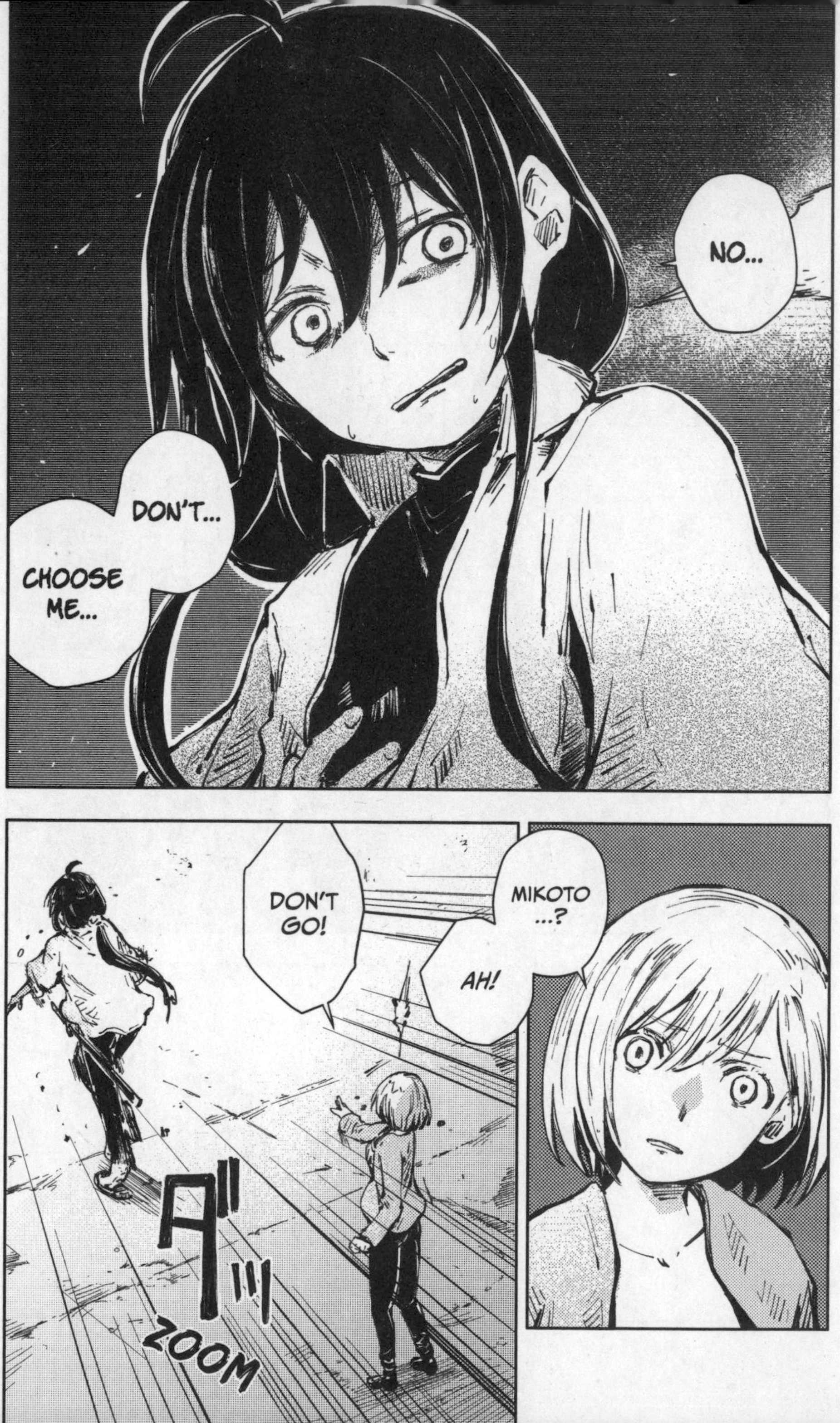
NO...
DON'T...
CHOOSE ME...
MIKOTO ...?
DON'T GO!
AH!
ZOOM

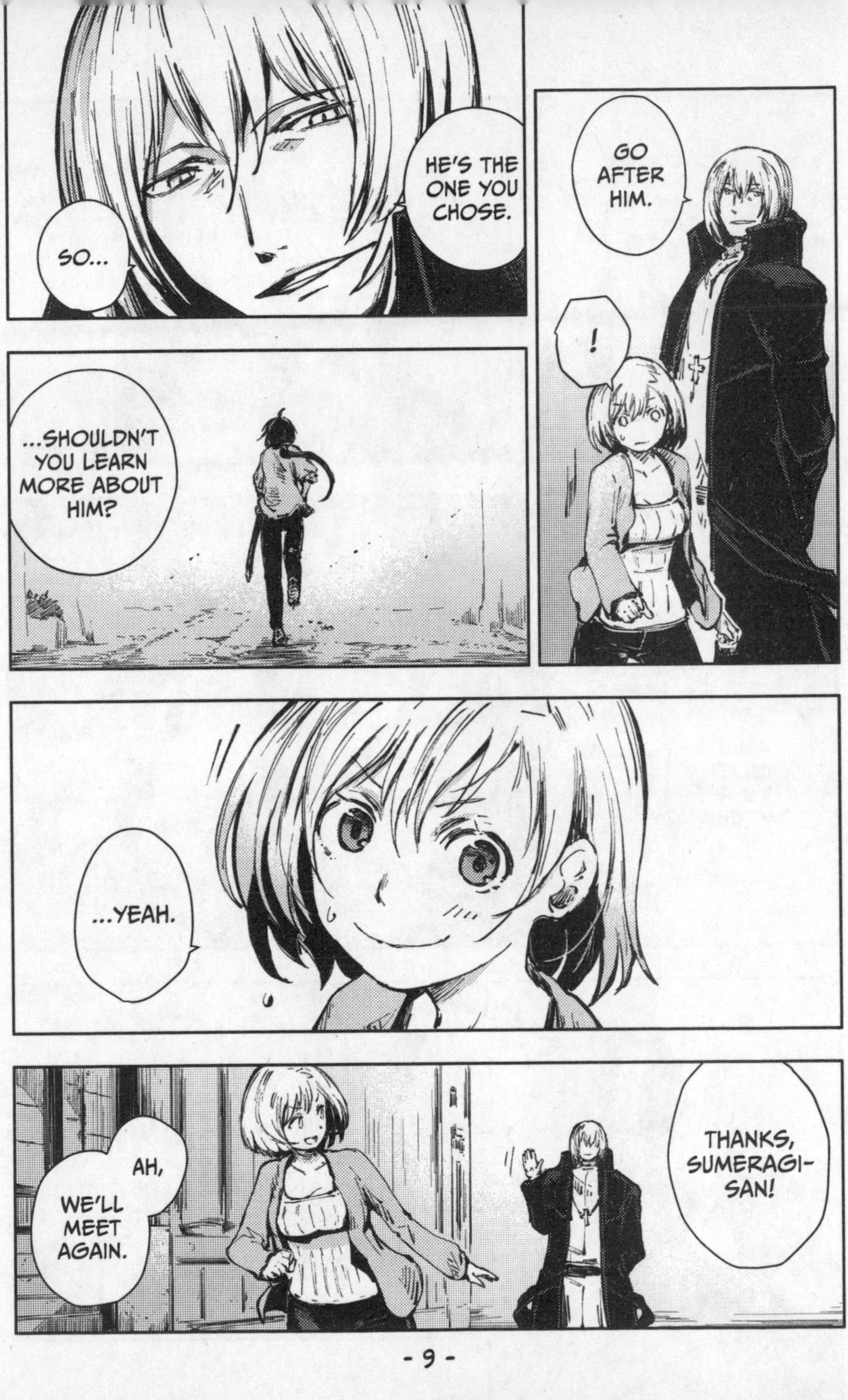
HE'S THE ONE YOU CHOSE.
SO...
...SHOULDN'T YOU LEARN MORE ABOUT HIM?
GO AFTER HIM.
!
...YEAH.
THANKS, SUMERAGI-SAN!
AH, WE'LL MEET AGAIN.

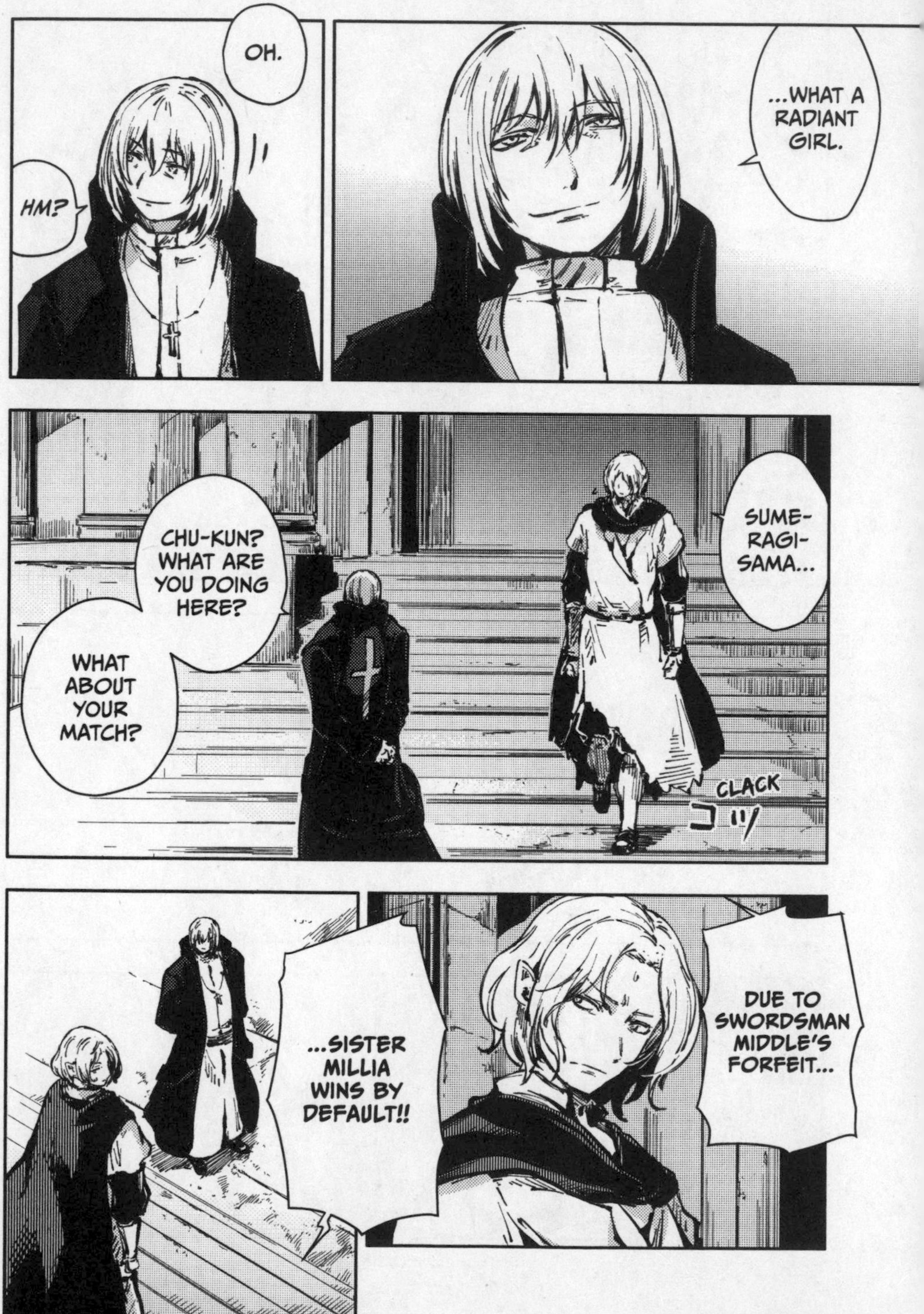
...WHAT A RADIANT GIRL.
OH.
HM?
SUME-RAGI-SAMA...
CLACK
コッ
CHU-KUN? WHAT ARE YOU DOING HERE?
WHAT ABOUT YOUR MATCH?
DUE TO SWORDSMAN MIDDLE'S FORFEIT...
...SISTER MILLIA WINS BY DEFAULT!!

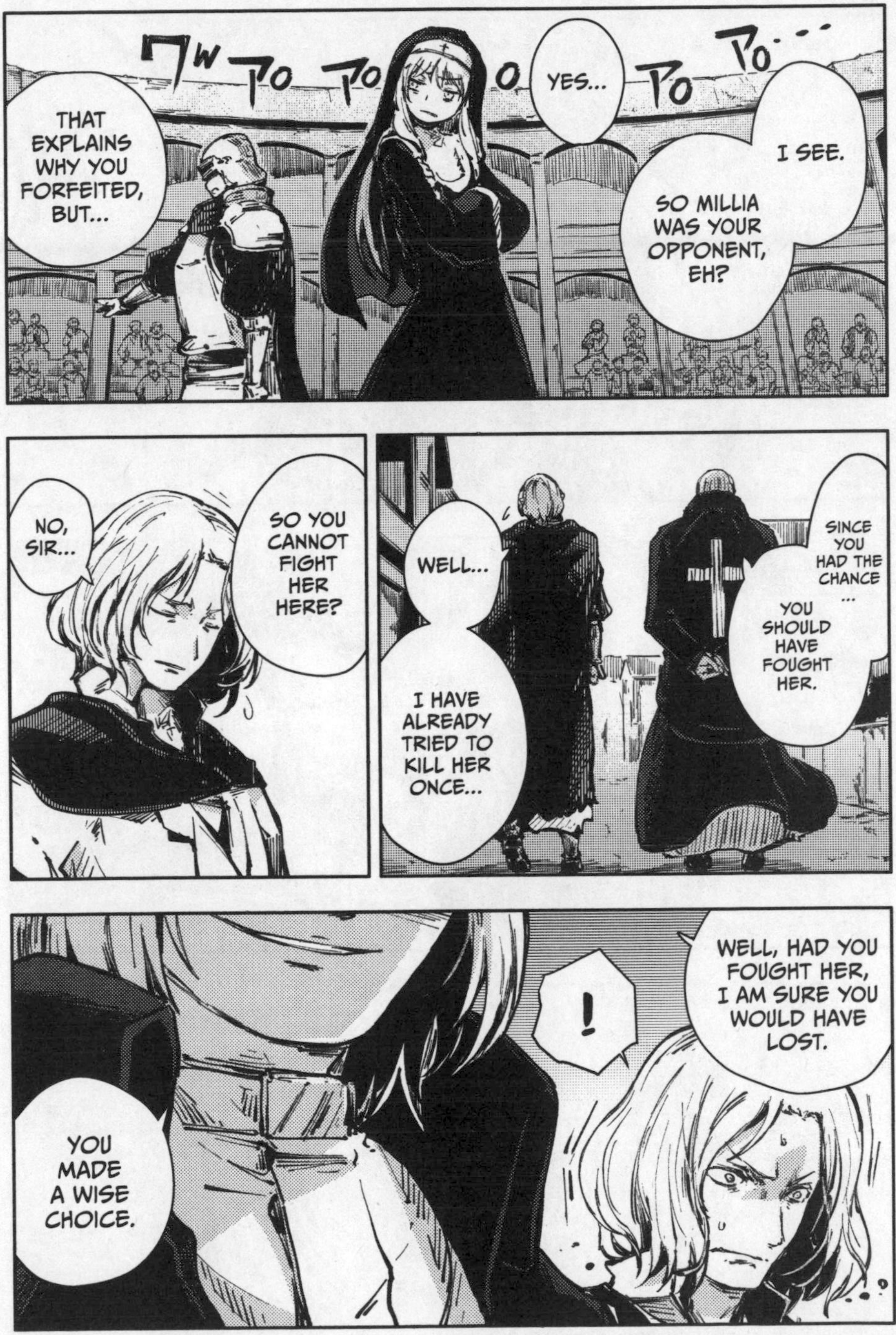
I SEE.
SO MILLIA WAS YOUR OPPONENT, EH?
YES...
THAT EXPLAINS WHY YOU FORFEITED, BUT...
SINCE YOU HAD THE CHANCE ...
YOU SHOULD HAVE FOUGHT HER.
WELL...
I HAVE ALREADY TRIED TO KILL HER ONCE...
SO YOU CANNOT FIGHT HER HERE?
NO, SIR...
WELL, HAD YOU FOUGHT HER, I AM SURE YOU WOULD HAVE LOST.
!
YOU MADE A WISE CHOICE.

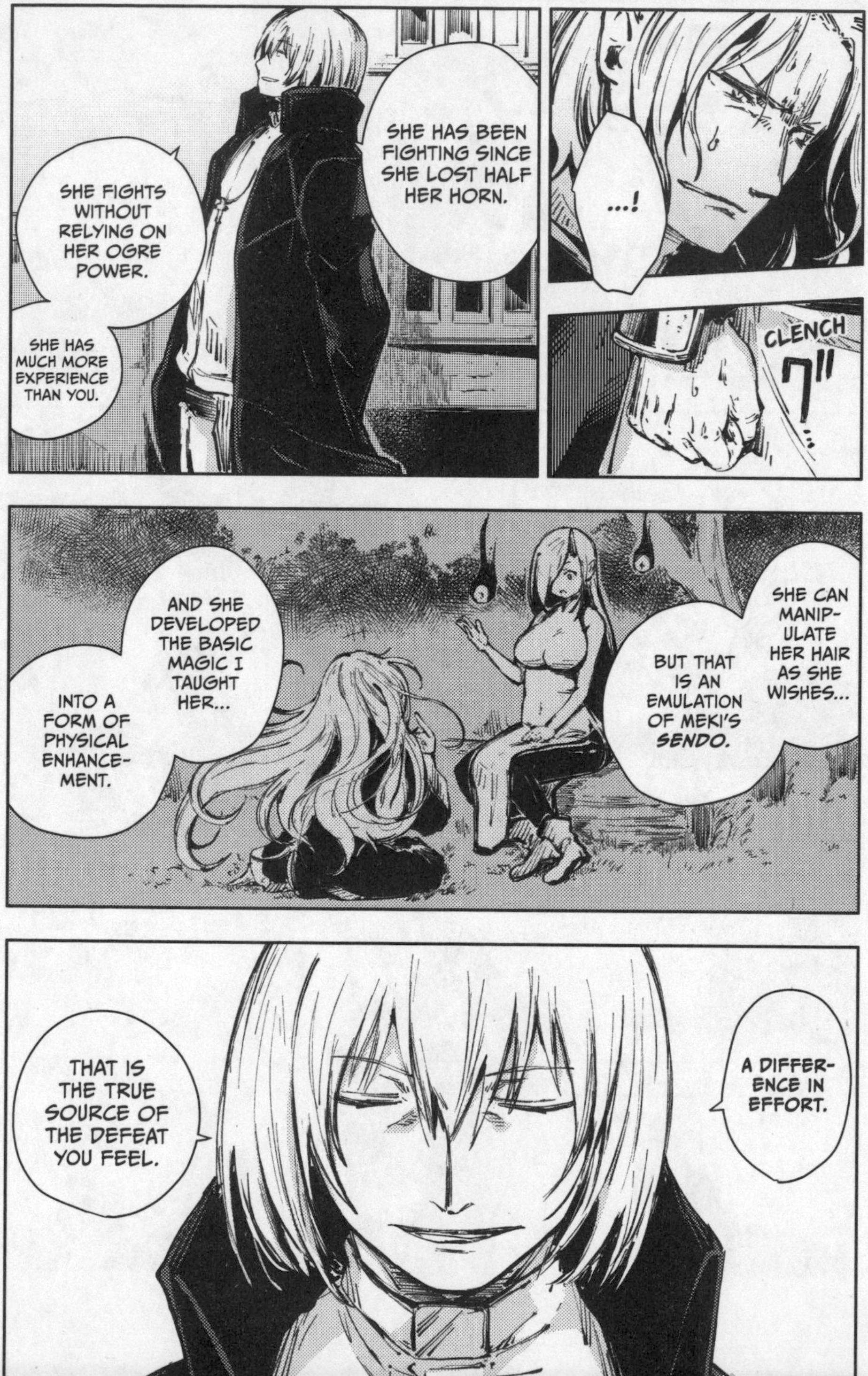
...!
CLENCH
SHE HAS BEEN FIGHTING SINCE SHE LOST HALF HER HORN.
SHE FIGHTS WITHOUT RELYING ON HER OGRE POWER.
SHE HAS MUCH MORE EXPERIENCE THAN YOU.
SHE CAN MANIPULATE HER HAIR AS SHE WISHES...
BUT THAT IS AN EMULATION OF MEKI'S *SENDO*.
AND SHE DEVELOPED THE BASIC MAGIC I TAUGHT HER...
INTO A FORM OF PHYSICAL ENHANCEMENT.
A DIFFERENCE IN EFFORT.
THAT IS THE TRUE SOURCE OF THE DEFEAT YOU FEEL.

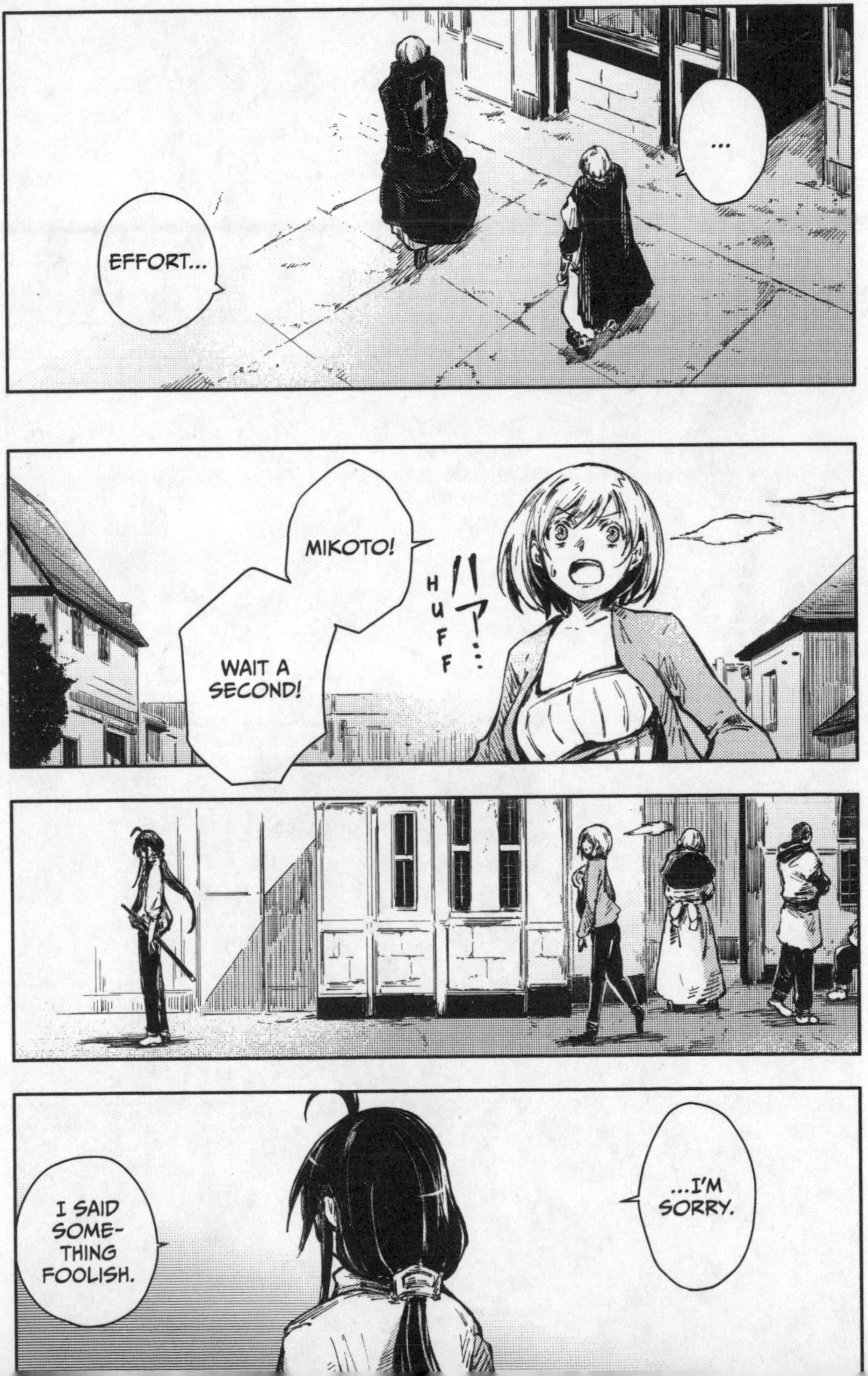
...
EFFORT...
ハァ…
HUFF
MIKOTO!
WAIT A SECOND!
...I'M SORRY.
I SAID SOMETHING FOOLISH.

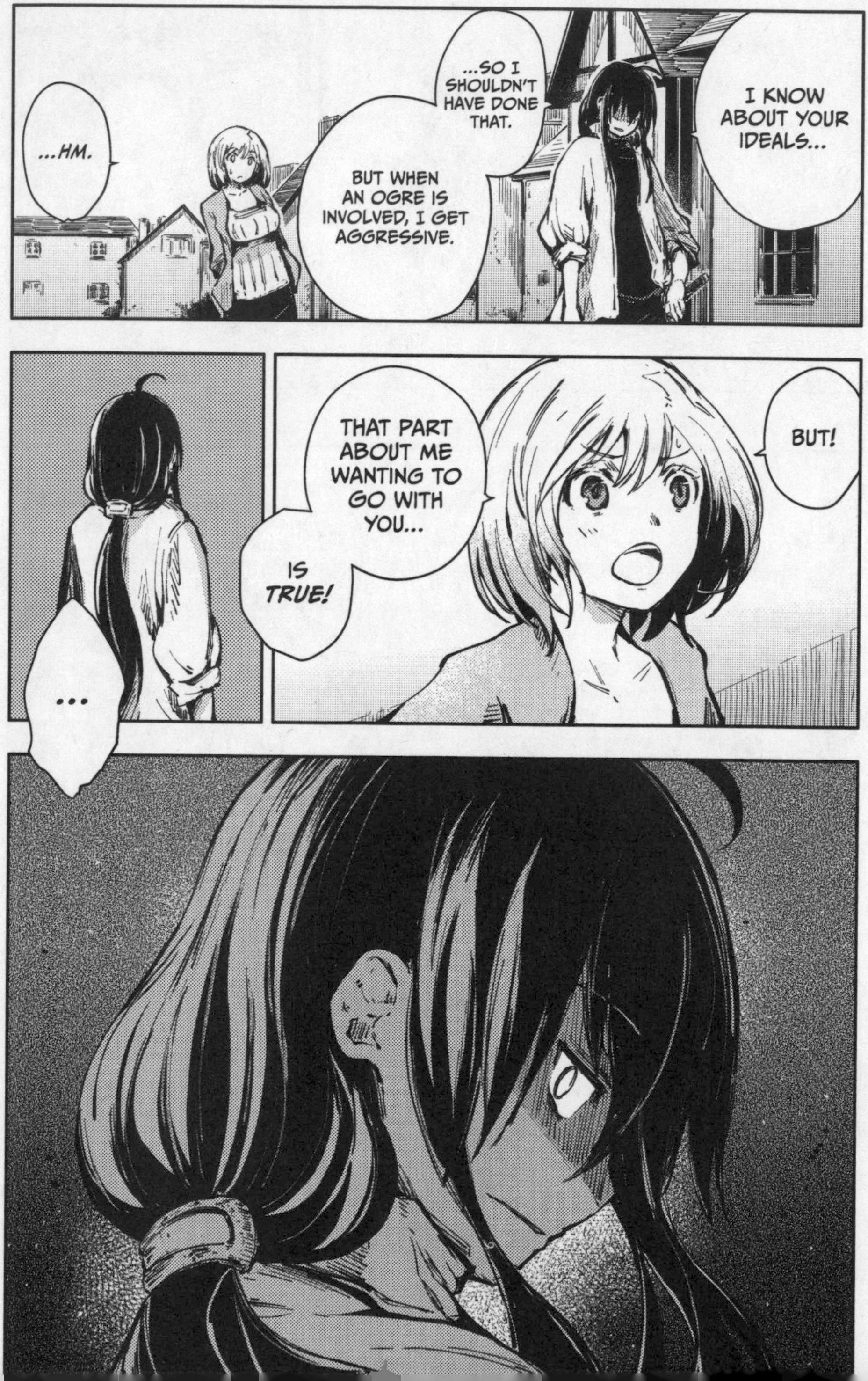
I KNOW ABOUT YOUR IDEALS...
...SO I SHOULDN'T HAVE DONE THAT.
BUT WHEN AN OGRE IS INVOLVED, I GET AGGRESSIVE.
...HM.
BUT!
THAT PART ABOUT ME WANTING TO GO WITH YOU...
IS *TRUE!*
...

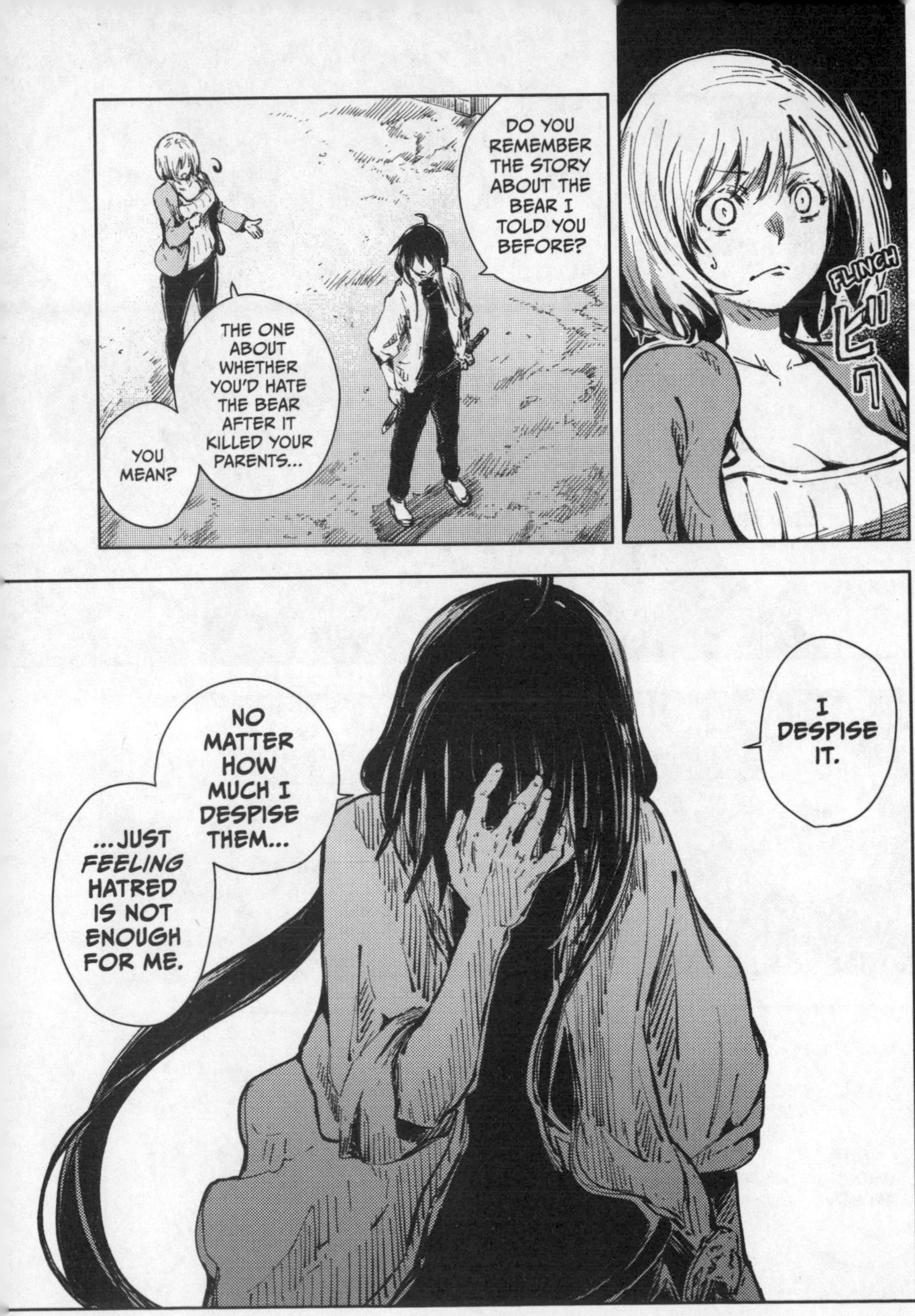

FLINCH
DO YOU REMEMBER THE STORY ABOUT THE BEAR I TOLD YOU BEFORE?
THE ONE ABOUT WHETHER YOU'D HATE THE BEAR AFTER IT KILLED YOUR PARENTS...
YOU MEAN?
I DESPISE IT.
NO MATTER HOW MUCH I DESPISE THEM...
...JUST *FEELING* HATRED IS NOT ENOUGH FOR ME.

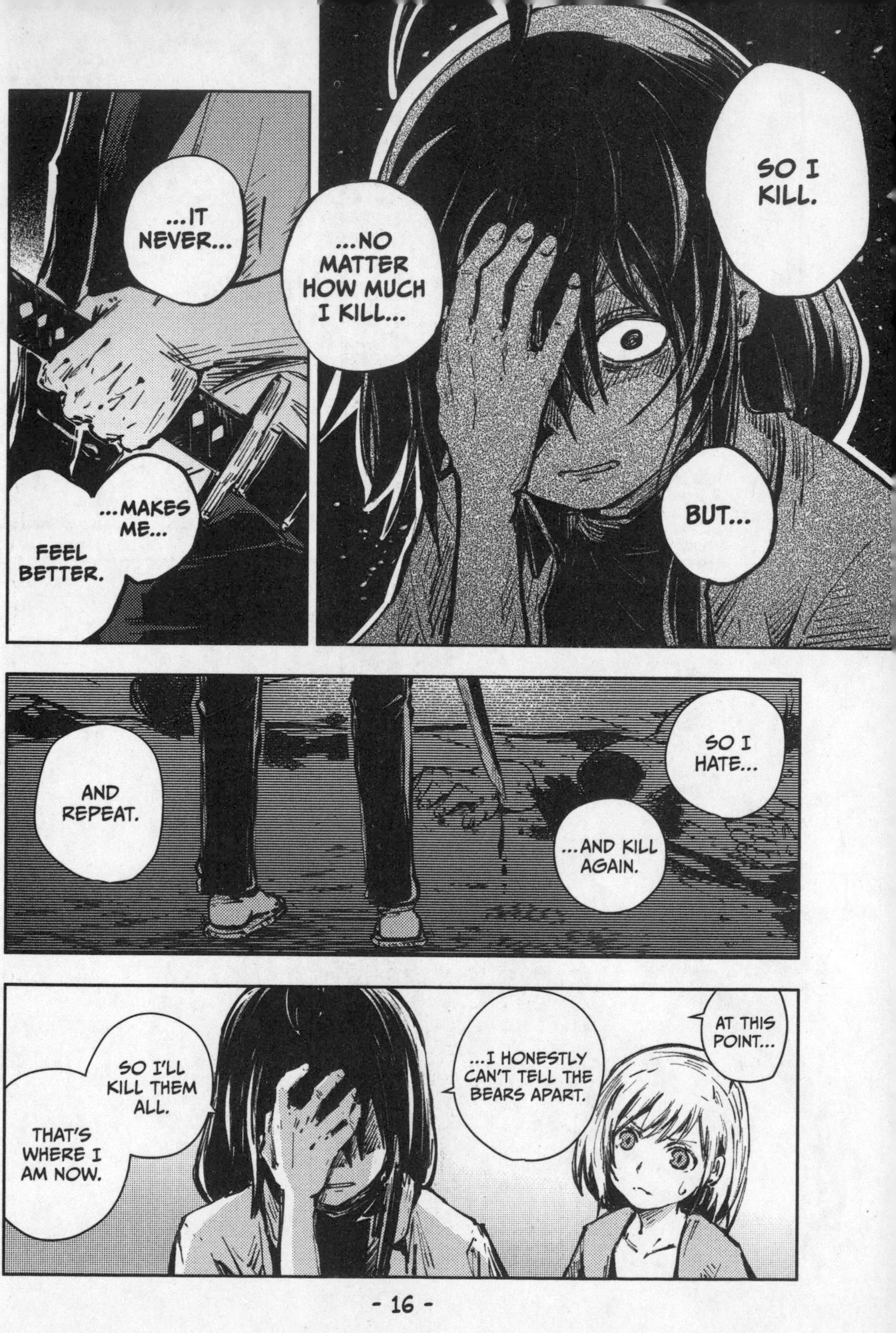
SO I KILL.
BUT...
...NO MATTER HOW MUCH I KILL...
...IT NEVER...
...MAKES ME...
FEEL BETTER.
SO I HATE...
...AND KILL AGAIN.
AND REPEAT.
AT THIS POINT...
...I HONESTLY CAN'T TELL THE BEARS APART.
SO I'LL KILL THEM ALL.
THAT'S WHERE I AM NOW.

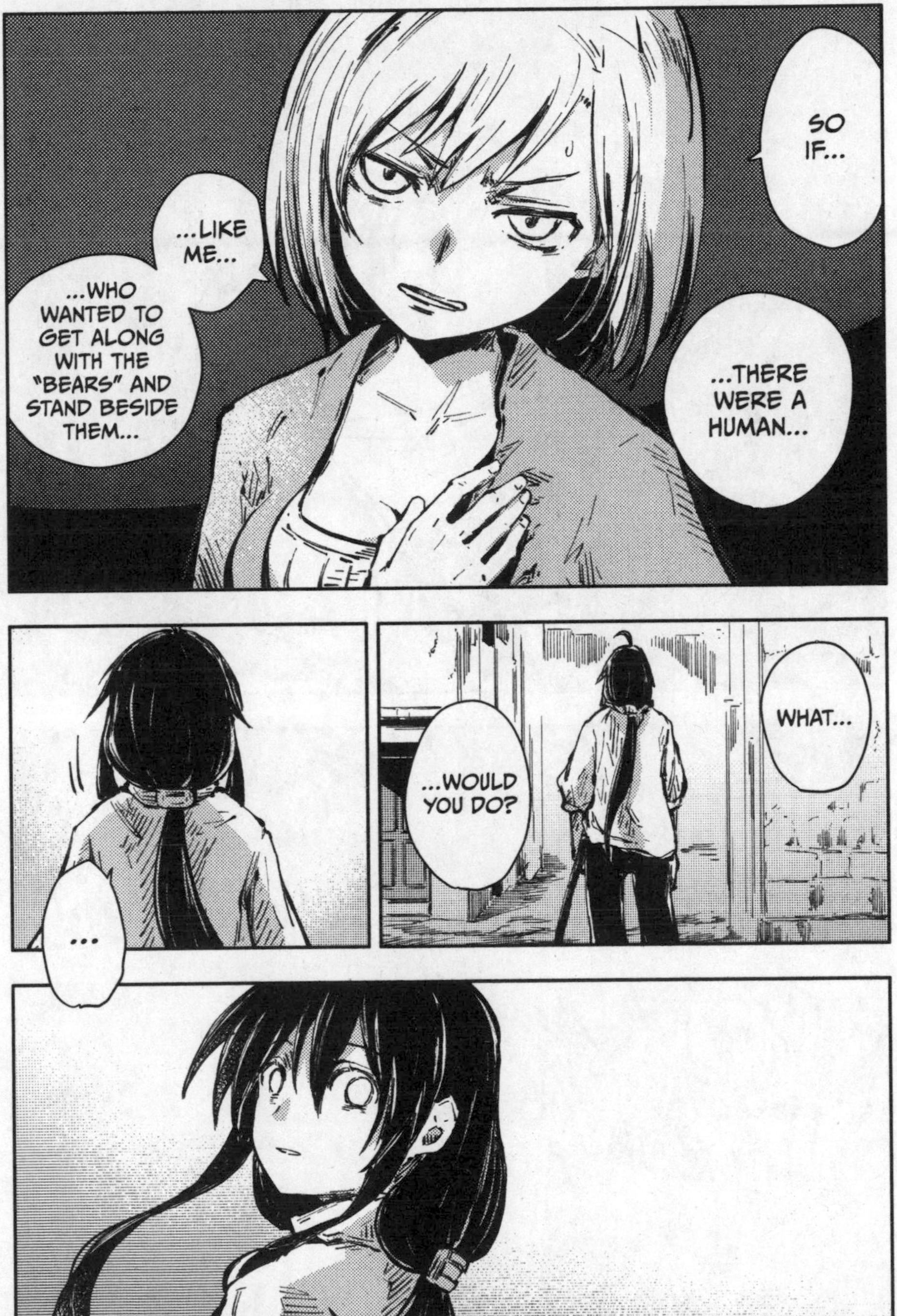
SO IF...
...THERE WERE A HUMAN...
...LIKE ME...
...WHO WANTED TO GET ALONG WITH THE "BEARS" AND STAND BESIDE THEM...
WHAT...
...WOULD YOU DO?
...

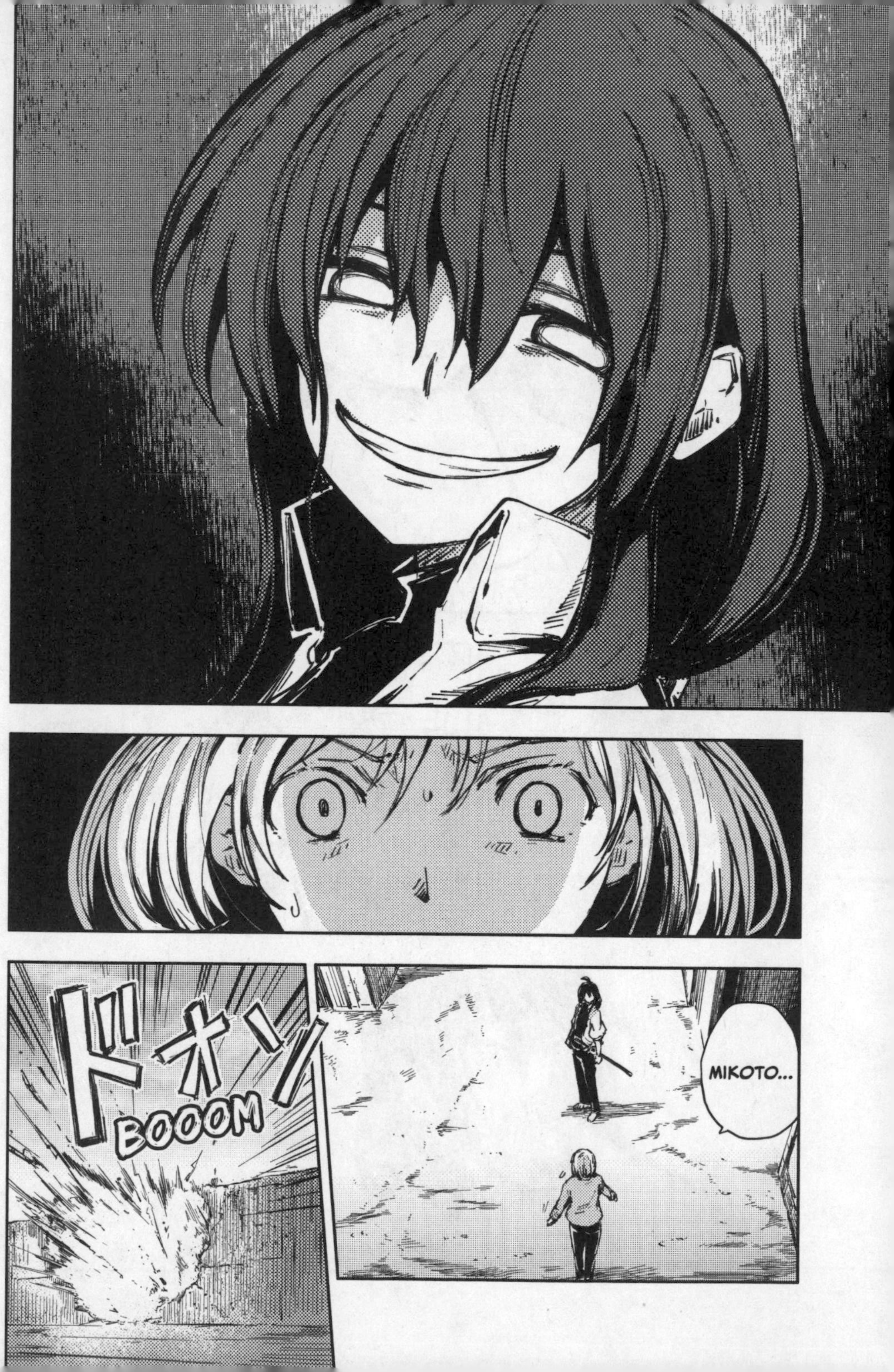
MIKOTO...
ドオン
BOOOM

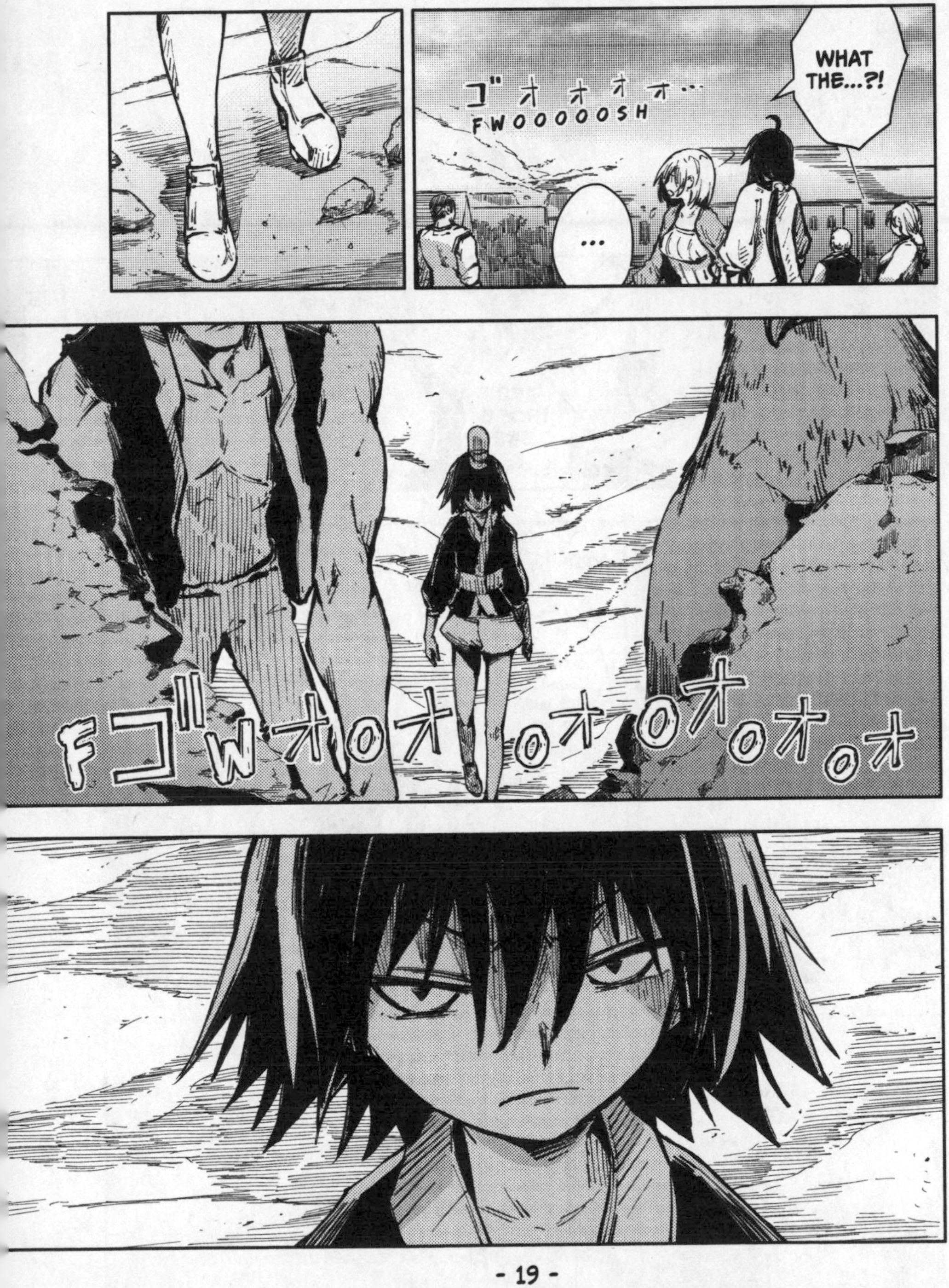
WHAT THE...?!
ゴオオオオ‥
FWOOOOOSH
...
FゴWオOオOオOオOオ

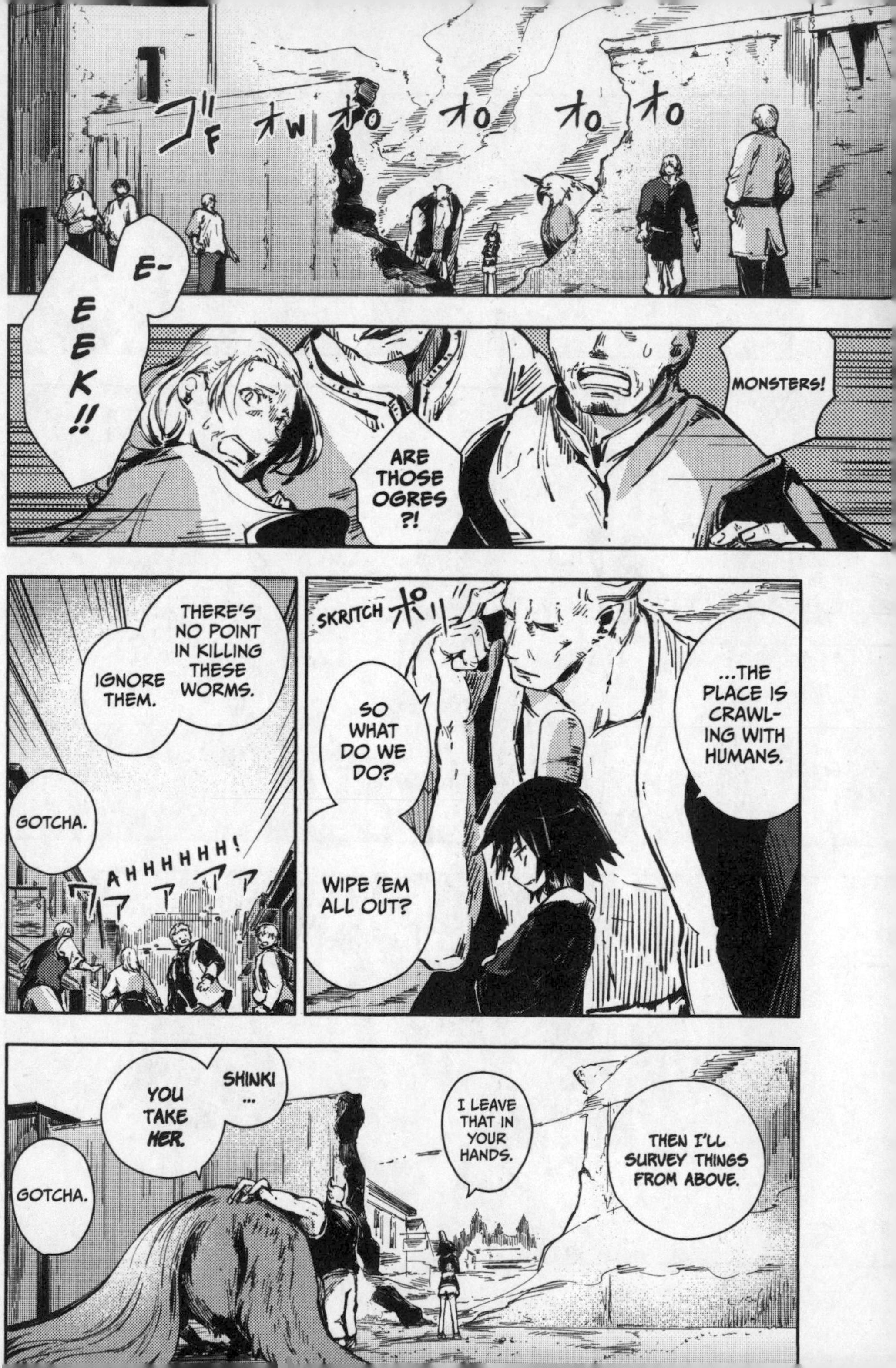
ゴF オW オO オO オO オ
E-EEEK!!
MONSTERS!
ARE THOSE OGRES?!
SKRITCH ポリ
...THE PLACE IS CRAWLING WITH HUMANS.
SO WHAT DO WE DO?
WIPE 'EM ALL OUT?
THERE'S NO POINT IN KILLING THESE WORMS.
IGNORE THEM.
GOTCHA.
AHHHHHHH! ワアアアア
THEN I'LL SURVEY THINGS FROM ABOVE.
I LEAVE THAT IN YOUR HANDS.
SHINKI...
YOU TAKE *HER*.
GOTCHA.

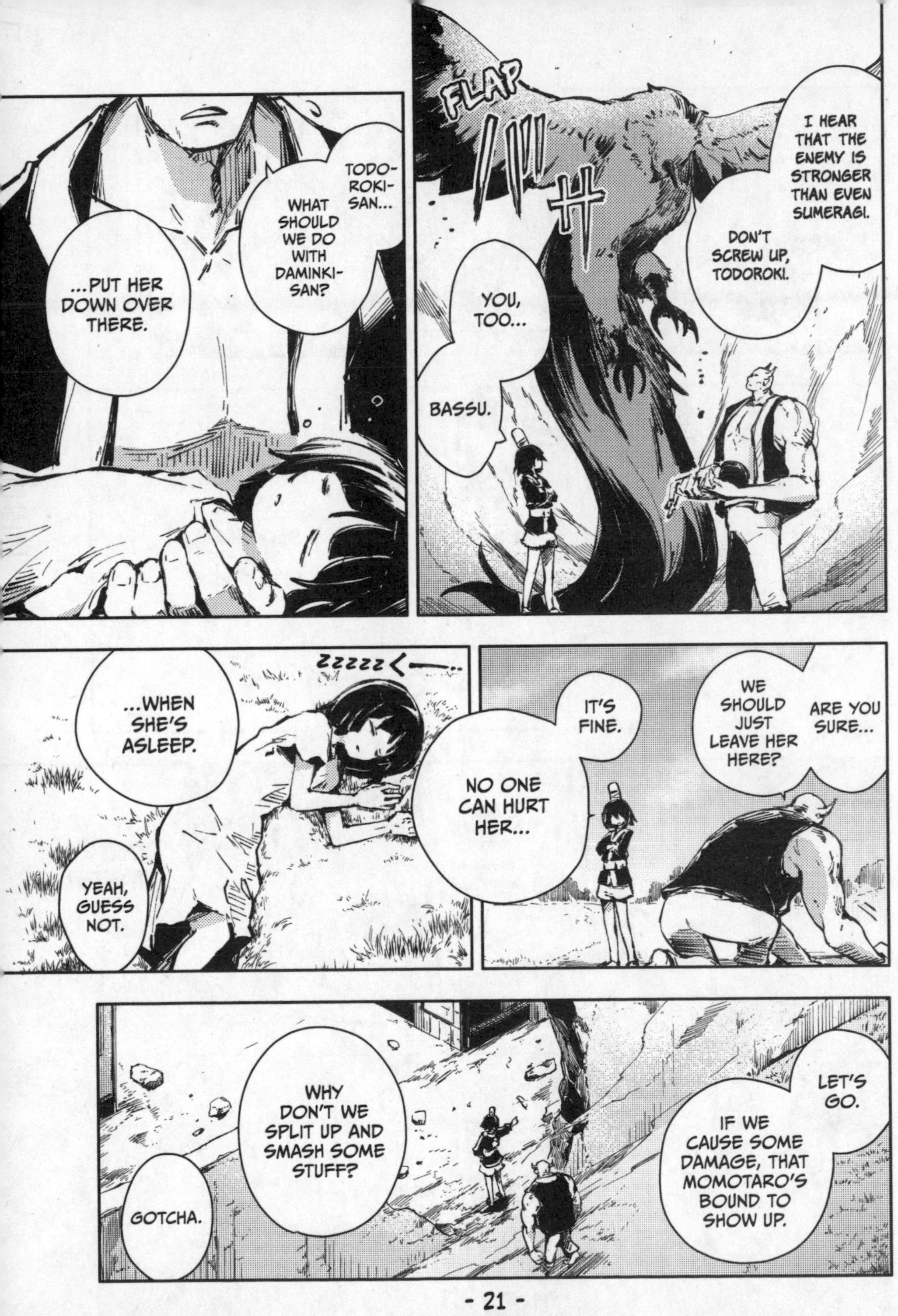
FLAP
I HEAR THAT THE ENEMY IS STRONGER THAN EVEN SUMERAGI.
DON'T SCREW UP, TODOROKI.
YOU, TOO...
BASSU.
TODOROKI-SAN...
WHAT SHOULD WE DO WITH DAMINKI-SAN?
...PUT HER DOWN OVER THERE.
ARE YOU SURE...
WE SHOULD JUST LEAVE HER HERE?
IT'S FINE.
NO ONE CAN HURT HER...
ZZZZZ
...WHEN SHE'S ASLEEP.
YEAH, GUESS NOT.
LET'S GO.
IF WE CAUSE SOME DAMAGE, THAT MOMOTARO'S BOUND TO SHOW UP.
WHY DON'T WE SPLIT UP AND SMASH SOME STUFF?
GOTCHA.

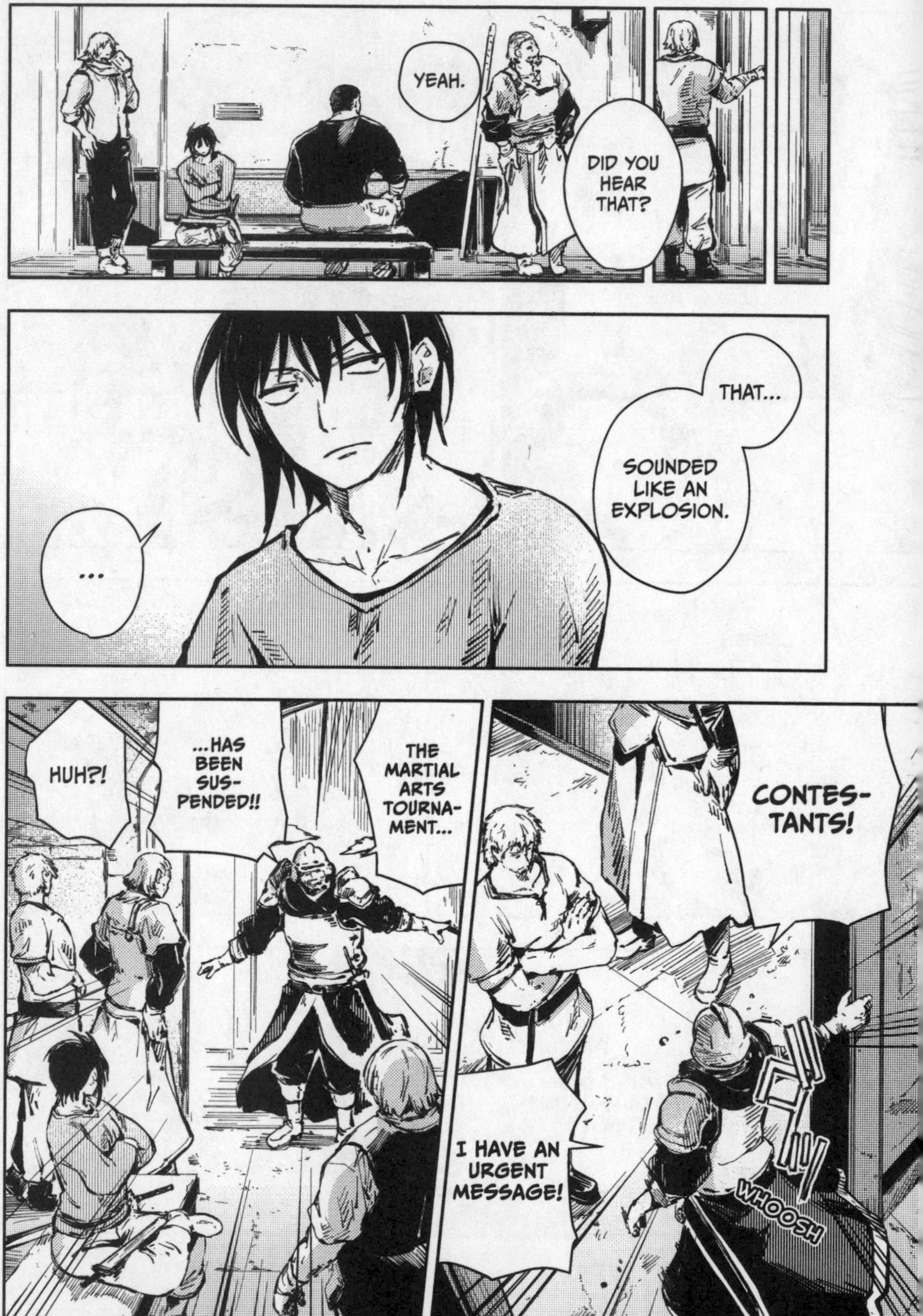
DID YOU HEAR THAT?
YEAH.
THAT...
SOUNDED LIKE AN EXPLOSION.
...
CONTES-TANTS!
I HAVE AN URGENT MESSAGE!
WHOOSH
THE MARTIAL ARTS TOURNA-MENT...
...HAS BEEN SUS-PENDED!!
HUH?!

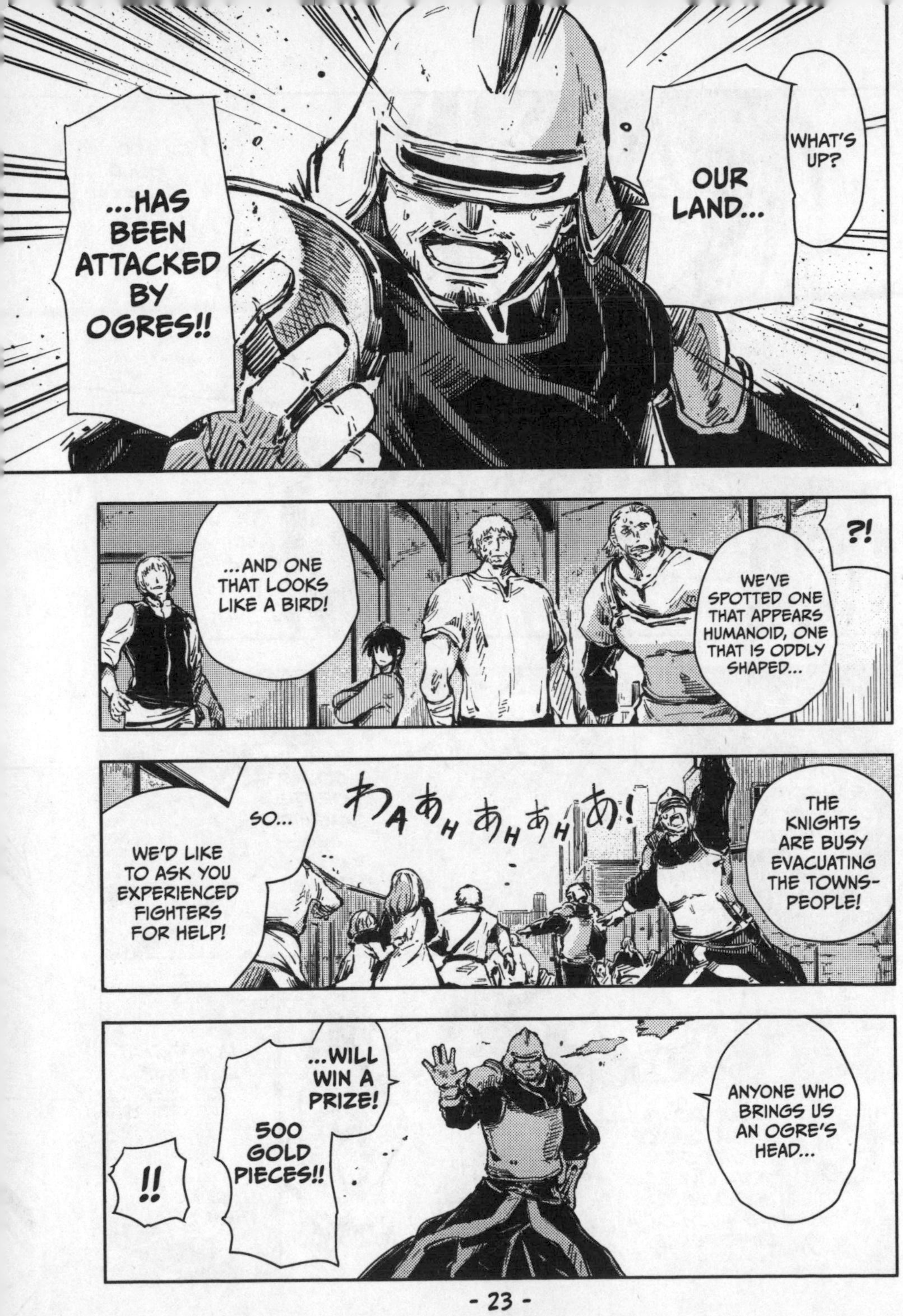
WHAT'S UP?
OUR LAND...
...HAS BEEN ATTACKED BY OGRES!!
?!
WE'VE SPOTTED ONE THAT APPEARS HUMANOID, ONE THAT IS ODDLY SHAPED...
...AND ONE THAT LOOKS LIKE A BIRD!
THE KNIGHTS ARE BUSY EVACUATING THE TOWNS-PEOPLE!
わAあHあHあHあ!
SO...
WE'D LIKE TO ASK YOU EXPERIENCED FIGHTERS FOR HELP!
ANYONE WHO BRINGS US AN OGRE'S HEAD...
...WILL WIN A PRIZE!
500 GOLD PIECES!!
!!

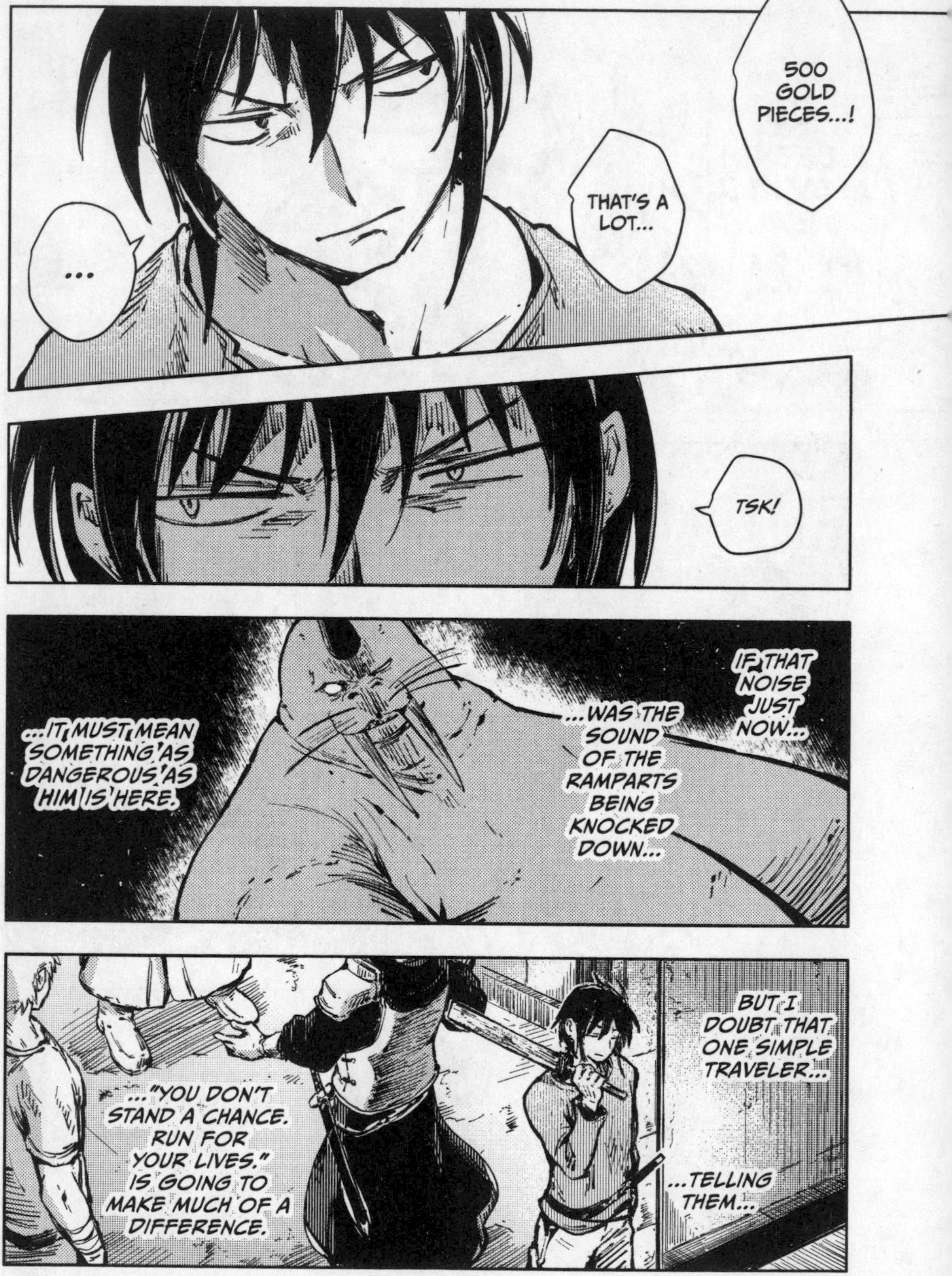
500 GOLD PIECES...!
THAT'S A LOT...
...
TSK!
IF THAT NOISE JUST NOW...
...WAS THE SOUND OF THE RAMPARTS BEING KNOCKED DOWN...
...IT MUST MEAN SOMETHING AS DANGEROUS AS HIM IS HERE.
BUT I DOUBT THAT ONE SIMPLE TRAVELER...
...TELLING THEM...
..."YOU DON'T STAND A CHANCE. RUN FOR YOUR LIVES." IS GOING TO MAKE MUCH OF A DIFFERENCE.

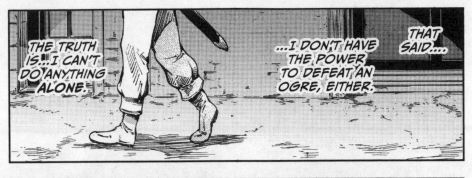

THAT SAID....
...I DON'T HAVE THE POWER TO DEFEAT AN OGRE, EITHER.
THE TRUTH IS...I CAN'T DO ANYTHING ALONE.
IN THE END...
I'M JUST GONNA HAVE TO RELY ON SALLY, EH?
SIGH
YO, PAL!
WHAP
!
HA HA HA!
BWA
Oh...
YOU'RE...
HUH...?
BALTHAS, RIGHT?
YEP!

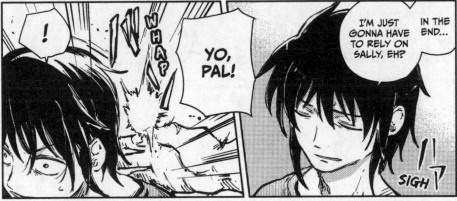

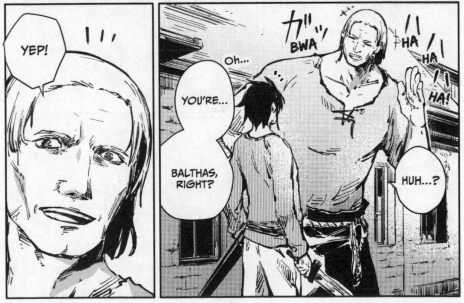

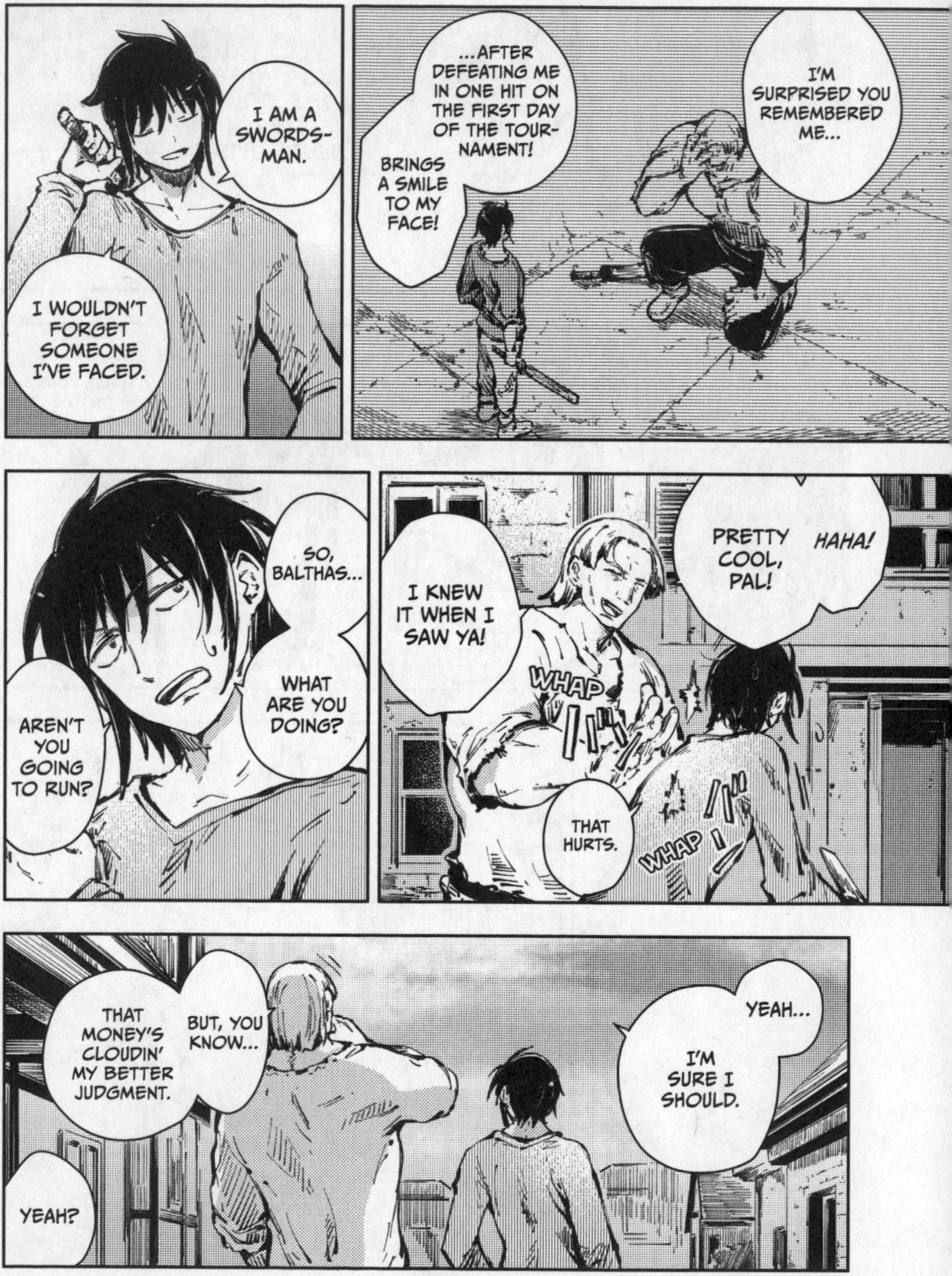
I'M SURPRISED YOU REMEMBERED ME...
...AFTER DEFEATING ME IN ONE HIT ON THE FIRST DAY OF THE TOURNAMENT!
BRINGS A SMILE TO MY FACE!
I AM A SWORDSMAN.
I WOULDN'T FORGET SOMEONE I'VE FACED.
HAHA!
PRETTY COOL, PAL!
I KNEW IT WHEN I SAW YA!
WHAP
THAT HURTS.
WHAP
SO, BALTHAS...
WHAT ARE YOU DOING?
AREN'T YOU GOING TO RUN?
YEAH...
I'M SURE I SHOULD.
BUT, YOU KNOW...
THAT MONEY'S CLOUDIN' MY BETTER JUDGMENT.
YEAH?

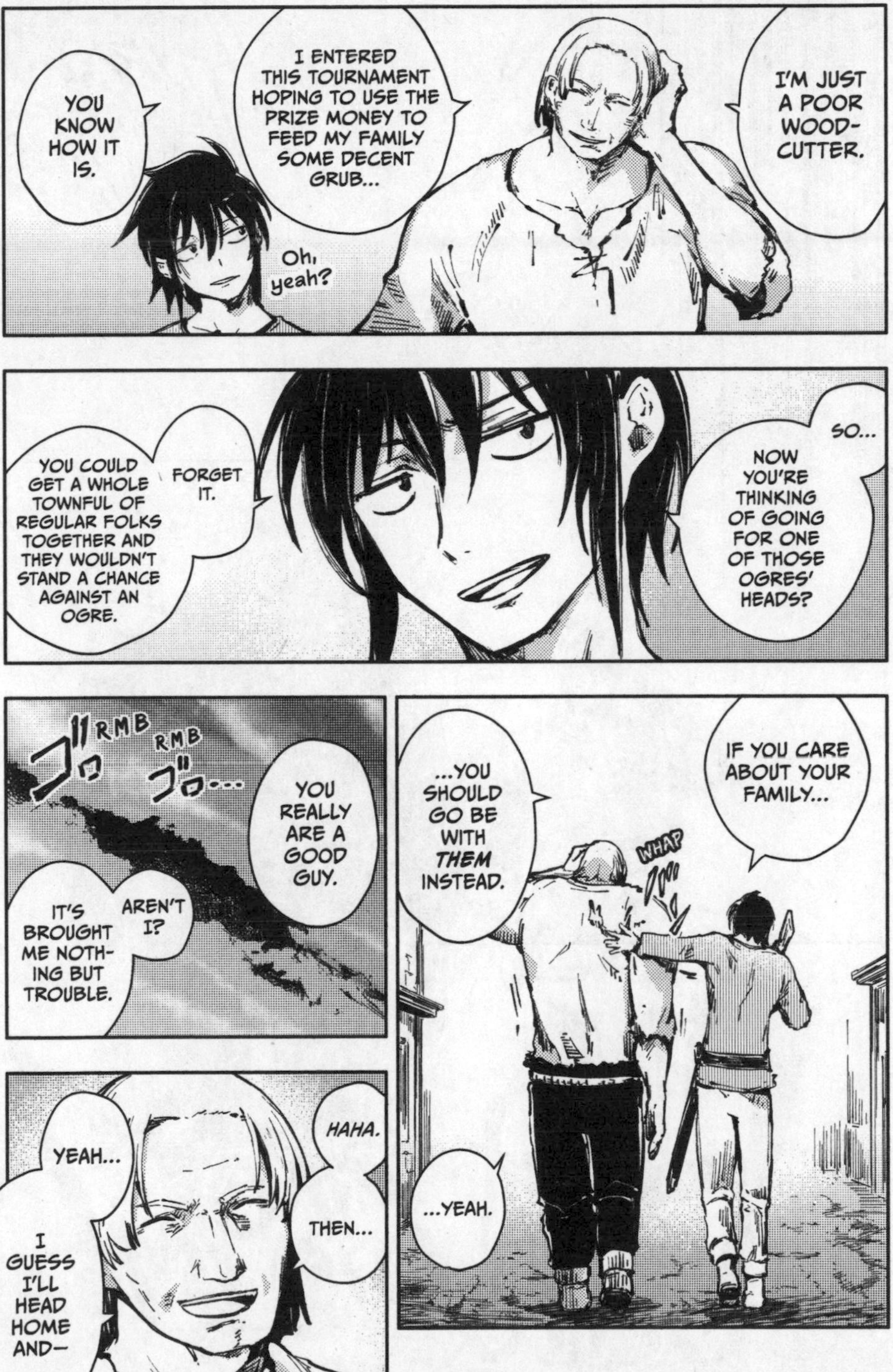
I'M JUST A POOR WOOD-CUTTER.
I ENTERED THIS TOURNAMENT HOPING TO USE THE PRIZE MONEY TO FEED MY FAMILY SOME DECENT GRUB...
YOU KNOW HOW IT IS.
Oh, yeah?
SO...
NOW YOU'RE THINKING OF GOING FOR ONE OF THOSE OGRES' HEADS?
FORGET IT.
YOU COULD GET A WHOLE TOWNFUL OF REGULAR FOLKS TOGETHER AND THEY WOULDN'T STAND A CHANCE AGAINST AN OGRE.
IF YOU CARE ABOUT YOUR FAMILY...
WHAP
...YOU SHOULD GO BE WITH *THEM* INSTEAD.
...YEAH.
RMB
RMB
YOU REALLY ARE A GOOD GUY.
AREN'T I?
IT'S BROUGHT ME NOTHING BUT TROUBLE.
HAHA.
THEN...
YEAH...
I GUESS I'LL HEAD HOME AND—

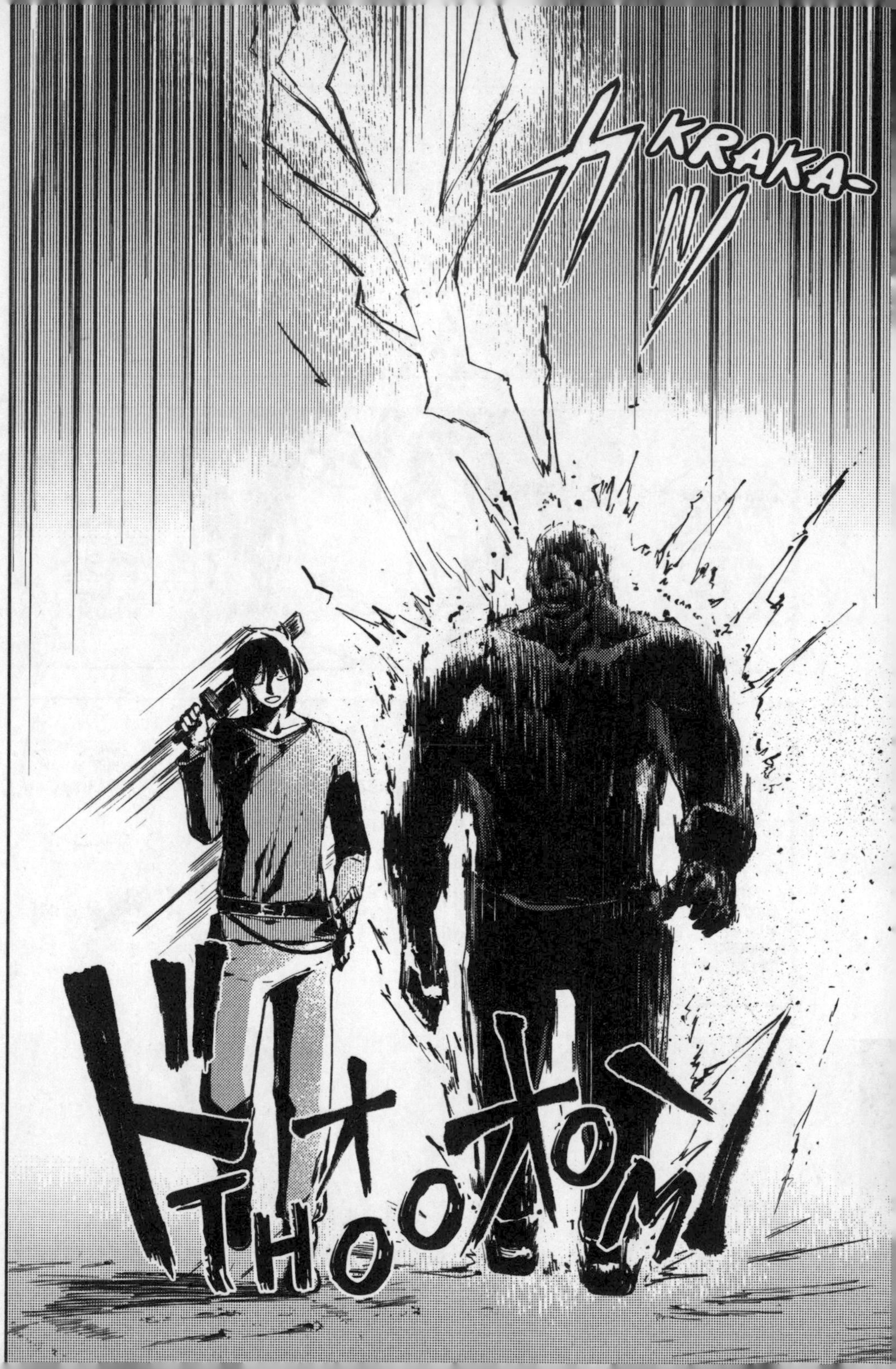
KRAKA-
THOOOOM

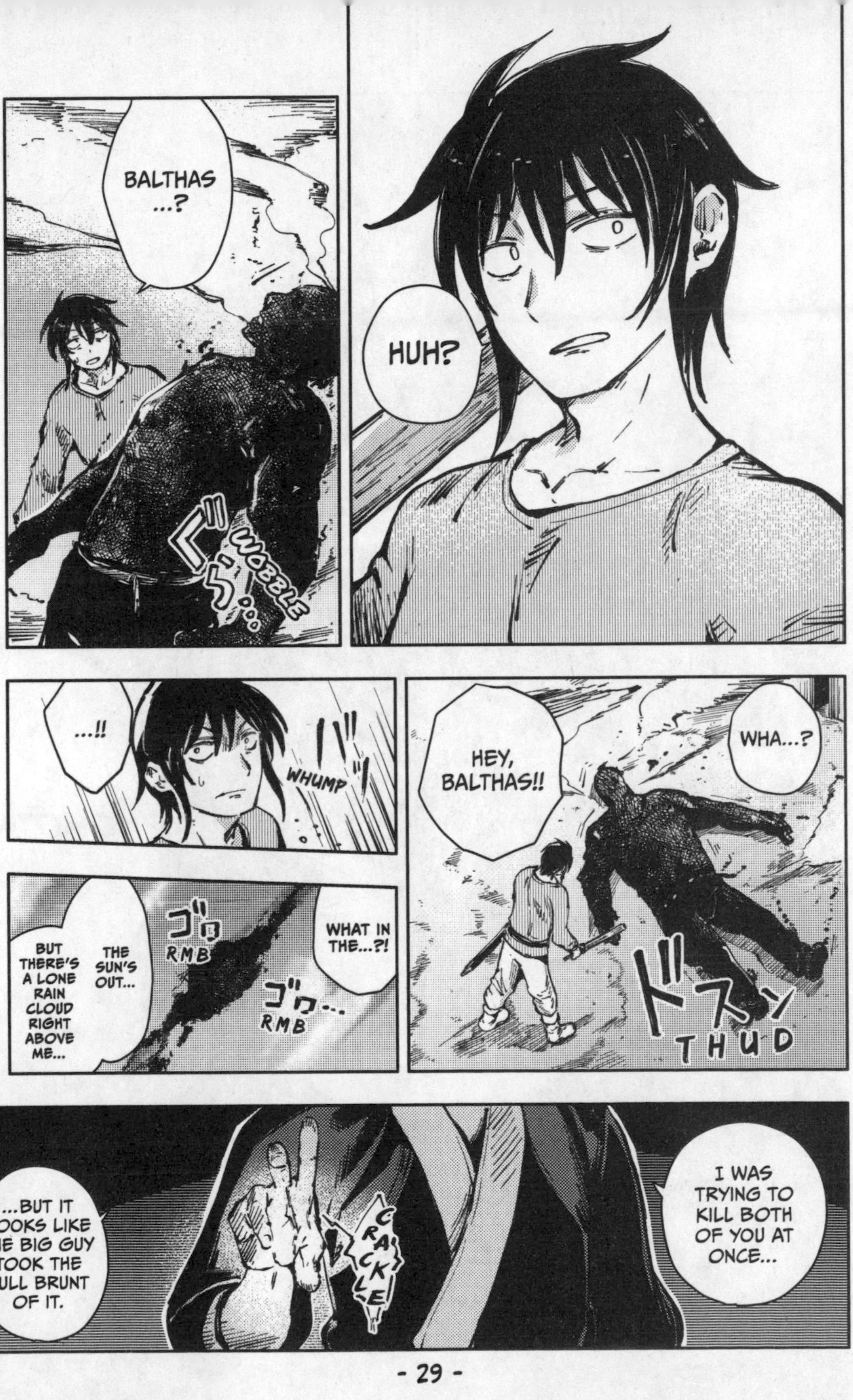
HUH?
BALTHAS ...?
WOBBLE
WHA...?
HEY, BALTHAS!!
THUD
...!!
WHUMP
WHAT IN THE...?!
RMB
THE SUN'S OUT...
BUT THERE'S A LONE RAIN CLOUD RIGHT ABOVE ME...
RMB
I WAS TRYING TO KILL BOTH OF YOU AT ONCE...
CRACKLE
...BUT IT LOOKS LIKE THE BIG GUY TOOK THE FULL BRUNT OF IT.

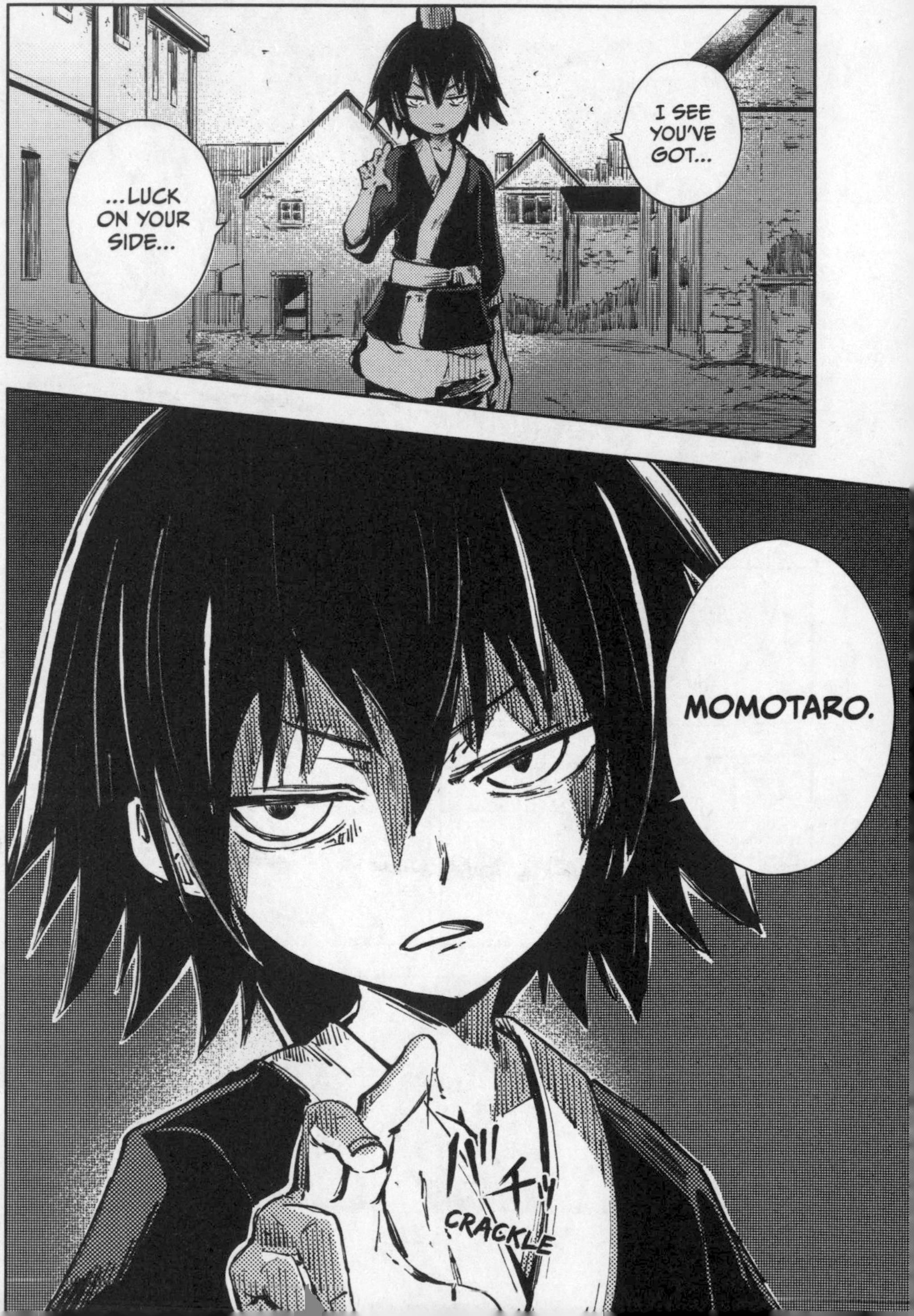
I SEE YOU'VE GOT...
...LUCK ON YOUR SIDE...
MOMOTARO.
バチッ
CRACKLE

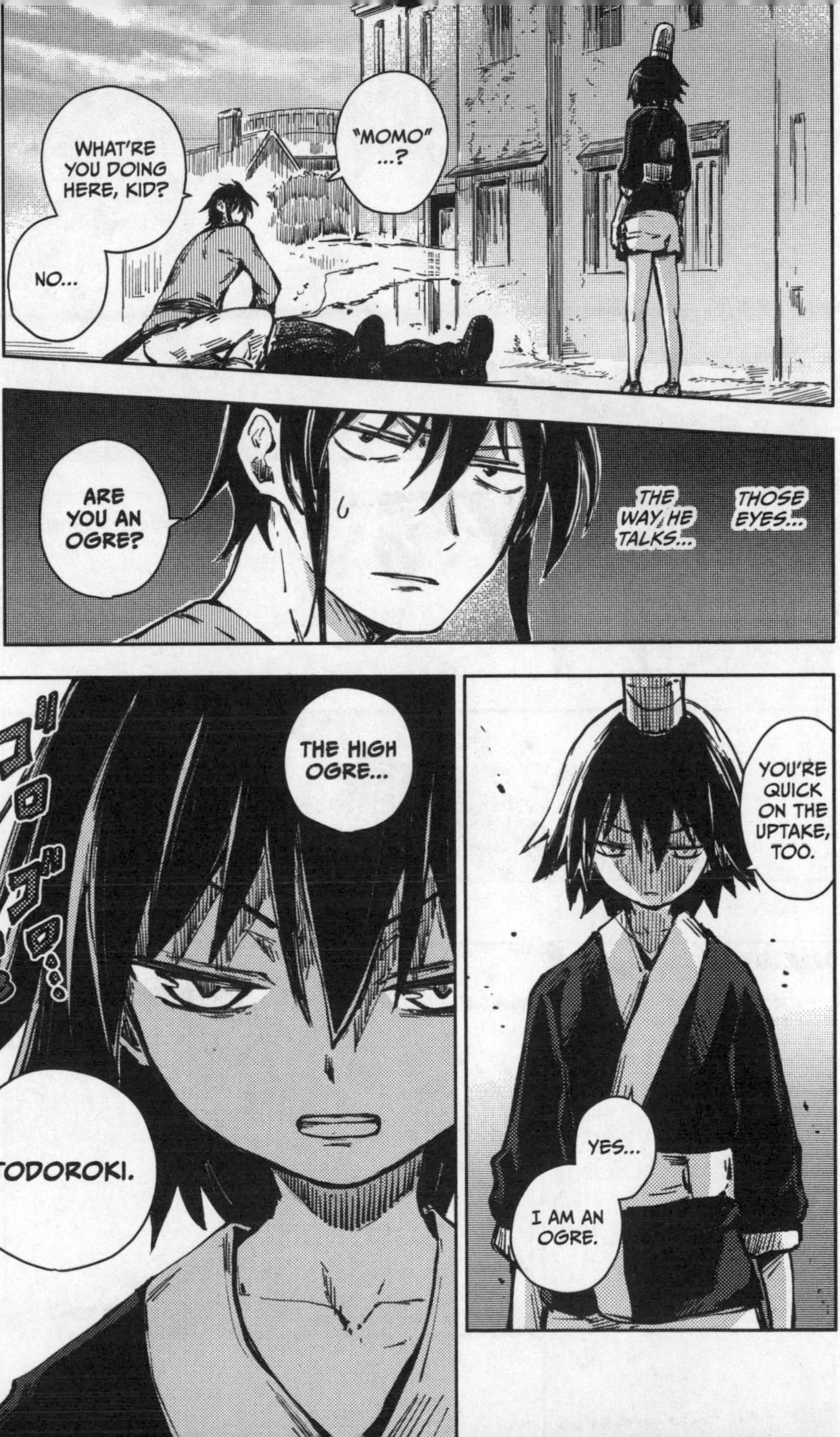
"MOMO" ...?
WHAT'RE YOU DOING HERE, KID?
NO...
THOSE EYES...
THE WAY HE TALKS...
ARE YOU AN OGRE?
YOU'RE QUICK ON THE UPTAKE, TOO.
YES...
I AM AN OGRE.
THE HIGH OGRE...
ゴロゴロ...
RMBRMB
TODOROKI.

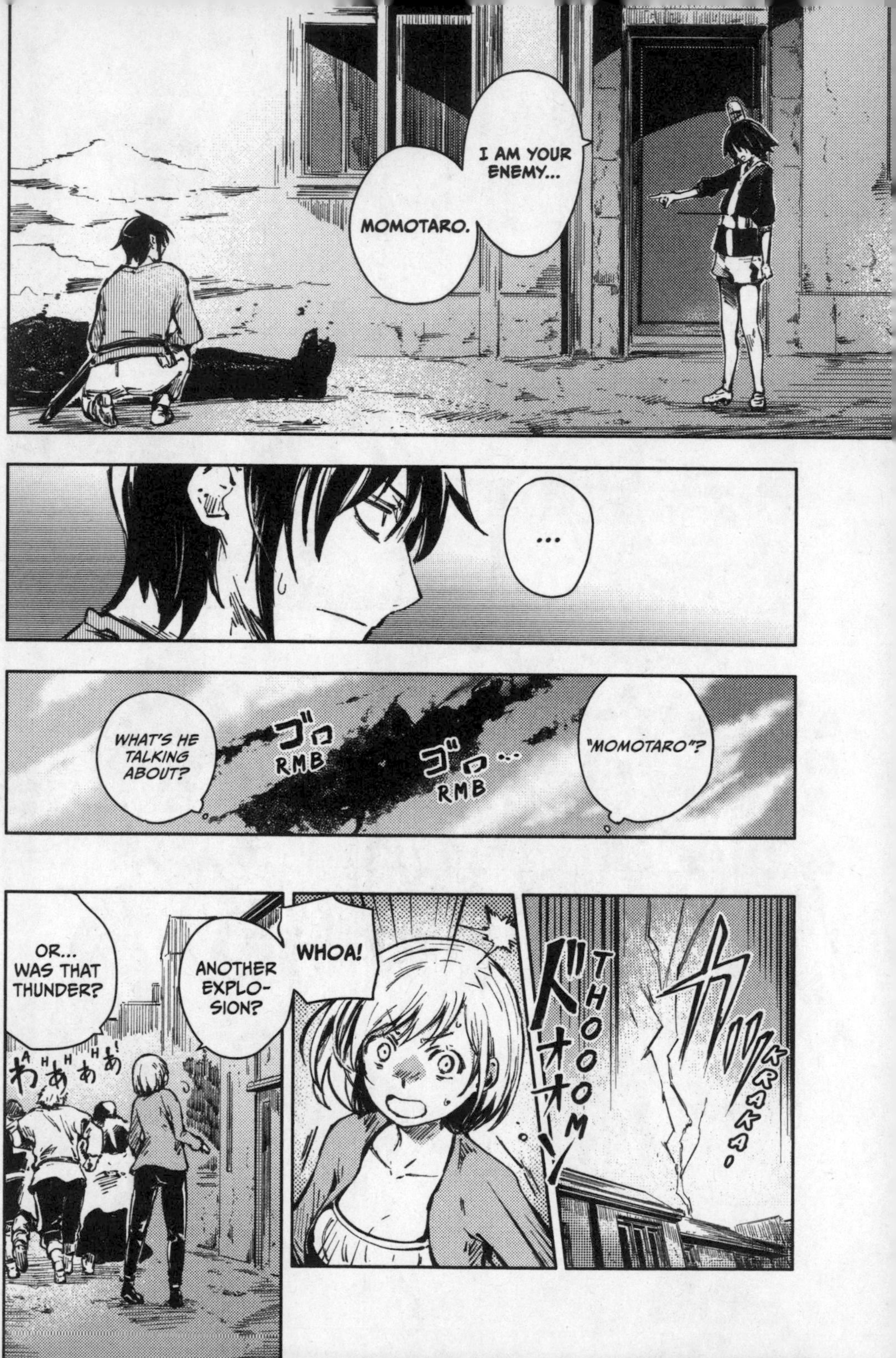
I AM YOUR ENEMY...
MOMOTARO.
...
"MOMOTARO"?
ゴロ...
RMB
ゴロ
RMB
WHAT'S HE TALKING ABOUT?
カッ
KRAKA.
ドオオオ
THOOOOM!
WHOA!
ANOTHER EXPLO-SION?
OR... WAS THAT THUNDER?
わあああ
AHHHH!

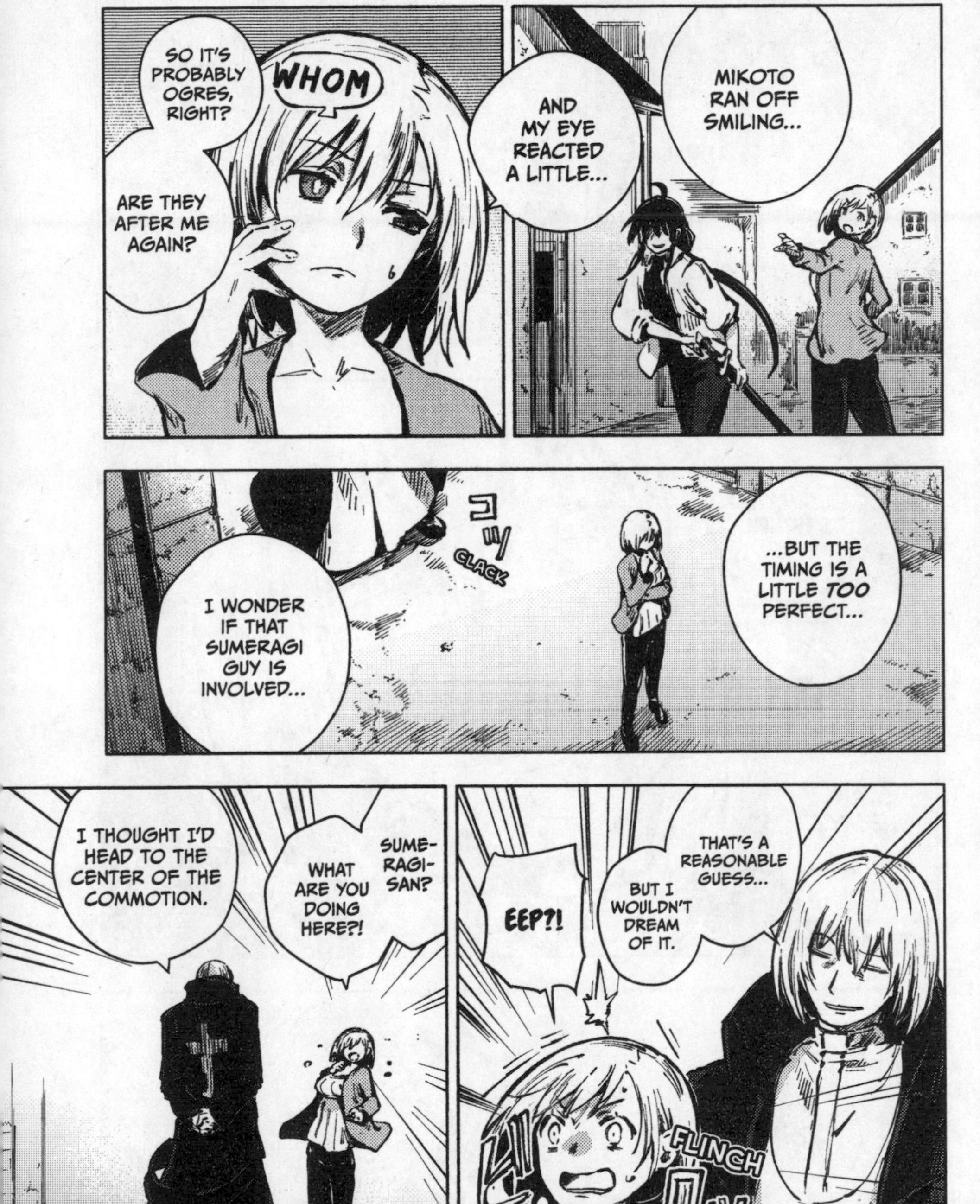
MIKOTO RAN OFF SMILING...
AND MY EYE REACTED A LITTLE...
WHOM
SO IT'S PROBABLY OGRES, RIGHT?
ARE THEY AFTER ME AGAIN?
...BUT THE TIMING IS A LITTLE *TOO* PERFECT...
CLACK
I WONDER IF THAT SUMERAGI GUY IS INVOLVED...
THAT'S A REASONABLE GUESS...
BUT I WOULDN'T DREAM OF IT.
EEP?!
FLINCH
SUME-RAGI-SAN?
WHAT ARE YOU DOING HERE?!
I THOUGHT I'D HEAD TO THE CENTER OF THE COMMOTION.

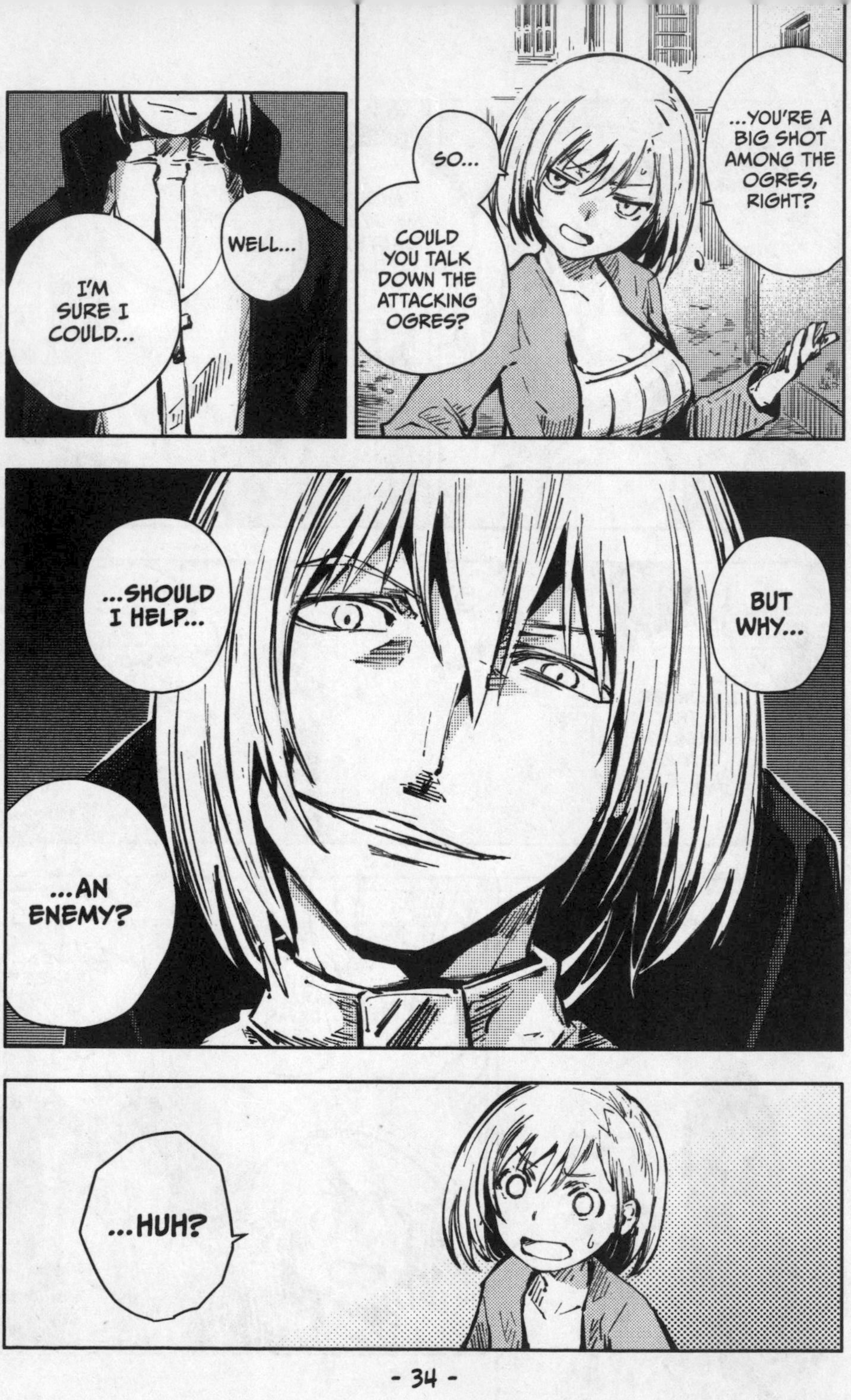
...YOU'RE A BIG SHOT AMONG THE OGRES, RIGHT?
SO...
COULD YOU TALK DOWN THE ATTACKING OGRES?
WELL...
I'M SURE I COULD...
BUT WHY...
...SHOULD I HELP...
...AN ENEMY?
...HUH?

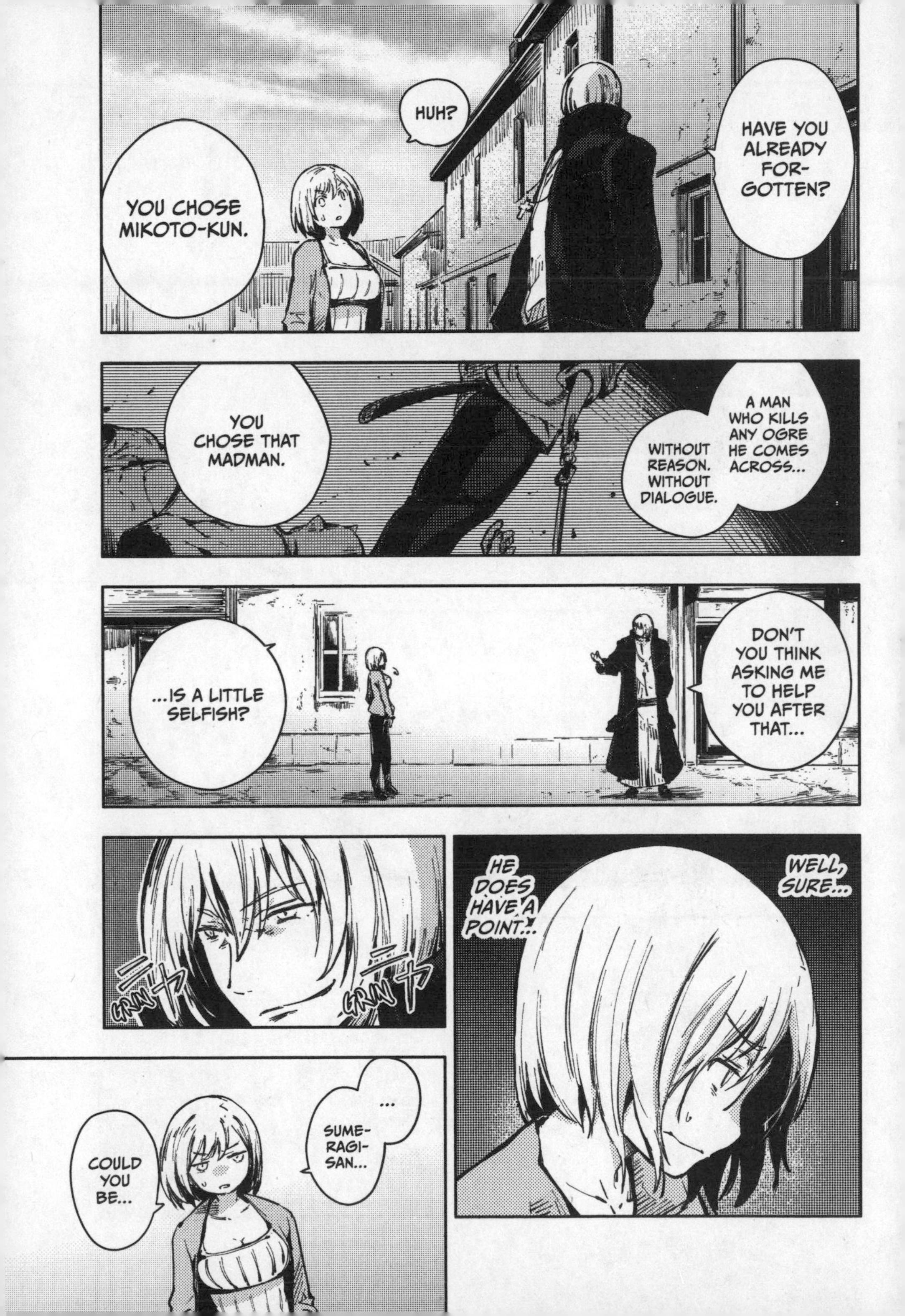
HAVE YOU ALREADY FOR-GOTTEN?
HUH?
YOU CHOSE MIKOTO-KUN.
A MAN WHO KILLS ANY OGRE HE COMES ACROSS...
WITHOUT REASON. WITHOUT DIALOGUE.
YOU CHOSE THAT MADMAN.
DON'T YOU THINK ASKING ME TO HELP YOU AFTER THAT...
...IS A LITTLE SELFISH?
WELL, SURE...
HE DOES HAVE A POINT...
GRIN
GRIN
... SUME-RAGI-SAN...
COULD YOU BE...

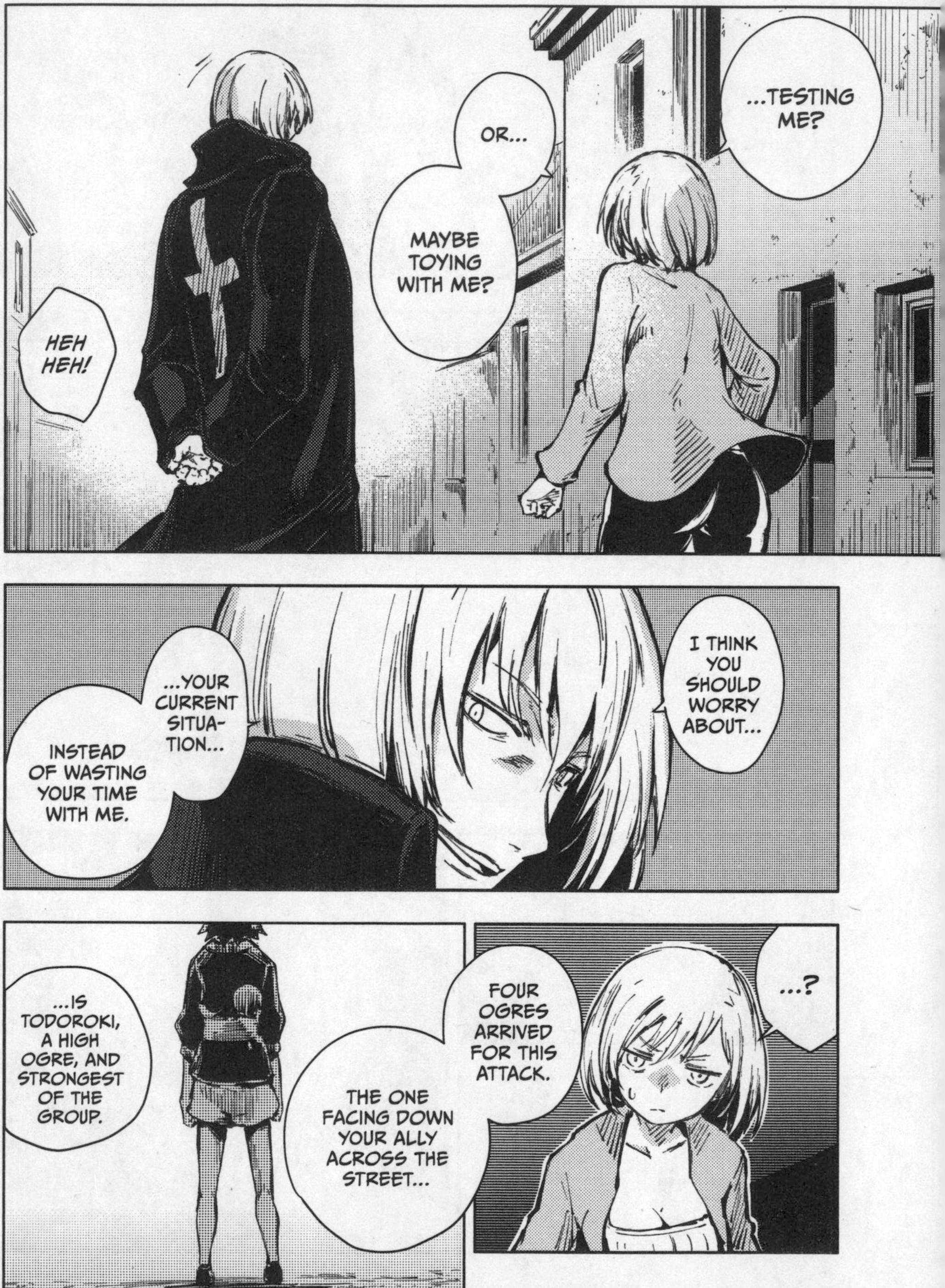
...TESTING ME?
OR...
MAYBE TOYING WITH ME?
HEH HEH!
I THINK YOU SHOULD WORRY ABOUT...
...YOUR CURRENT SITUA-TION...
INSTEAD OF WASTING YOUR TIME WITH ME.
...?
FOUR OGRES ARRIVED FOR THIS ATTACK.
THE ONE FACING DOWN YOUR ALLY ACROSS THE STREET...
...IS TODOROKI, A HIGH OGRE, AND STRONGEST OF THE GROUP.

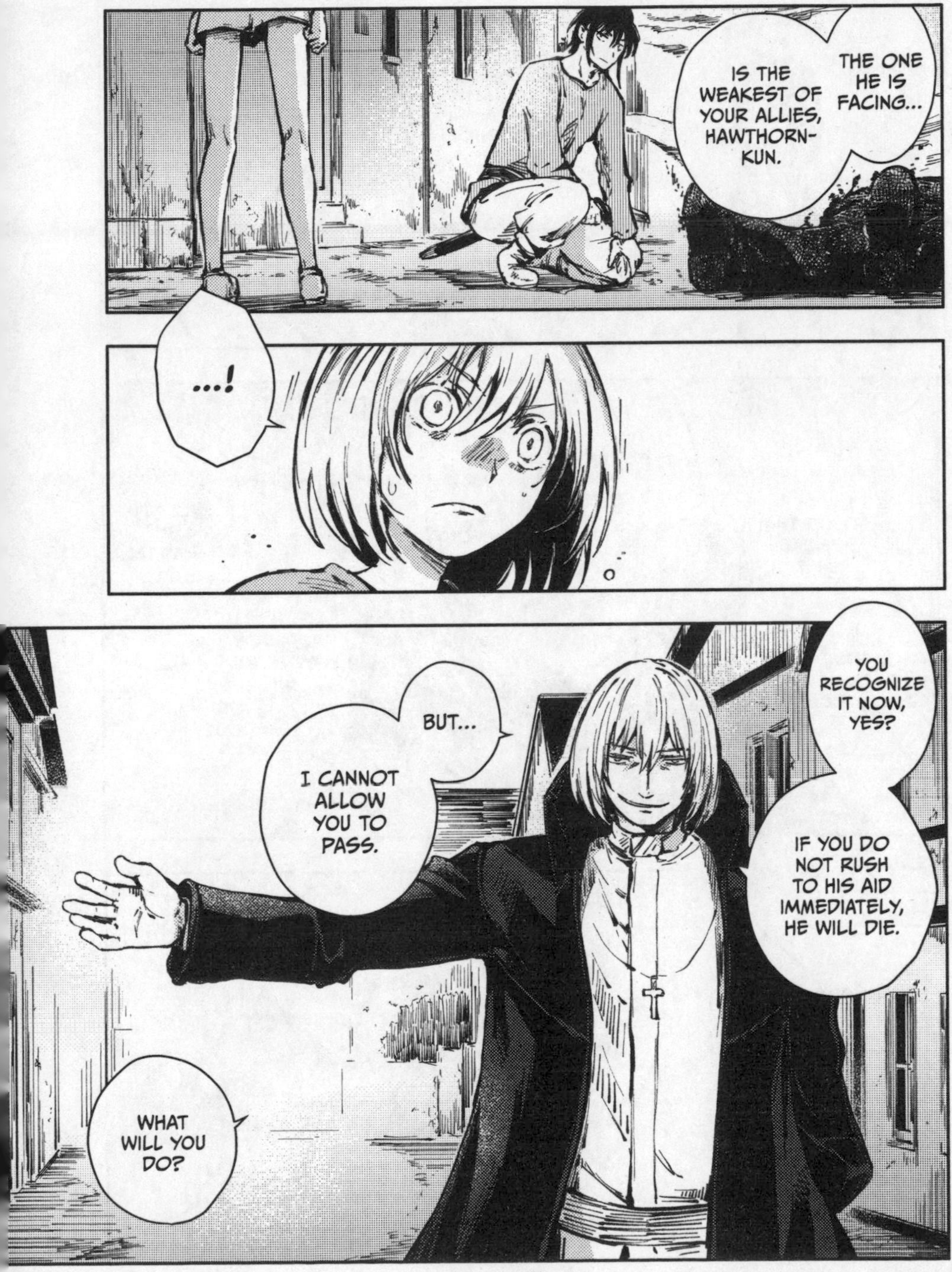
THE ONE HE IS FACING...
IS THE WEAKEST OF YOUR ALLIES, HAWTHORN-KUN.
...!
YOU RECOGNIZE IT NOW, YES?
IF YOU DO NOT RUSH TO HIS AID IMMEDIATELY, HE WILL DIE.
BUT...
I CANNOT ALLOW YOU TO PASS.
WHAT WILL YOU DO?

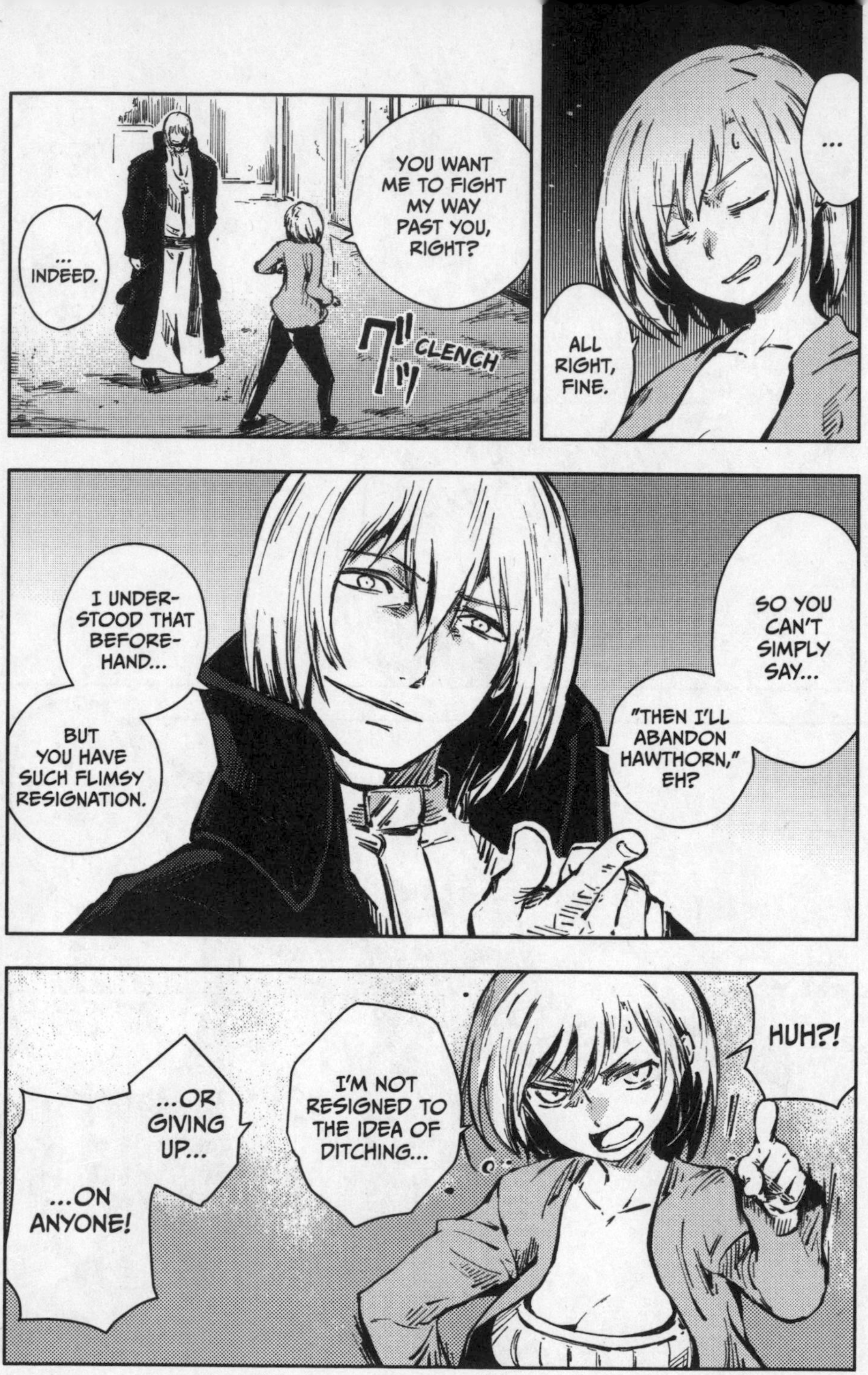
...
ALL RIGHT, FINE.
YOU WANT ME TO FIGHT MY WAY PAST YOU, RIGHT?
CLENCH
... INDEED.
SO YOU CAN'T SIMPLY SAY...
"THEN I'LL ABANDON HAWTHORN," EH?
I UNDER-STOOD THAT BEFORE-HAND...
BUT YOU HAVE SUCH FLIMSY RESIGNATION.
HUH?!
I'M NOT RESIGNED TO THE IDEA OF DITCHING...
...OR GIVING UP...
...ON ANYONE!

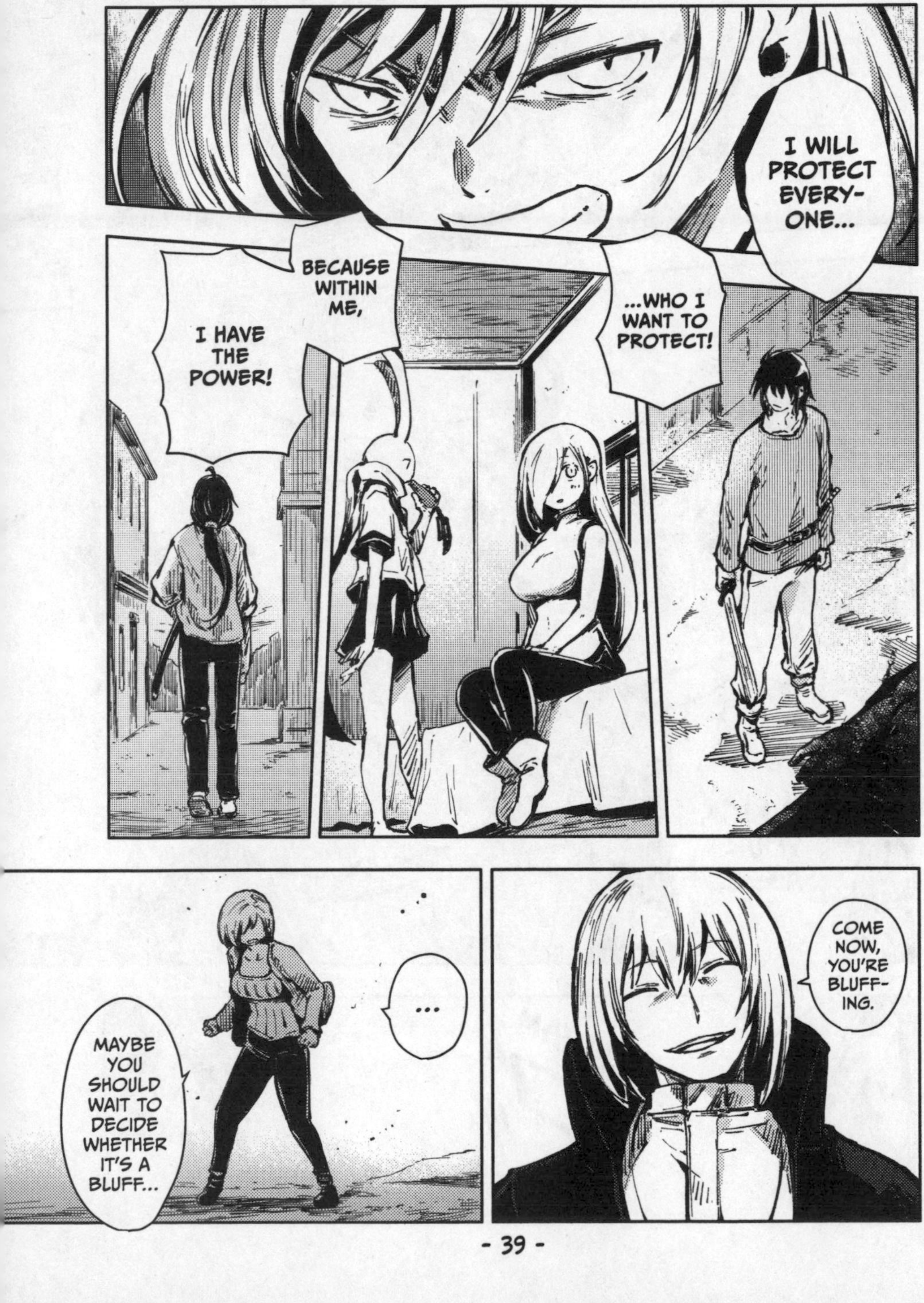
I WILL PROTECT EVERY-ONE...
...WHO I WANT TO PROTECT!
BECAUSE WITHIN ME,
I HAVE THE POWER!
COME NOW, YOU'RE BLUFF-ING.
...
MAYBE YOU SHOULD WAIT TO DECIDE WHETHER IT'S A BLUFF...

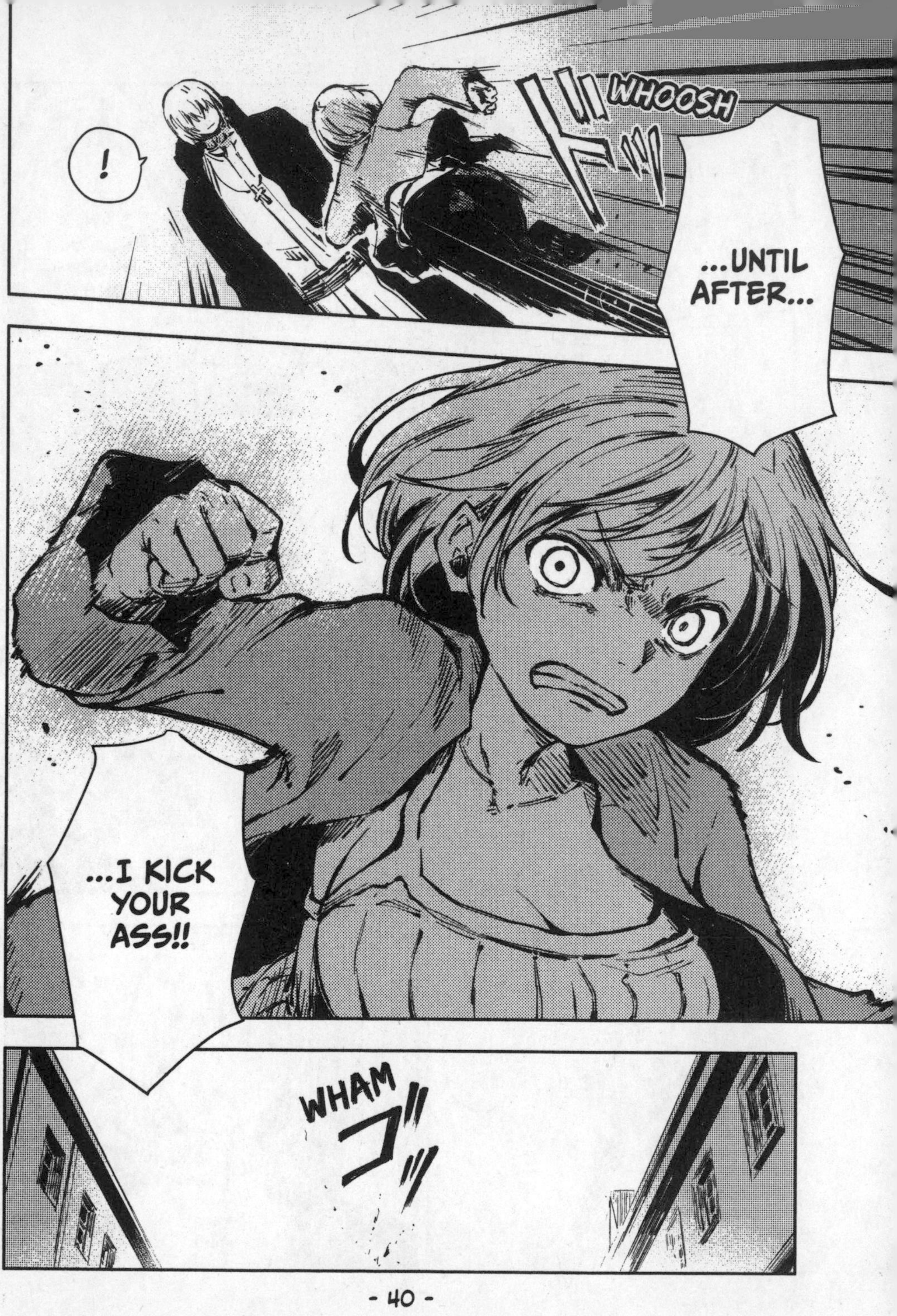
WHOOSH
...UNTIL AFTER...
!
...I KICK YOUR ASS!!
WHAM

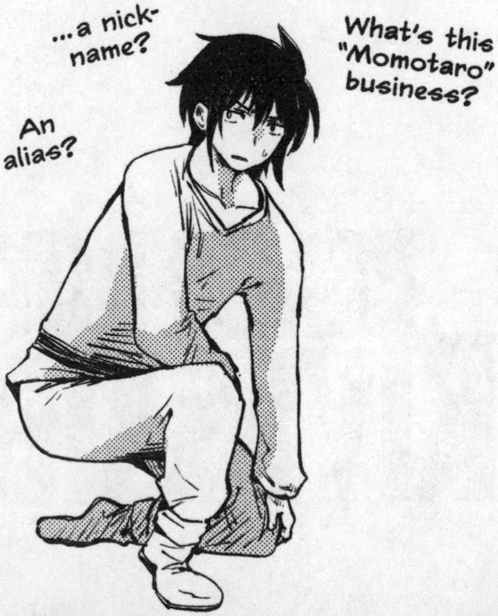
What's this "Momotaro" business?
...a nick-name?
An alias?

PEACH BOY RIVERSIDE

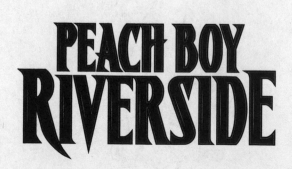

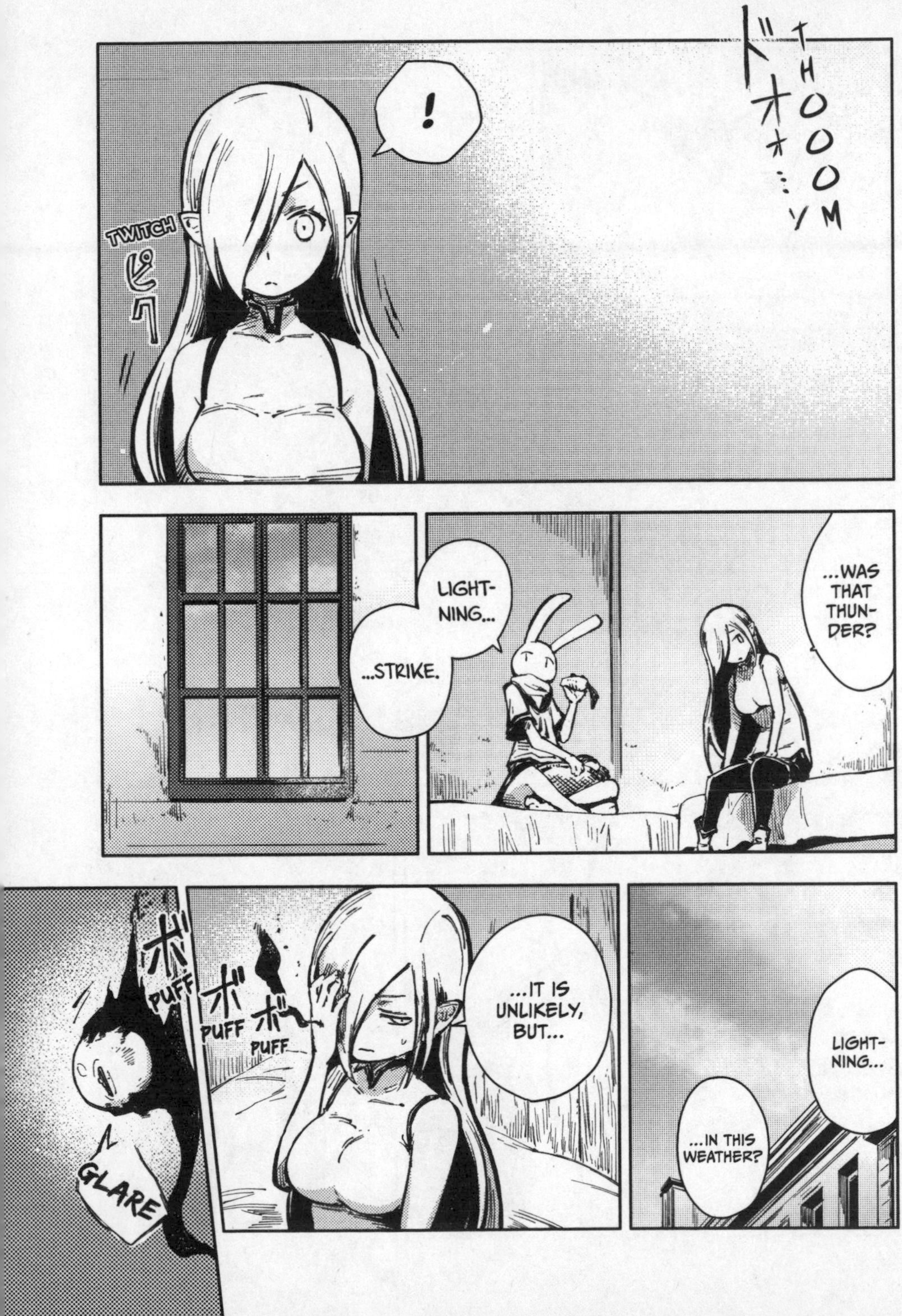
THOOOOM
!
TWITCH
ピク
...WAS THAT THUNDER?
LIGHTNING...
...STRIKE.
LIGHTNING...
...IN THIS WEATHER?
...IT IS UNLIKELY, BUT...
PUFF
PUFF
PUFF
GLARE

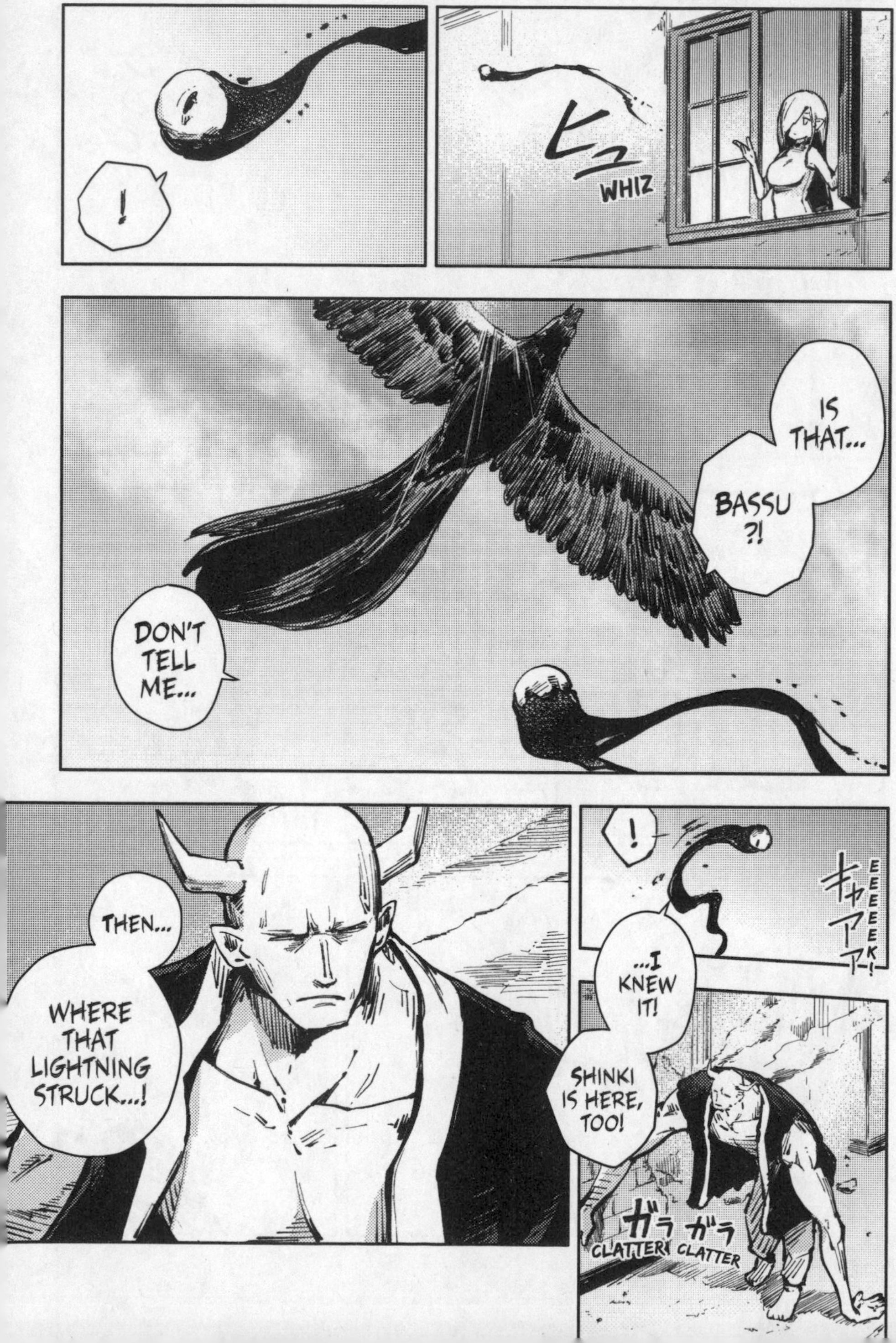
ヒュ
WHIZ
!
IS THAT...
BASSU?!
DON'T TELL ME...
!
キャアアー
EEEEEK!
THEN...
WHERE THAT LIGHTNING STRUCK...!
...I KNEW IT!
SHINKI IS HERE, TOO!
ガラガラ
CLATTER CLATTER

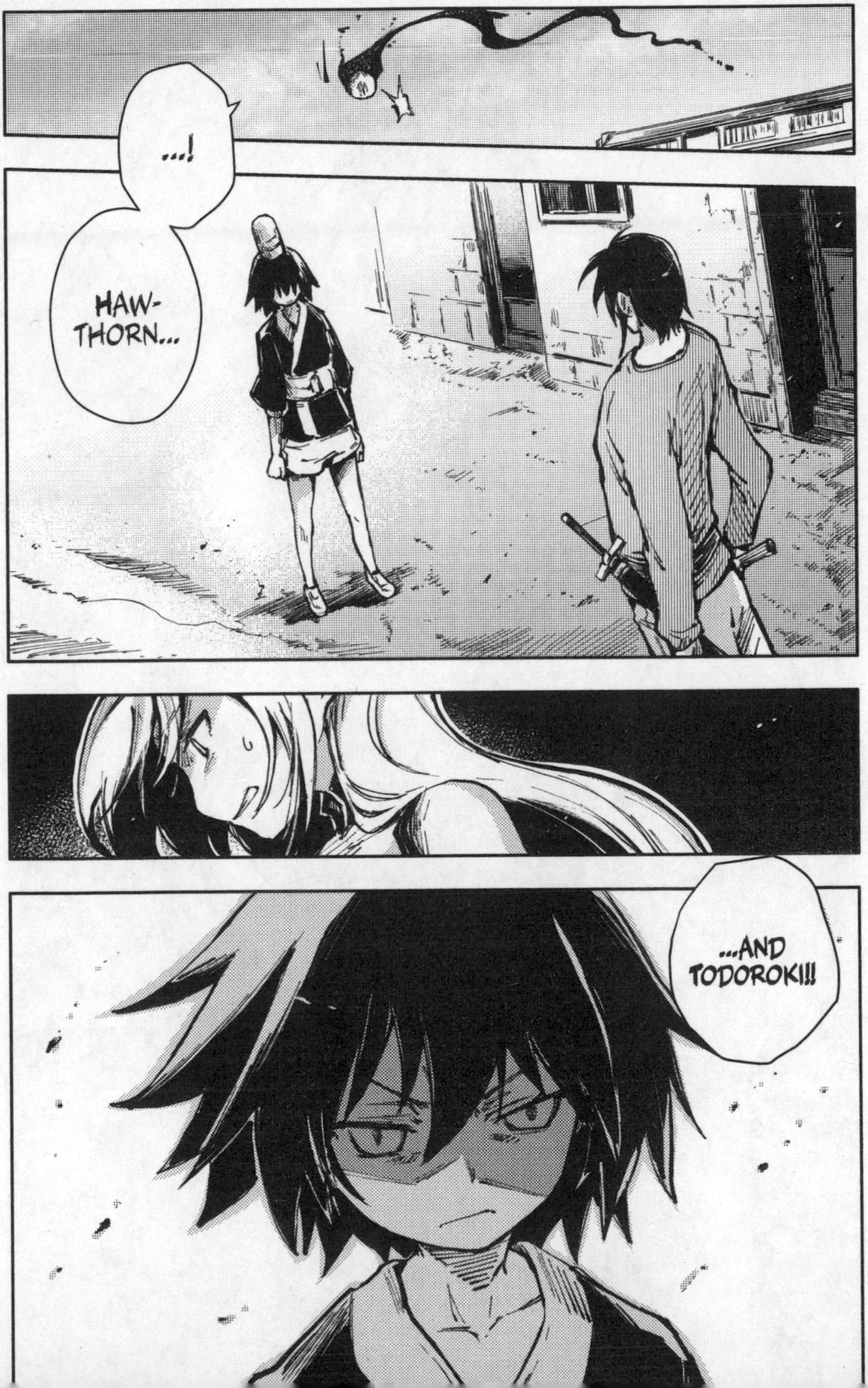
...!
HAW-THORN...
...AND TODOROKI!!!

CHAPTER 21:-MEKI AND CARROT

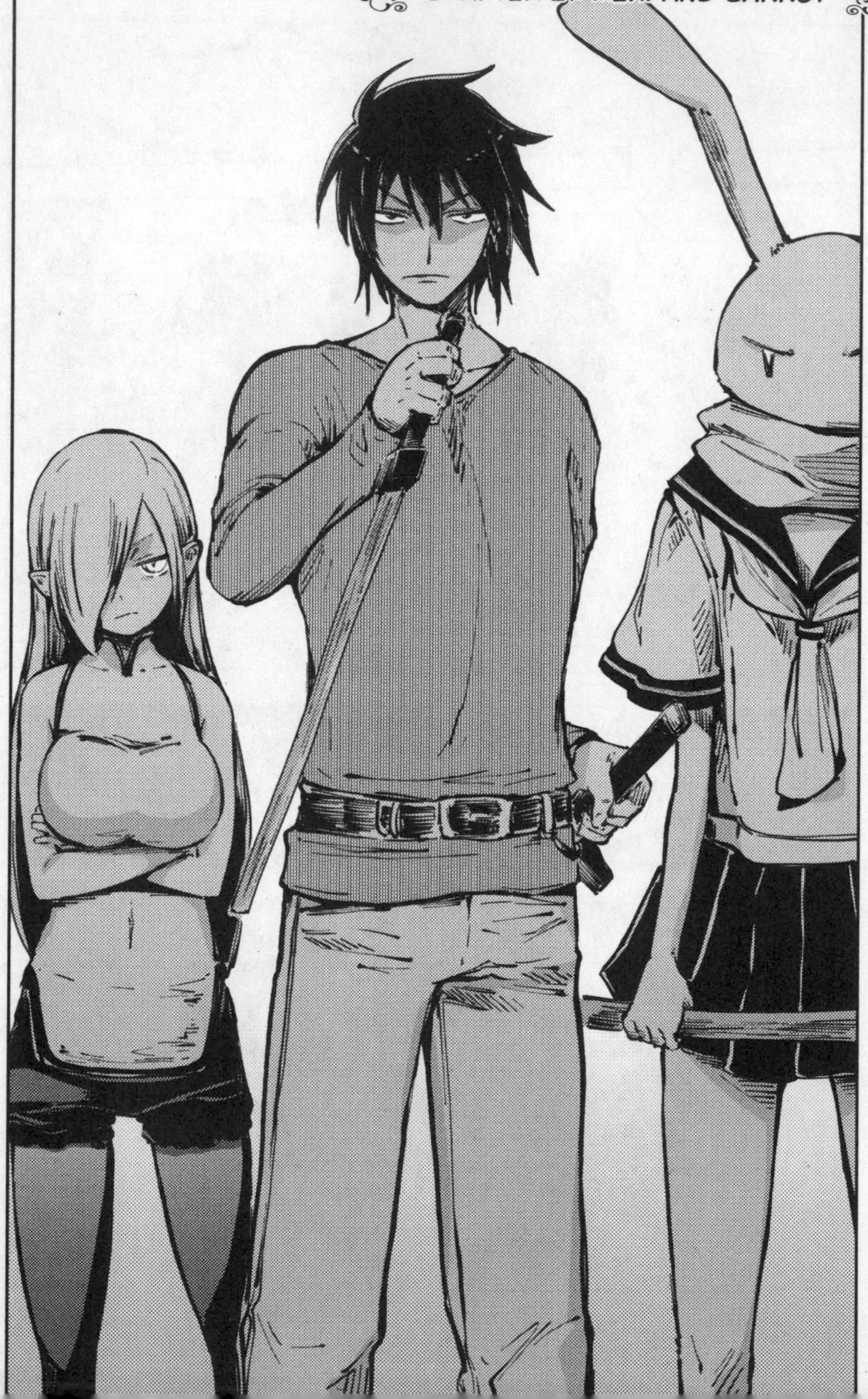

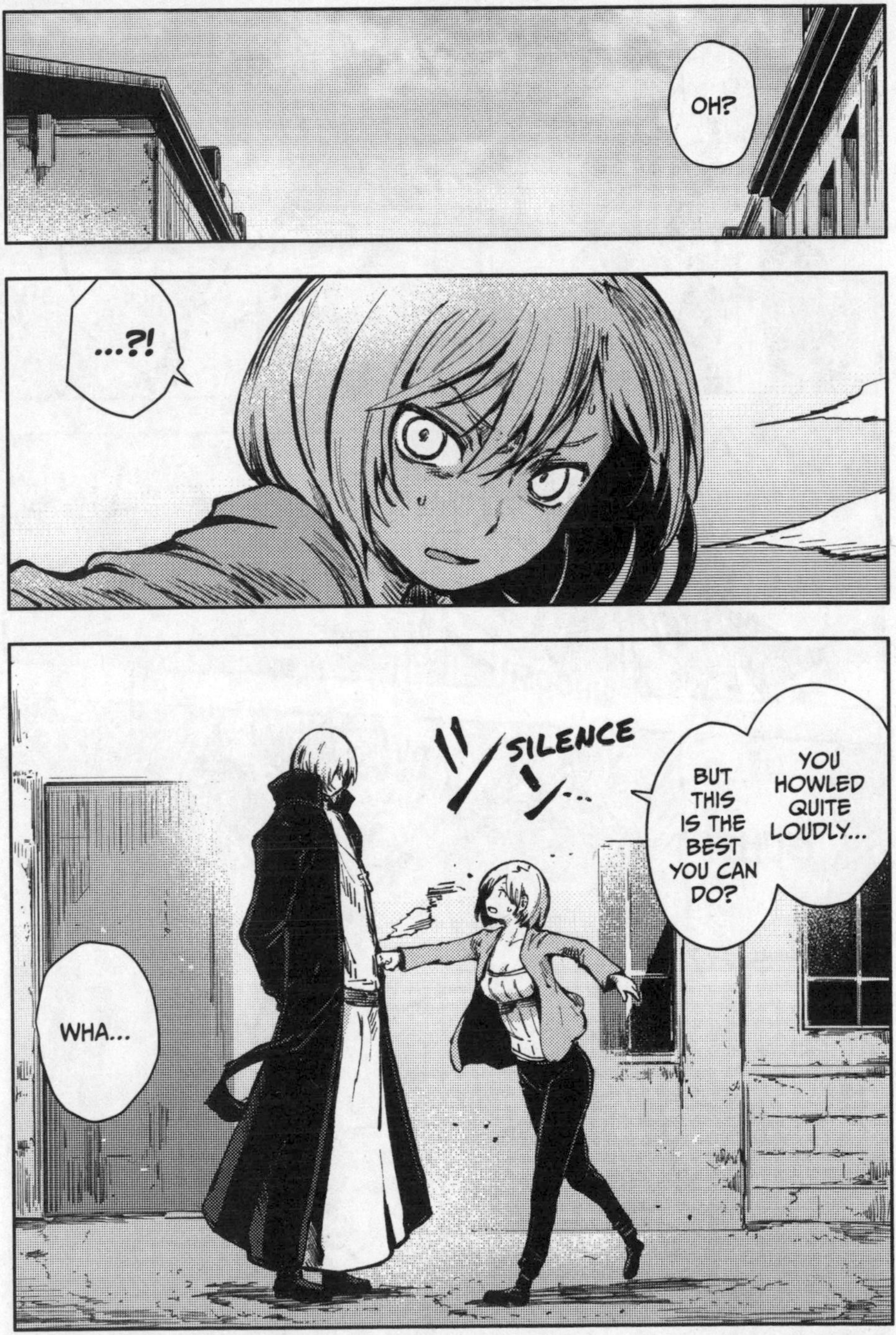
OH?
...?!
YOU HOWLED QUITE LOUDLY...
BUT THIS IS THE BEST YOU CAN DO?
SILENCE...
WHA...

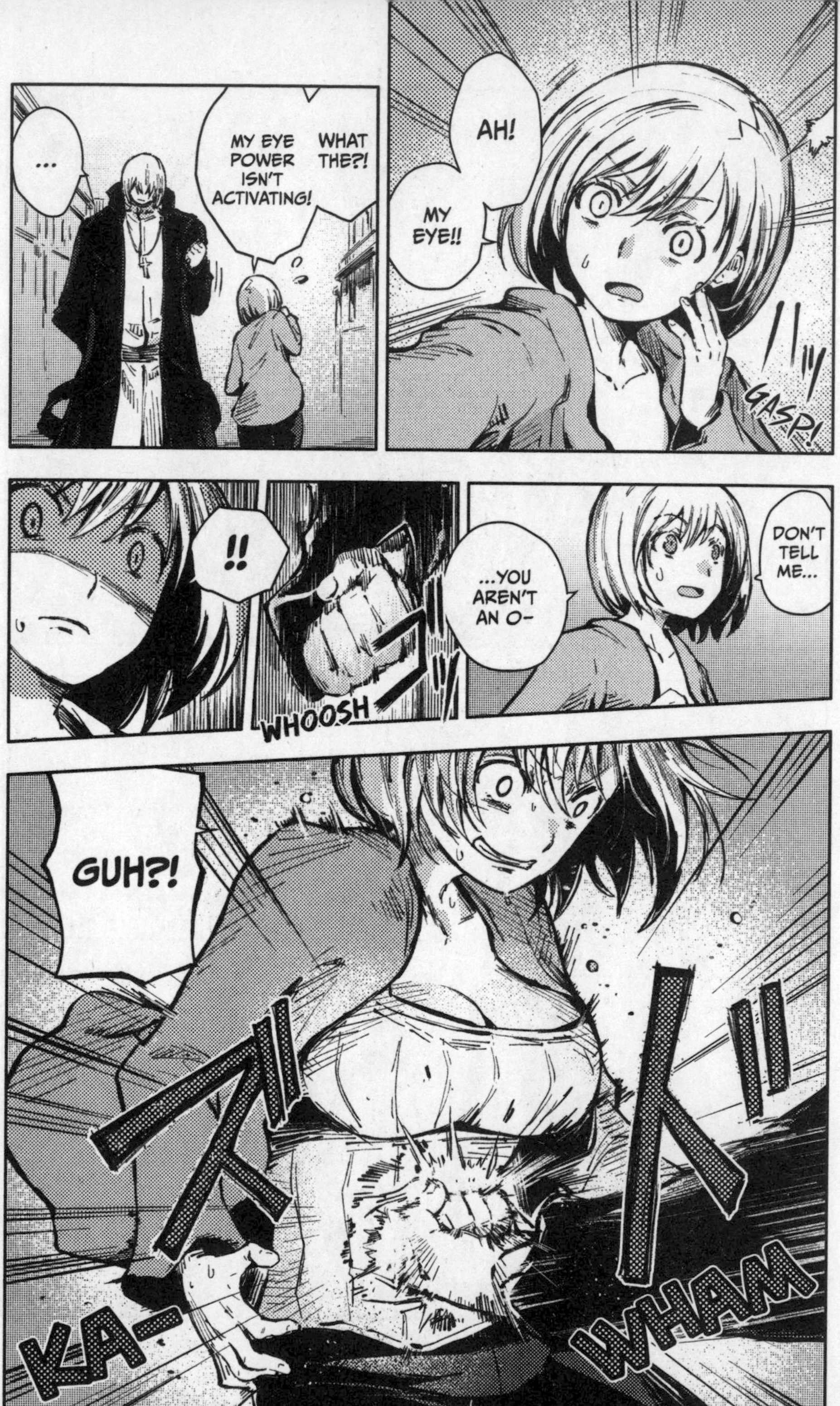
AH!
MY EYE!!
GASP!
WHAT THE?!
MY EYE POWER ISN'T ACTIVATING!
...
DON'T TELL ME...
...YOU AREN'T AN O-
WHOOSH
!!
GUH?!
KA-
WHAM

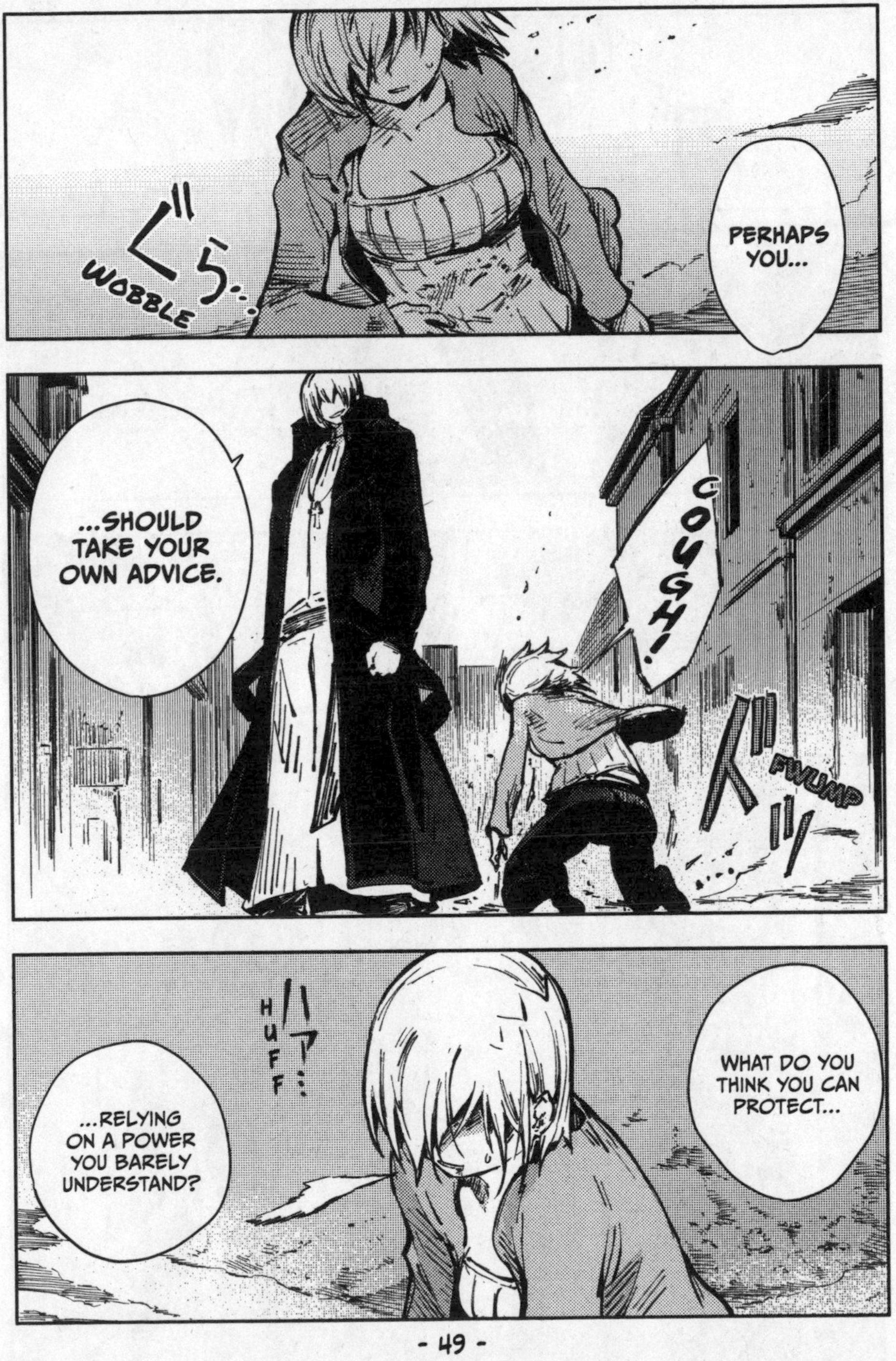
PERHAPS YOU...
WOBBLE
COUGH!
FWUMP
...SHOULD TAKE YOUR OWN ADVICE.
WHAT DO YOU THINK YOU CAN PROTECT...
HUFF
...RELYING ON A POWER YOU BARELY UNDERSTAND?

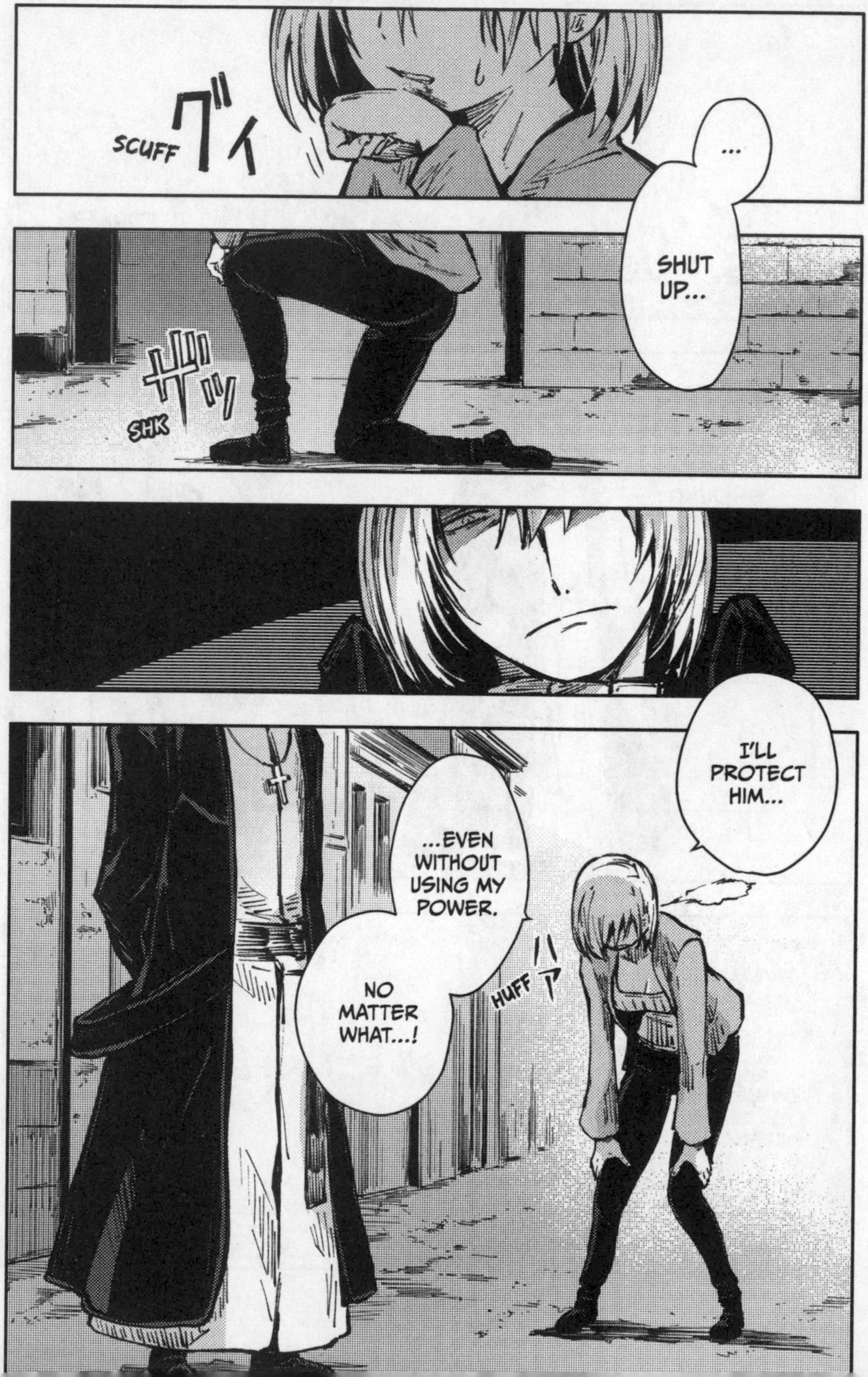

SCUFF
グイ
...
SHUT UP...
ザッ
SHK
I'LL PROTECT HIM...
...EVEN WITHOUT USING MY POWER.
NO MATTER WHAT...!
HUFF
ハァ

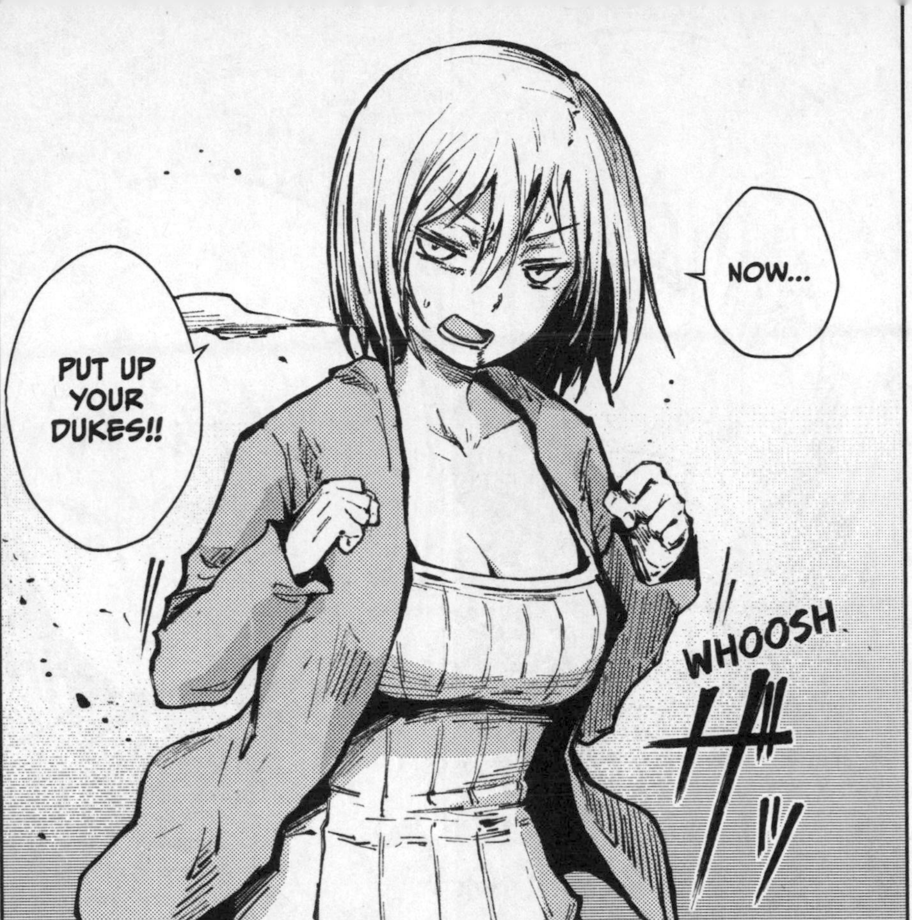
NOW...
PUT UP YOUR DUKES!!
WHOOSH

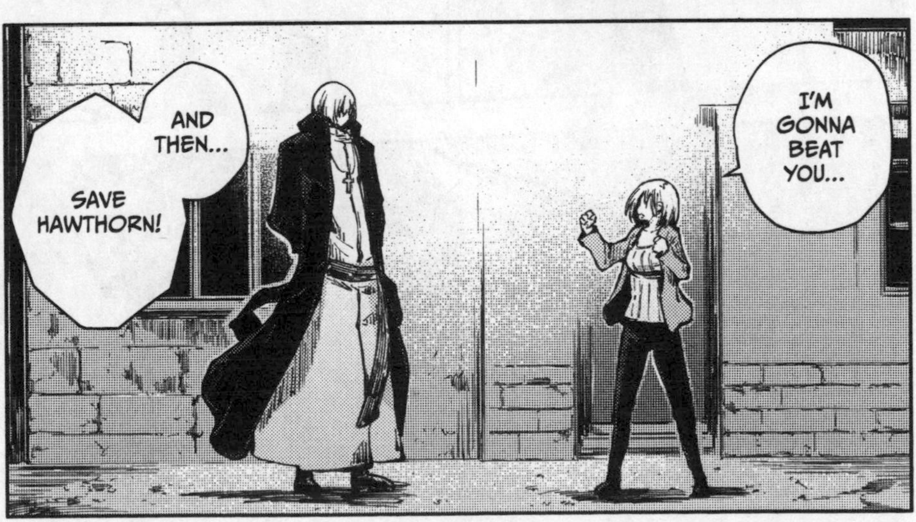
I'M GONNA BEAT YOU...
AND THEN...
SAVE HAWTHORN!

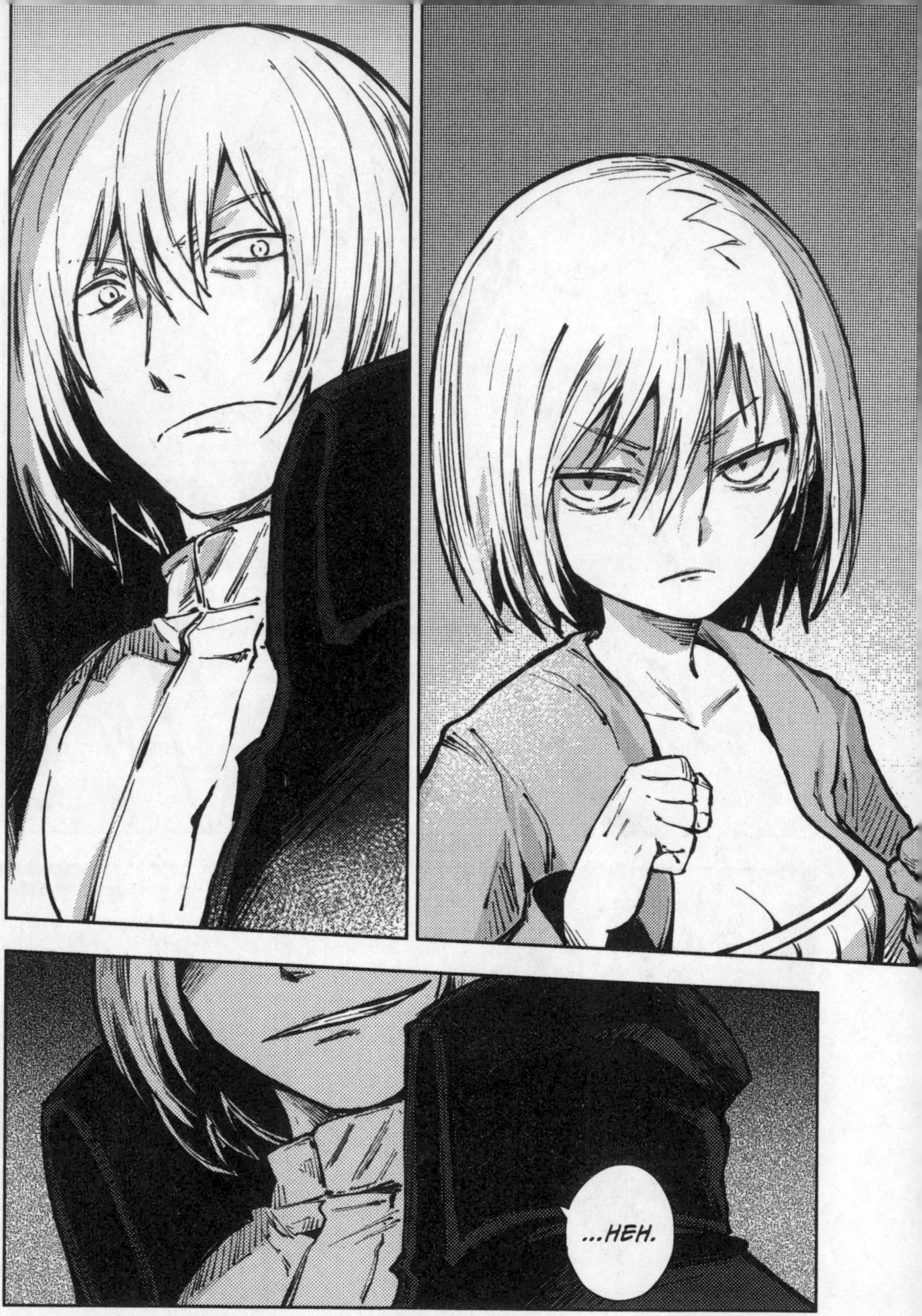
...HEH.

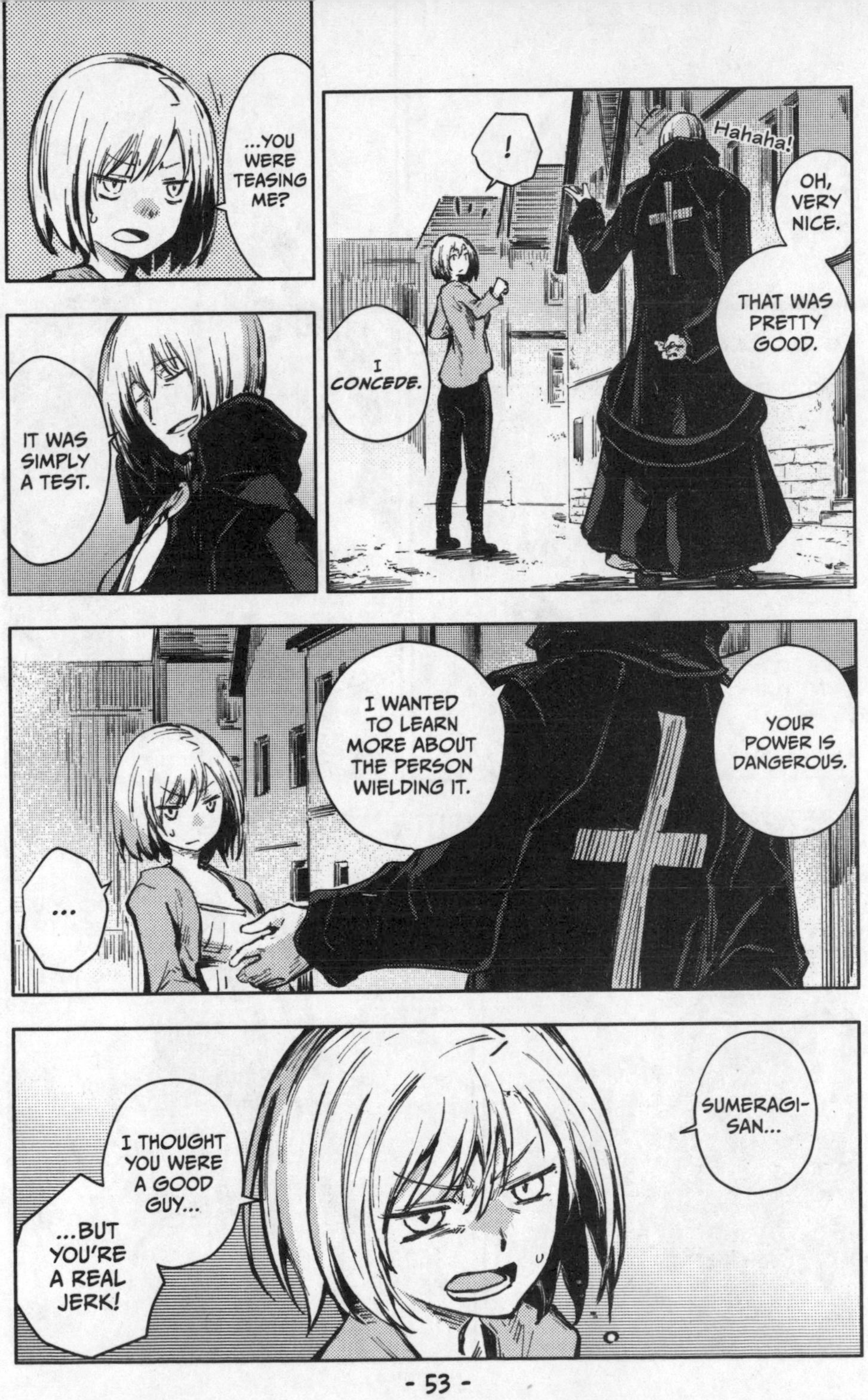
Hahaha!
OH, VERY NICE.
THAT WAS PRETTY GOOD.
!
I CONCEDE.
...YOU WERE TEASING ME?
IT WAS SIMPLY A TEST.
YOUR POWER IS DANGEROUS.
I WANTED TO LEARN MORE ABOUT THE PERSON WIELDING IT.
...
SUMERAGI-SAN...
I THOUGHT YOU WERE A GOOD GUY...
...BUT YOU'RE A REAL JERK!

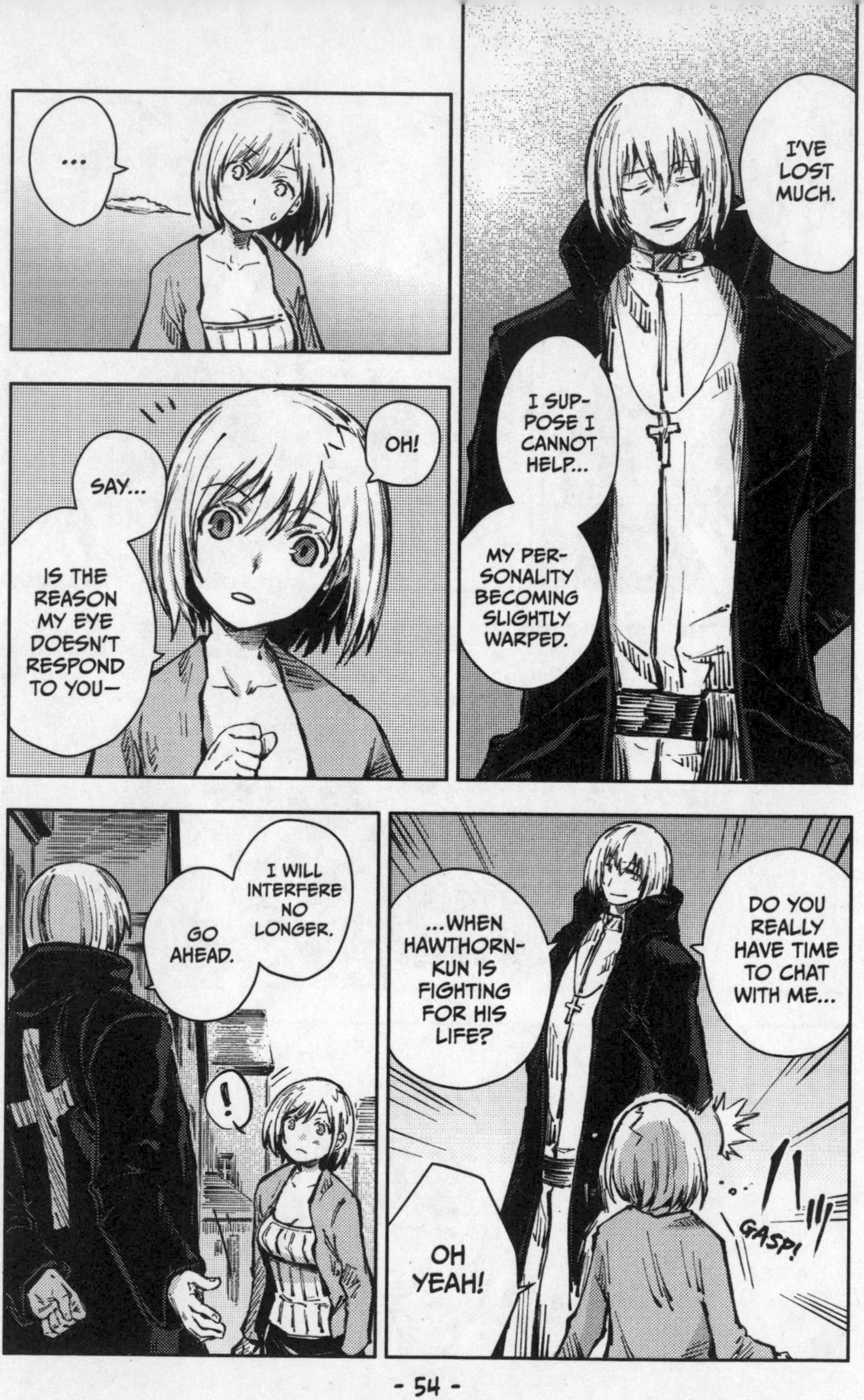
I'VE LOST MUCH.
I SUP-POSE I CANNOT HELP...
MY PER-SONALITY BECOMING SLIGHTLY WARPED.
...
OH!
SAY...
IS THE REASON MY EYE DOESN'T RESPOND TO YOU—
DO YOU REALLY HAVE TIME TO CHAT WITH ME...
...WHEN HAWTHORN-KUN IS FIGHTING FOR HIS LIFE?
GASP!
OH YEAH!
I WILL INTERFERE NO LONGER.
GO AHEAD.
!

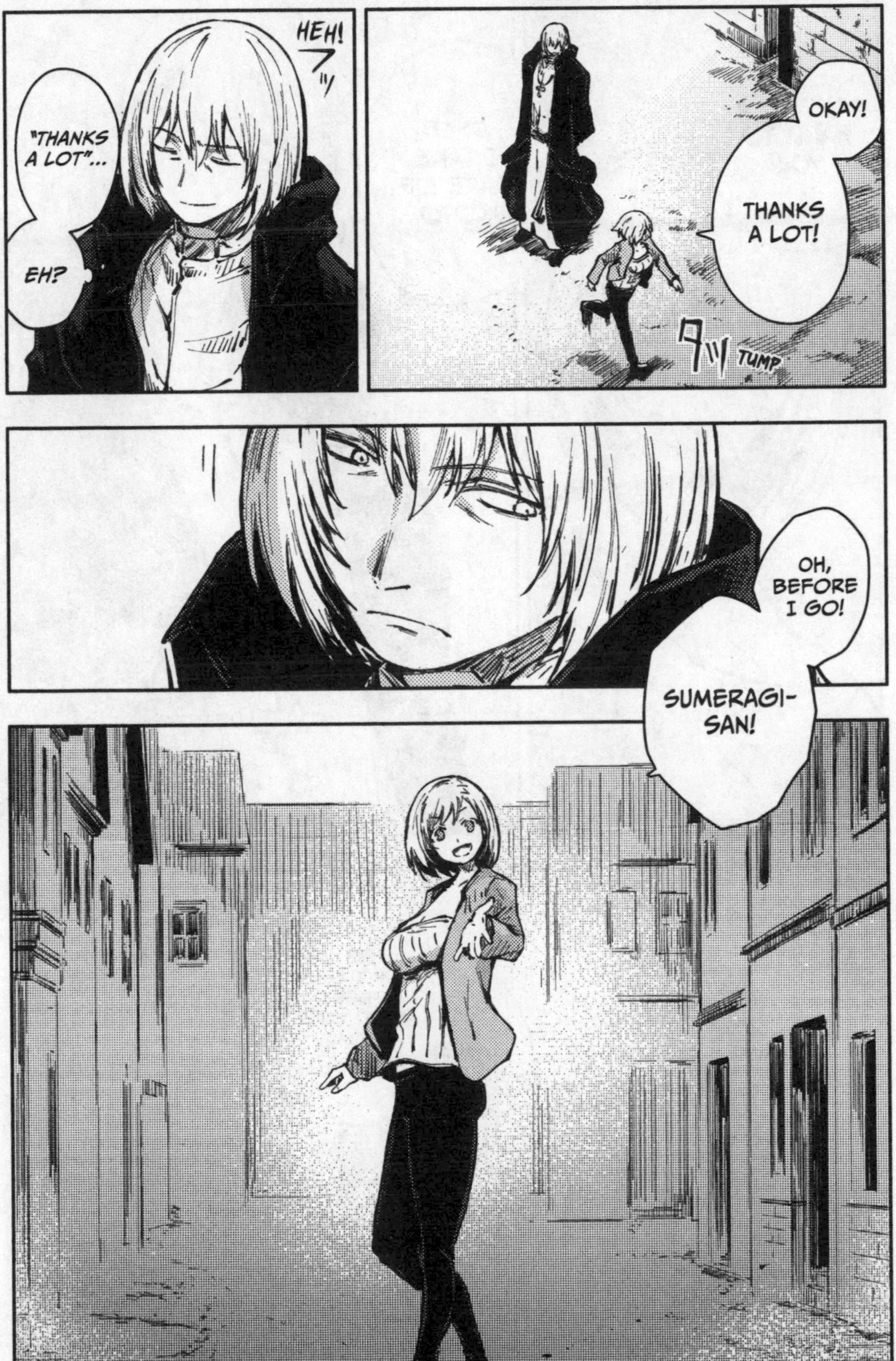
OKAY!
THANKS A LOT!
タッ TUMP
HEH!
フッ
"THANKS A LOT"...
EH?
OH, BEFORE I GO!
SUMERAGI-SAN!

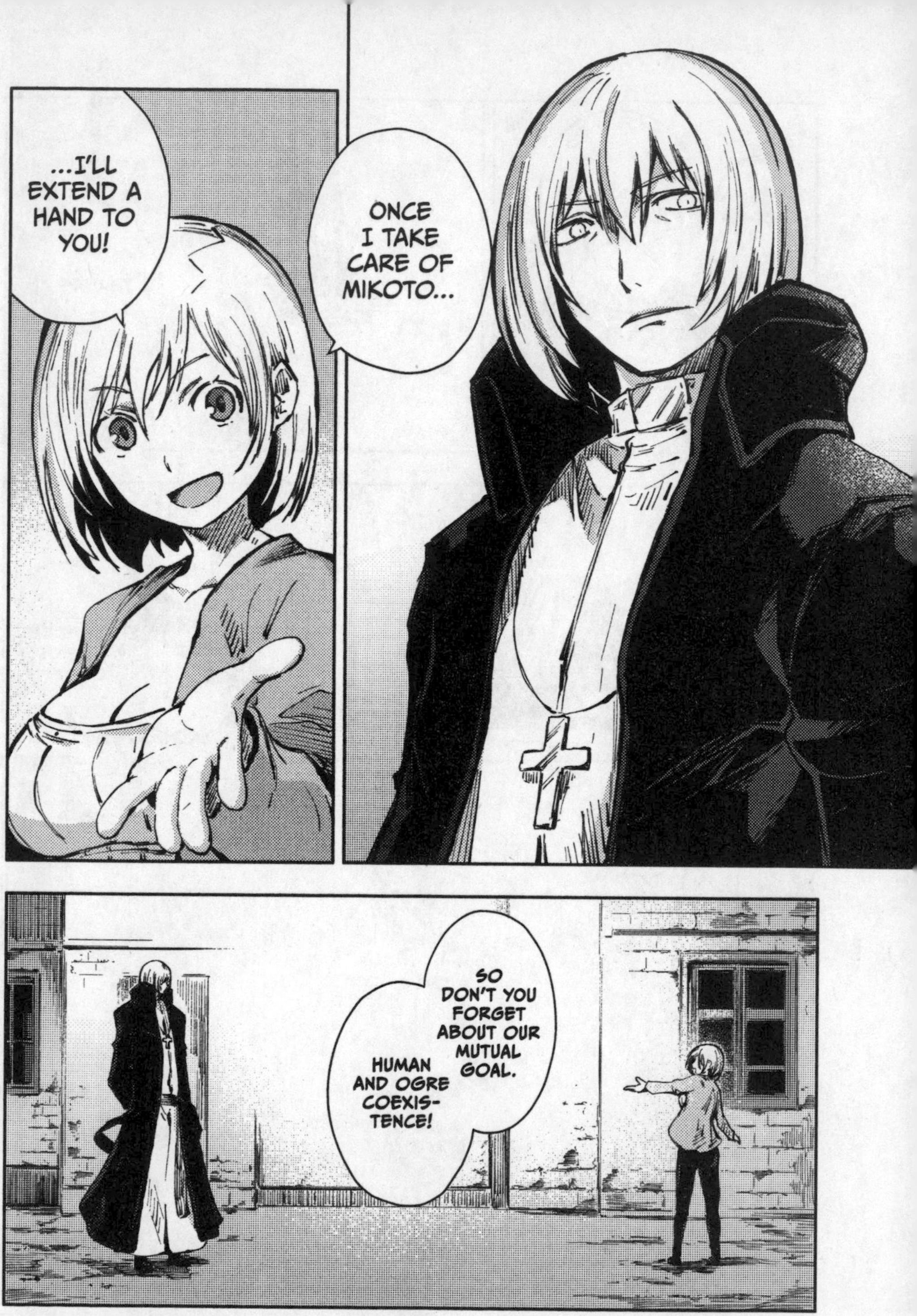
ONCE I TAKE CARE OF MIKOTO...
...I'LL EXTEND A HAND TO YOU!
SO DON'T YOU FORGET ABOUT OUR MUTUAL GOAL.
HUMAN AND OGRE COEXIS-TENCE!

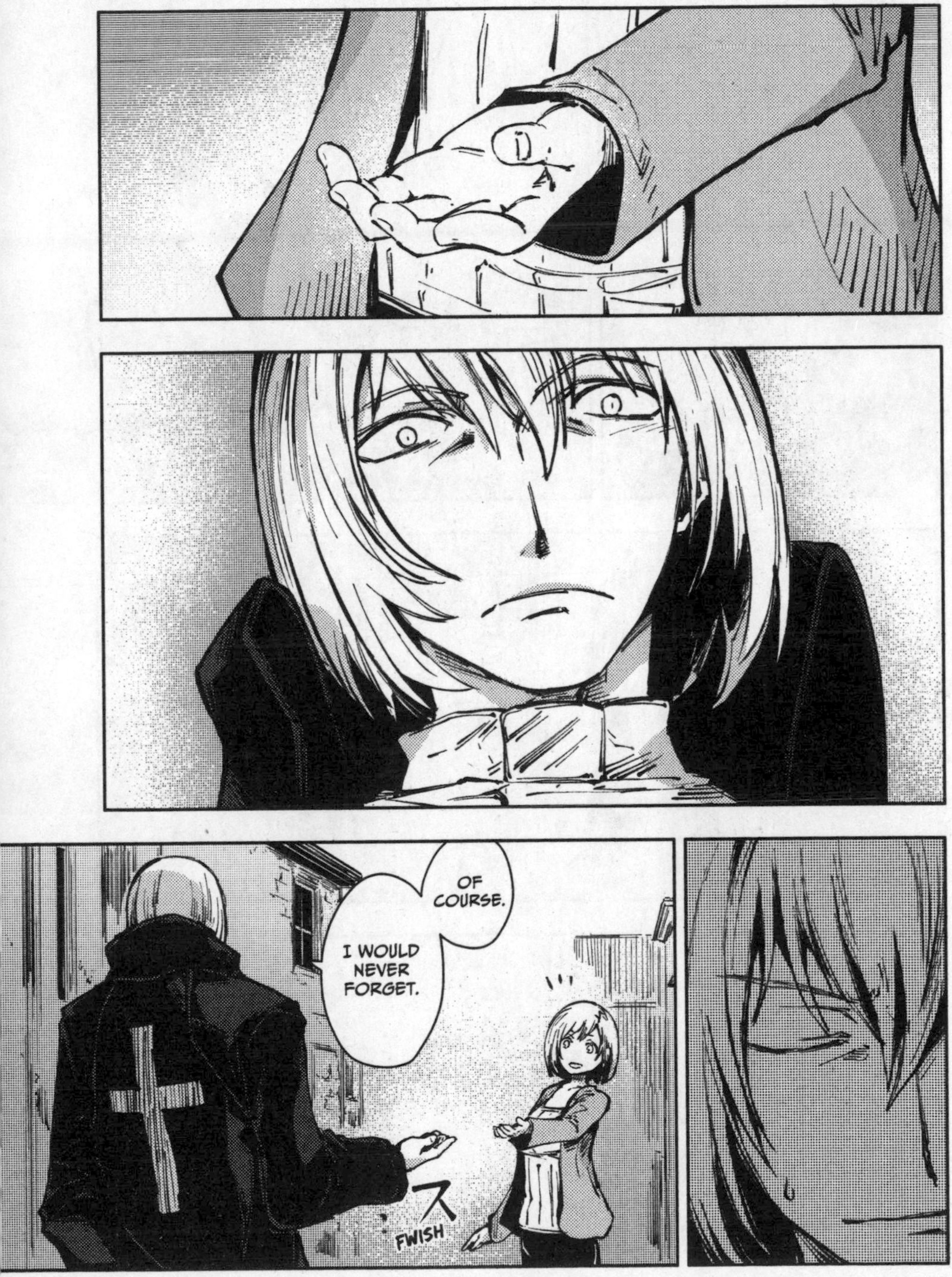
OF COURSE.
I WOULD NEVER FORGET.
ス
FWISH

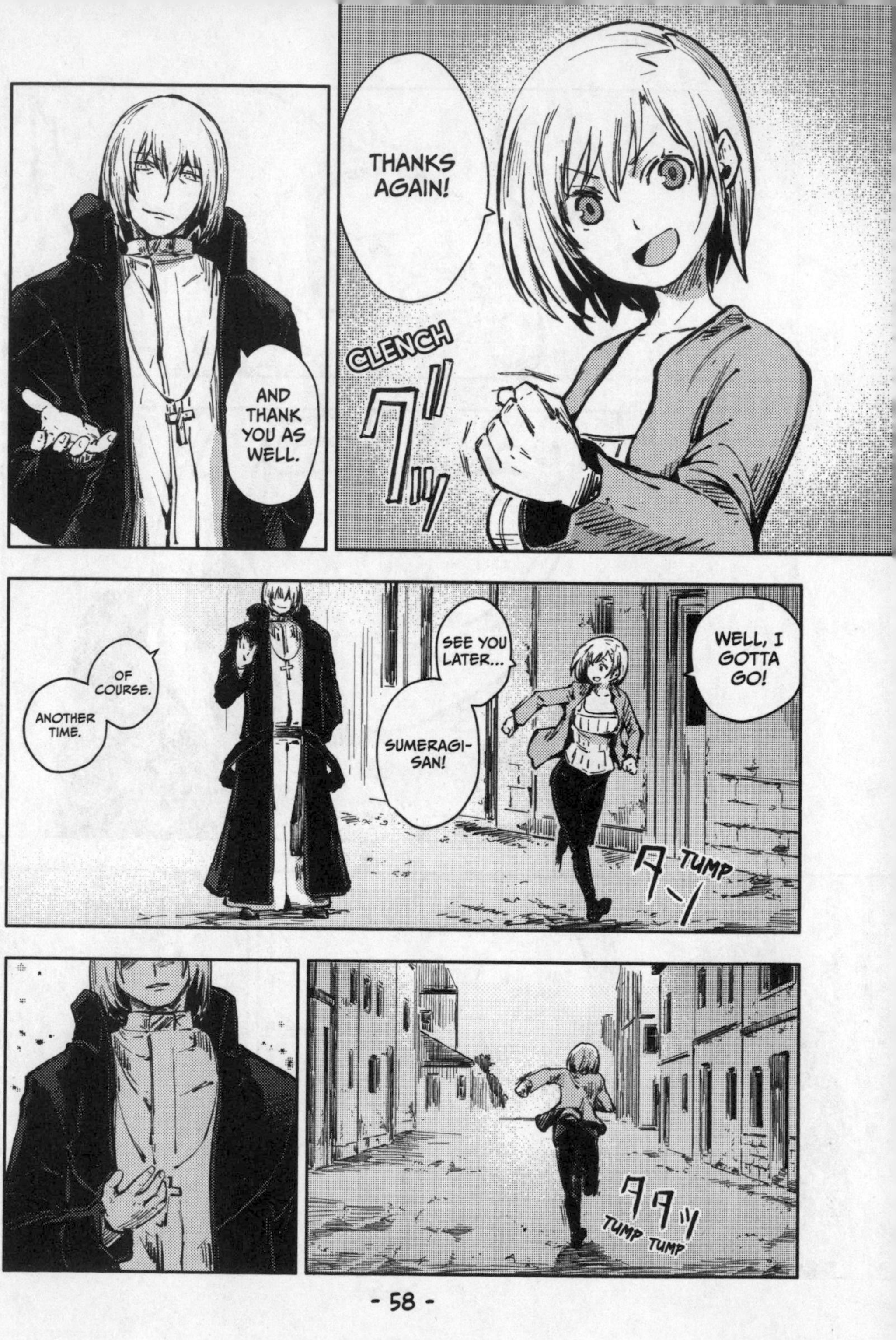
THANKS AGAIN!
CLENCH
グッ
AND THANK YOU AS WELL.
WELL, I GOTTA GO!
SEE YOU LATER...
SUMERAGI-SAN!
TUMP
OF COURSE.
ANOTHER TIME.
タタッ
TUMP TUMP

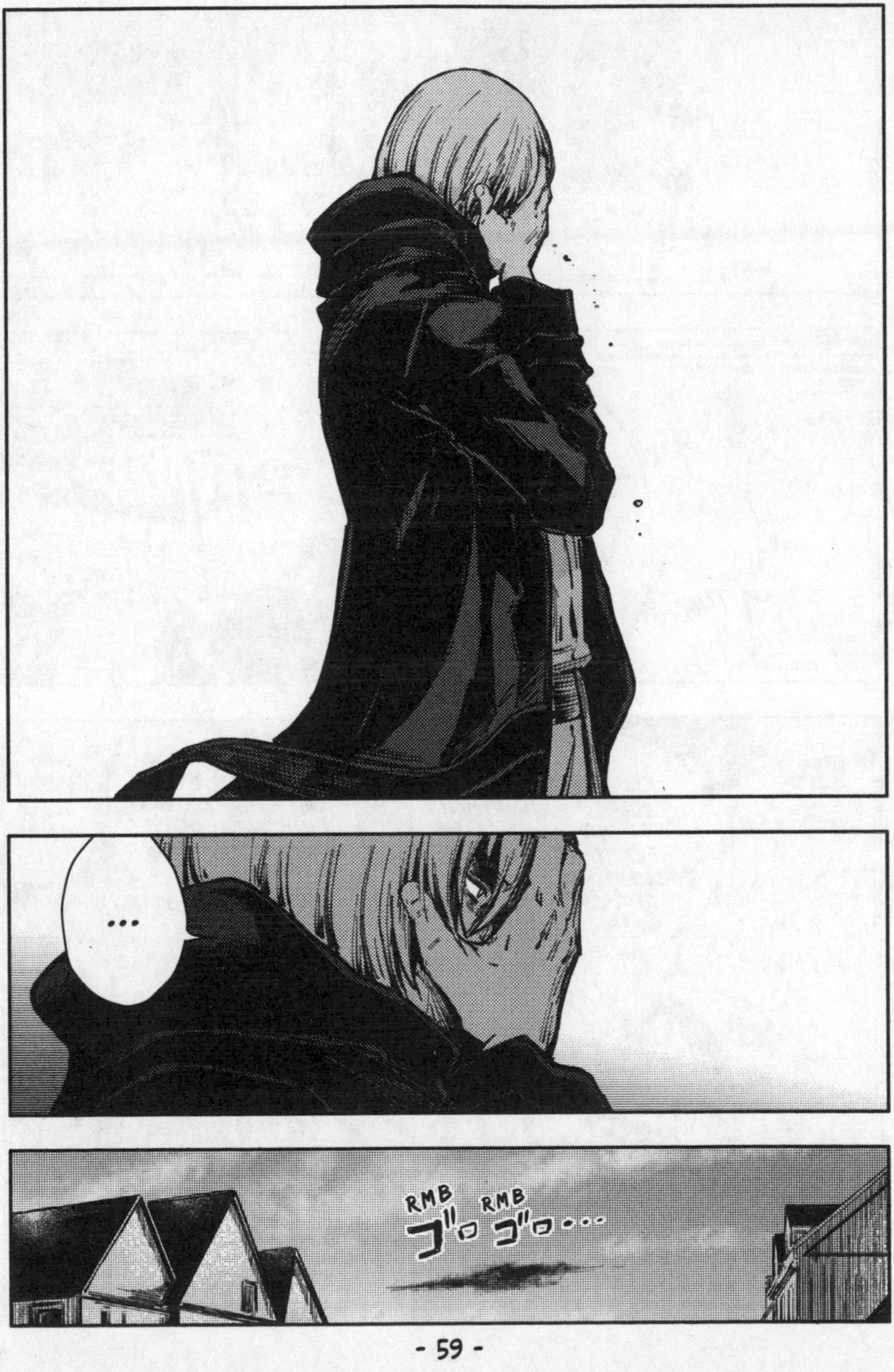
...
RMB RMB
ゴロ ゴロ...

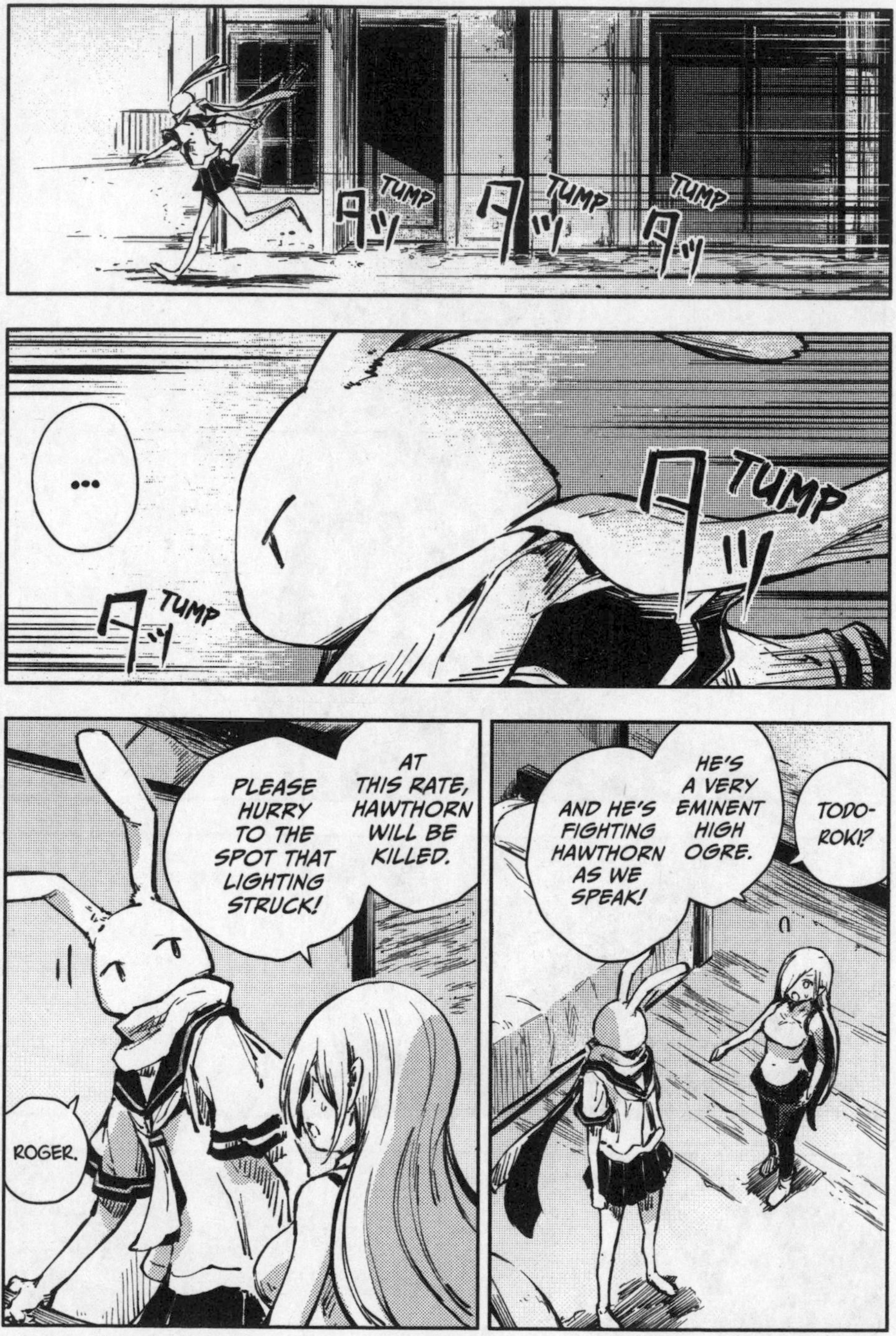
タッ
TUMP
タッ
TUMP
タッ
TUMP
TUMP
タッ
...
TUMP
タッ
TODO-ROKI!?
HE'S A VERY EMINENT HIGH OGRE.
AND HE'S FIGHTING HAWTHORN AS WE SPEAK!
AT THIS RATE, HAWTHORN WILL BE KILLED.
PLEASE HURRY TO THE SPOT THAT LIGHTING STRUCK!
ROGER.

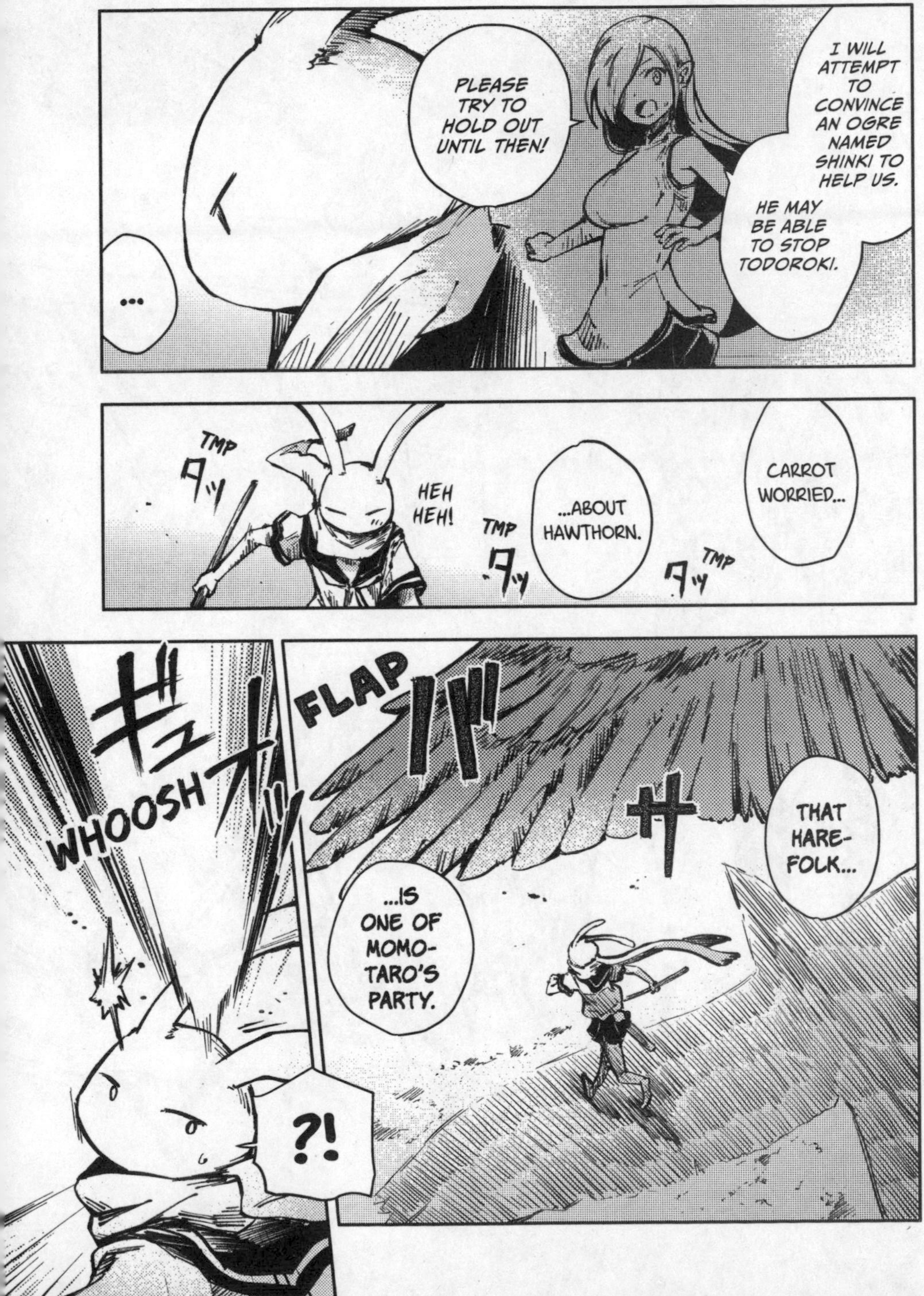
I WILL ATTEMPT TO CONVINCE AN OGRE NAMED SHINKI TO HELP US.
HE MAY BE ABLE TO STOP TODOROKI.
PLEASE TRY TO HOLD OUT UNTIL THEN!
...
CARROT WORRIED...
TMP
タッ
...ABOUT HAWTHORN.
TMP
タッ
HEH HEH!
TMP
タッ
FLAP
バ
サ
THAT HARE-FOLK...
...IS ONE OF MOMO-TARO'S PARTY.
ギュオッ
WHOOSH
?!

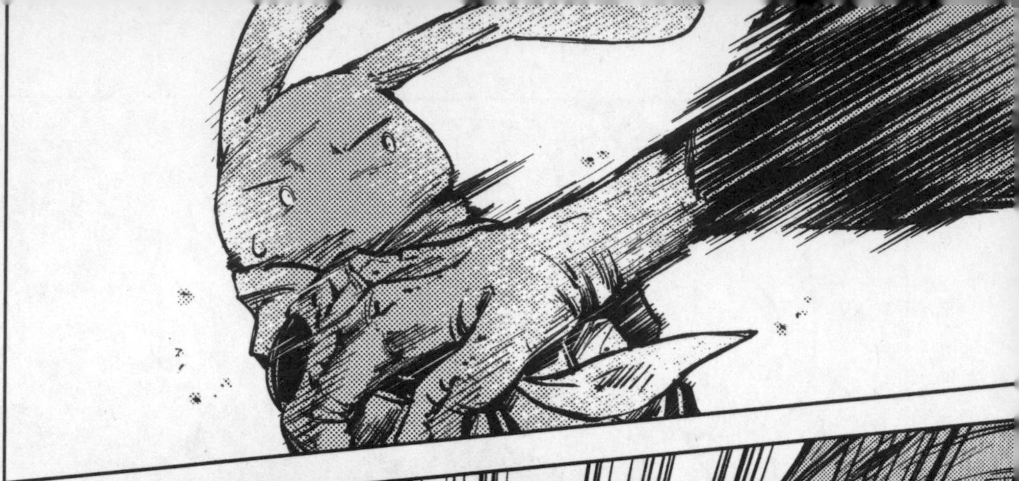

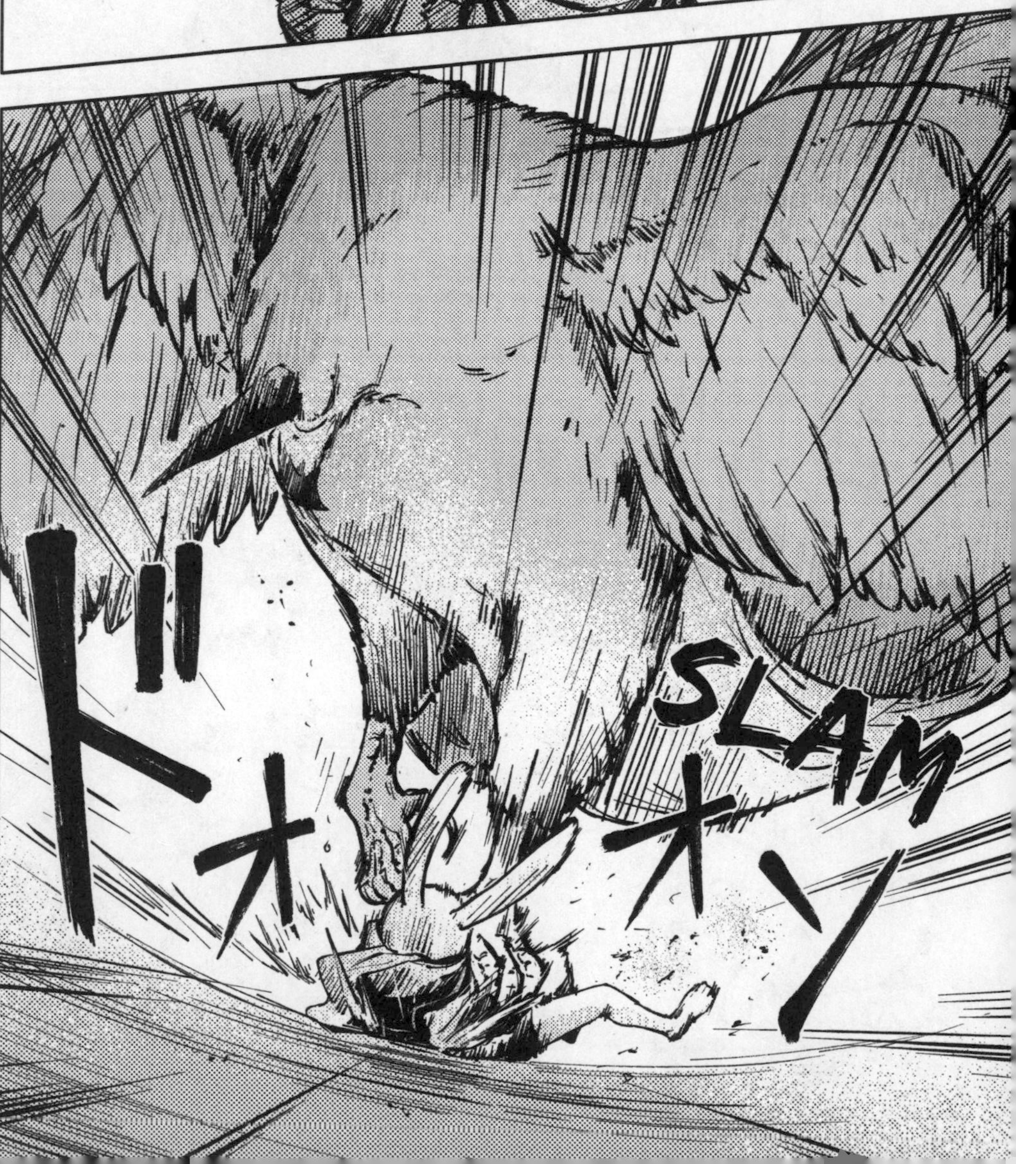
ドオオン
SLAM

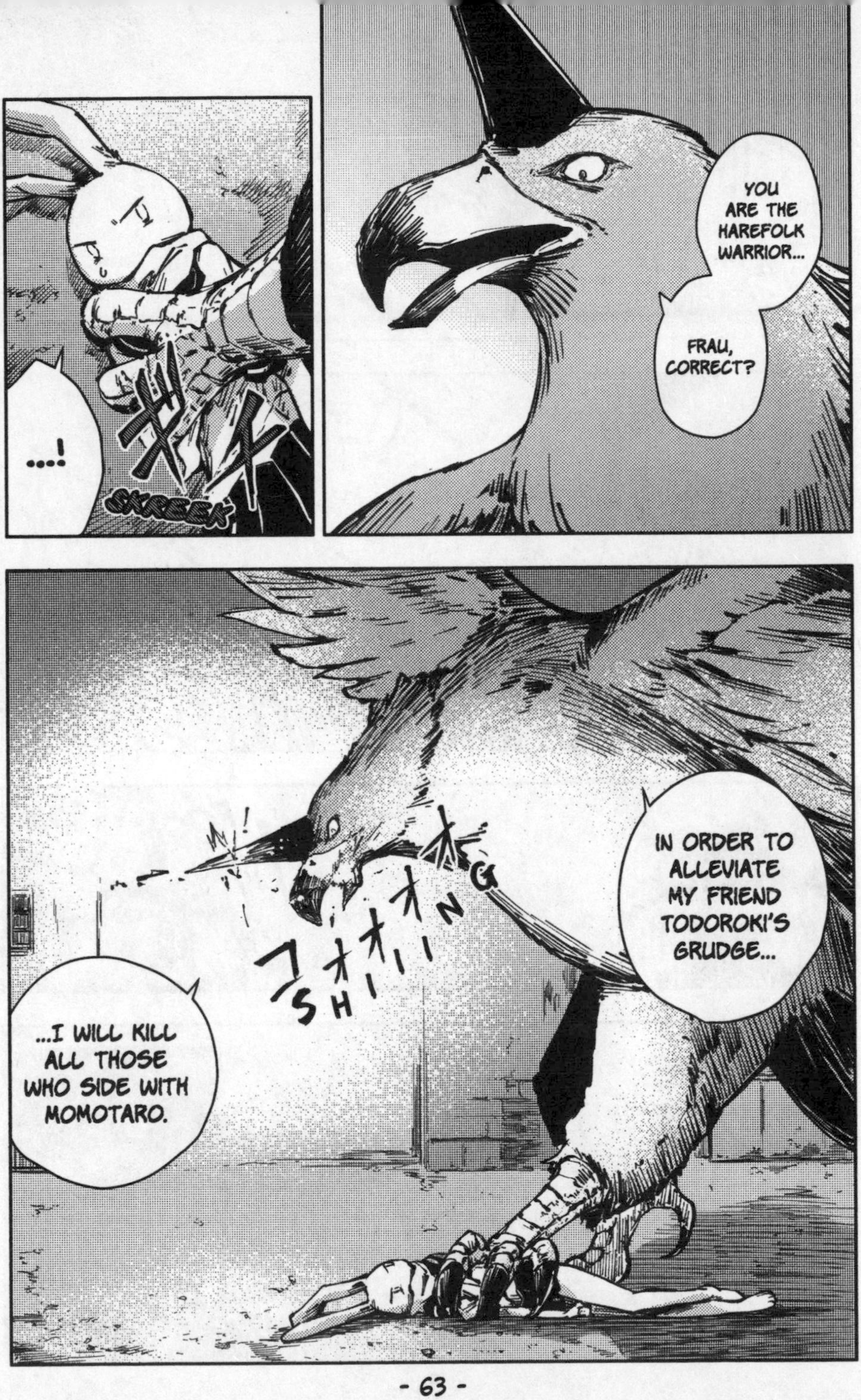
YOU ARE THE HAREFOLK WARRIOR...
FRAU, CORRECT?
...!
SKREEK
IN ORDER TO ALLEVIATE MY FRIEND TODOROKI'S GRUDGE...
SHIIIING
...I WILL KILL ALL THOSE WHO SIDE WITH MOMOTARO.

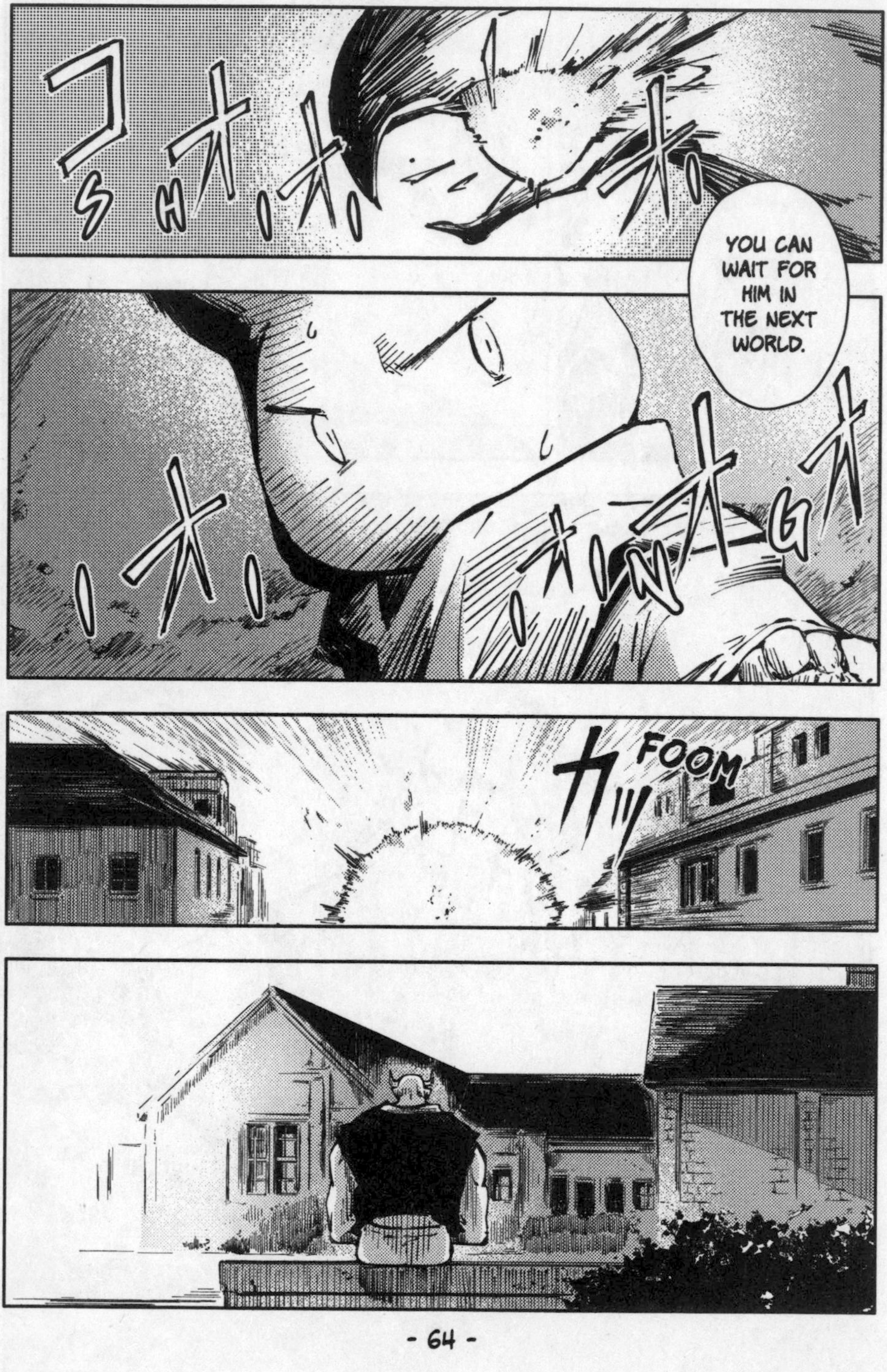
YOU CAN WAIT FOR HIM IN THE NEXT WORLD.
カッ
FOOM

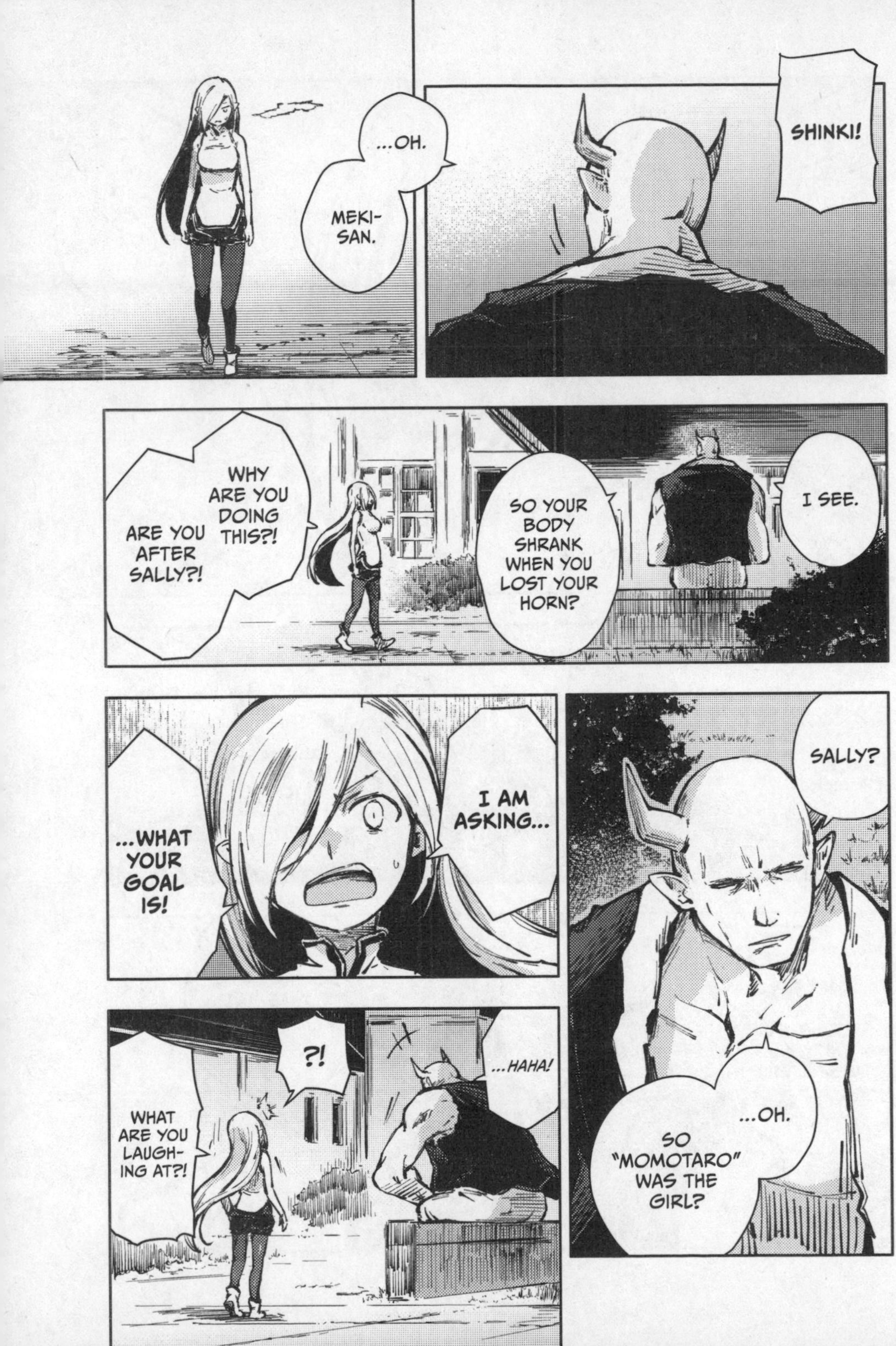
SHINKI!
...OH.
MEKI-SAN.
I SEE.
SO YOUR BODY SHRANK WHEN YOU LOST YOUR HORN?
WHY ARE YOU DOING THIS?!
ARE YOU AFTER SALLY?!
SALLY?
...OH.
SO "MOMOTARO" WAS THE GIRL?
I AM ASKING...
...WHAT YOUR GOAL IS!
...HAHA!
?!
WHAT ARE YOU LAUGHING AT?!

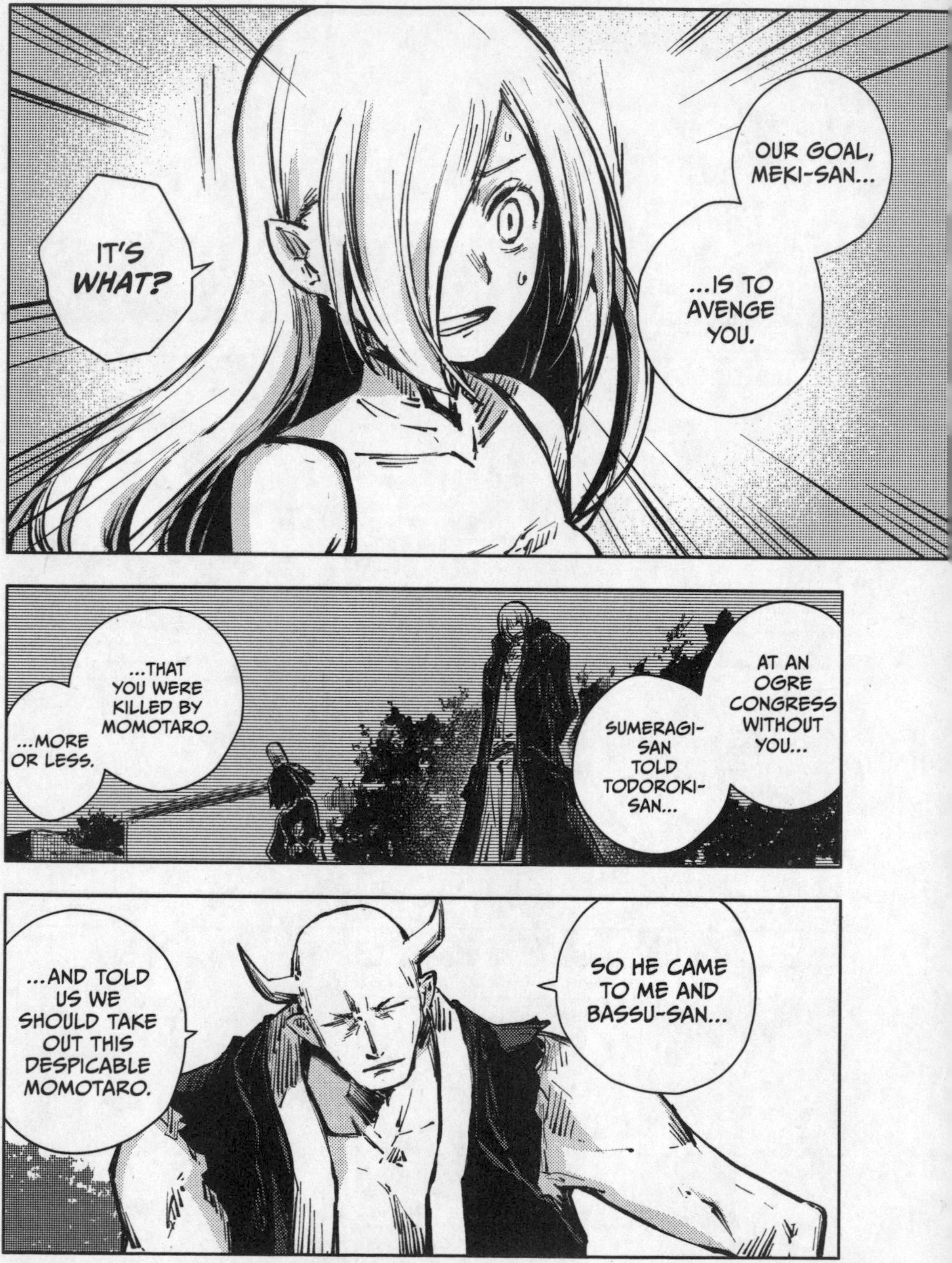
OUR GOAL, MEKI-SAN...
...IS TO AVENGE YOU.
IT'S *WHAT?*
AT AN OGRE CONGRESS WITHOUT YOU...
SUMERAGI-SAN TOLD TODOROKI-SAN...
...THAT YOU WERE KILLED BY MOMOTARO.
...MORE OR LESS.
SO HE CAME TO ME AND BASSU-SAN...
...AND TOLD US WE SHOULD TAKE OUT THIS DESPICABLE MOMOTARO.

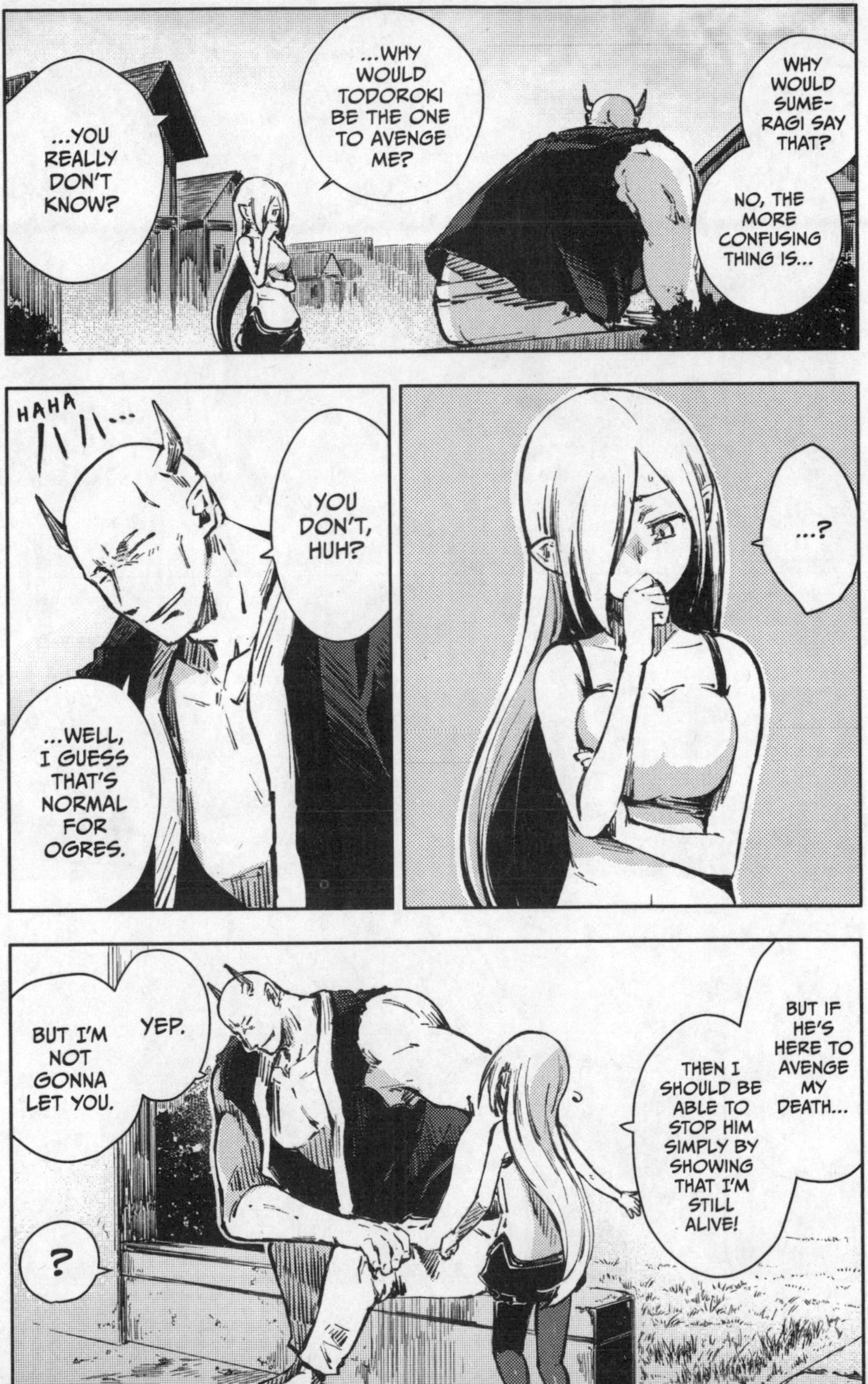
WHY WOULD SUME-RAGI SAY THAT?
NO, THE MORE CONFUSING THING IS...
...WHY WOULD TODOROKI BE THE ONE TO AVENGE ME?
...YOU REALLY DON'T KNOW?
...?
HAHA ハハ...
YOU DON'T, HUH?
...WELL, I GUESS THAT'S NORMAL FOR OGRES.
BUT IF HE'S HERE TO AVENGE MY DEATH...
THEN I SHOULD BE ABLE TO STOP HIM SIMPLY BY SHOWING THAT I'M STILL ALIVE!
YEP.
BUT I'M NOT GONNA LET YOU.
?

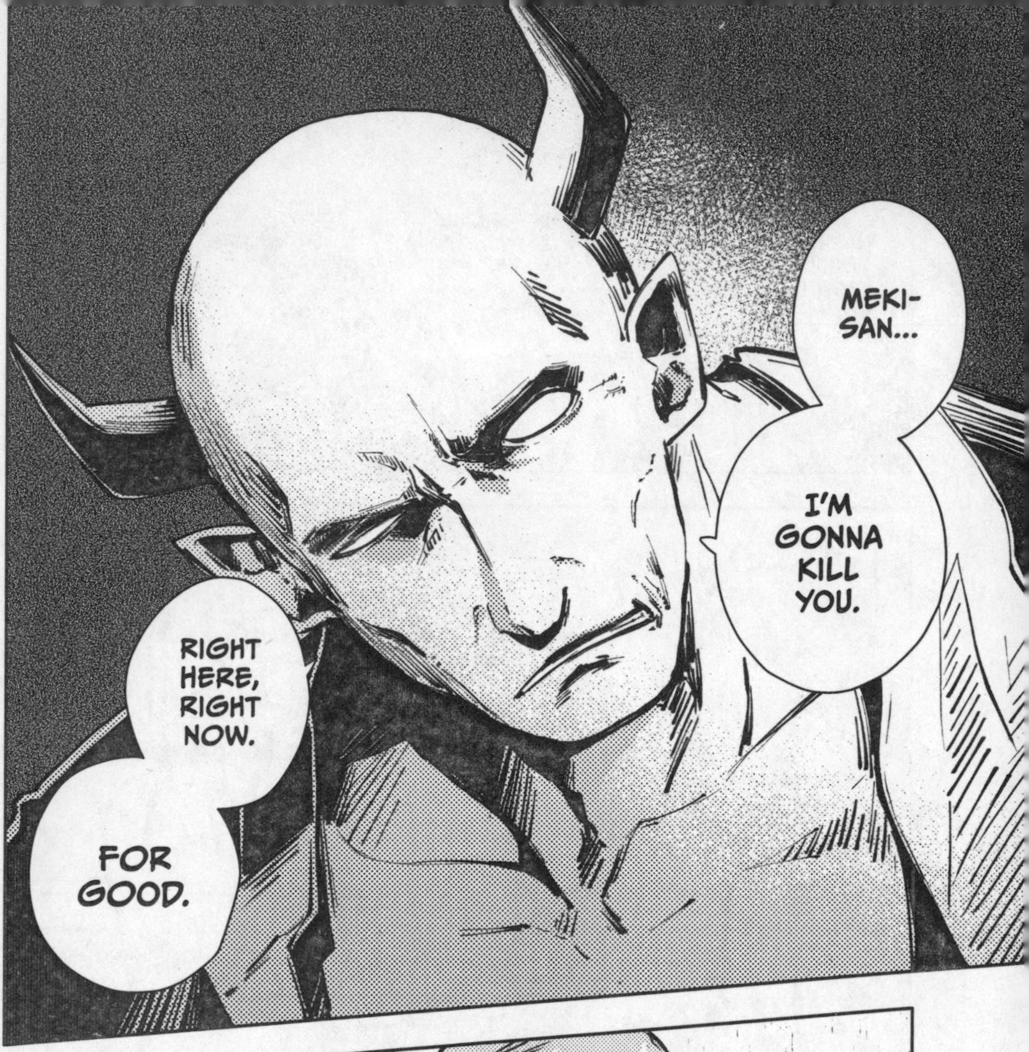
MEKI-SAN...
I'M GONNA KILL YOU.
RIGHT HERE, RIGHT NOW.
FOR GOOD.

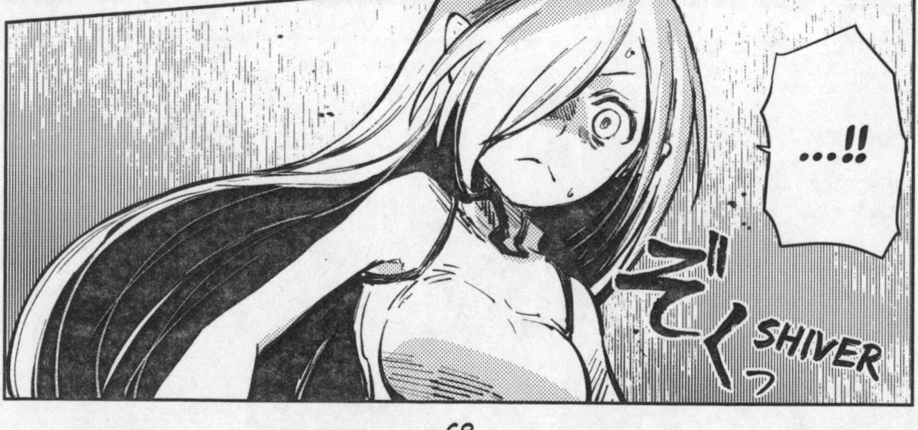
...!!
SHIVER

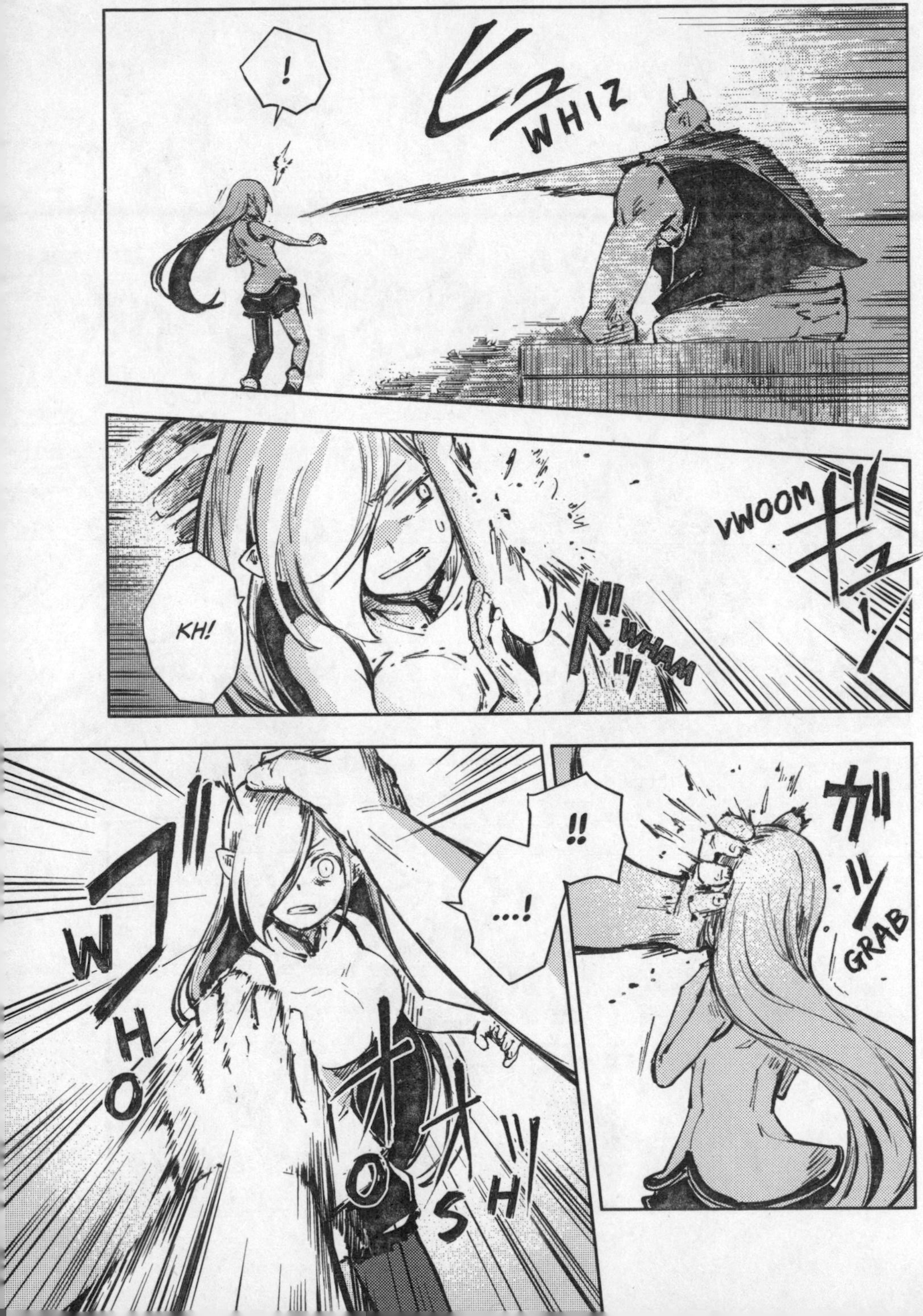

!
WHIZ
VWOOM
WHAM
KH!
GRAB
!!
...!
WHOOSH

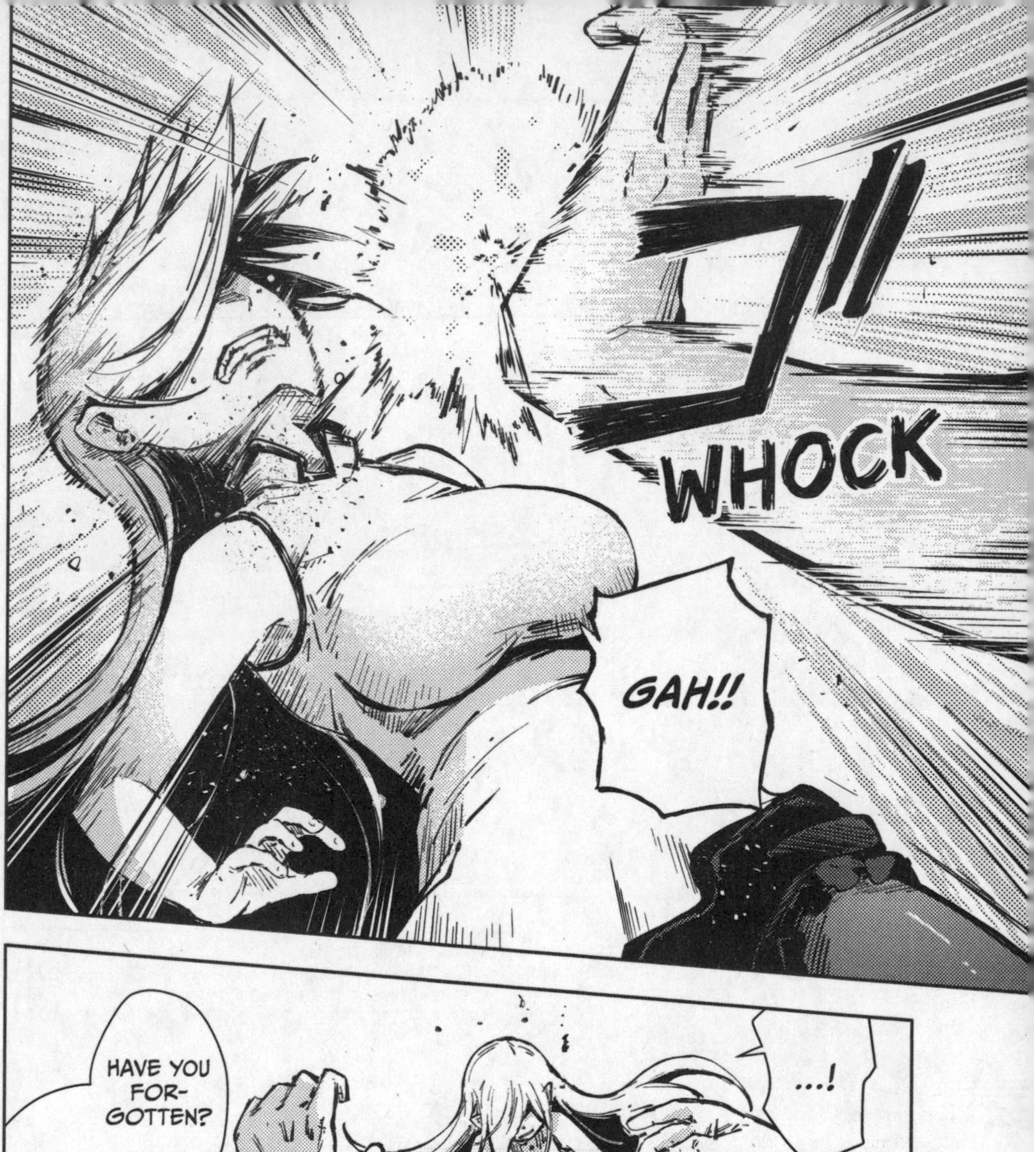
WHOCK
GAH!!

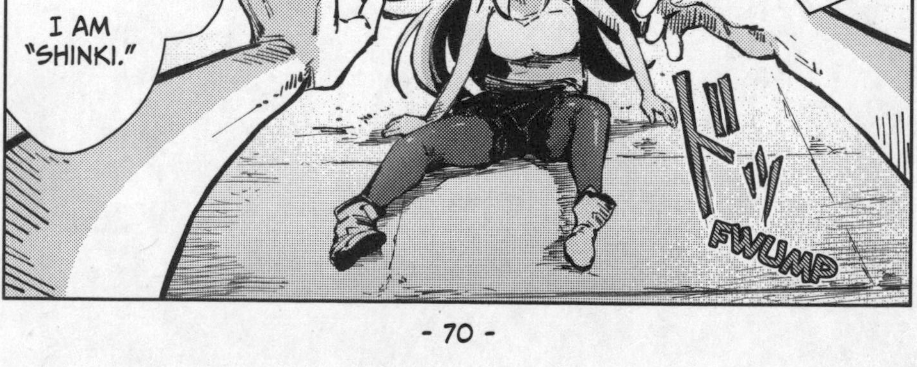
...!
HAVE YOU FOR-GOTTEN?
I AM "SHINKI."
FWUMP

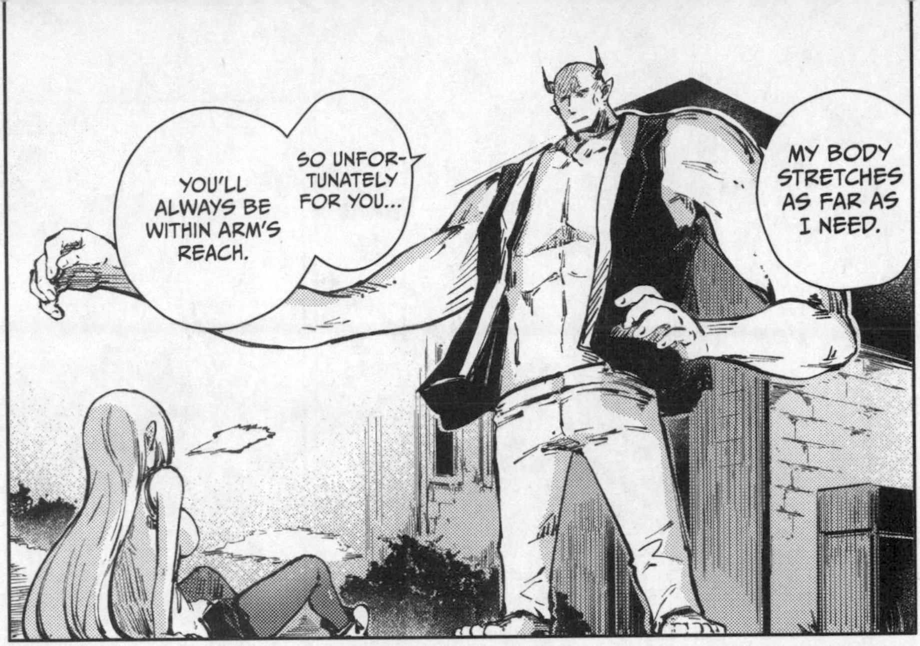
MY BODY STRETCHES AS FAR AS I NEED.
SO UNFOR-TUNATELY FOR YOU...
YOU'LL ALWAYS BE WITHIN ARM'S REACH.

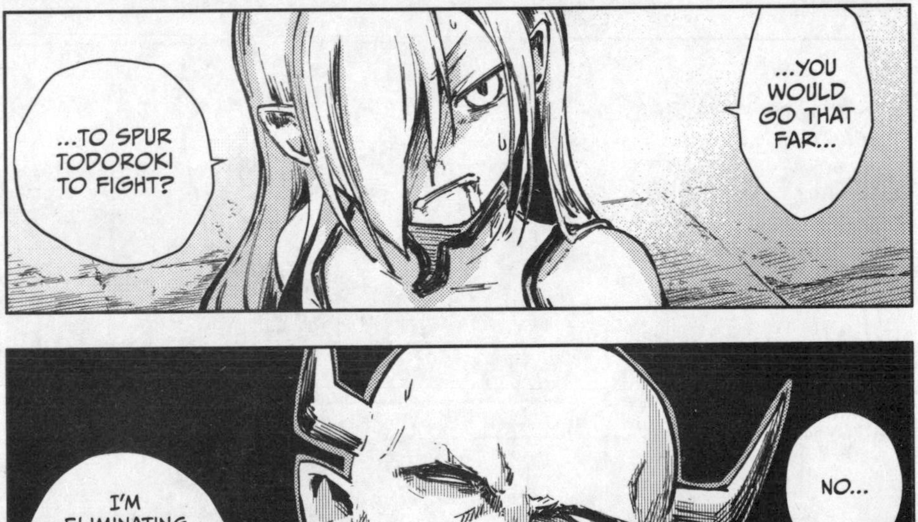
...YOU WOULD GO THAT FAR...
...TO SPUR TODOROKI TO FIGHT?

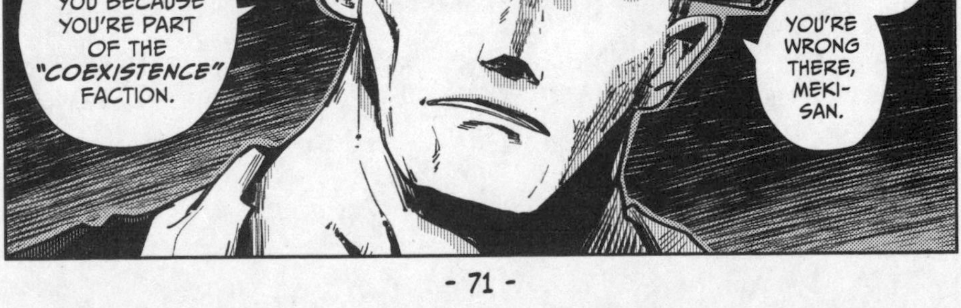
NO...
YOU'RE WRONG THERE, MEKI-SAN.
I'M ELIMINATING YOU BECAUSE YOU'RE PART OF THE *"COEXISTENCE"* FACTION.

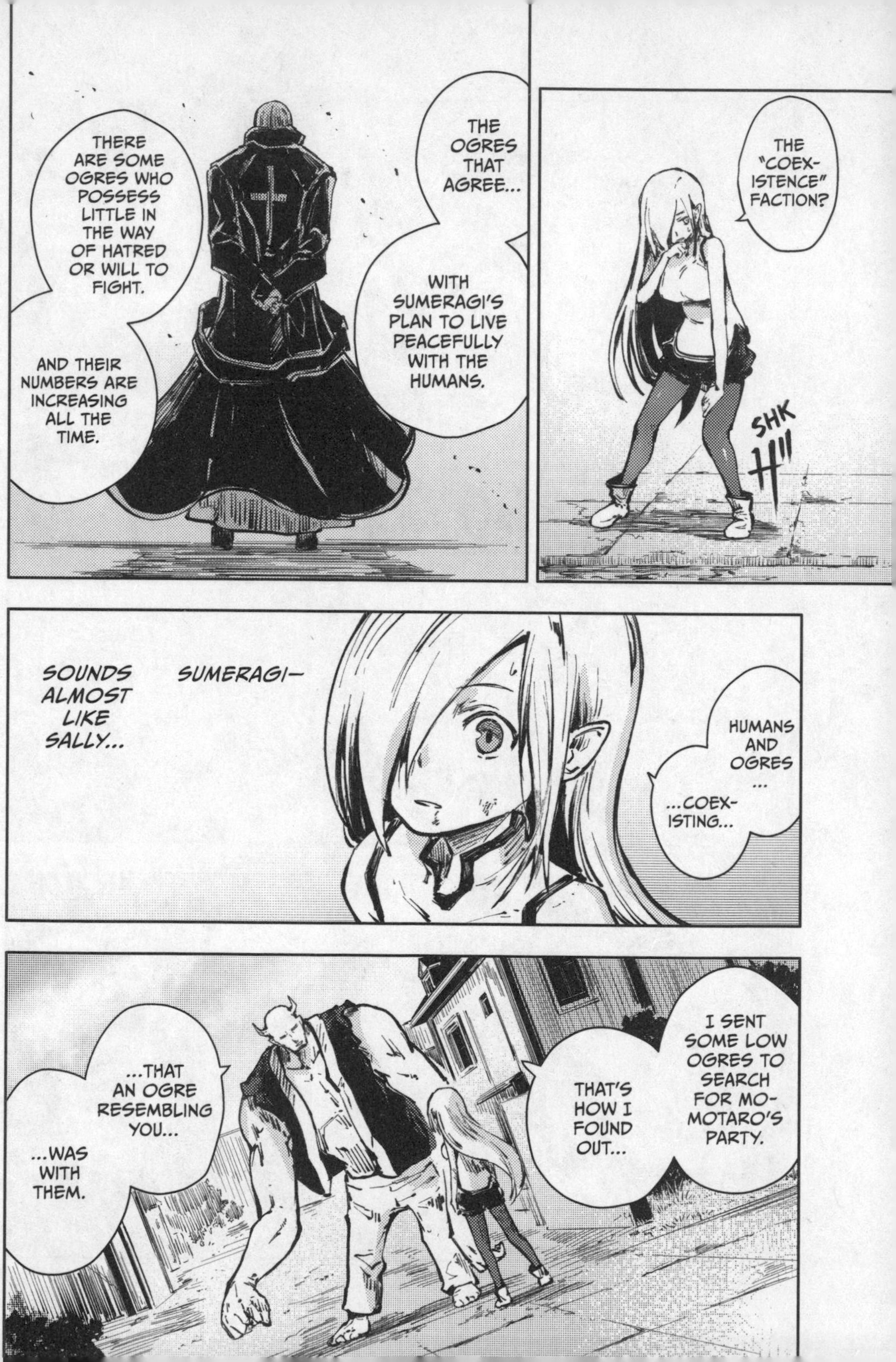
THE "COEXISTENCE" FACTION?
SHK
THE OGRES THAT AGREE...
WITH SUMERAGI'S PLAN TO LIVE PEACEFULLY WITH THE HUMANS.
THERE ARE SOME OGRES WHO POSSESS LITTLE IN THE WAY OF HATRED OR WILL TO FIGHT.
AND THEIR NUMBERS ARE INCREASING ALL THE TIME.
HUMANS AND OGRES...
...COEXISTING...
SUMERAGI—
SOUNDS ALMOST LIKE SALLY...
I SENT SOME LOW OGRES TO SEARCH FOR MOMOTARO'S PARTY.
THAT'S HOW I FOUND OUT...
...THAT AN OGRE RESEMBLING YOU...
...WAS WITH THEM.

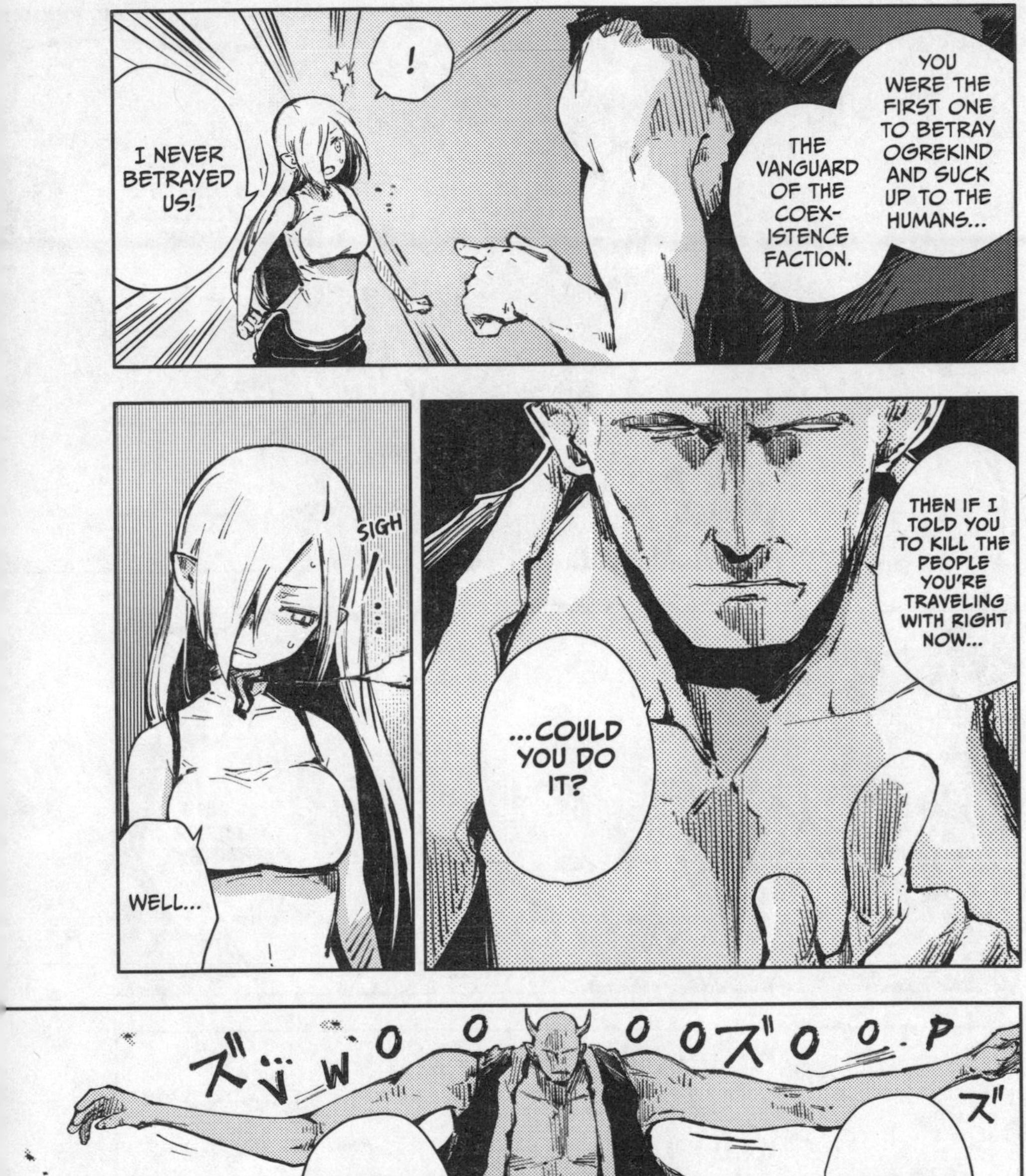
YOU WERE THE FIRST ONE TO BETRAY OGREKIND AND SUCK UP TO THE HUMANS...
THE VANGUARD OF THE COEX-ISTENCE FACTION.
!
I NEVER BETRAYED US!
THEN IF I TOLD YOU TO KILL THE PEOPLE YOU'RE TRAVELING WITH RIGHT NOW...
...COULD YOU DO IT?
SIGH
...
WELL...
WOOOOOOP
SEE? YOU HESITATED.
THAT'S ENOUGH TO PROVE...
...YOU'RE NO LONGER AN OGRE.

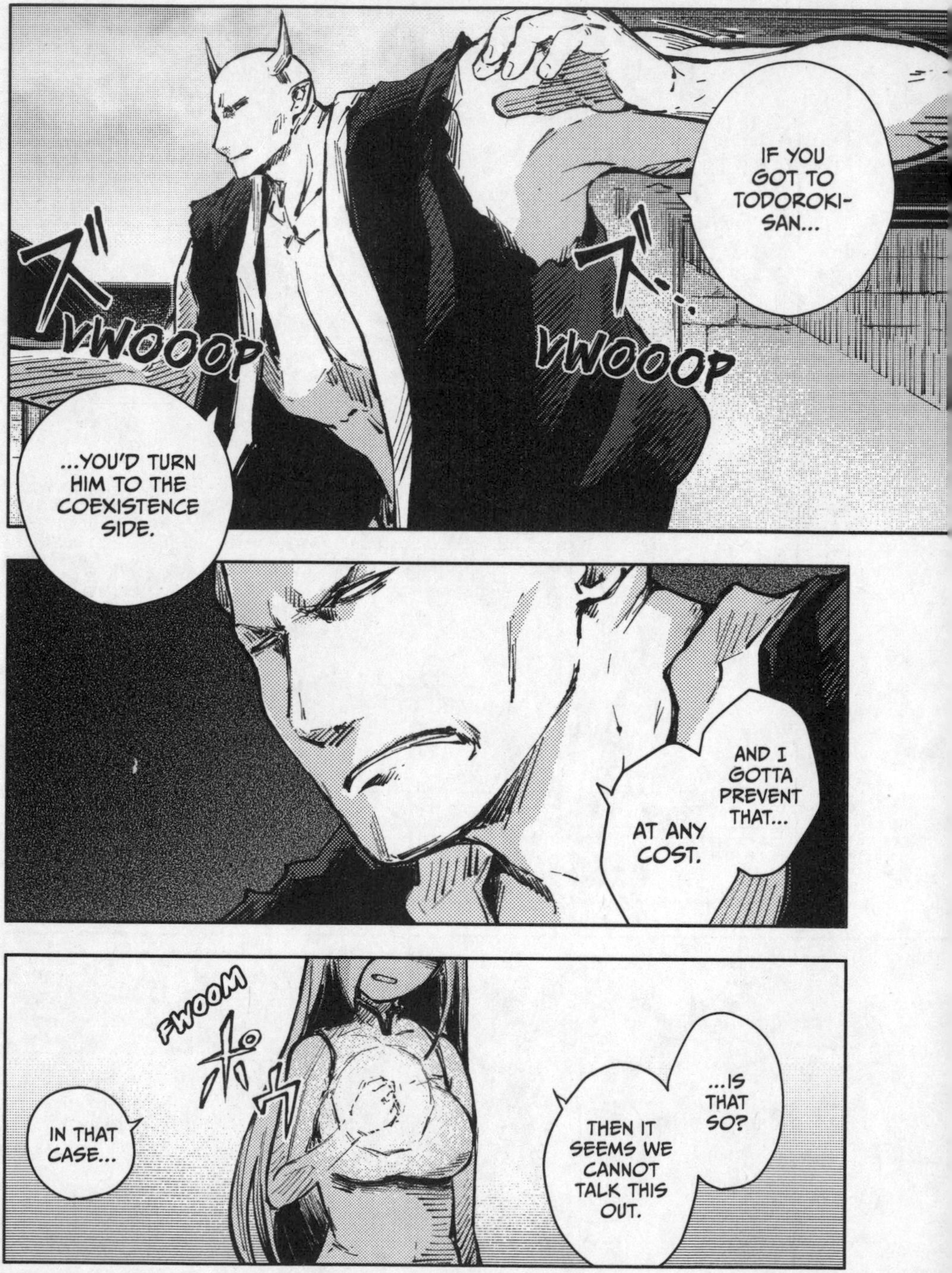
IF YOU GOT TO TODOROKI-SAN...
VWOOOP
VWOOOP
...YOU'D TURN HIM TO THE COEXISTENCE SIDE.
AND I GOTTA PREVENT THAT...
AT ANY COST.
...IS THAT SO?
THEN IT SEEMS WE CANNOT TALK THIS OUT.
FWOOM
IN THAT CASE...

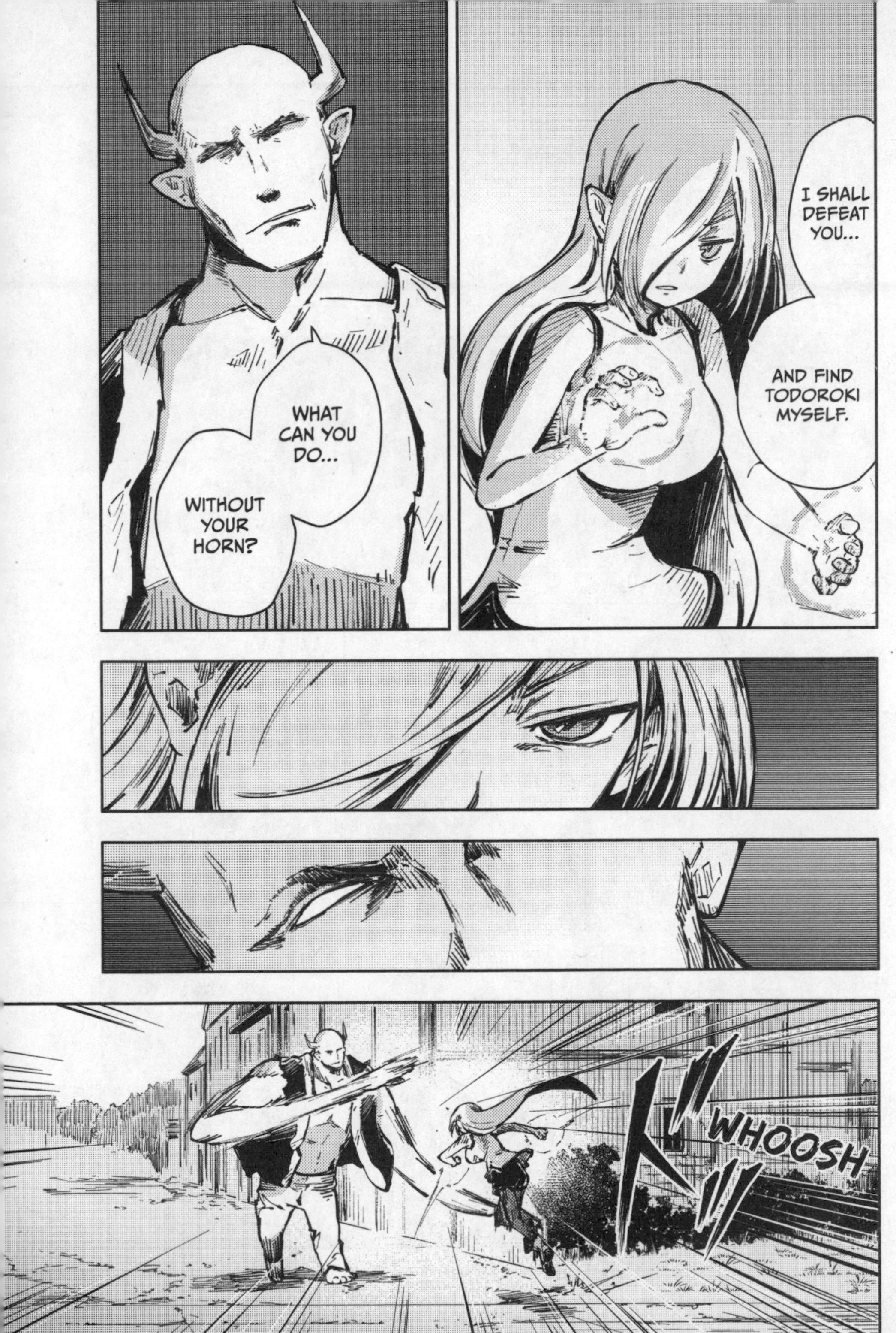
I SHALL DEFEAT YOU...
AND FIND TODOROKI MYSELF.
WHAT CAN YOU DO...
WITHOUT YOUR HORN?
WHOOSH

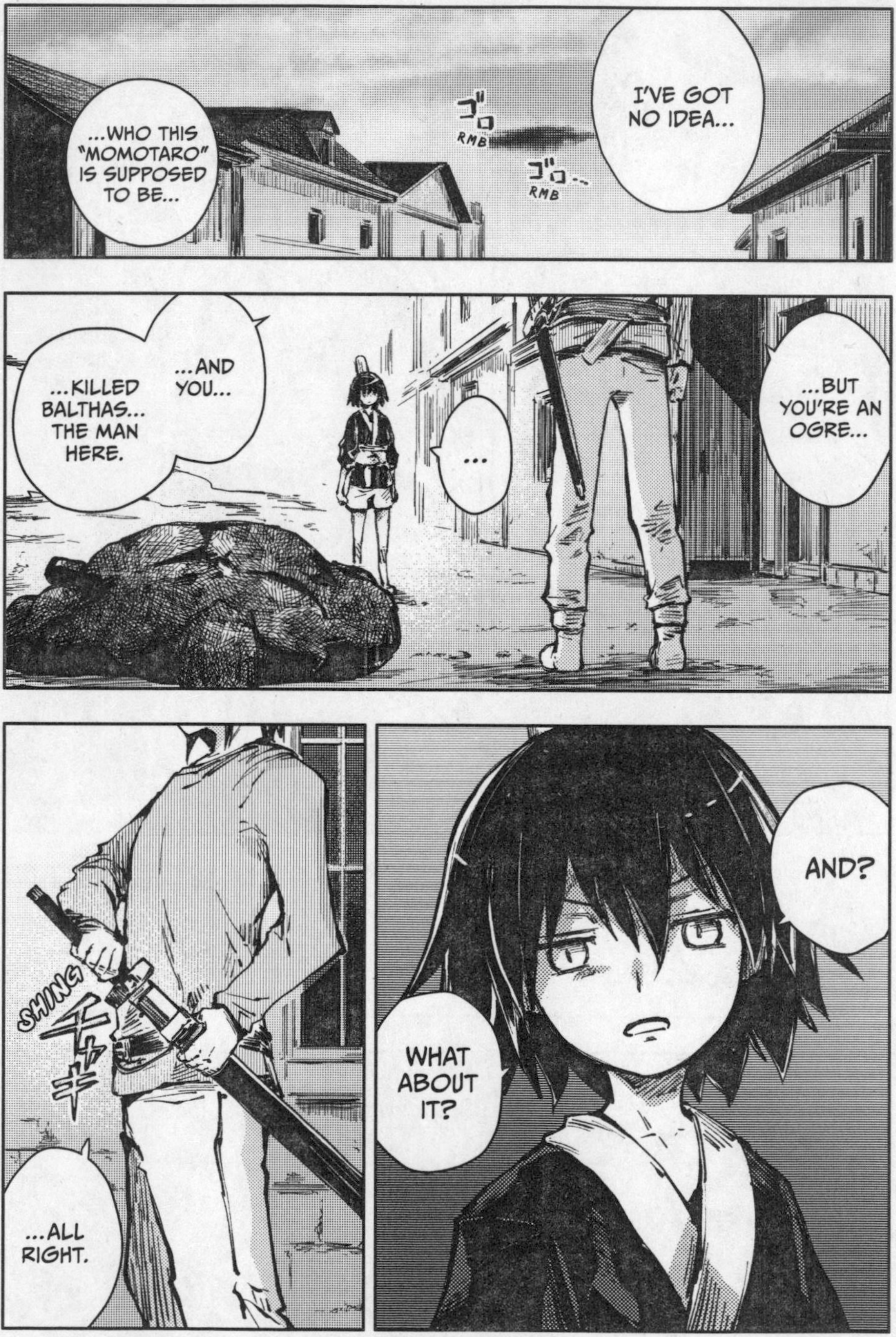
I'VE GOT NO IDEA...
ゴロ RMB
ゴロ... RMB
...WHO THIS "MOMOTARO" IS SUPPOSED TO BE...
...BUT YOU'RE AN OGRE...
...
...AND YOU...
...KILLED BALTHAS... THE MAN HERE.
AND?
WHAT ABOUT IT?
SHING チャキ
...ALL RIGHT.

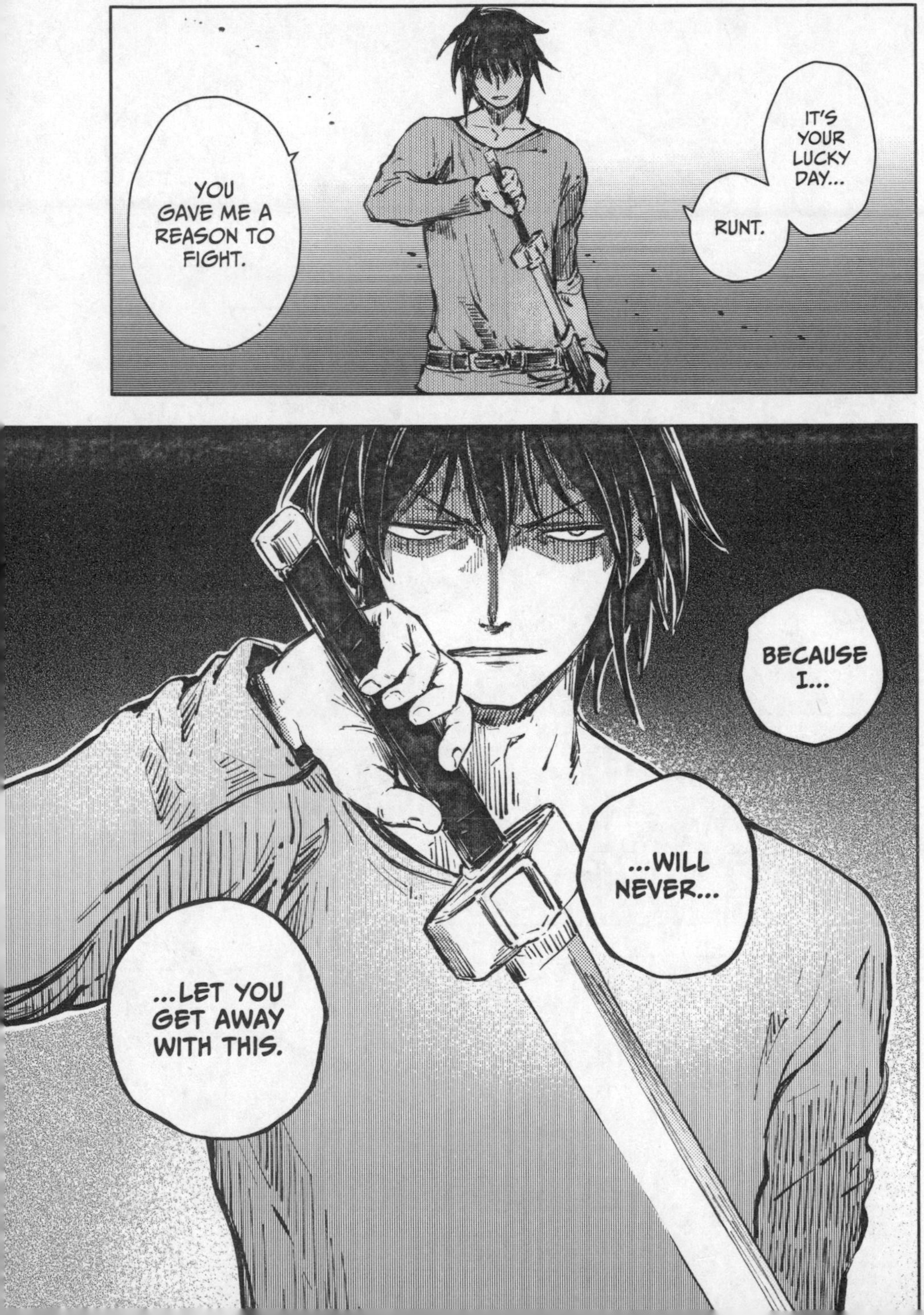
IT'S YOUR LUCKY DAY...
RUNT.
YOU GAVE ME A REASON TO FIGHT.
BECAUSE I...
...WILL NEVER...
...LET YOU GET AWAY WITH THIS.

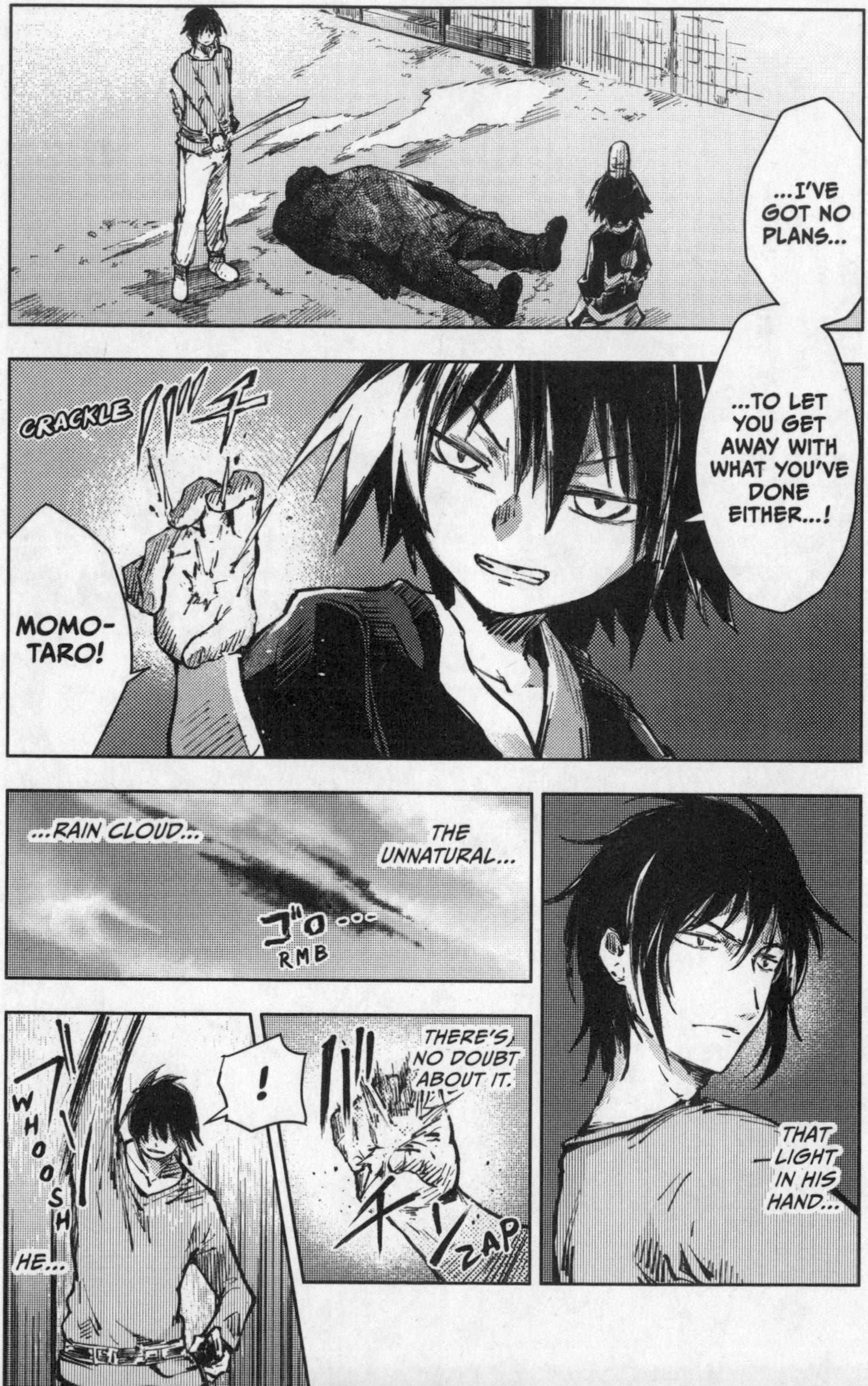
...I'VE GOT NO PLANS...
...TO LET YOU GET AWAY WITH WHAT YOU'VE DONE EITHER...!
パチ
CRACKLE
MOMO-TARO!
THAT LIGHT IN HIS HAND...
THE UNNATURAL...
...RAIN CLOUD...
ゴロ…
RMB
THERE'S NO DOUBT ABOUT IT.
ZAP
!
WHOOSH
HE...

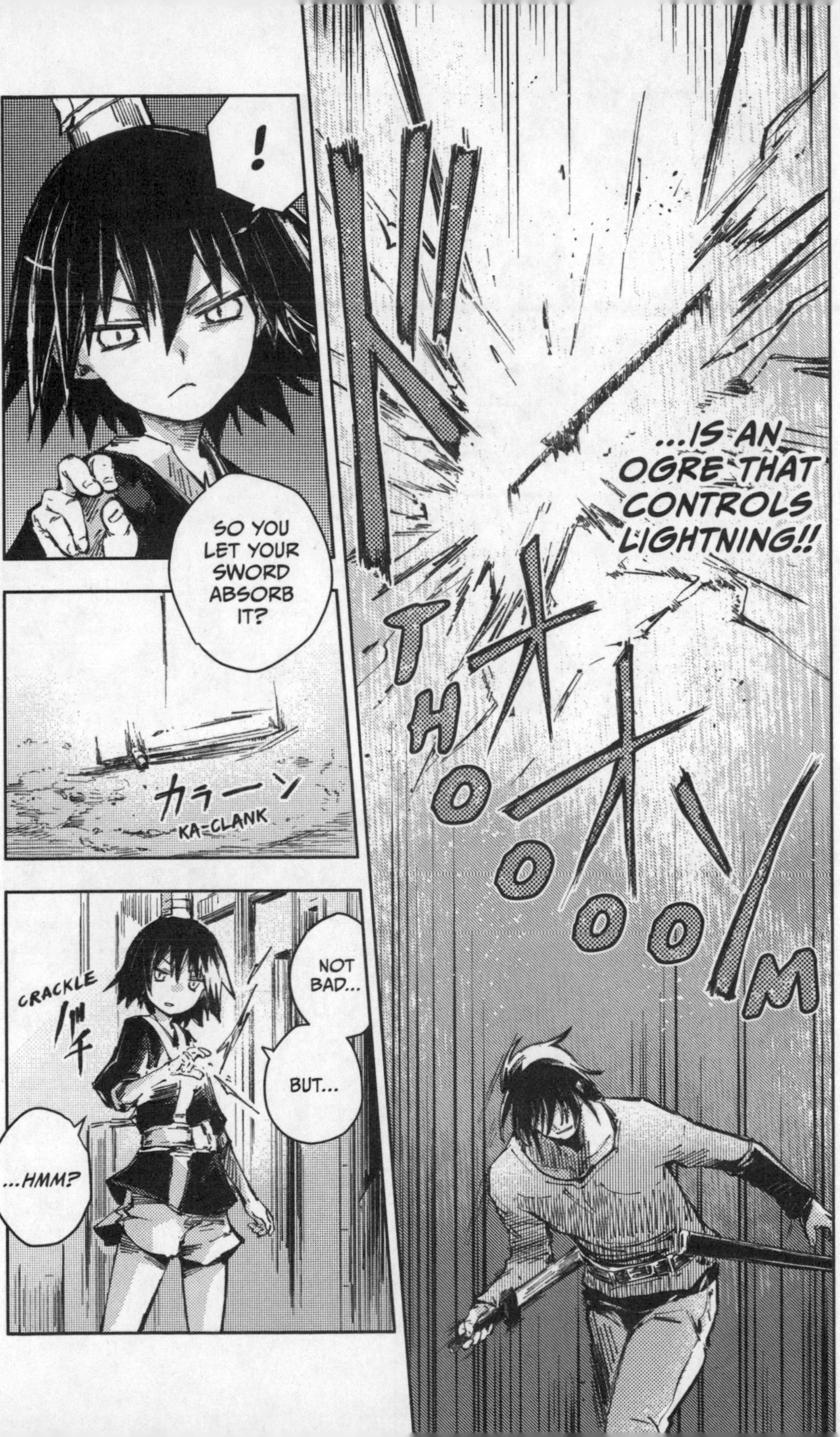
...IS AN OGRE THAT CONTROLS LIGHTNING!!
THOOOOOM
!
SO YOU LET YOUR SWORD ABSORB IT?
カラーン
KA-CLANK
CRACKLE
NOT BAD...
BUT...
...HMM?

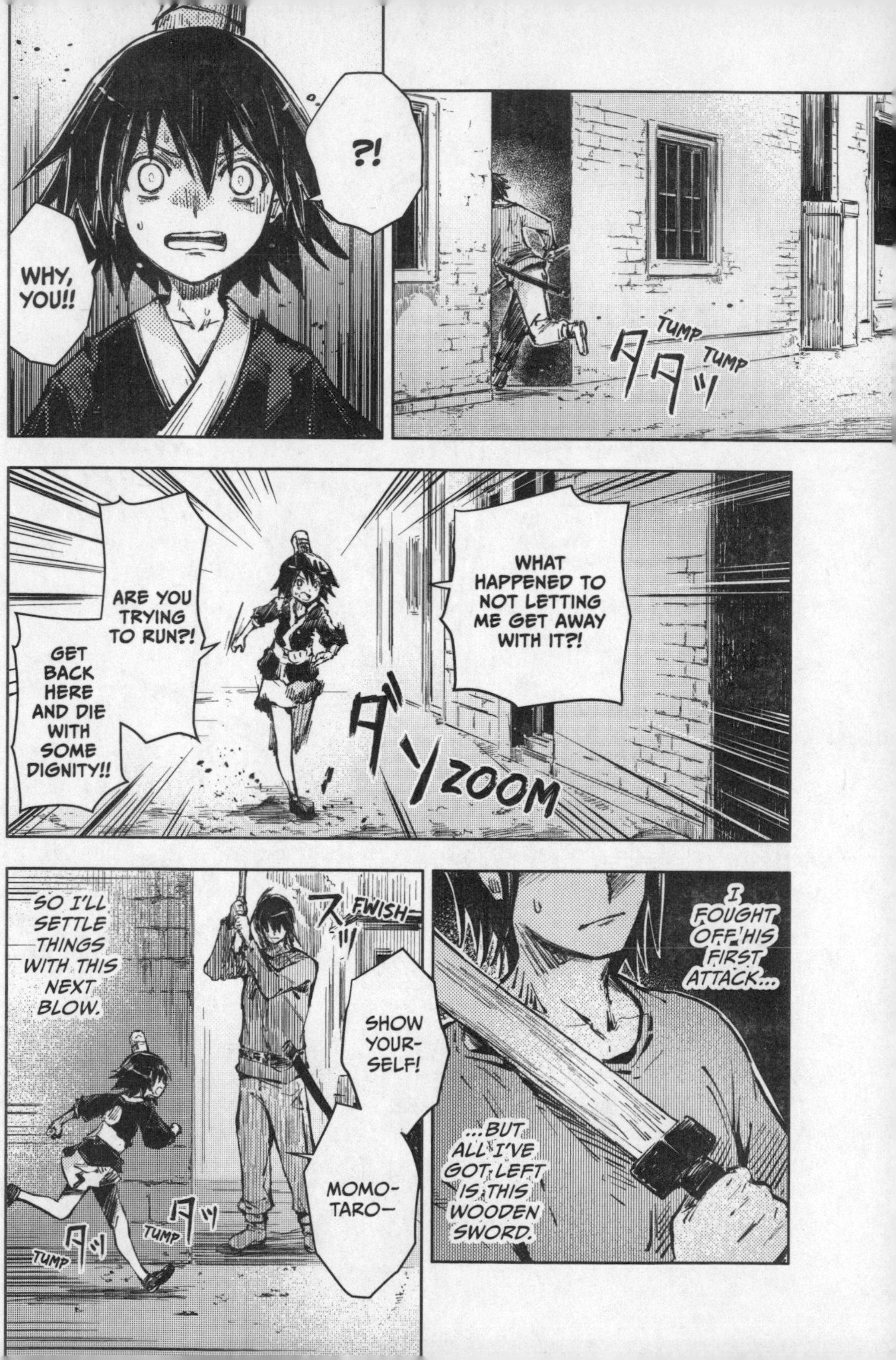
TUMP TUMP
タタッ
?!
WHY, YOU!!
WHAT HAPPENED TO NOT LETTING ME GET AWAY WITH IT?!
ARE YOU TRYING TO RUN?!
GET BACK HERE AND DIE WITH SOME DIGNITY!!
ダッ ZOOM
I FOUGHT OFF HIS FIRST ATTACK...
...BUT ALL I'VE GOT LEFT IS THIS WOODEN SWORD.
スッ FWISH
SO I'LL SETTLE THINGS WITH THIS NEXT BLOW.
SHOW YOUR-SELF!
MOMO-TARO—
タッ TUMP
タッ TUMP

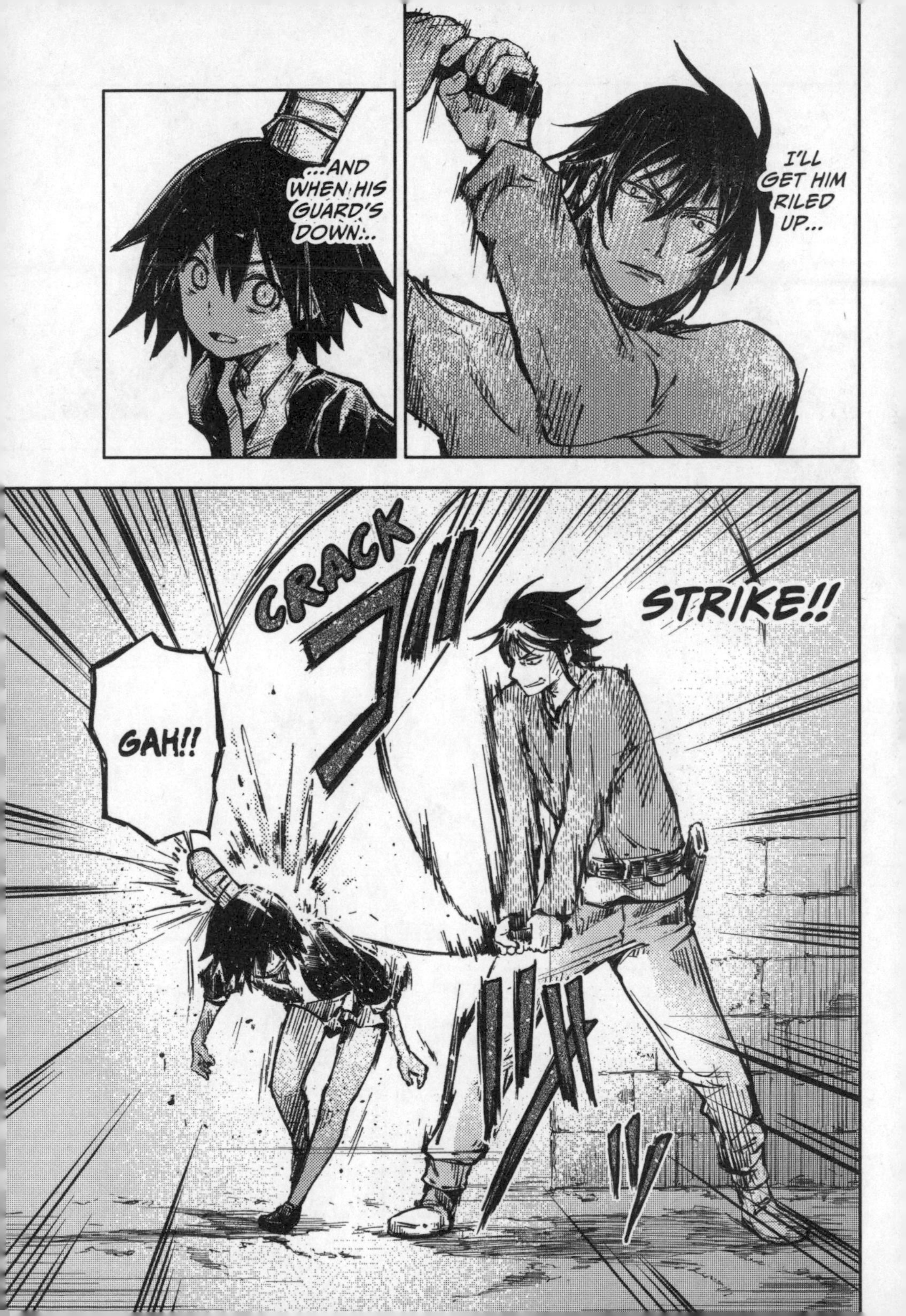
I'LL GET HIM RILED UP...
...AND WHEN HIS GUARD'S DOWN...
STRIKE!!
CRACK
GAH!!

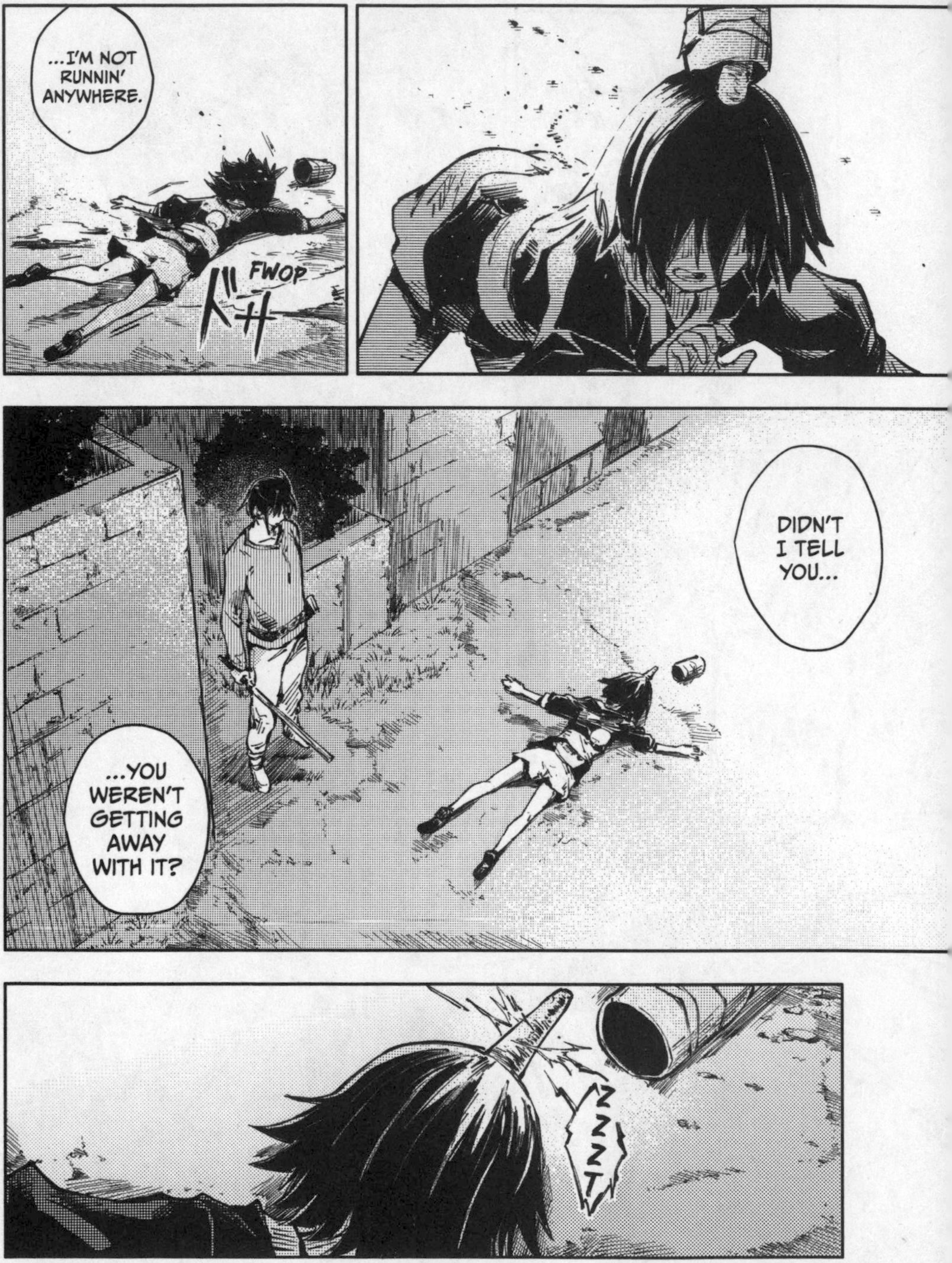
...I'M NOT RUNNIN' ANYWHERE.
ドッ
FWOP
DIDN'T I TELL YOU...
...YOU WEREN'T GETTING AWAY WITH IT?
ZZZT

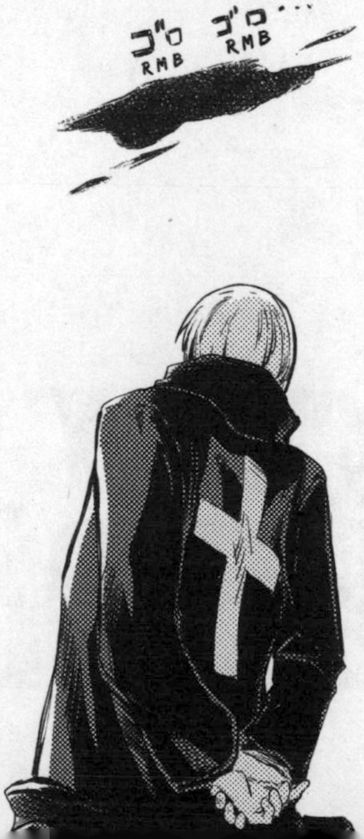
ゴロ
RMB
ゴロ…
RMB

PEACH BOY
RIVERSIDE

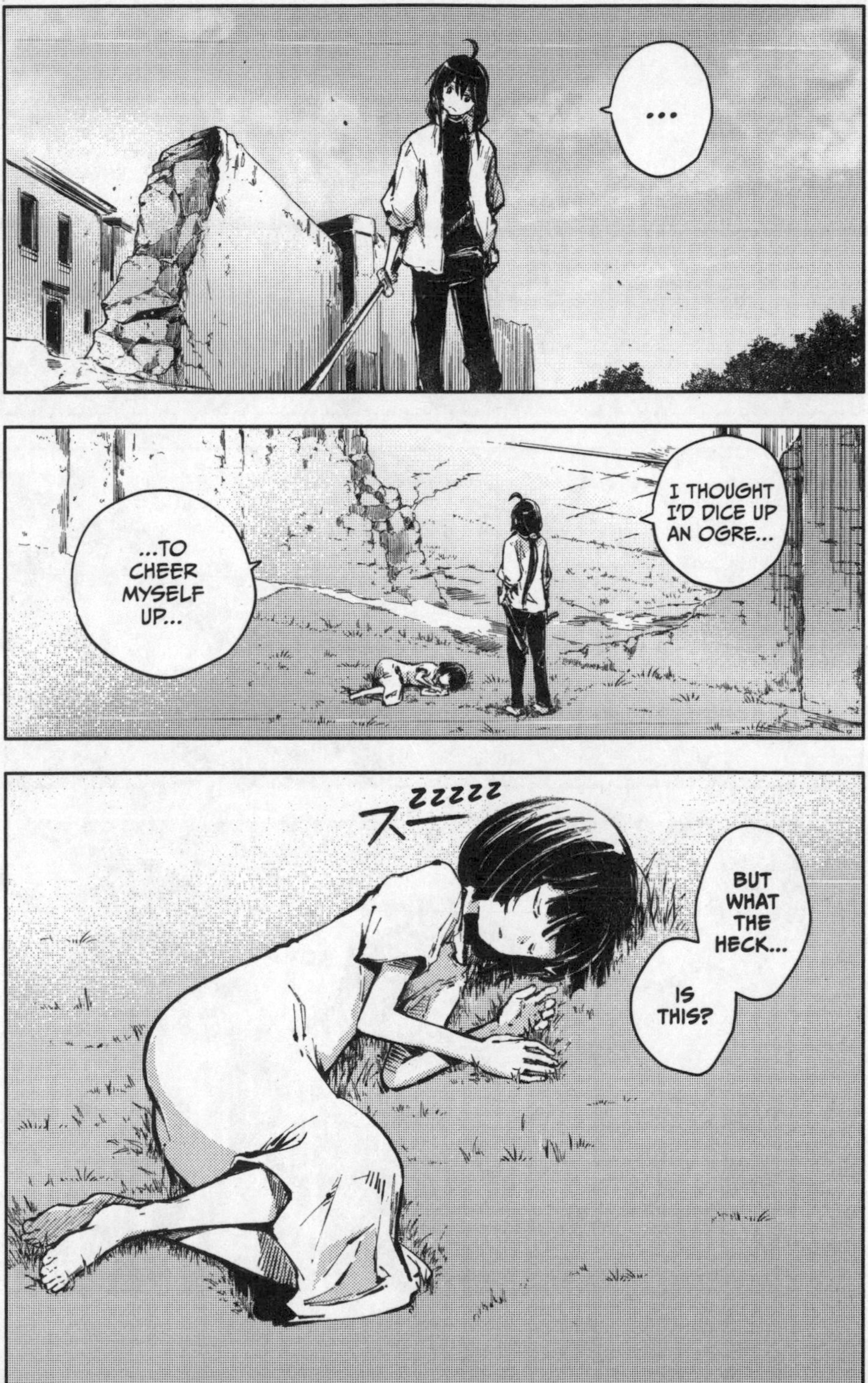
...
I THOUGHT I'D DICE UP AN OGRE...
...TO CHEER MYSELF UP...
ZZZZZ
スー
BUT WHAT THE HECK...
IS THIS?

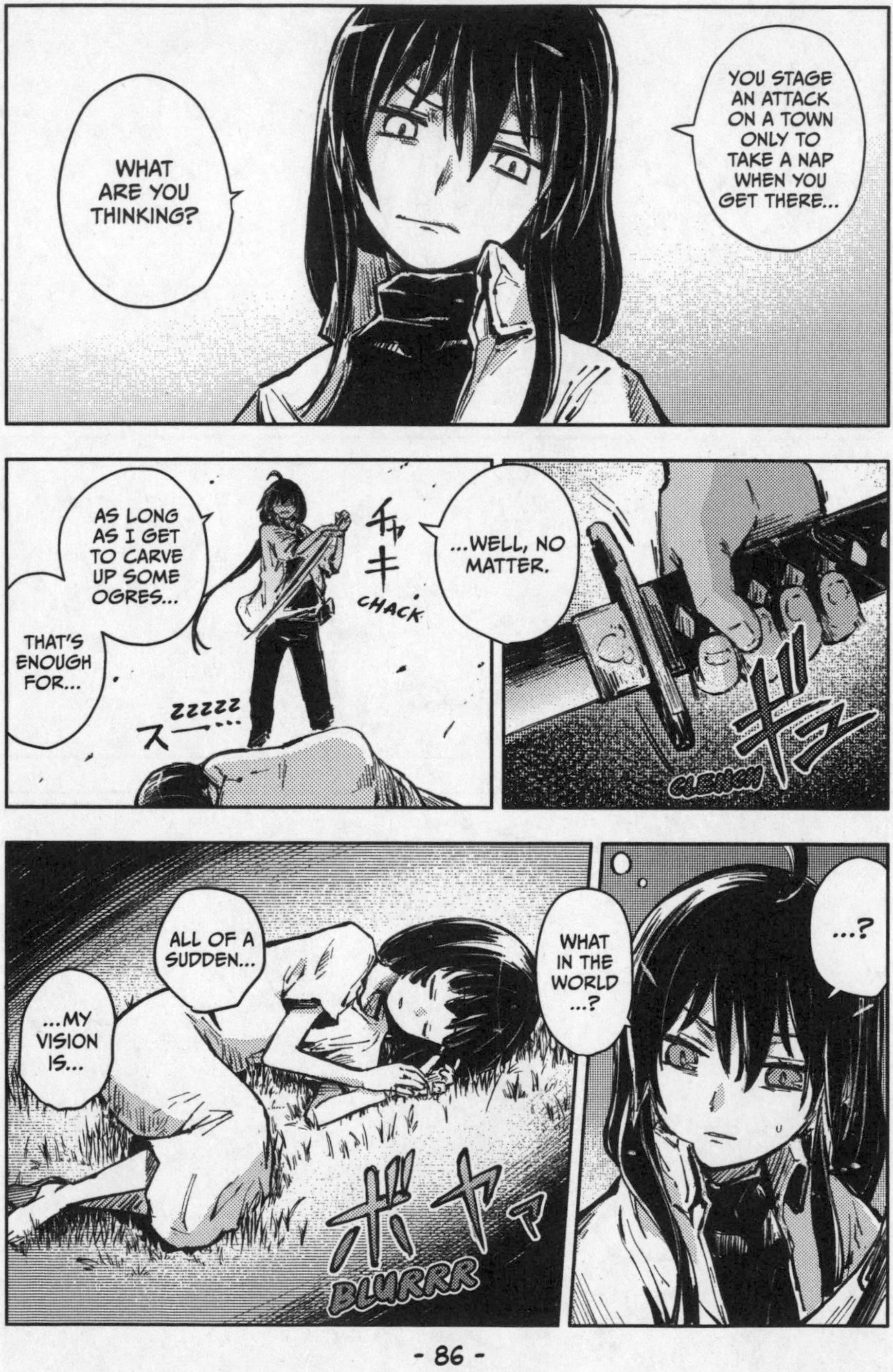
YOU STAGE AN ATTACK ON A TOWN ONLY TO TAKE A NAP WHEN YOU GET THERE...
WHAT ARE YOU THINKING?
ギュ
CLENCH
...WELL, NO MATTER.
AS LONG AS I GET TO CARVE UP SOME OGRES...
チャキ
CHACK
THAT'S ENOUGH FOR...
ZZZZZ
スー…
...?
WHAT IN THE WORLD ...?
ALL OF A SUDDEN...
...MY VISION IS...
ボヤァ
BLURRR

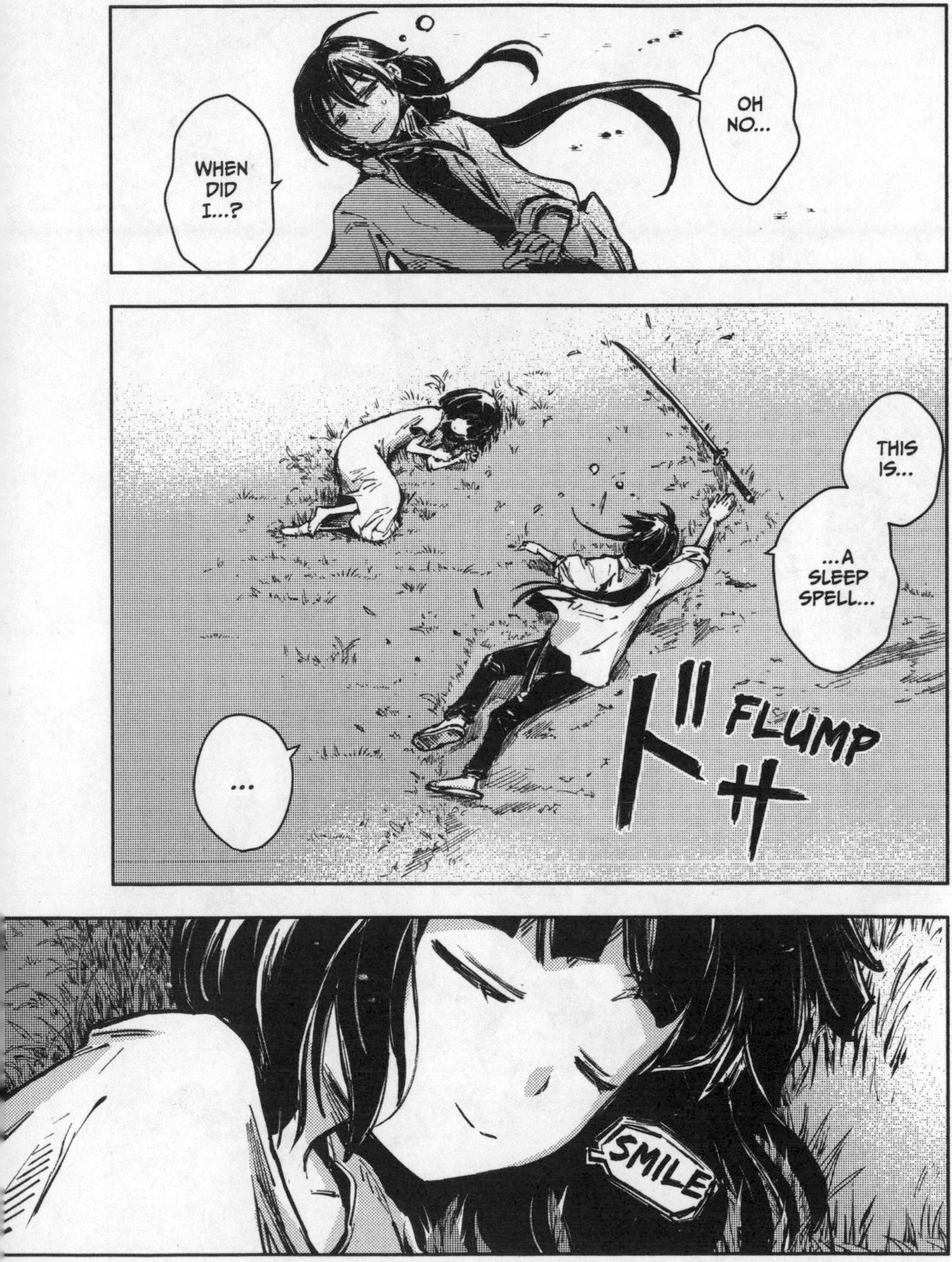

OH NO...
WHEN DID I...?
THIS IS...
...A SLEEP SPELL...
FLUMP
...
SMILE

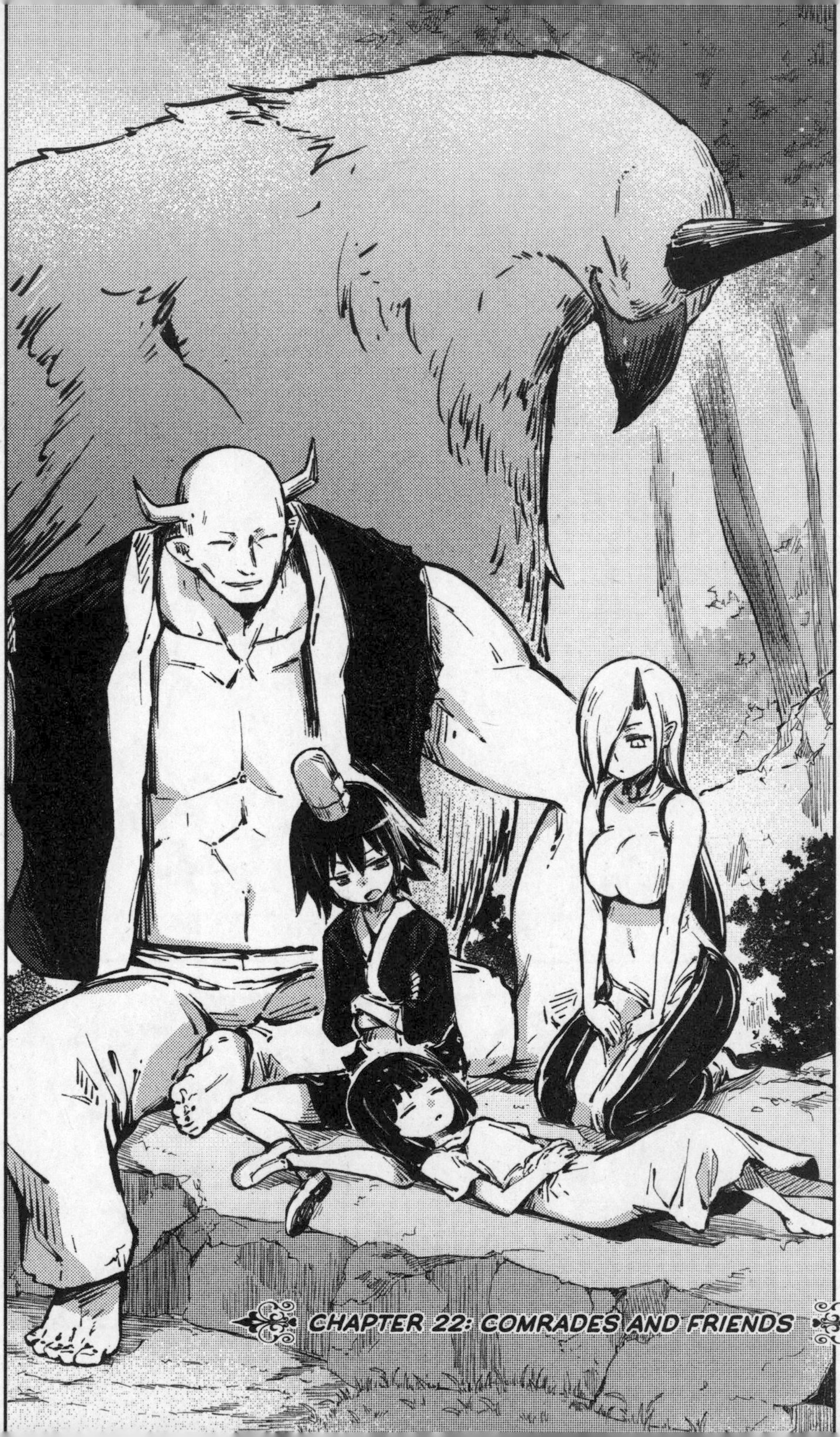
CHAPTER 22: COMRADES AND FRIENDS

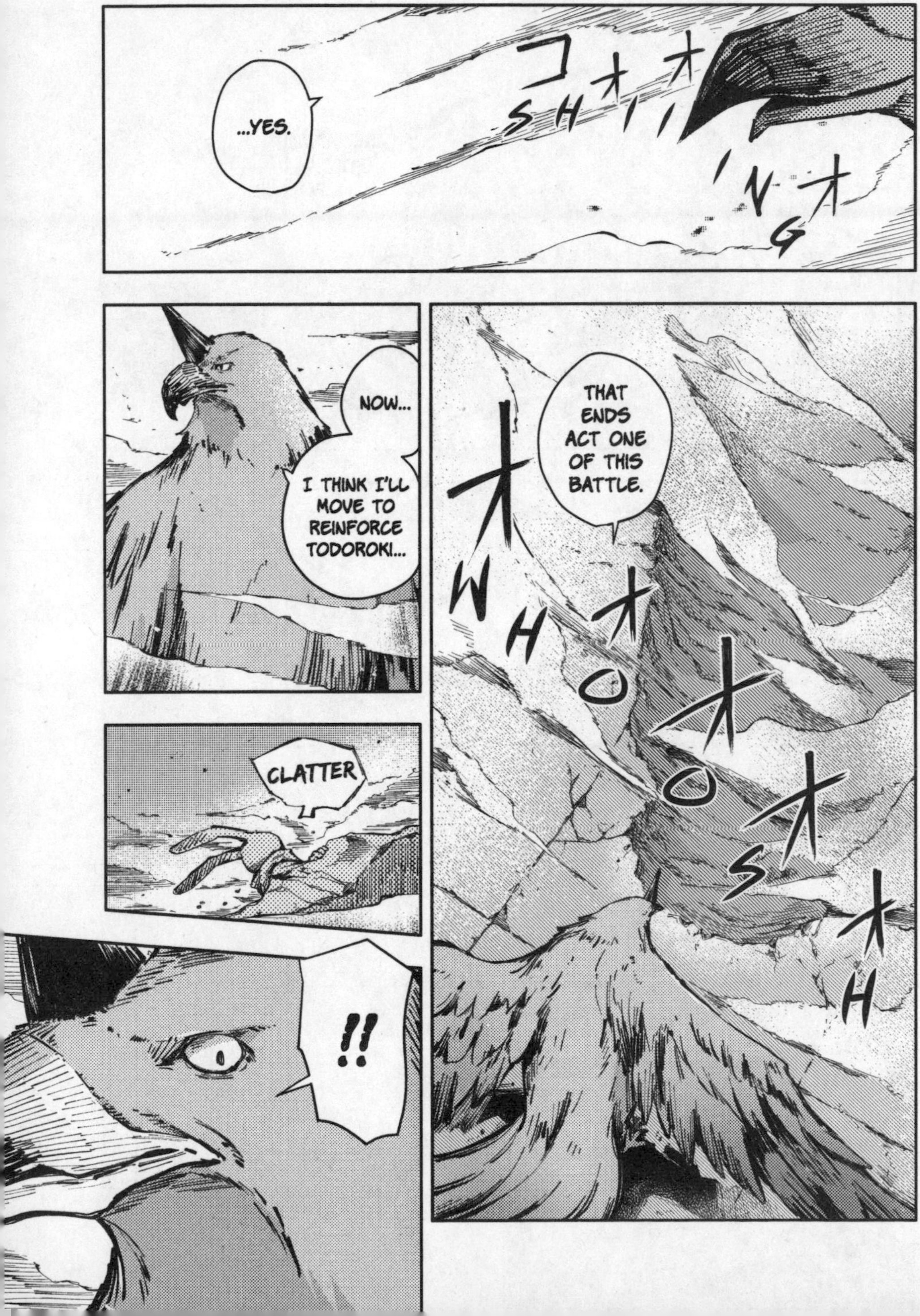
...YES.
SHIING
THAT ENDS ACT ONE OF THIS BATTLE.
WHOOSH
NOW...
I THINK I'LL MOVE TO REINFORCE TODOROKI...
CLATTER
!!

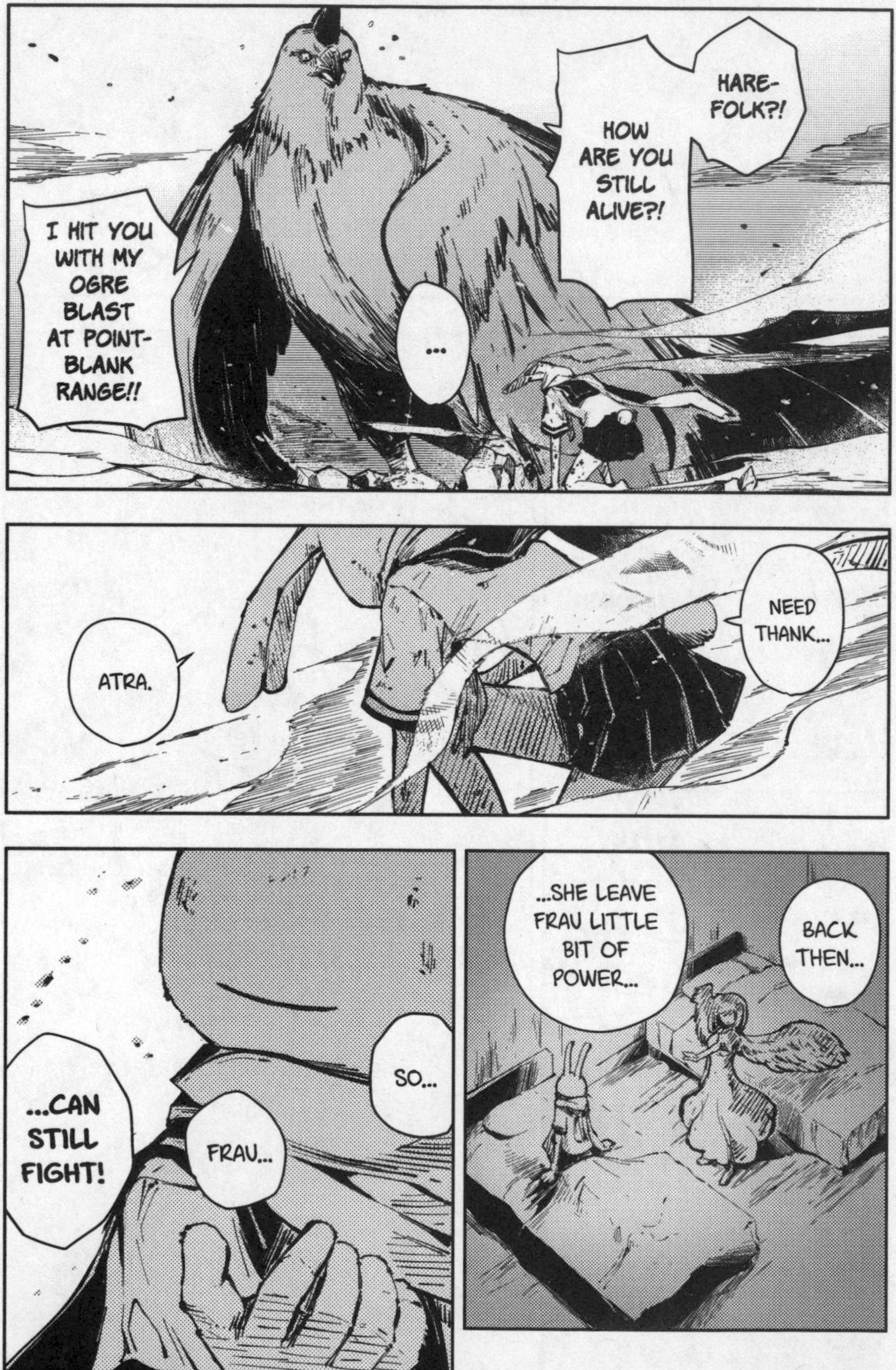
HARE-FOLK?!
HOW ARE YOU STILL ALIVE?!
I HIT YOU WITH MY OGRE BLAST AT POINT-BLANK RANGE!!
...
NEED THANK...
ATRA.
BACK THEN...
...SHE LEAVE FRAU LITTLE BIT OF POWER...
SO...
FRAU...
...CAN STILL FIGHT!

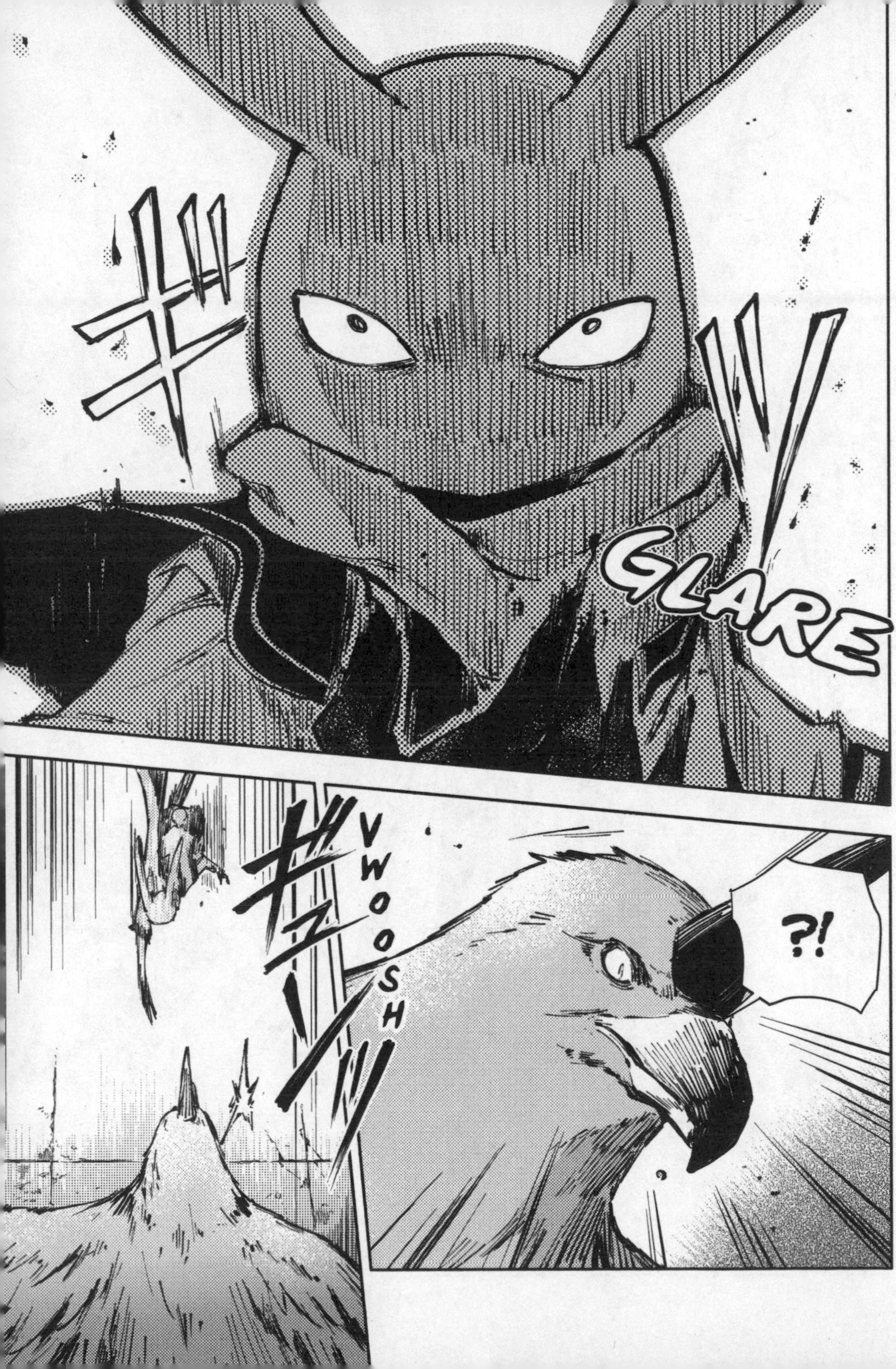
GLARE
?!
VWOOSH

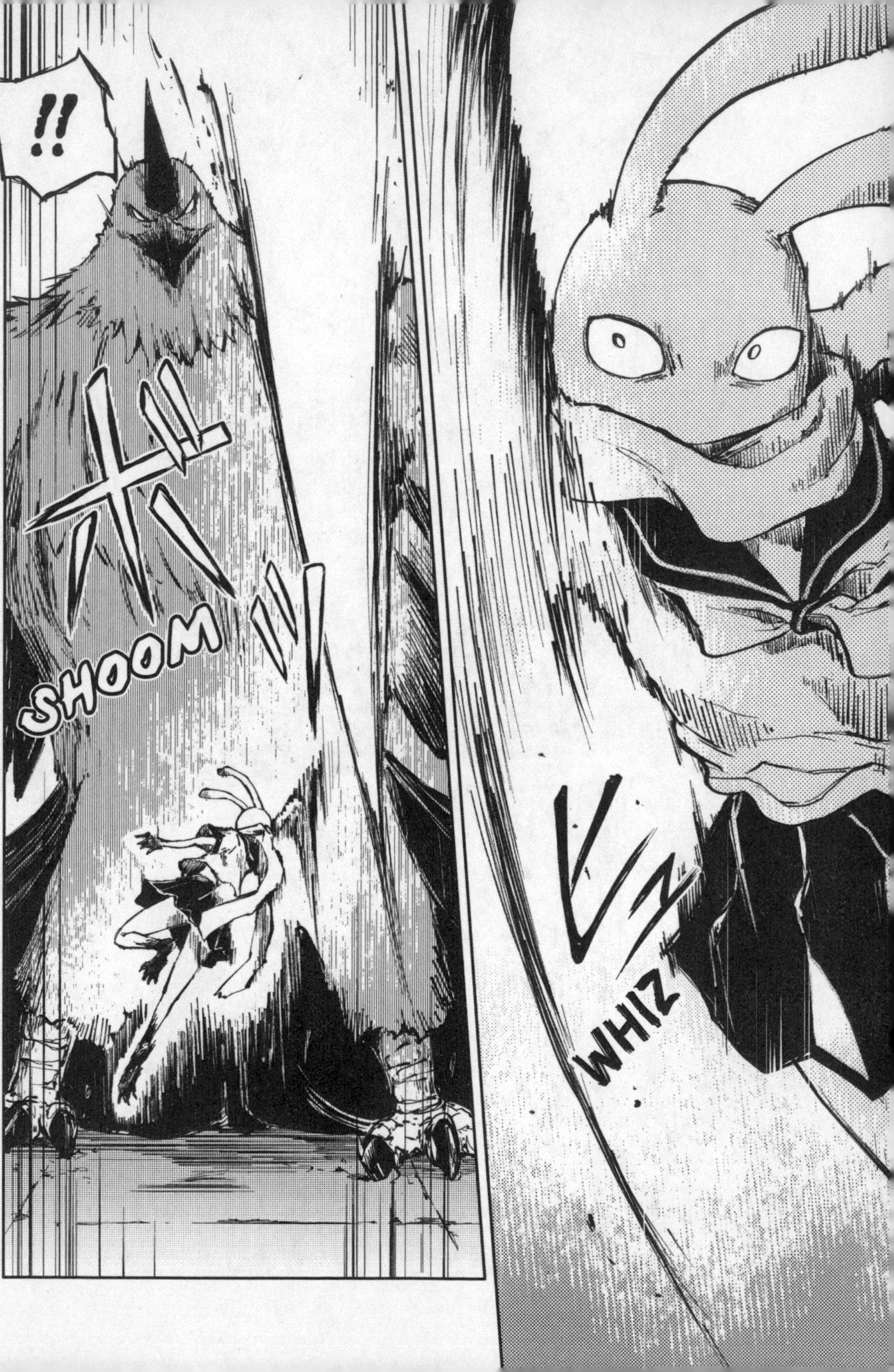
WHIZ
!!
SHOOM

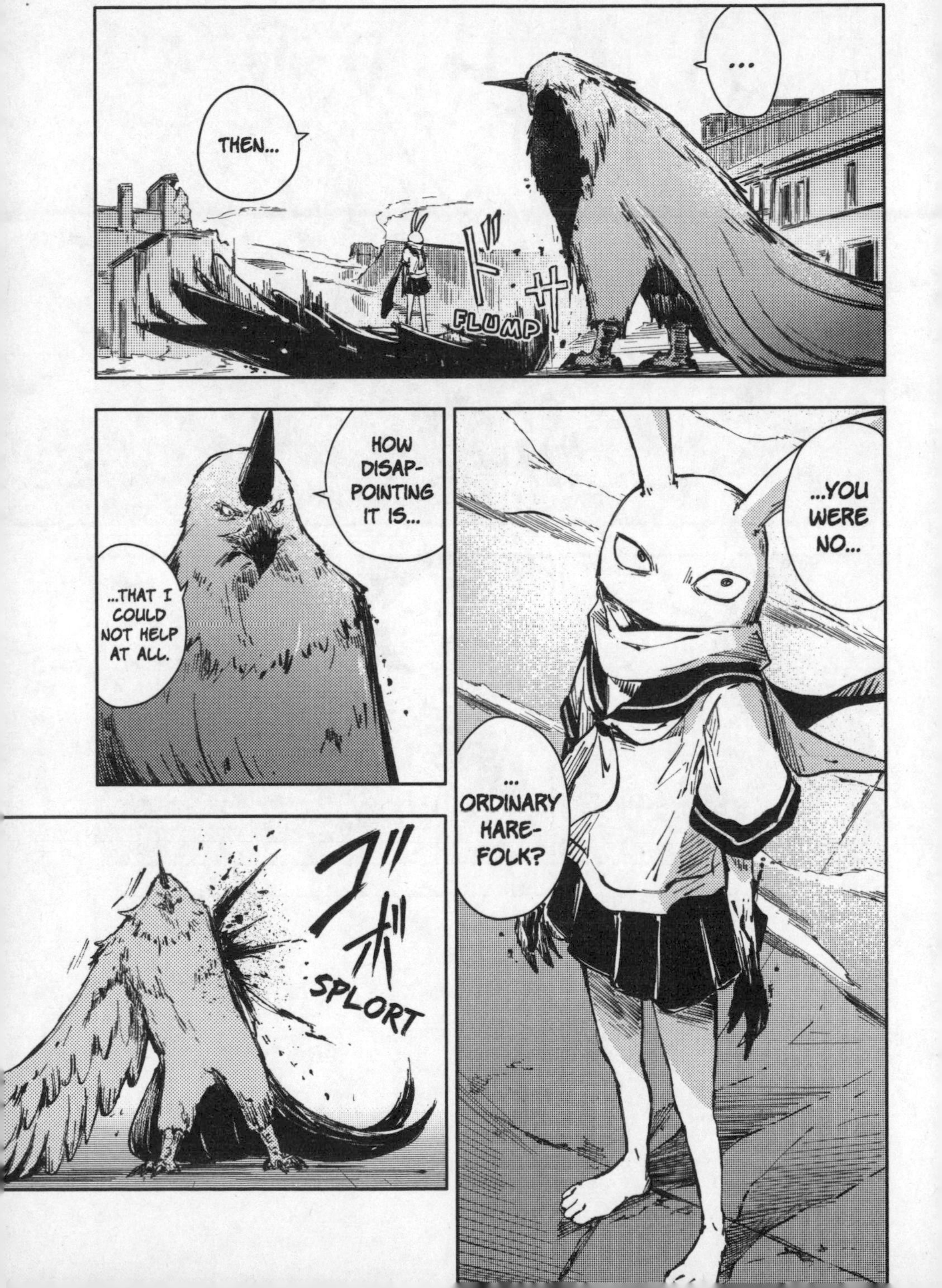
...
THEN...
FLUMP
...YOU WERE NO...
... ORDINARY HARE-FOLK?
HOW DISAP-POINTING IT IS...
...THAT I COULD NOT HELP AT ALL.
SPLORT

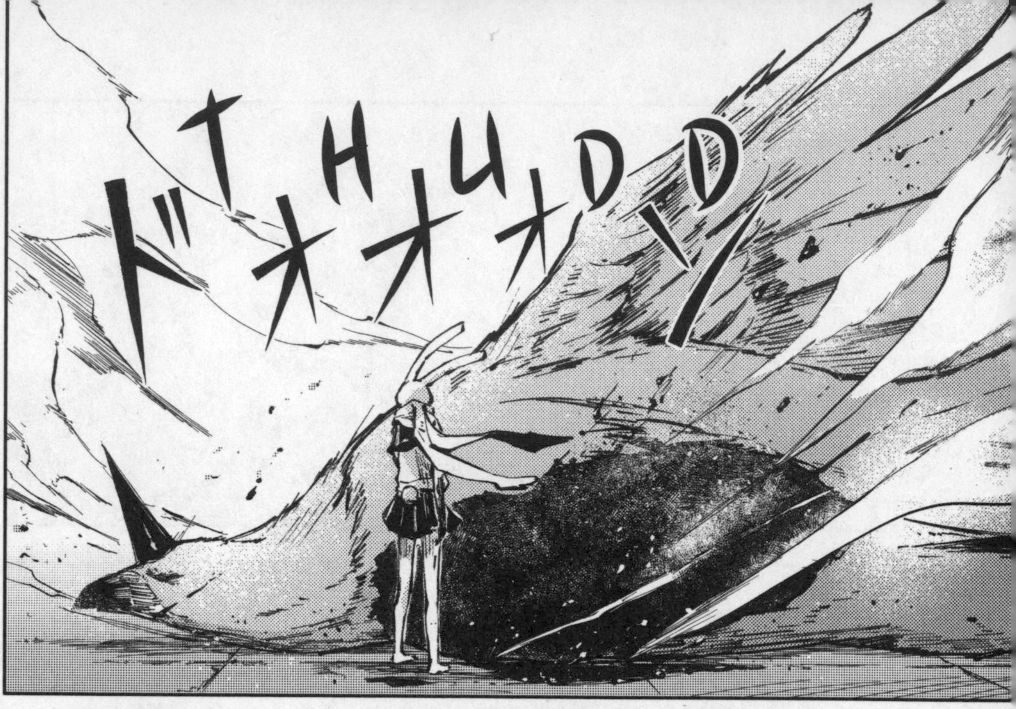
THUDD

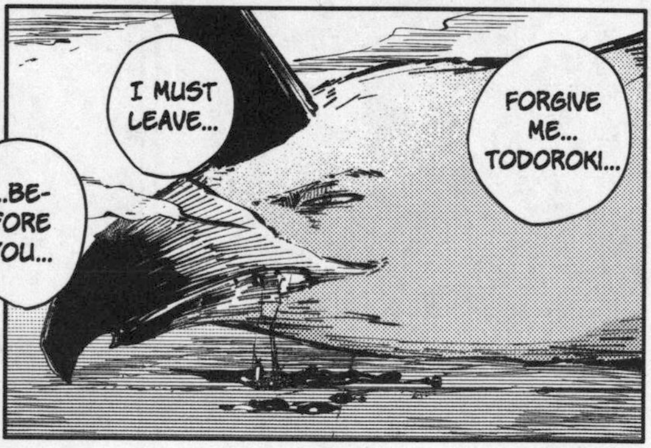
FORGIVE ME... TODOROKI...
I MUST LEAVE...
...BE-FORE YOU...

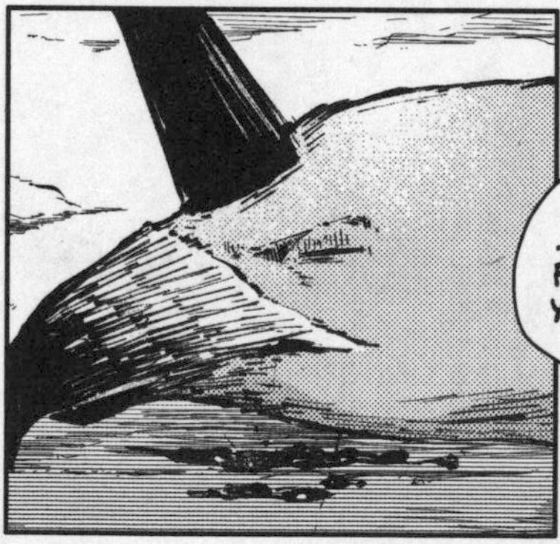

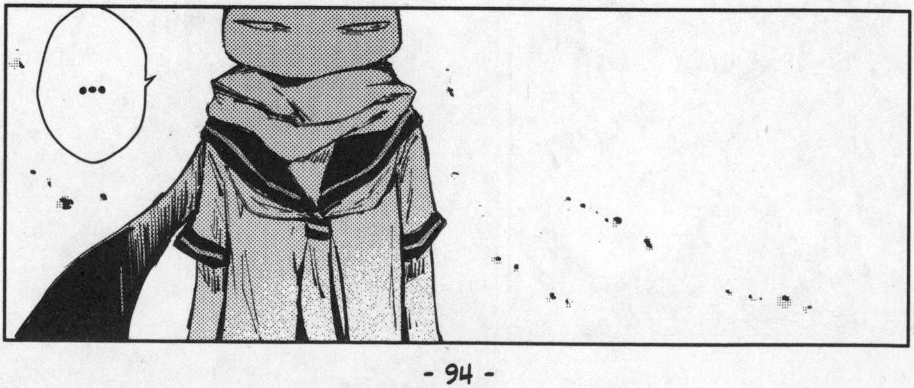
...

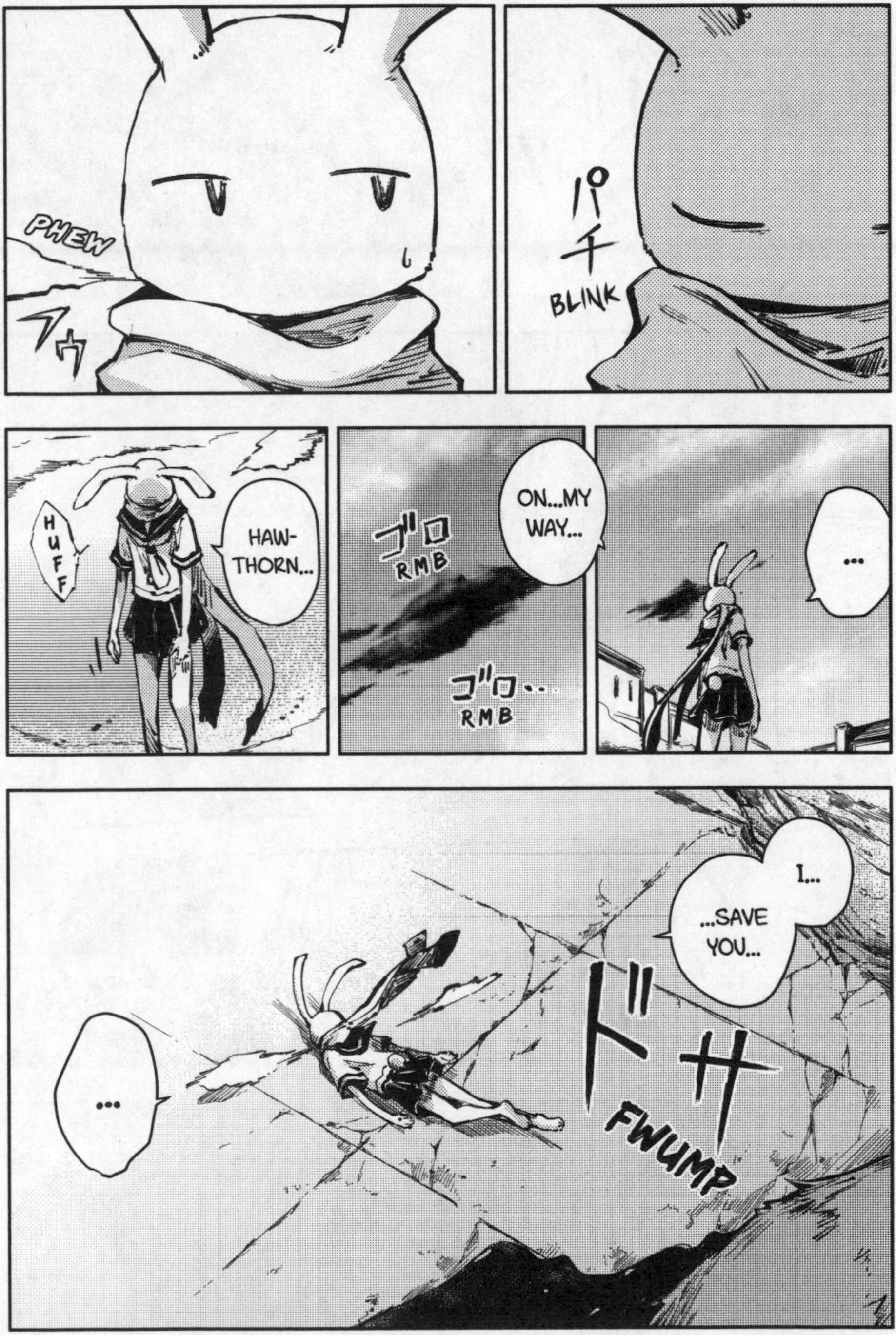
パチ
BLINK
PHEW
フウ
...
ON...MY WAY...
ゴロ
RMB
ゴロ...
RMB
HAW-THORN...
HUFF
I...
...SAVE YOU...
ドサ
FWUMP
...

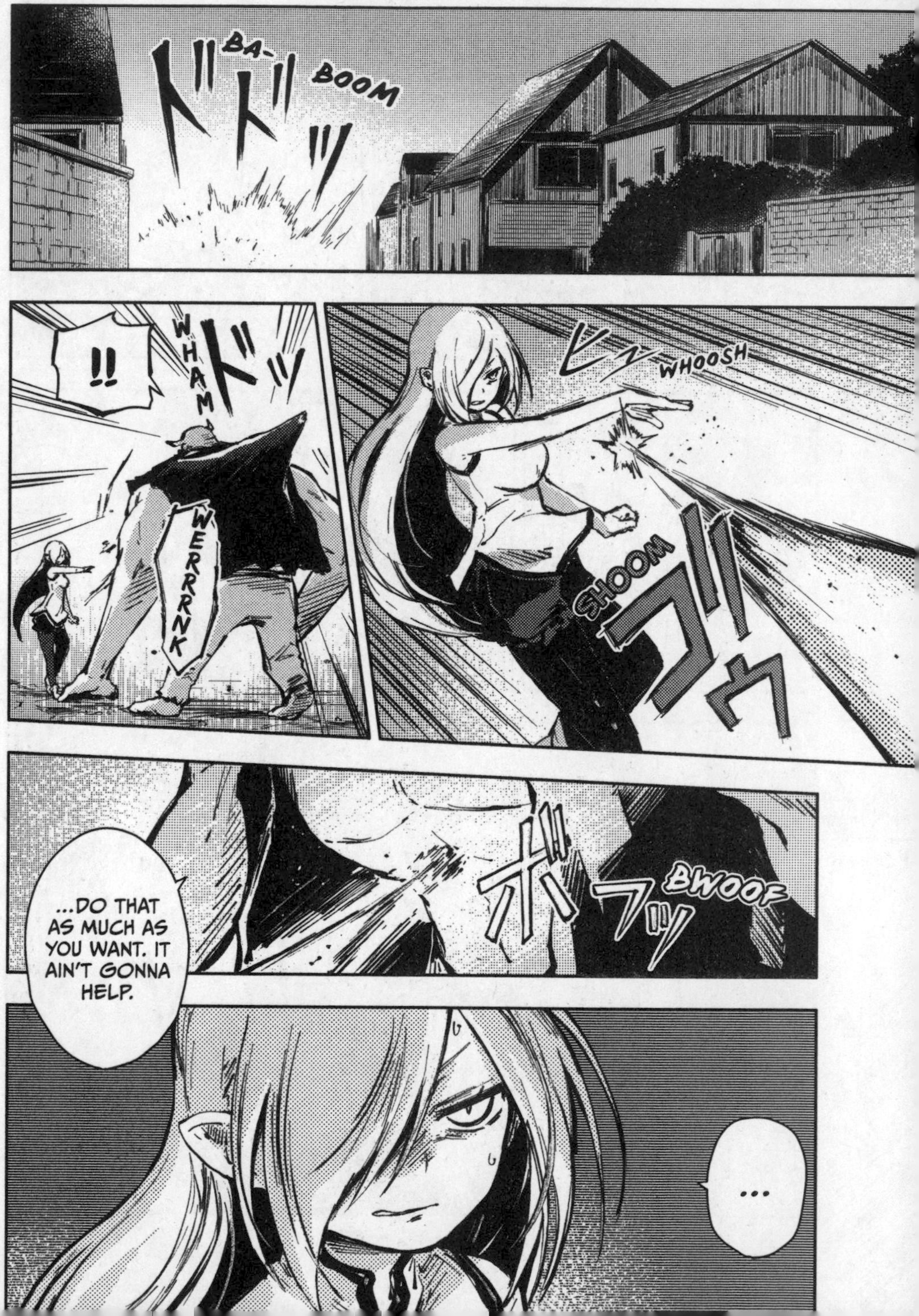
BA-BOOM
WHOOSH
SHOOM
!!
WHAM
WERRRNK
BWOOF
...DO THAT AS MUCH AS YOU WANT. IT AIN'T GONNA HELP.
...

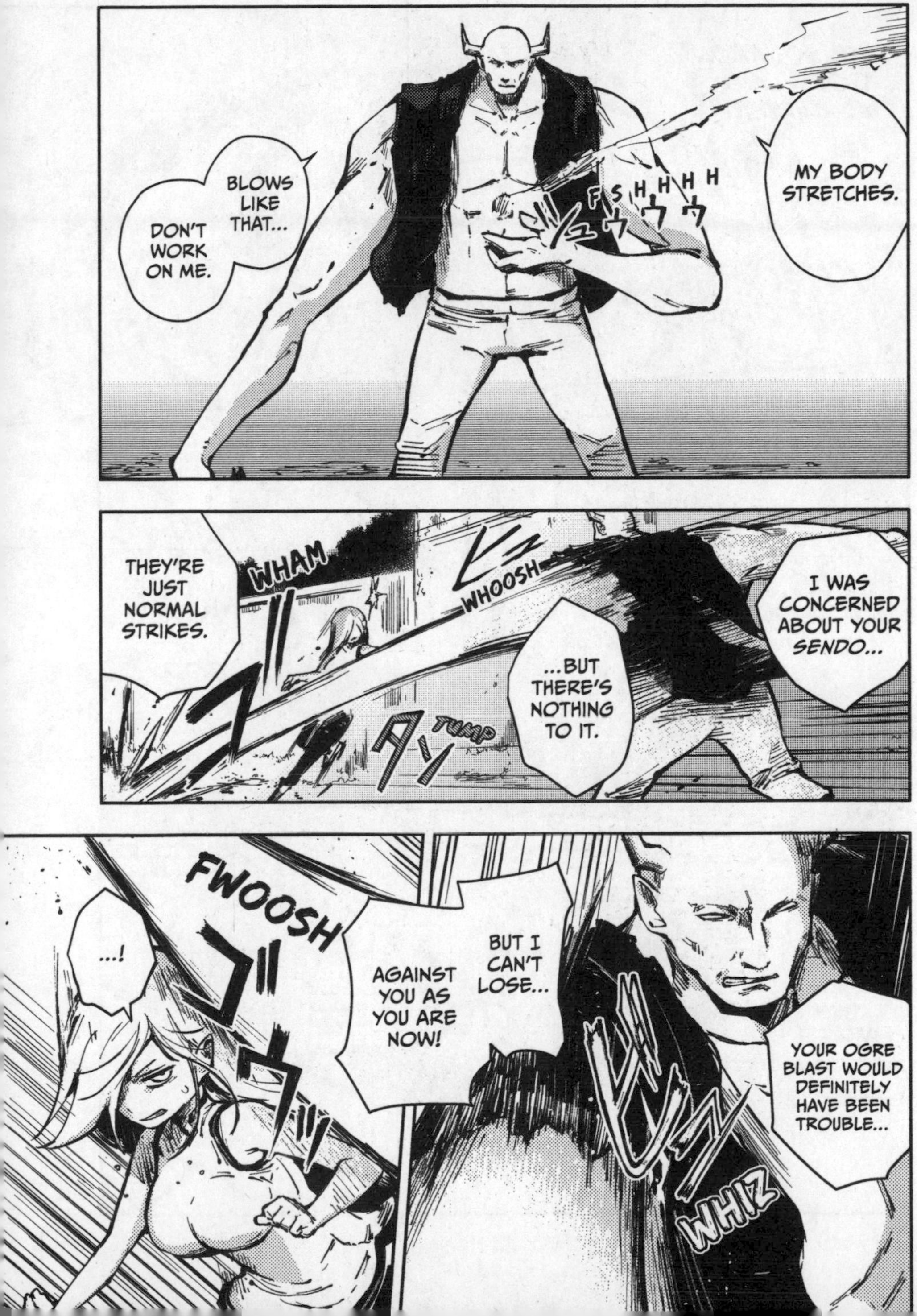
MY BODY STRETCHES.
FSHHHH
BLOWS LIKE THAT... DON'T WORK ON ME.
I WAS CONCERNED ABOUT YOUR SENDO...
...BUT THERE'S NOTHING TO IT.
WHOOSH
WHAM
TUMP
THEY'RE JUST NORMAL STRIKES.
YOUR OGRE BLAST WOULD DEFINITELY HAVE BEEN TROUBLE...
WHIZ
BUT I CAN'T LOSE...
AGAINST YOU AS YOU ARE NOW!
FWOOSH
...!

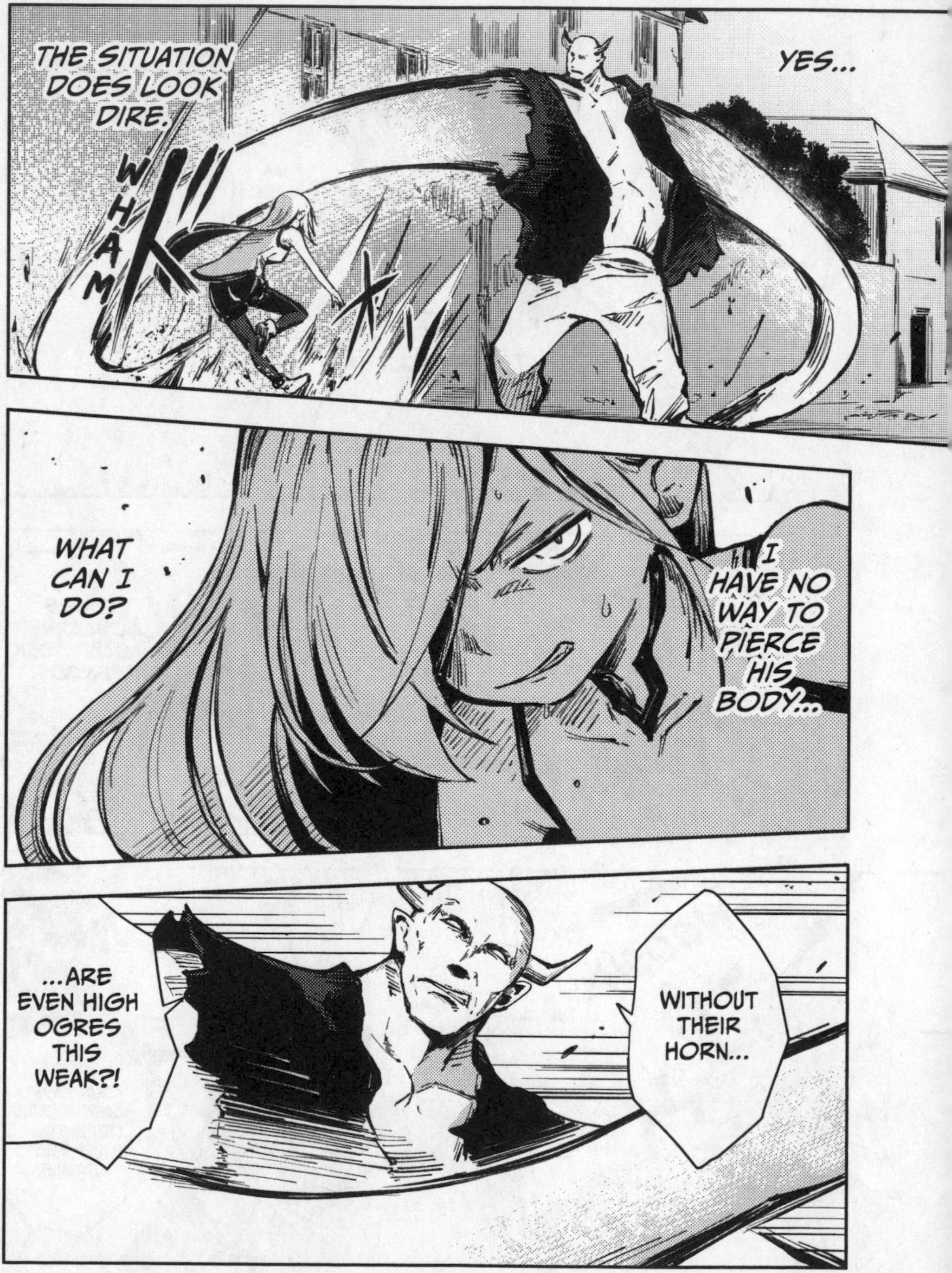
YES...
THE SITUATION DOES LOOK DIRE.
WHAM
I HAVE NO WAY TO PIERCE HIS BODY...
WHAT CAN I DO?
WITHOUT THEIR HORN...
...ARE EVEN HIGH OGRES THIS WEAK?!

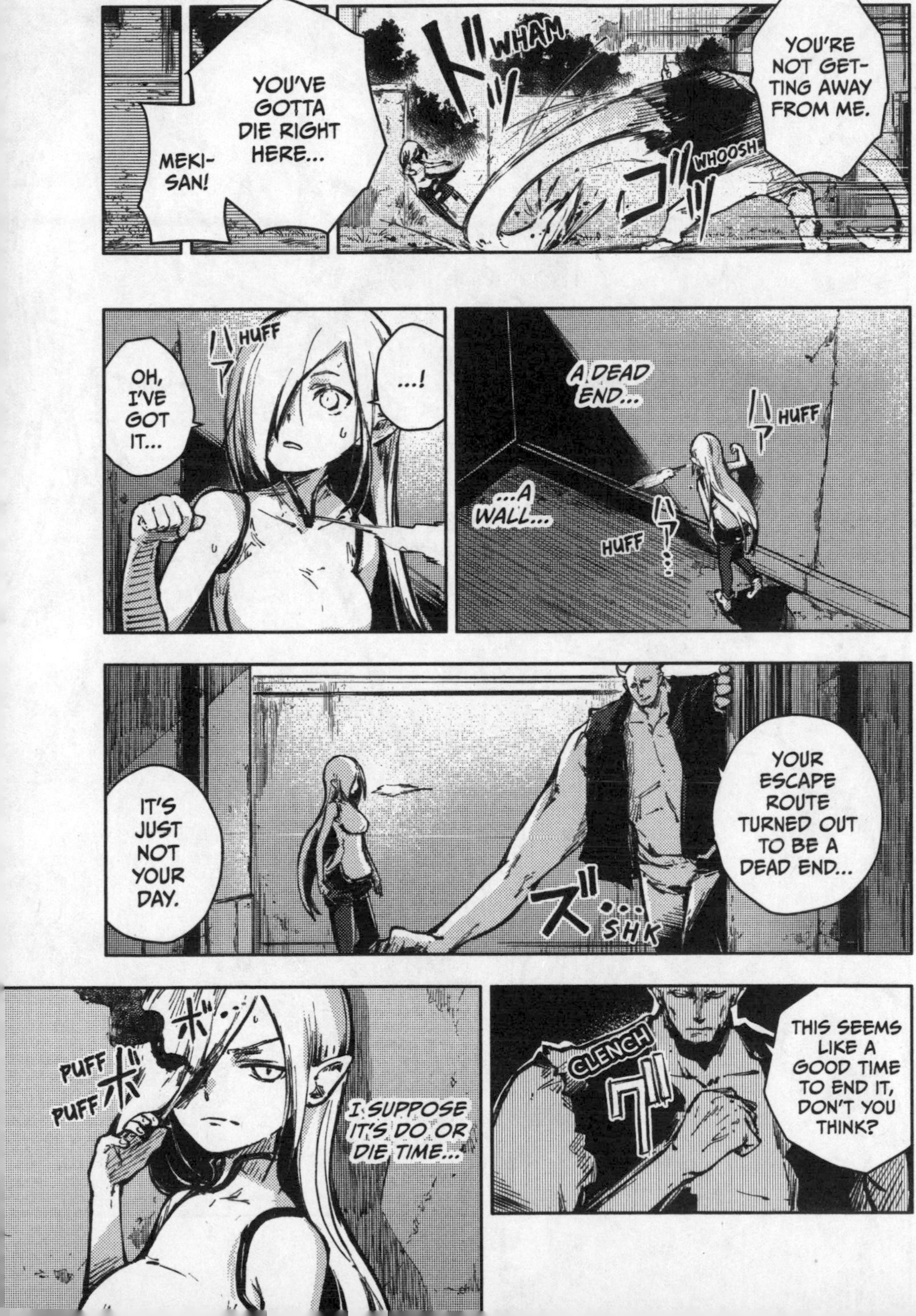
YOU'RE NOT GET-TING AWAY FROM ME.
WHAM
WHOOSH
YOU'VE GOTTA DIE RIGHT HERE...
MEKI-SAN!
A DEAD END...
HUFF
...A WALL...
HUFF
HUFF
...!
OH, I'VE GOT IT...
YOUR ESCAPE ROUTE TURNED OUT TO BE A DEAD END...
SHK
IT'S JUST NOT YOUR DAY.
THIS SEEMS LIKE A GOOD TIME TO END IT, DON'T YOU THINK?
CLENCH
I SUPPOSE IT'S DO OR DIE TIME...
PUFF
PUFF

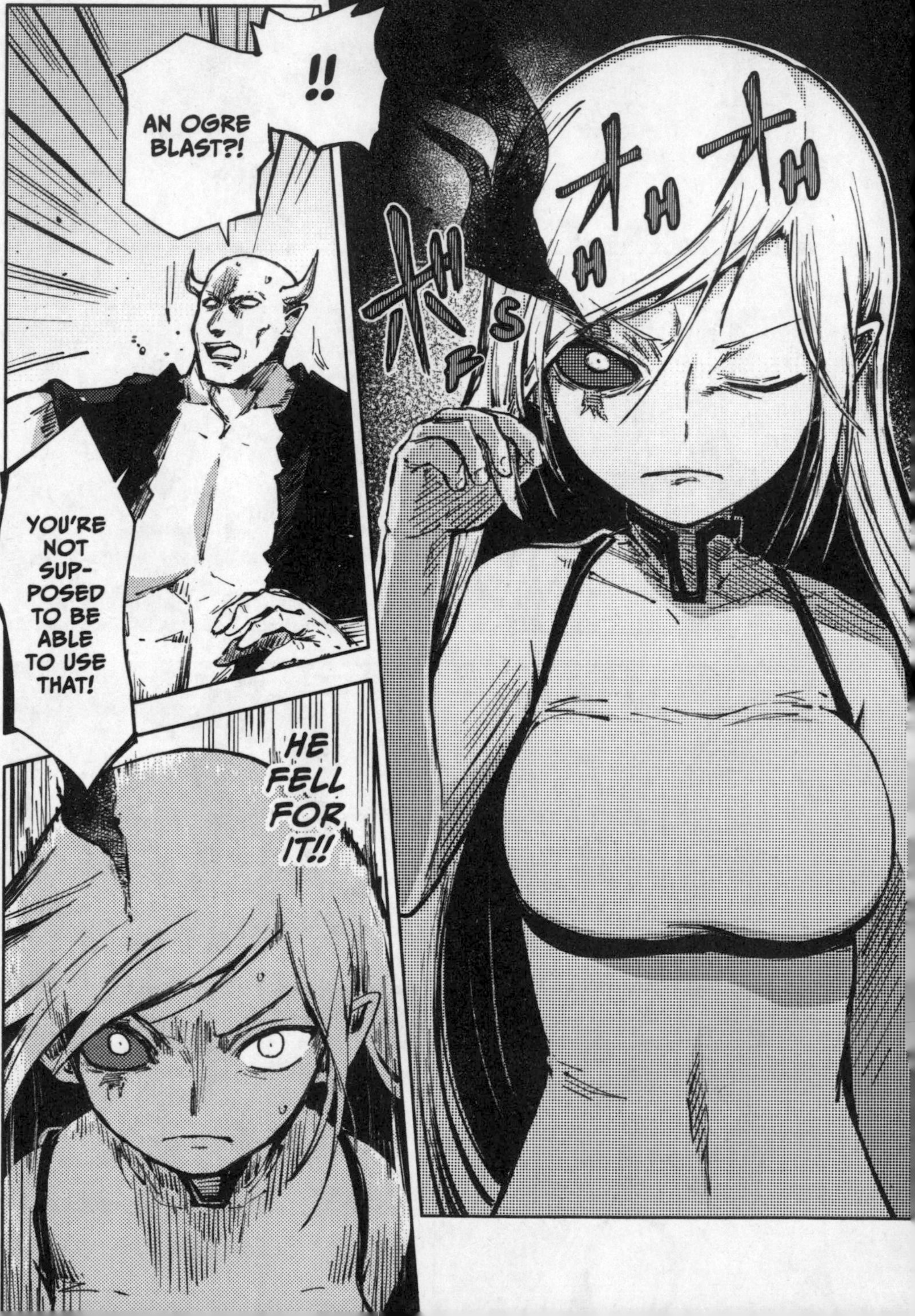
!!
AN OGRE BLAST?!
YOU'RE NOT SUP-POSED TO BE ABLE TO USE THAT!
HE FELL FOR IT!!

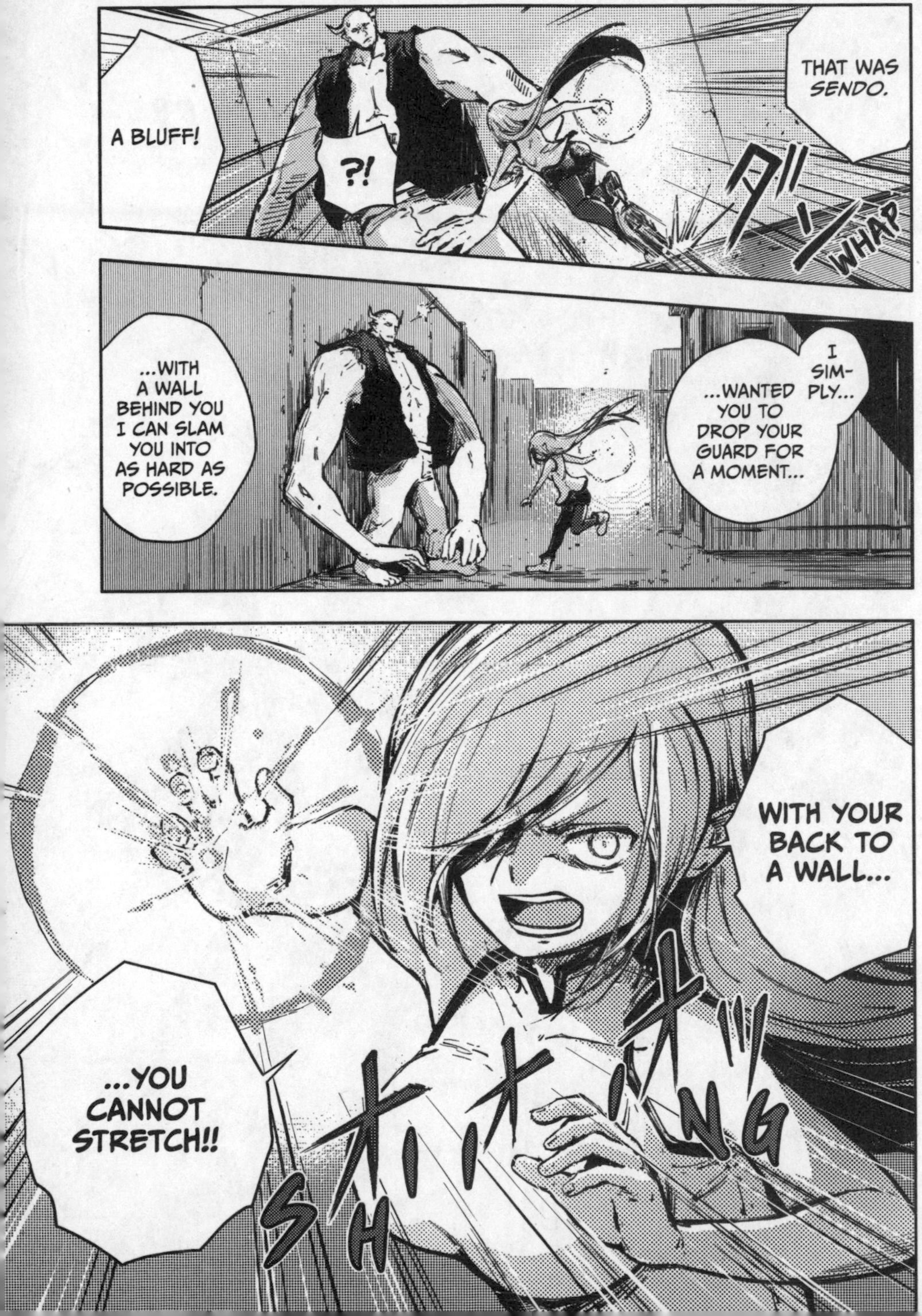
THAT WAS SENDO.
ダン
WHAP
?!
A BLUFF!
I SIMPLY...
...WANTED YOU TO DROP YOUR GUARD FOR A MOMENT...
...WITH A WALL BEHIND YOU I CAN SLAM YOU INTO AS HARD AS POSSIBLE.
WITH YOUR BACK TO A WALL...
...YOU CANNOT STRETCH!!
SHIIING

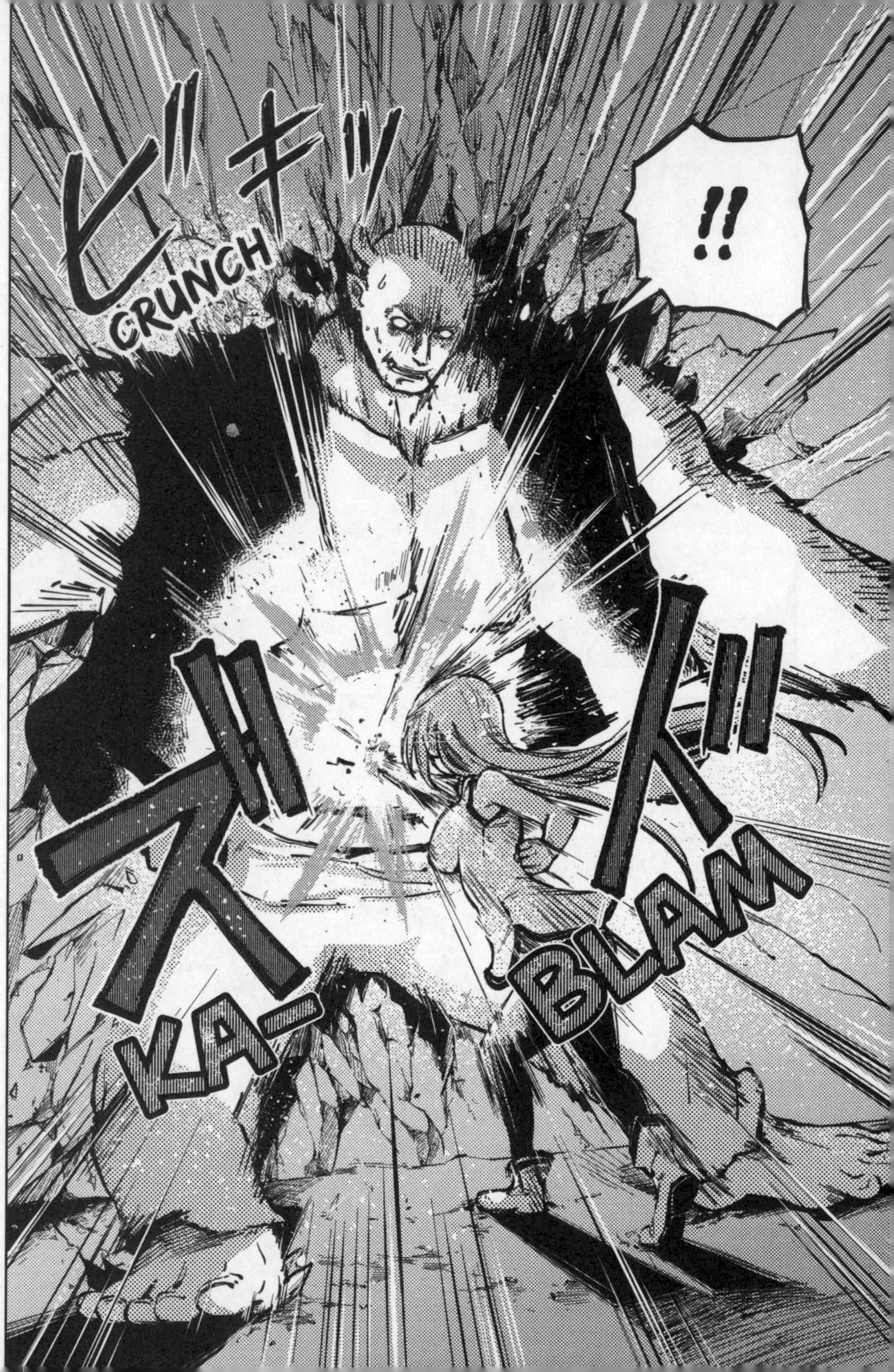
!!
ビギッ
CRUNCH
ズド
KA-
BLAM

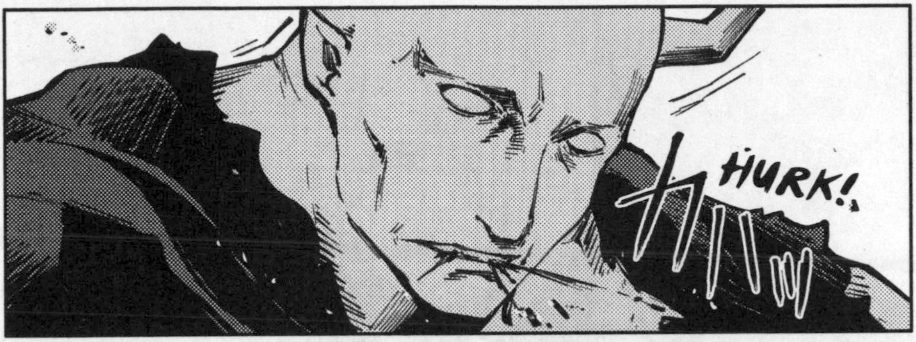
HURK!

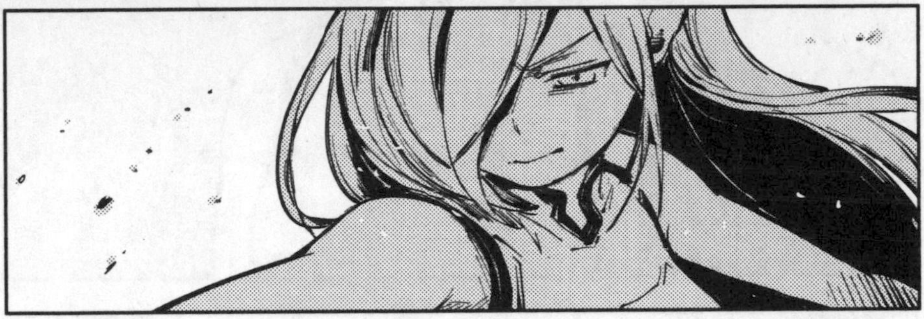

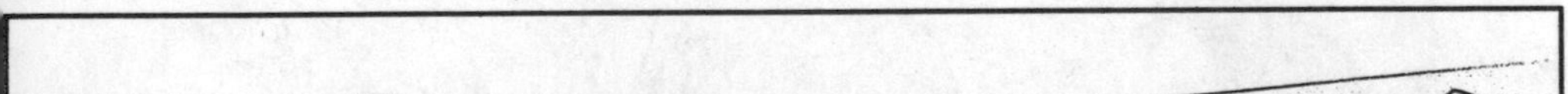
HA... HA...
YOU BEAT ME...
SHINKI...
...HEY... I WAS JUST AN ENEMY WHO WAS IN YOUR WAY...
SO...

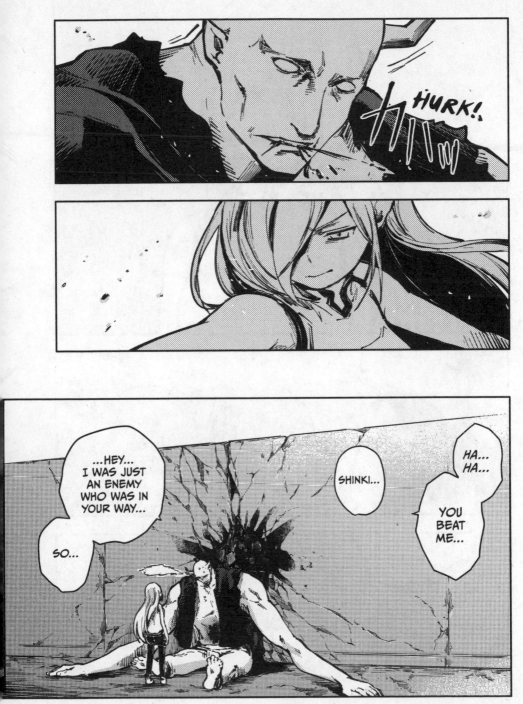

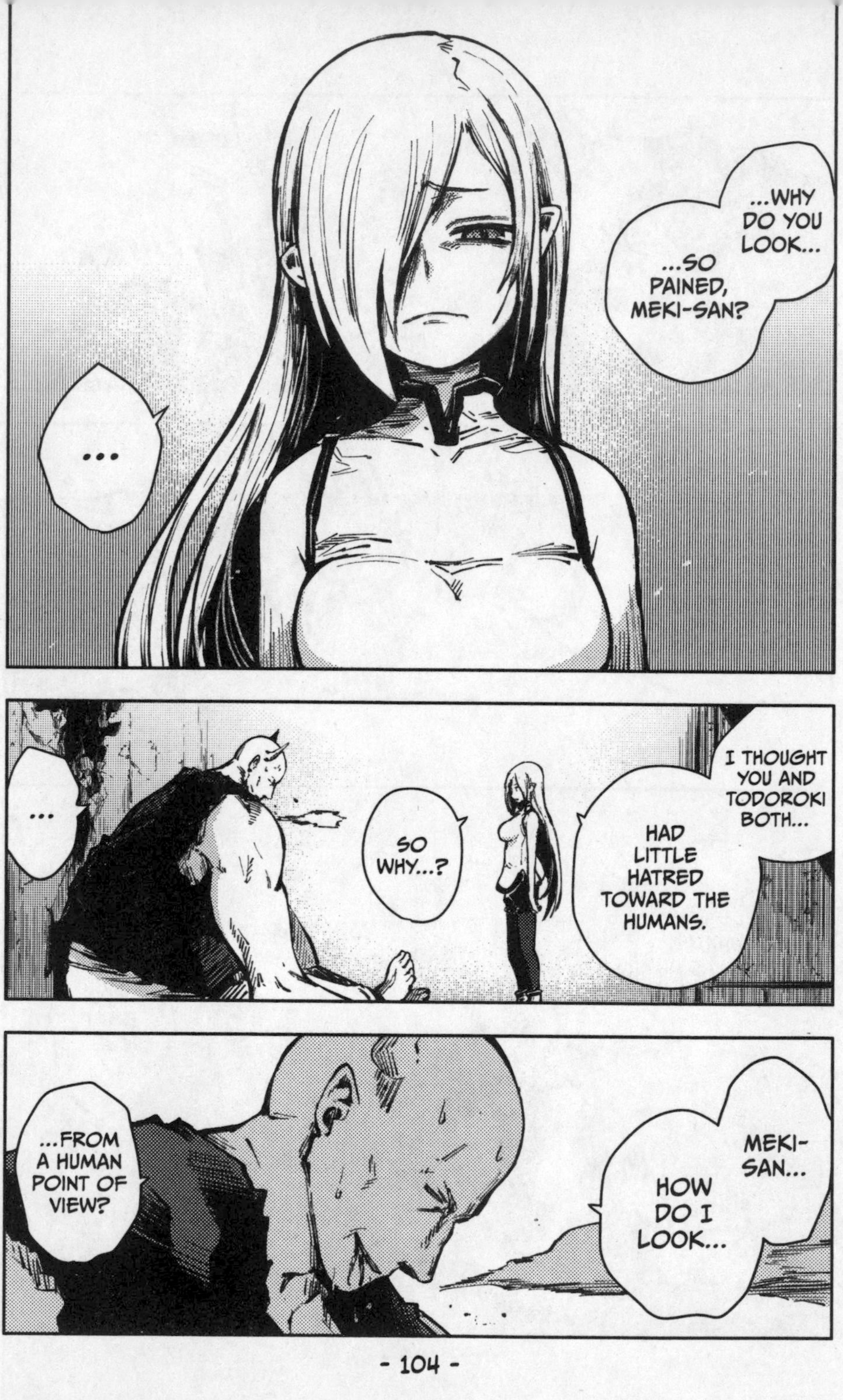
...WHY DO YOU LOOK...
...SO PAINED, MEKI-SAN?
...
I THOUGHT YOU AND TODOROKI BOTH...
HAD LITTLE HATRED TOWARD THE HUMANS.
SO WHY...?
...
MEKI-SAN...
HOW DO I LOOK...
...FROM A HUMAN POINT OF VIEW?

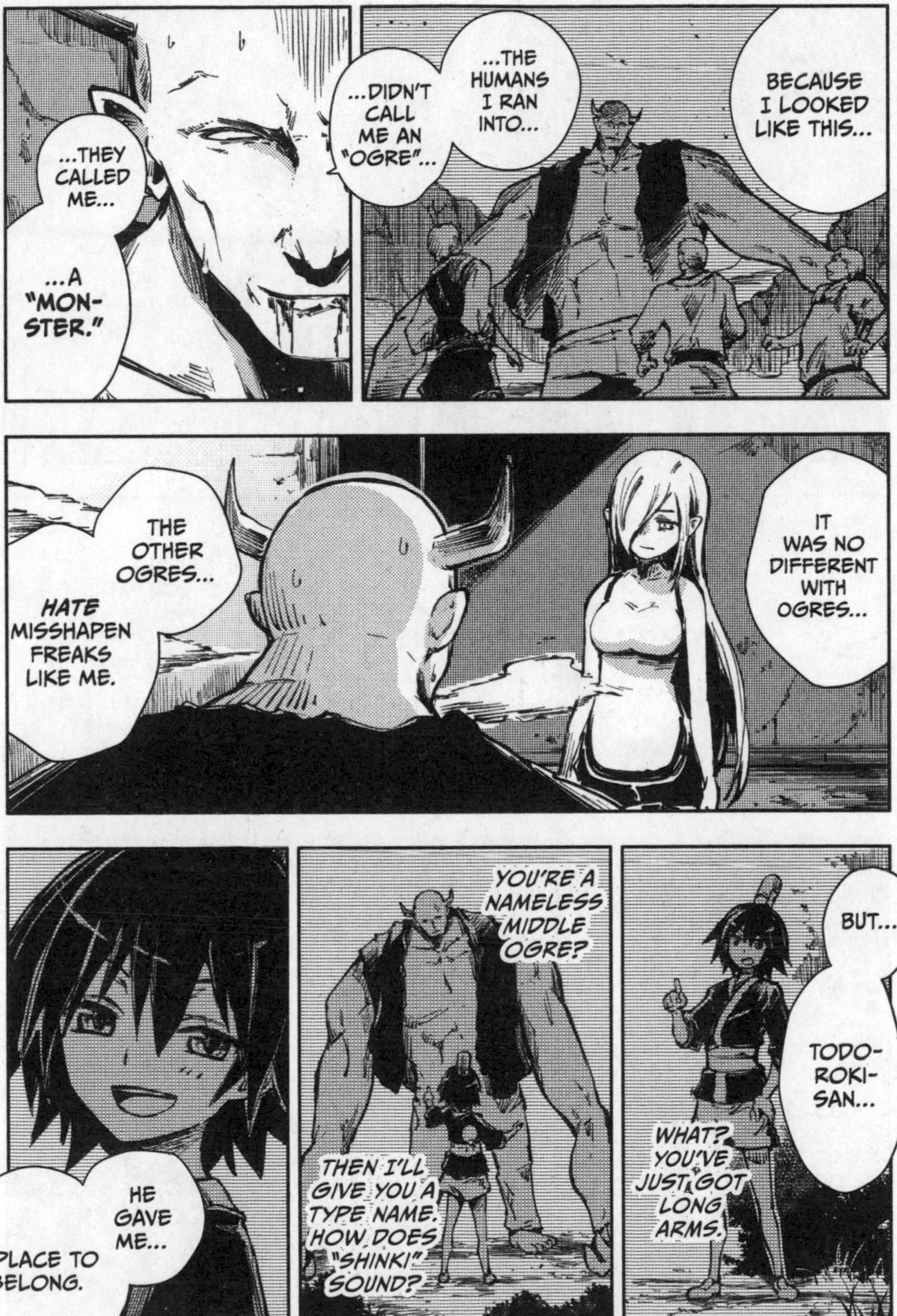
BECAUSE I LOOKED LIKE THIS...
...THE HUMANS I RAN INTO...
...DIDN'T CALL ME AN "OGRE"...
...THEY CALLED ME...
...A "MONSTER."
IT WAS NO DIFFERENT WITH OGRES...
THE OTHER OGRES...
HATE MISSHAPEN FREAKS LIKE ME.
BUT...
TODOROKI-SAN...
WHAT? YOU'VE JUST GOT LONG ARMS.
YOU'RE A NAMELESS MIDDLE OGRE?
THEN I'LL GIVE YOU A TYPE NAME. HOW DOES "SHINKI" SOUND?
HE GAVE ME...
A PLACE TO BELONG.

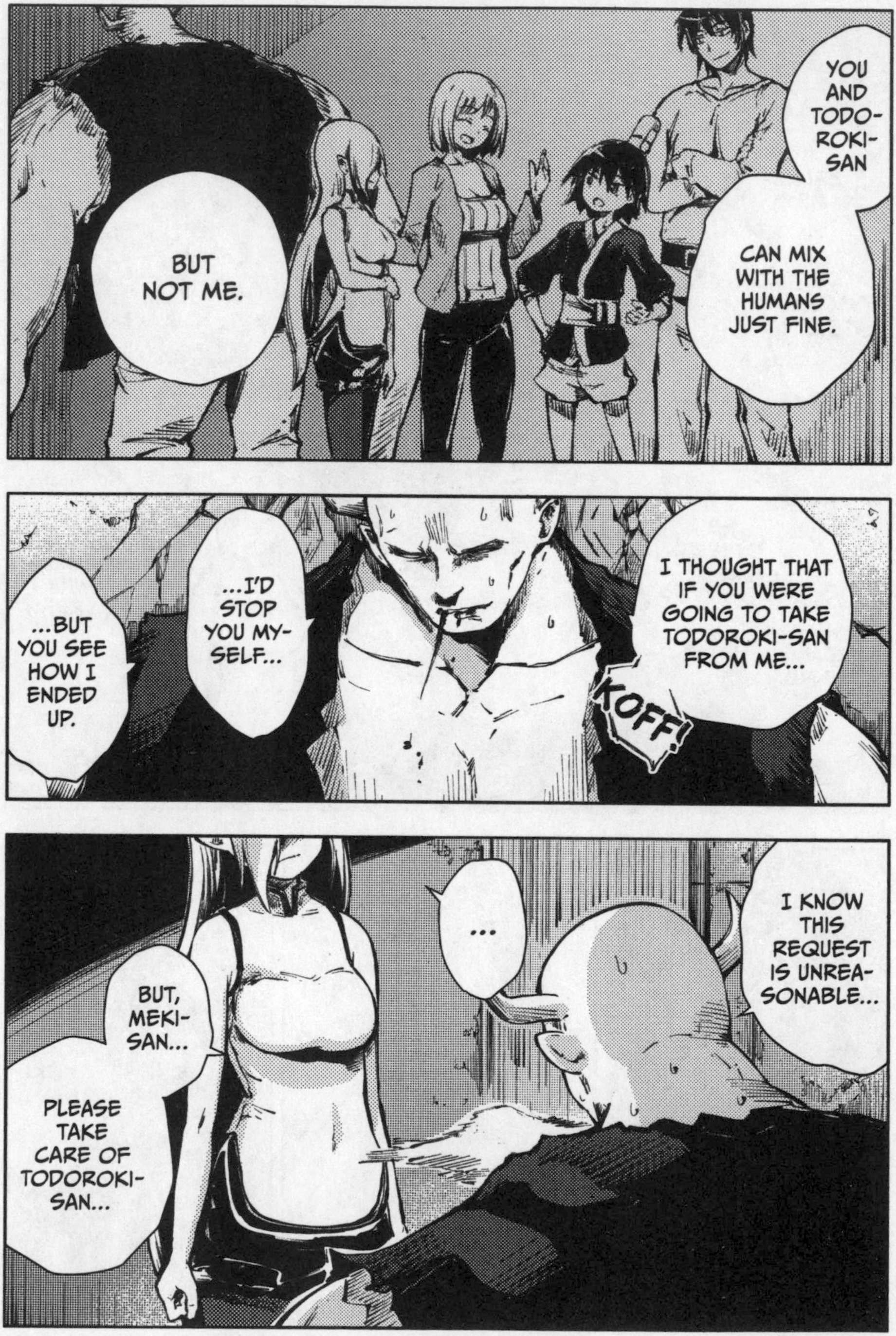
YOU AND TODO-ROKI-SAN
CAN MIX WITH THE HUMANS JUST FINE.
BUT NOT ME.
I THOUGHT THAT IF YOU WERE GOING TO TAKE TODOROKI-SAN FROM ME...
KOFF!
...I'D STOP YOU MY-SELF...
...BUT YOU SEE HOW I ENDED UP.
I KNOW THIS REQUEST IS UNREA-SONABLE...
...
BUT, MEKI-SAN...
PLEASE TAKE CARE OF TODOROKI-SAN...

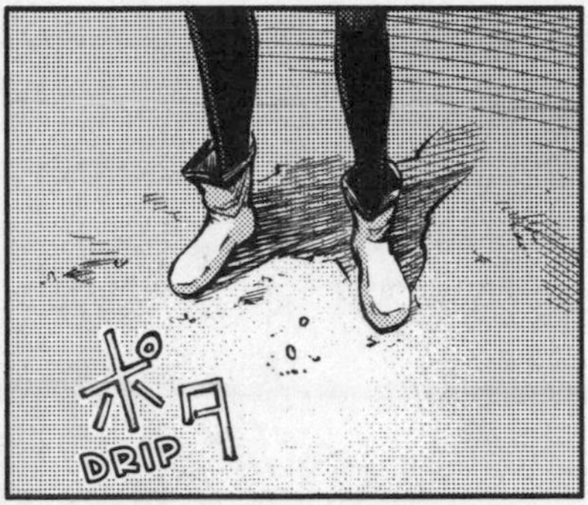
ポタ
DRIP
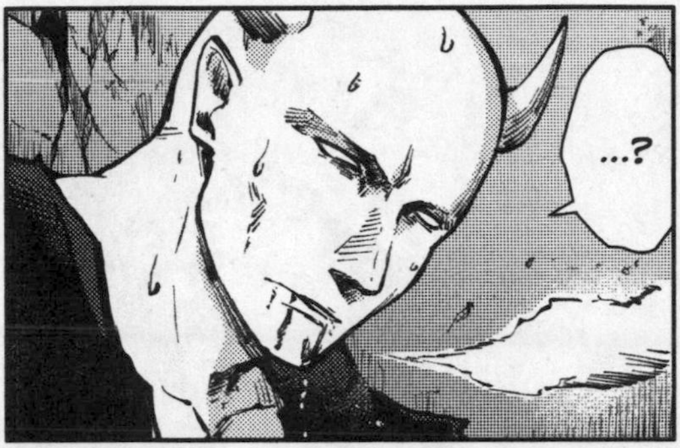
...?
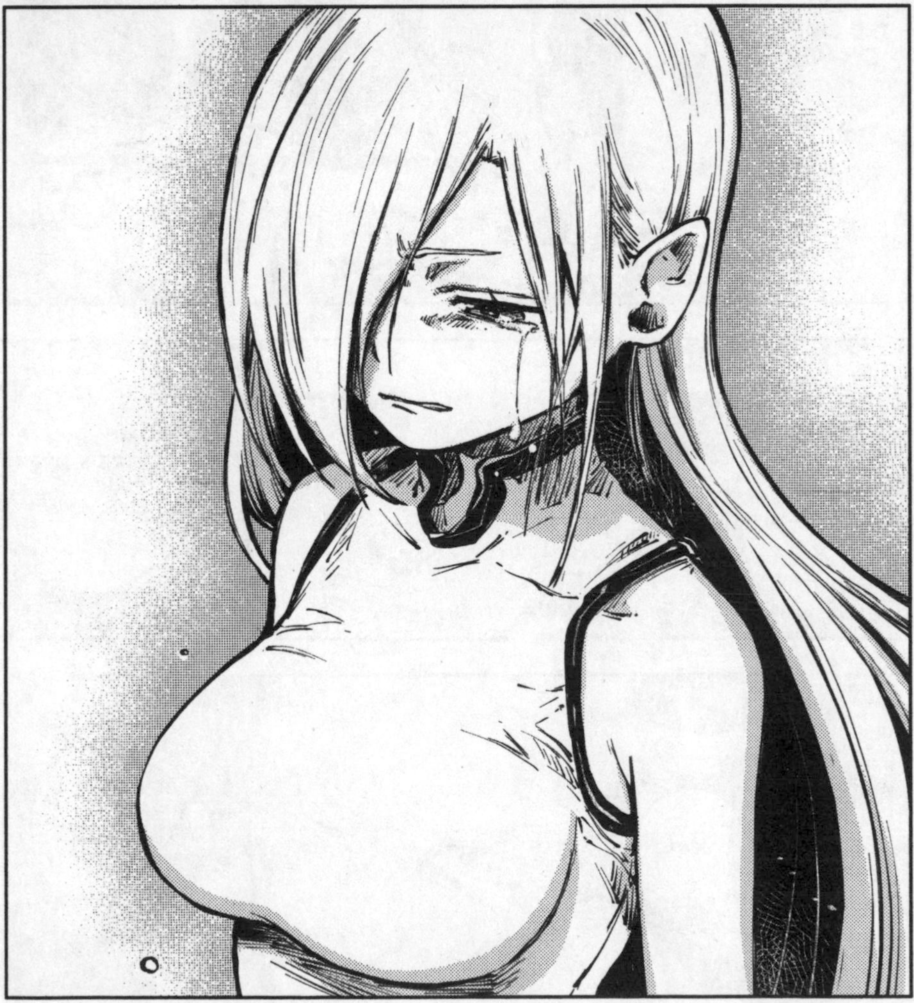

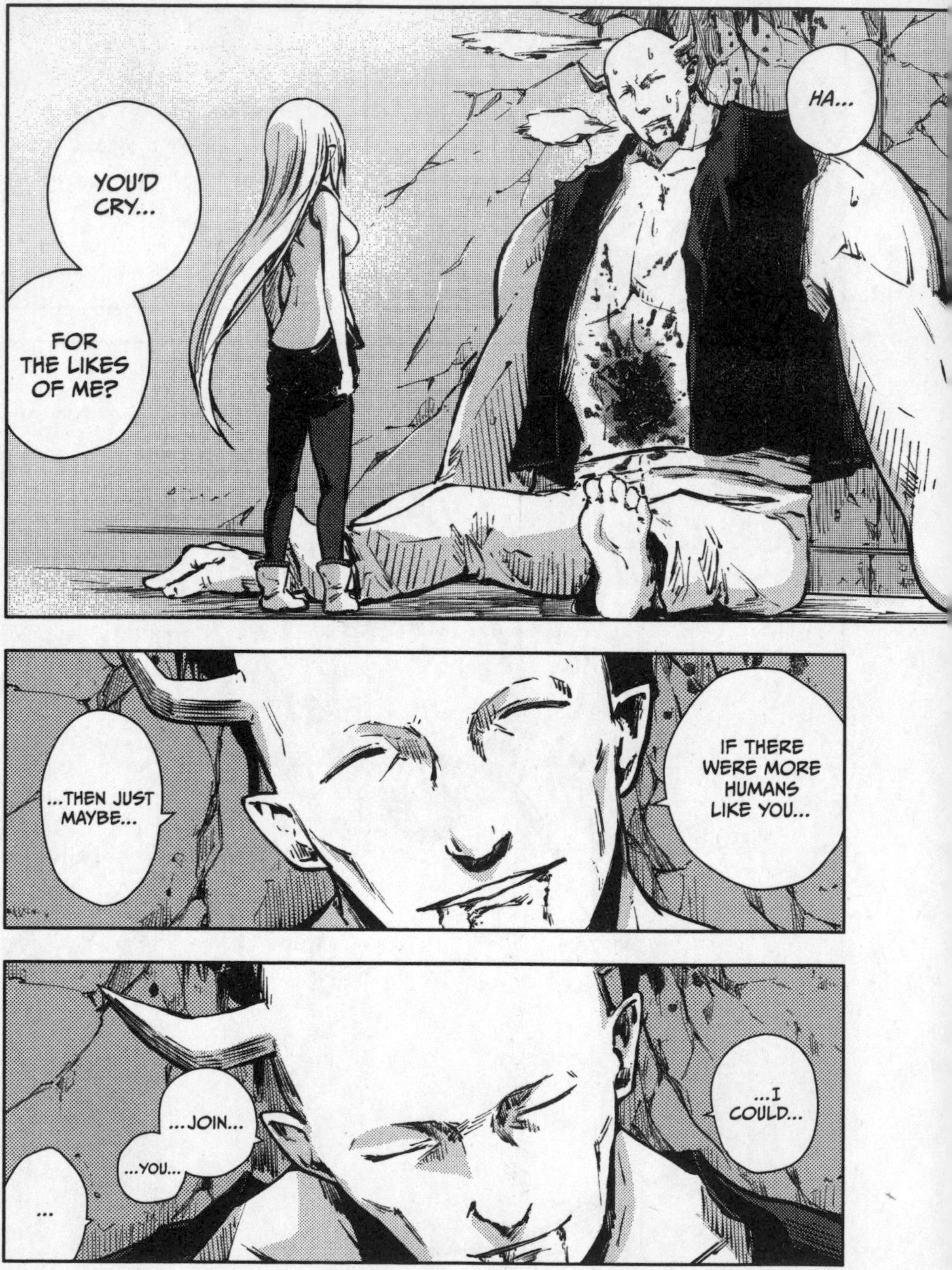
HA...
YOU'D CRY...
FOR THE LIKES OF ME?
IF THERE WERE MORE HUMANS LIKE YOU...
...THEN JUST MAYBE...
...I COULD...
...JOIN...
...YOU...
...

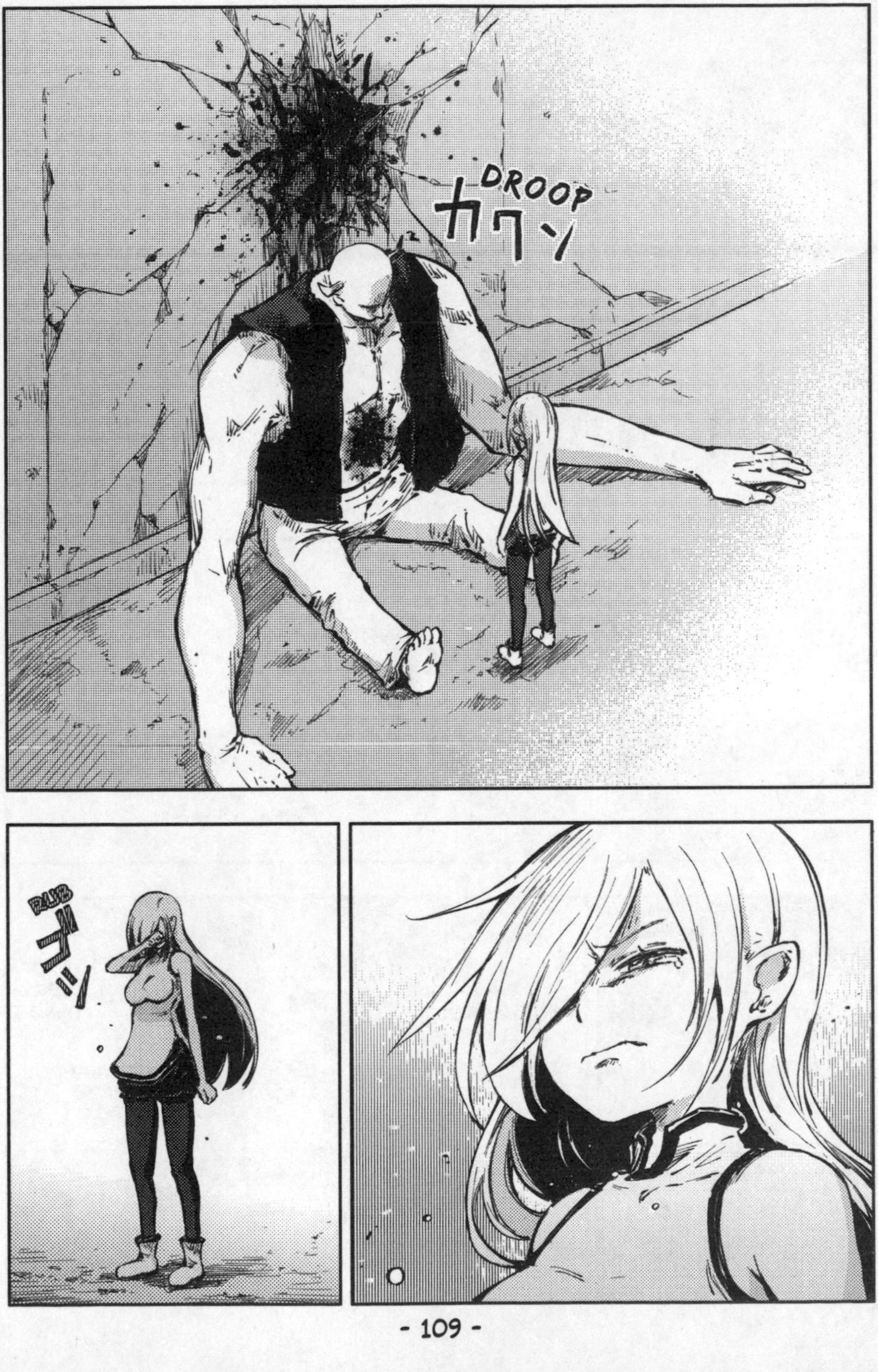
DROOP
カクン
ゴシッ

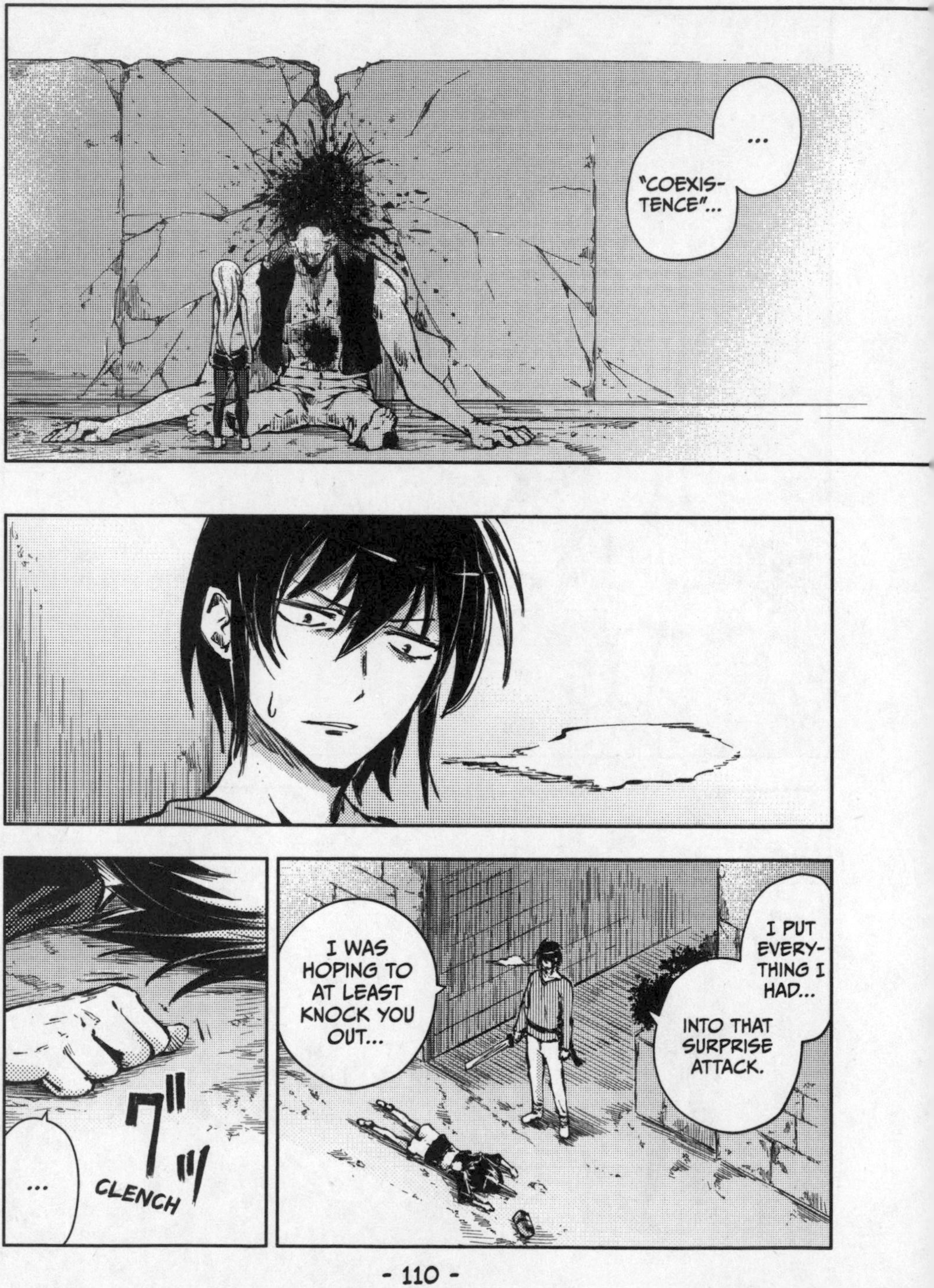
...
"COEXIS-TENCE"...
I PUT EVERY-THING I HAD...
INTO THAT SURPRISE ATTACK.
I WAS HOPING TO AT LEAST KNOCK YOU OUT...
グッ
CLENCH
...

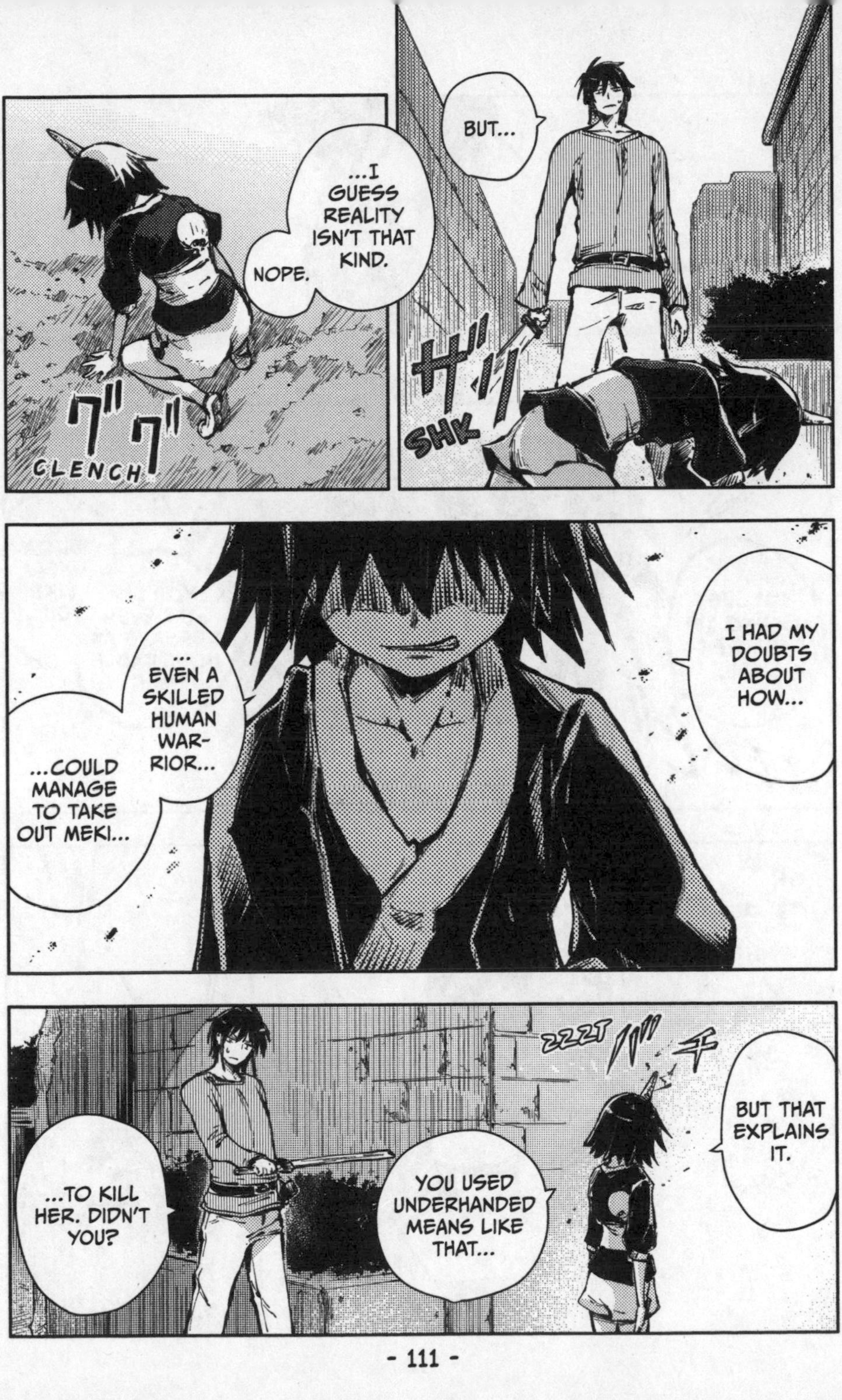
BUT...
SHK
...I GUESS REALITY ISN'T THAT KIND.
NOPE.
CLENCH
I HAD MY DOUBTS ABOUT HOW...
... EVEN A SKILLED HUMAN WAR-RIOR...
...COULD MANAGE TO TAKE OUT MEKI...
ZZZT
BUT THAT EXPLAINS IT.
YOU USED UNDERHANDED MEANS LIKE THAT...
...TO KILL HER. DIDN'T YOU?

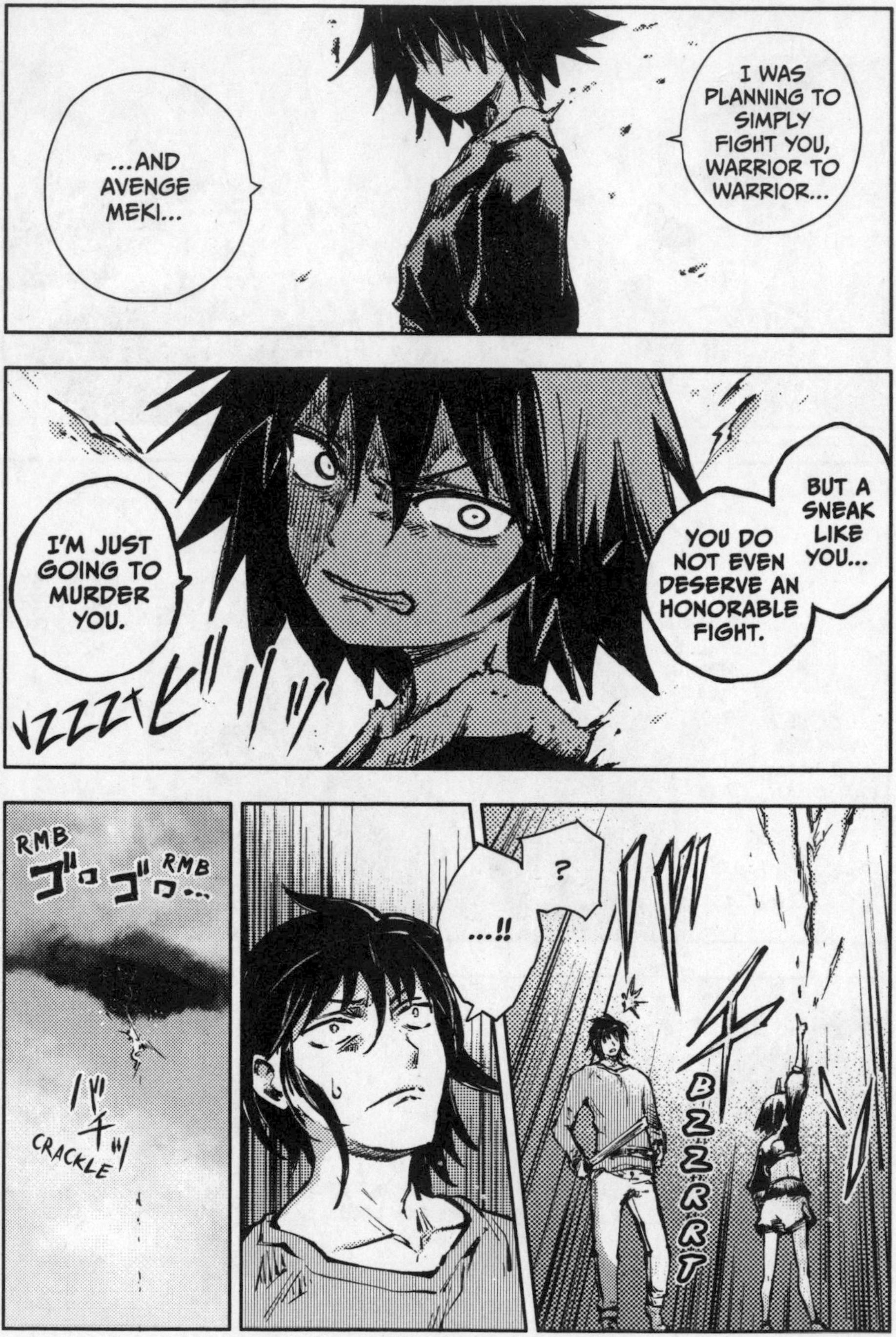
I WAS PLANNING TO SIMPLY FIGHT YOU, WARRIOR TO WARRIOR...
...AND AVENGE MEKI...
BUT A SNEAK LIKE YOU...
YOU DO NOT EVEN DESERVE AN HONORABLE FIGHT.
I'M JUST GOING TO MURDER YOU.
VZZZZT
BZZZRRRT
?
...!!
RMB ゴロ RMB ゴロ...
バチッ CRACKLE

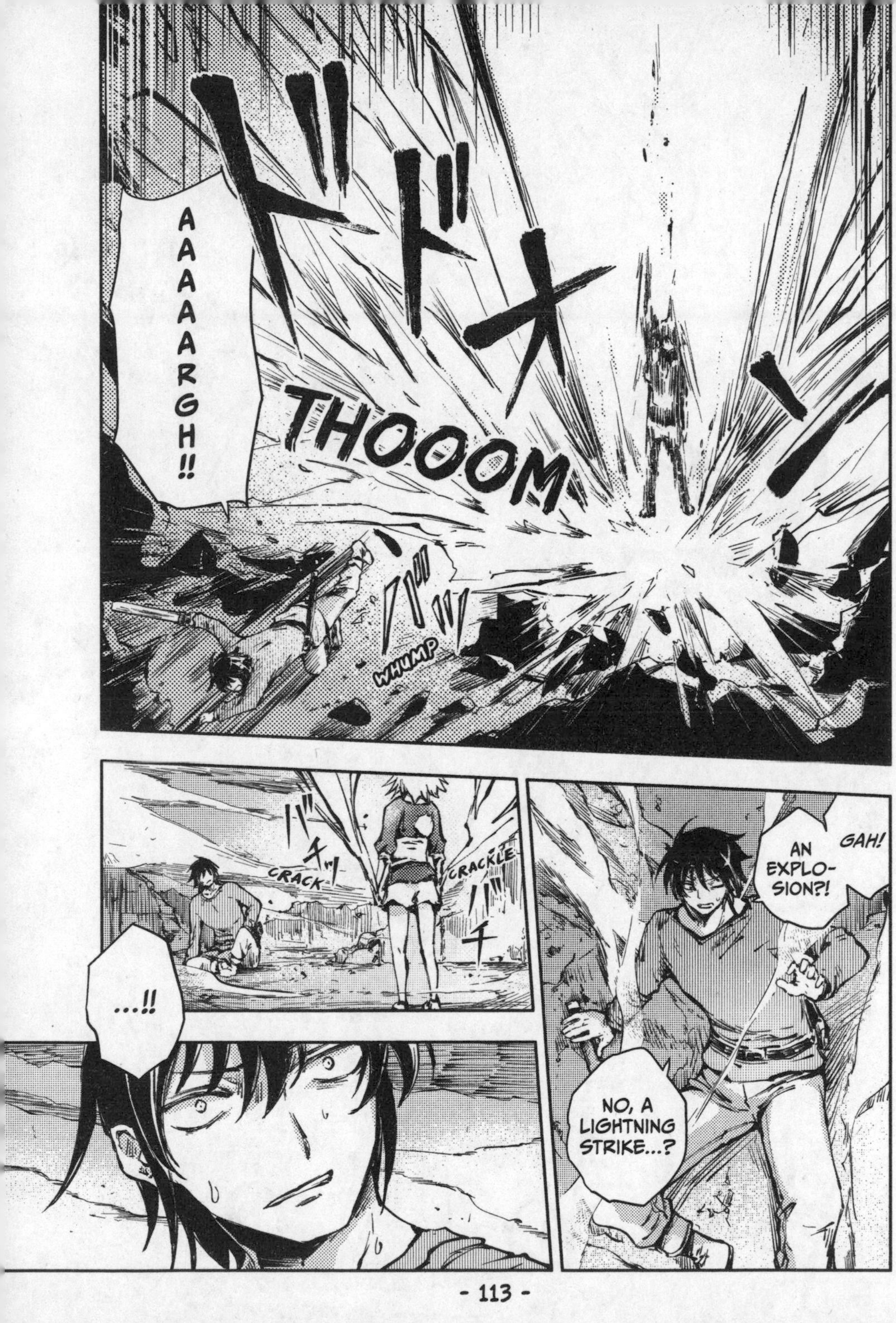
THOOOM
AAAAAARGH!!
WHUMP
GAH!
AN EXPLOSION?!
NO, A LIGHTNING STRIKE...?
CRACKLE
CRACK
...!!

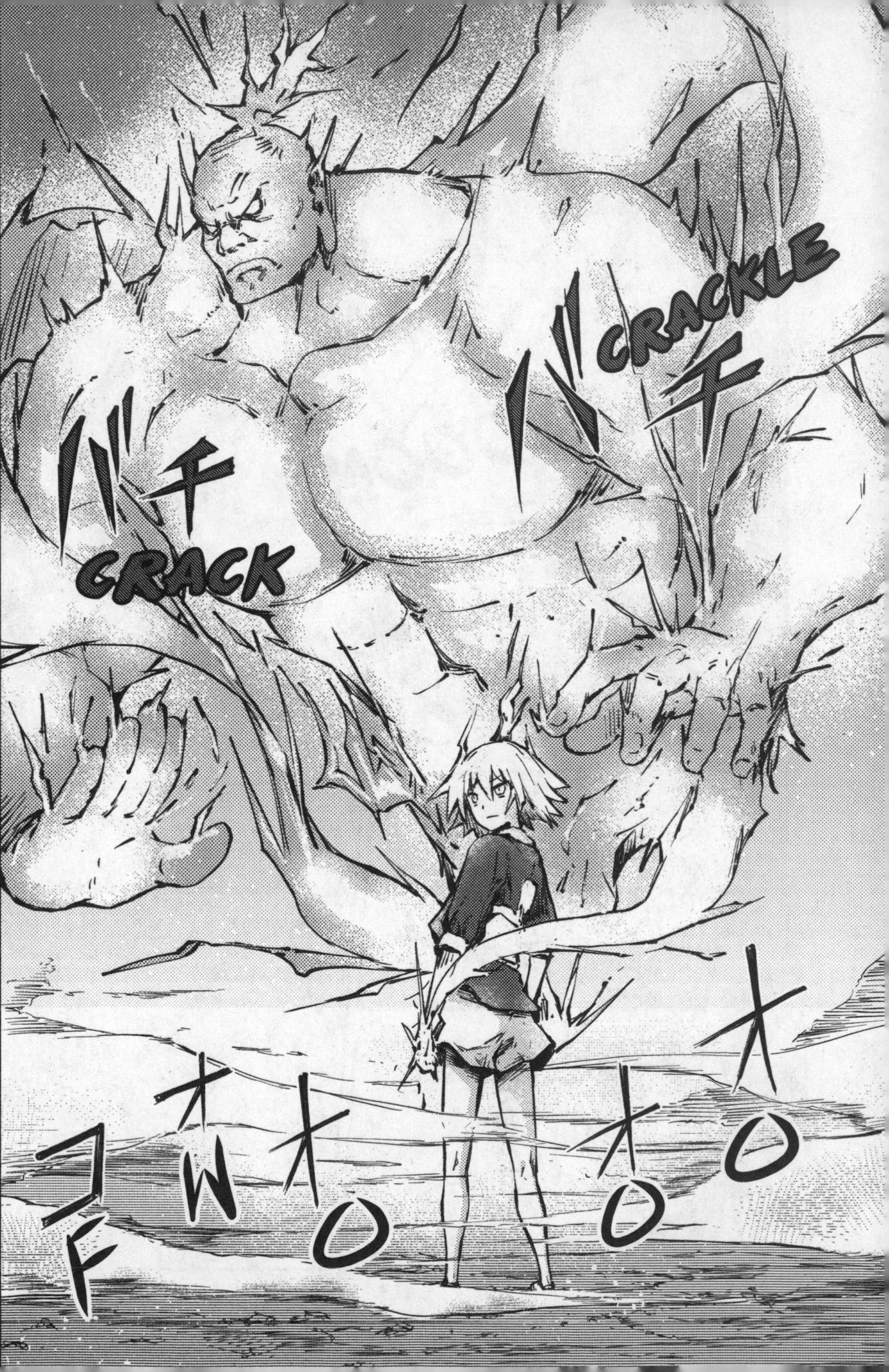
バチ
CRACKLE
バチ
CRACK
ゴオオオオ
FWOOOO

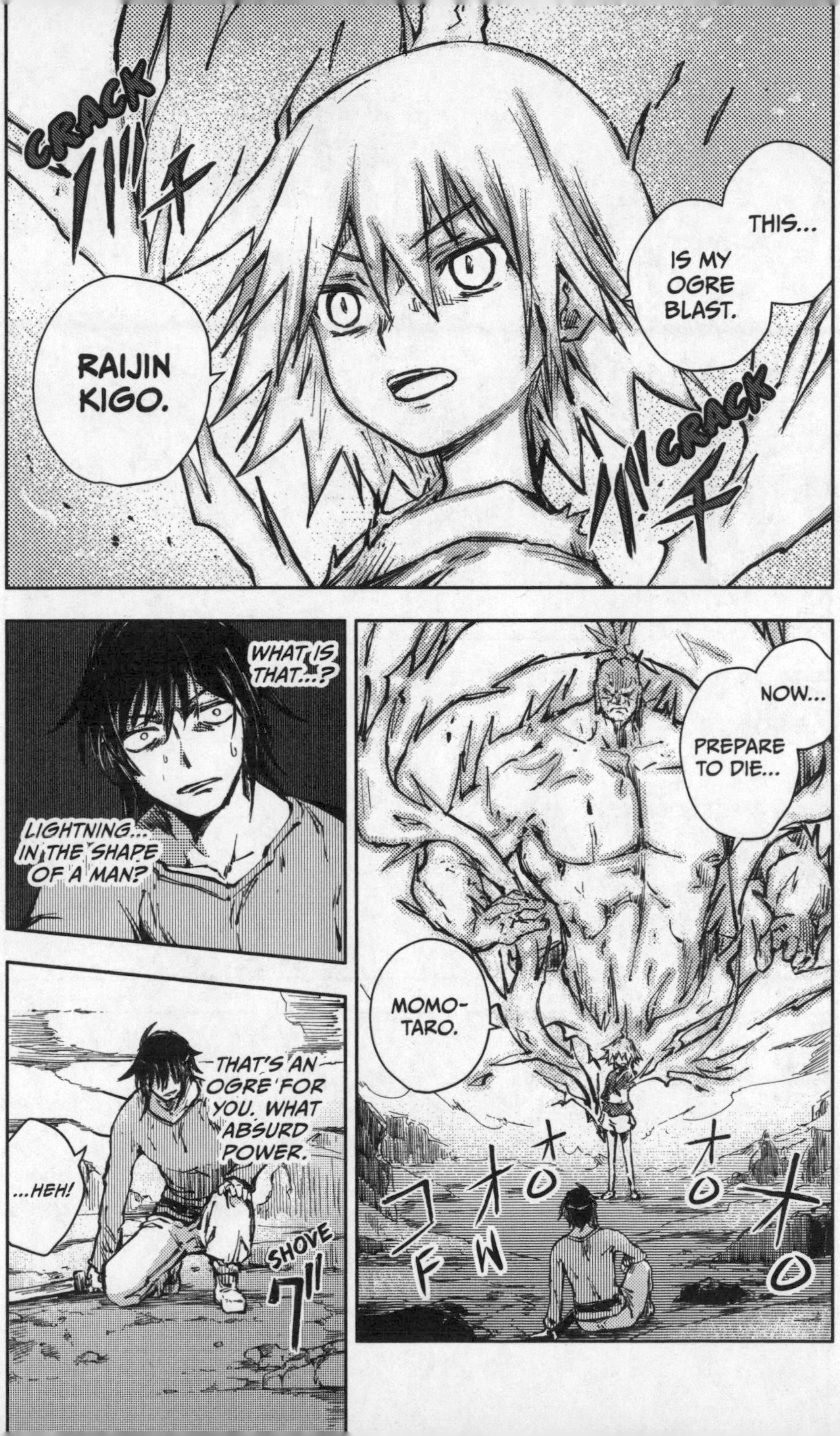
CRACK
THIS...
IS MY OGRE BLAST.
CRACK
RAIJIN KIGO.
NOW...
PREPARE TO DIE...
MOMO-TARO.
FWOOO
WHAT IS THAT...?
LIGHTNING... IN THE SHAPE OF A MAN?
THAT'S AN OGRE FOR YOU. WHAT ABSURD POWER.
...HEH!
SHOVE

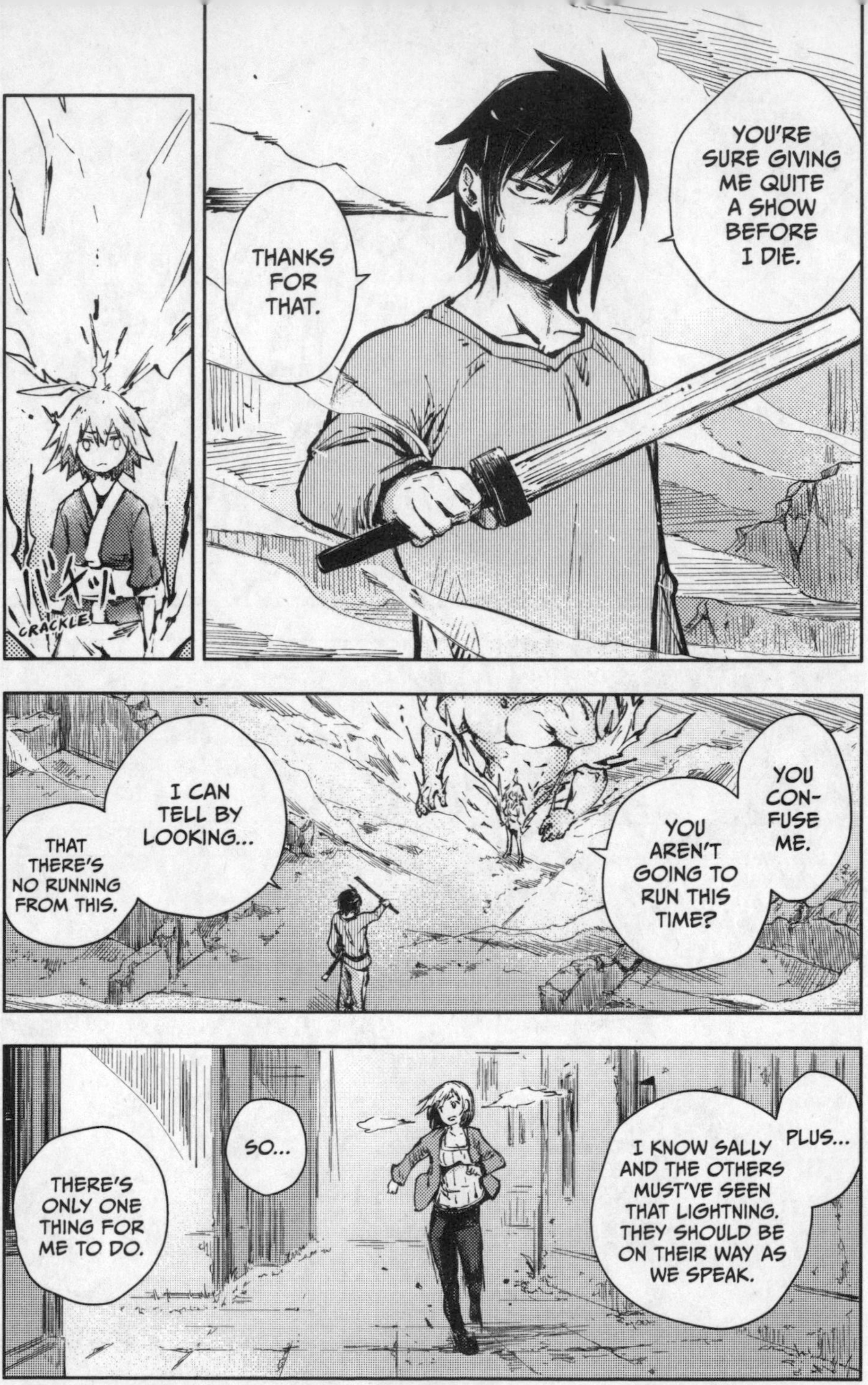
YOU'RE SURE GIVING ME QUITE A SHOW BEFORE I DIE.
THANKS FOR THAT.
バキッ
CRACKLE
YOU CONFUSE ME.
YOU AREN'T GOING TO RUN THIS TIME?
I CAN TELL BY LOOKING...
THAT THERE'S NO RUNNING FROM THIS.
PLUS...
I KNOW SALLY AND THE OTHERS MUST'VE SEEN THAT LIGHTNING. THEY SHOULD BE ON THEIR WAY AS WE SPEAK.
SO...
THERE'S ONLY ONE THING FOR ME TO DO.

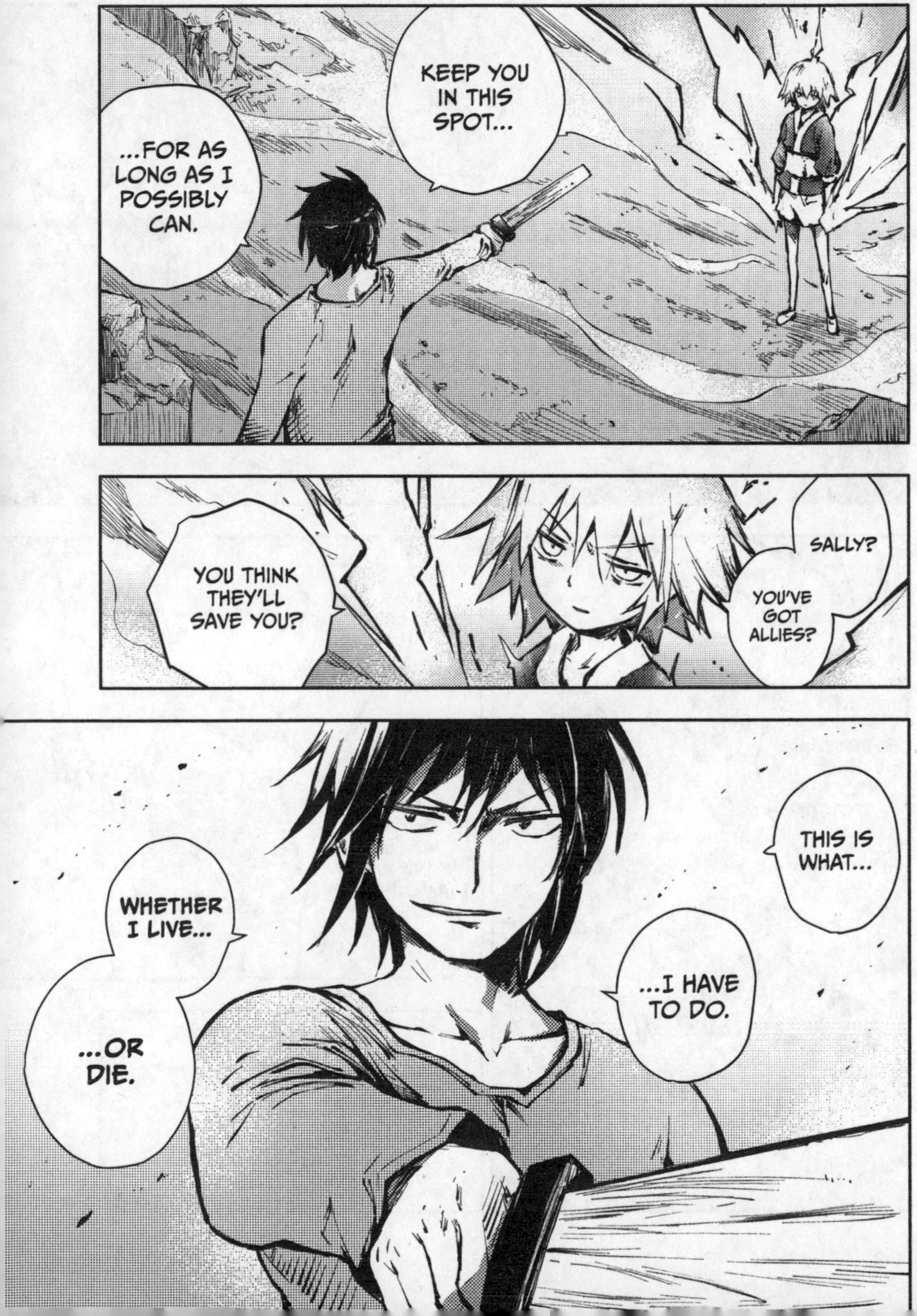
KEEP YOU IN THIS SPOT...
...FOR AS LONG AS I POSSIBLY CAN.
SALLY?
YOU'VE GOT ALLIES?
YOU THINK THEY'LL SAVE YOU?
THIS IS WHAT...
...I HAVE TO DO.
WHETHER I LIVE...
...OR DIE.

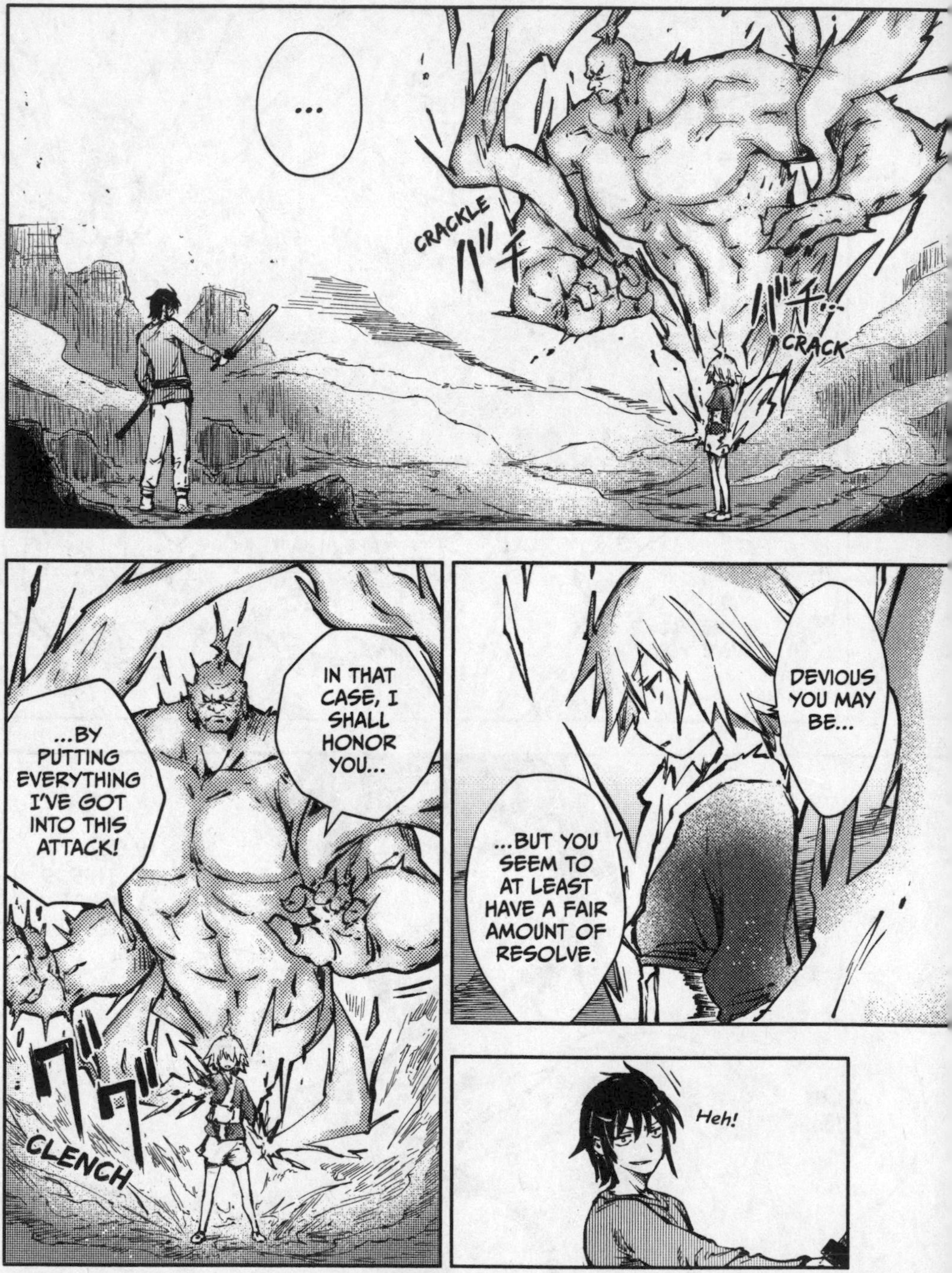
CRACKLE
バチ
バチ...
CRACK
...
DEVIOUS YOU MAY BE...
...BUT YOU SEEM TO AT LEAST HAVE A FAIR AMOUNT OF RESOLVE.
Heh!
IN THAT CASE, I SHALL HONOR YOU...
...BY PUTTING EVERYTHING I'VE GOT INTO THIS ATTACK!
CLENCH

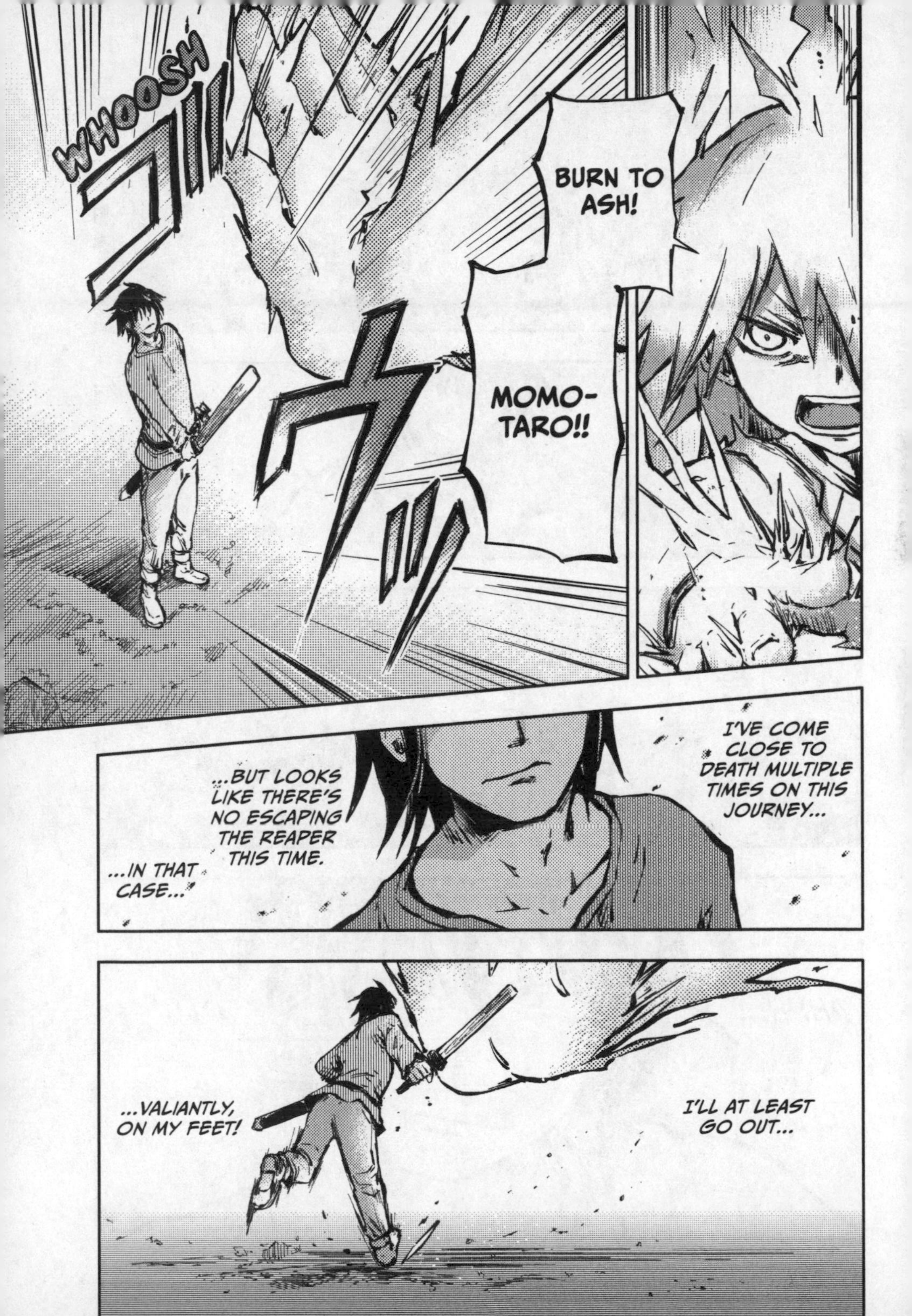
BURN TO ASH!
MOMO-TARO!!
WHOOSH
I'VE COME CLOSE TO DEATH MULTIPLE TIMES ON THIS JOURNEY...
...BUT LOOKS LIKE THERE'S NO ESCAPING THE REAPER THIS TIME.
...IN THAT CASE...
I'LL AT LEAST GO OUT...
...VALIANTLY, ON MY FEET!

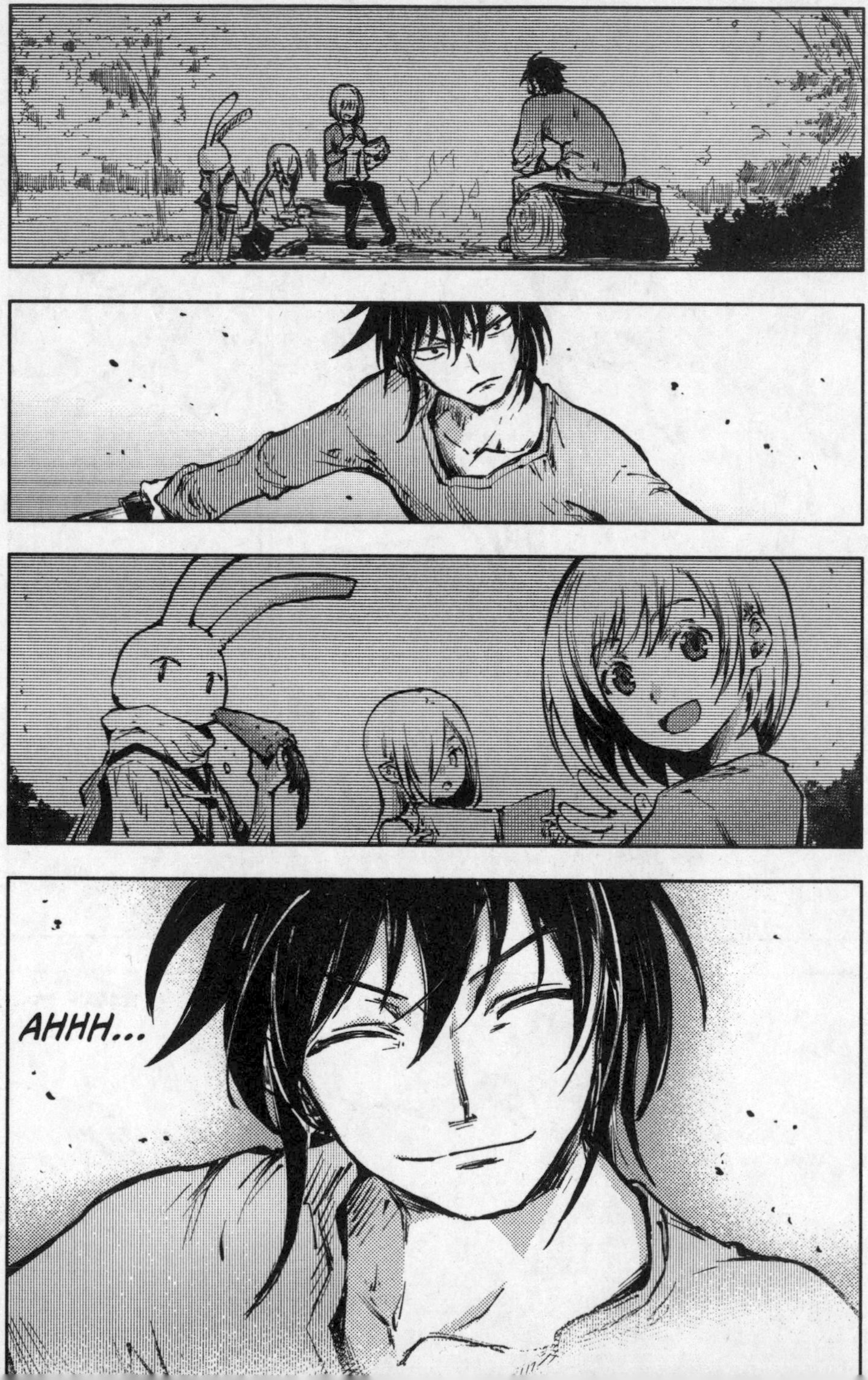
AHHH...

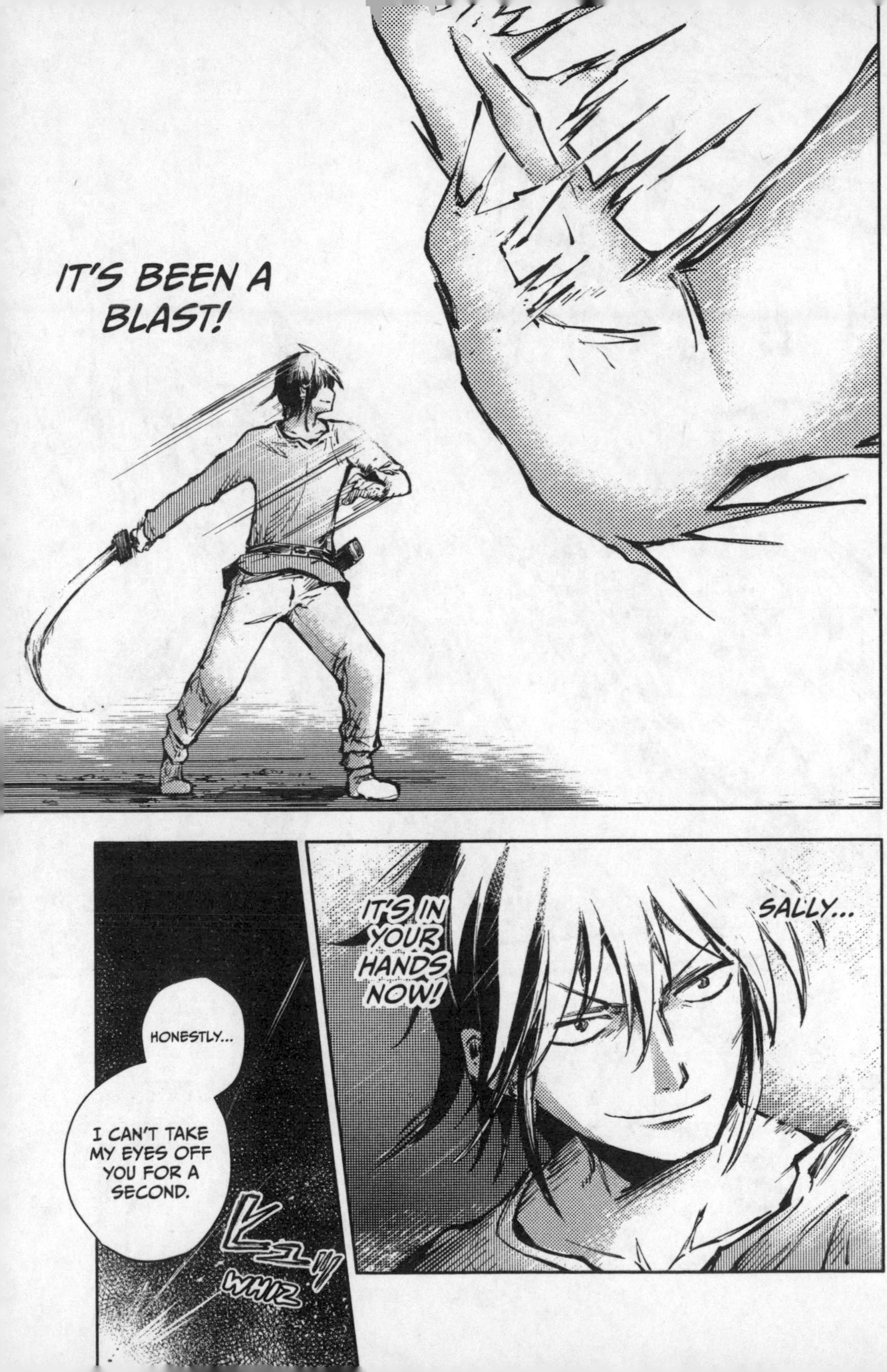
IT'S BEEN A BLAST!
SALLY...
IT'S IN YOUR HANDS NOW!
HONESTLY...
I CAN'T TAKE MY EYES OFF YOU FOR A SECOND.
WHIZ

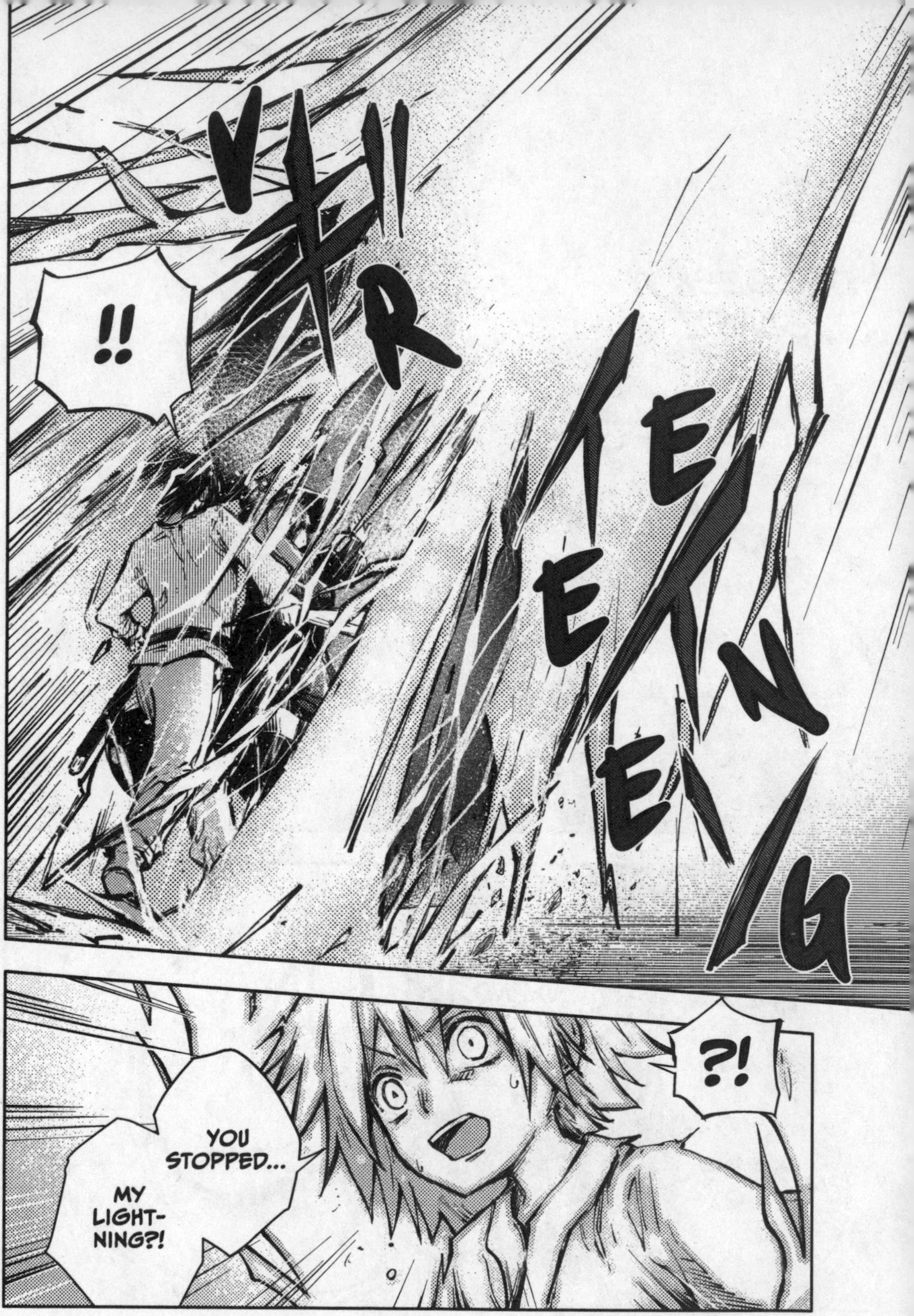
!!
?!
YOU STOPPED...
MY LIGHTNING?!

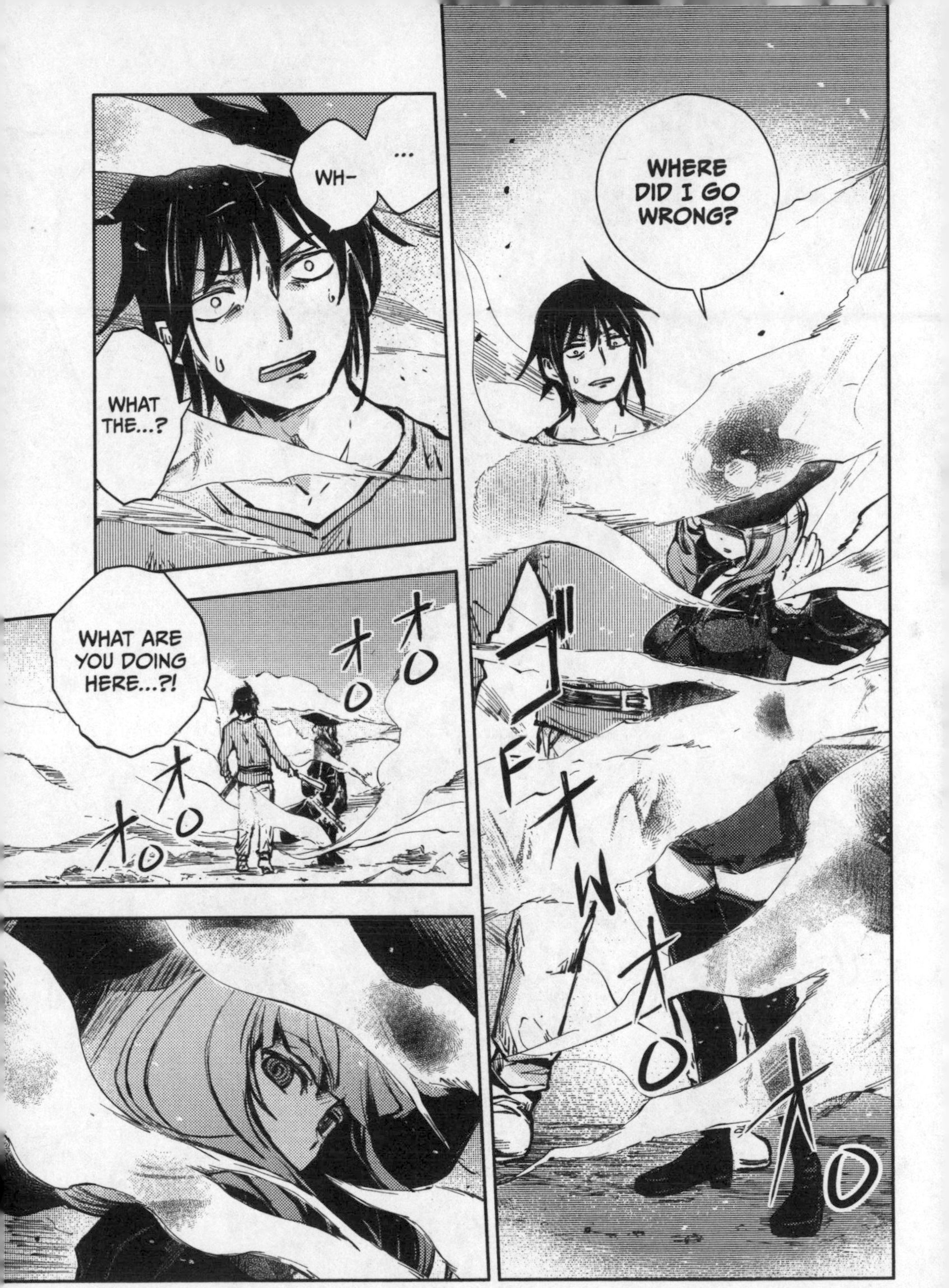
WHERE DID I GO WRONG?
FWOO
...
WH-
WHAT THE...?
WHAT ARE YOU DOING HERE...?!

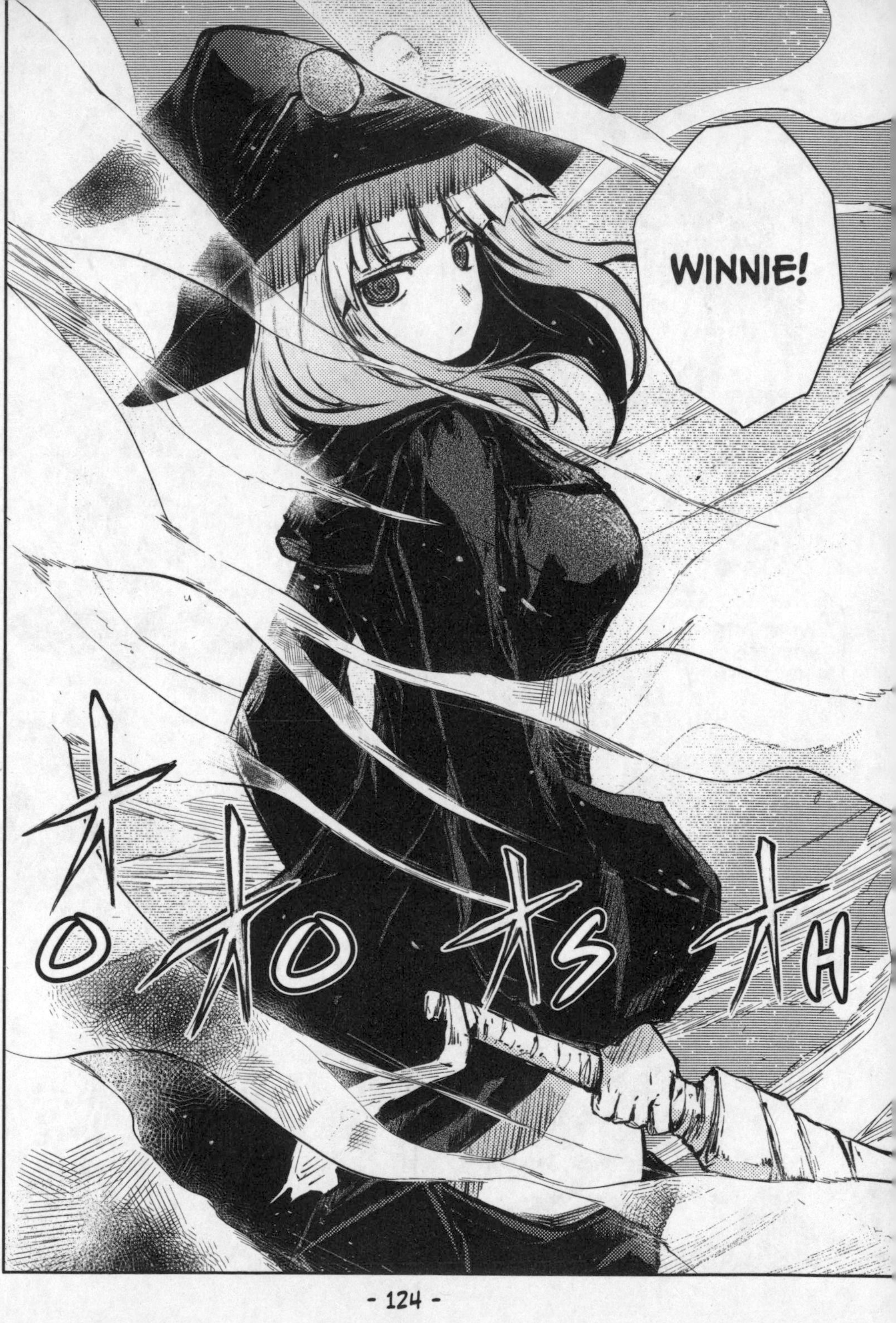
WINNIE!

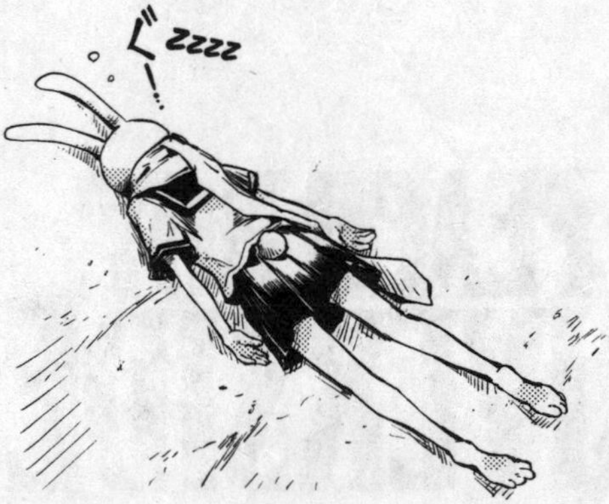
zzzz

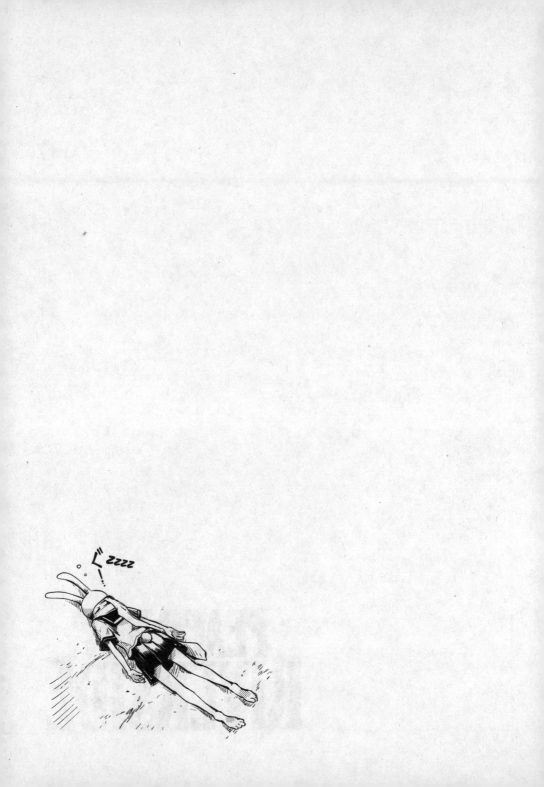

PEACH BOY
RIVERSIDE

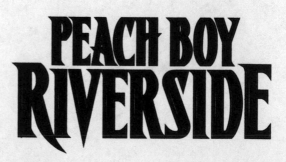

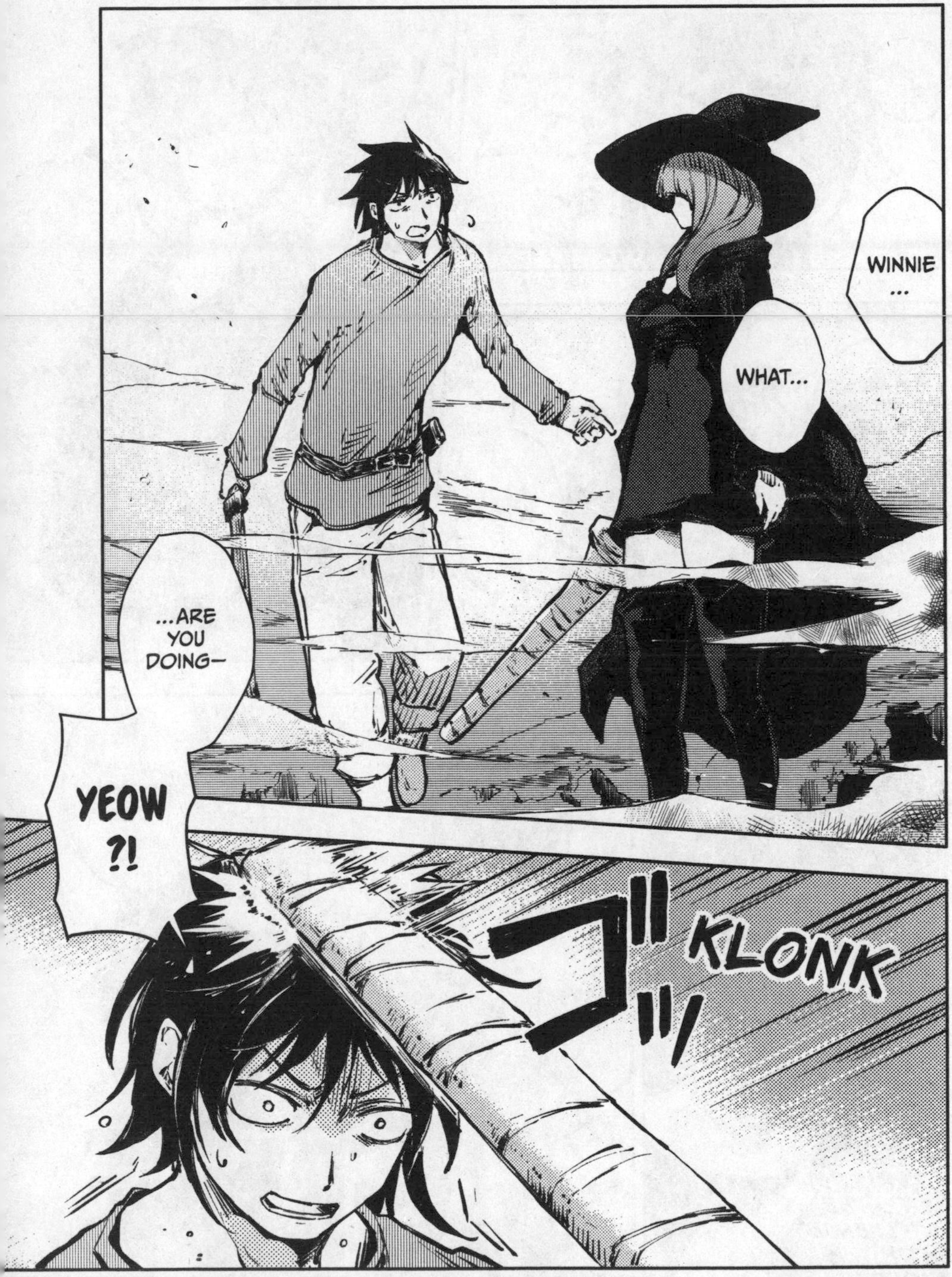
WINNIE ...
WHAT...
...ARE YOU DOING—
KLONK
YEOW ?!

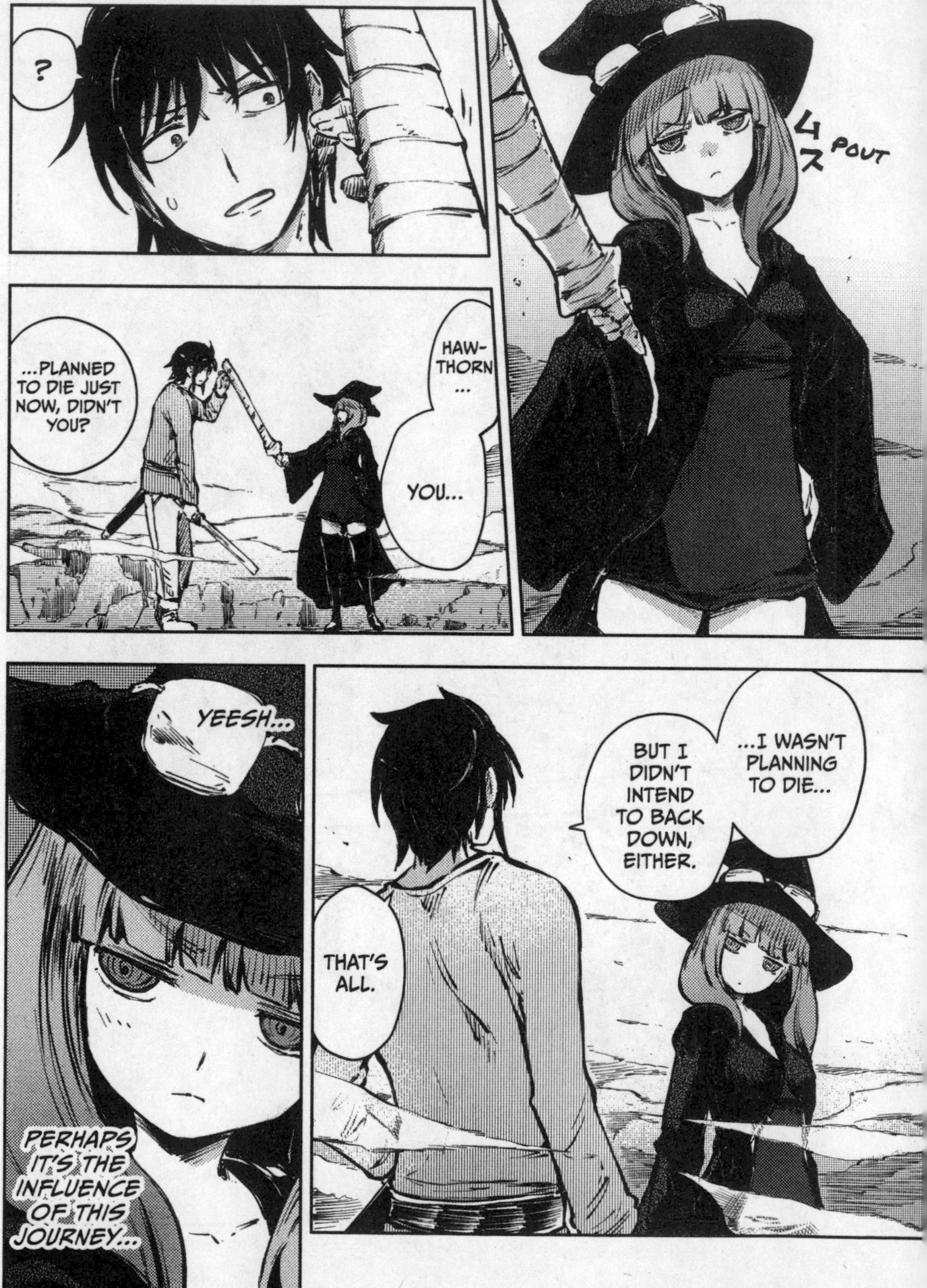
ムス POUT
?
HAW-THORN ...
YOU...
...PLANNED TO DIE JUST NOW, DIDN'T YOU?
...I WASN'T PLANNING TO DIE...
BUT I DIDN'T INTEND TO BACK DOWN, EITHER.
THAT'S ALL.
YEESH...
PERHAPS IT'S THE INFLUENCE OF THIS JOURNEY...

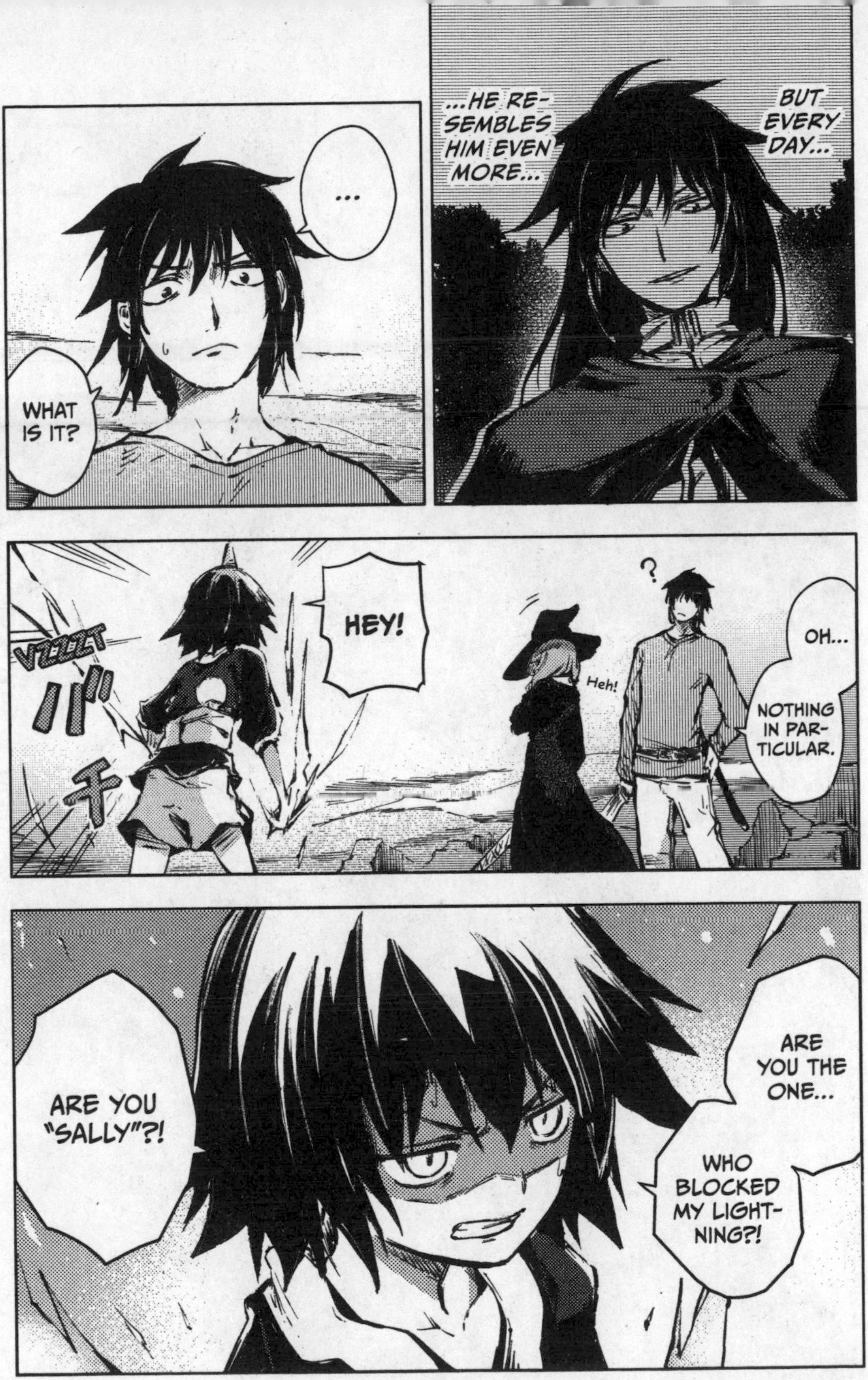
BUT EVERY DAY...
...HE RE-SEMBLES HIM EVEN MORE...
...
WHAT IS IT?
?
OH...
NOTHING IN PAR-TICULAR.
Heh!
HEY!
VZZZT
バチ
ARE YOU THE ONE...
WHO BLOCKED MY LIGHT-NING?!
ARE YOU "SALLY"?!

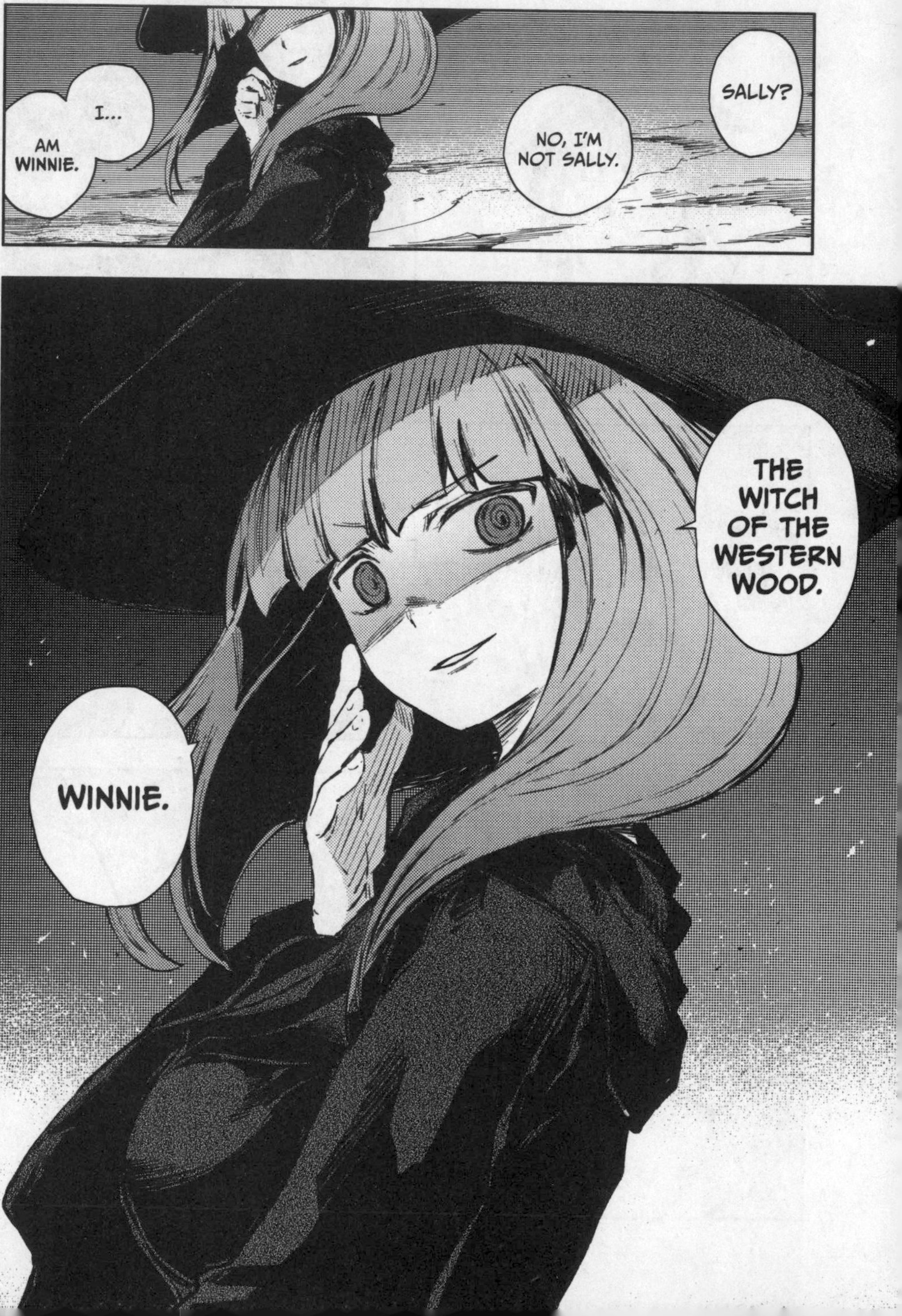
SALLY?
NO, I'M NOT SALLY.
I...
AM WINNIE.
THE WITCH OF THE WESTERN WOOD.
WINNIE.

CHAPTER 23: THE RAVAGES OF WAR AND HATRED

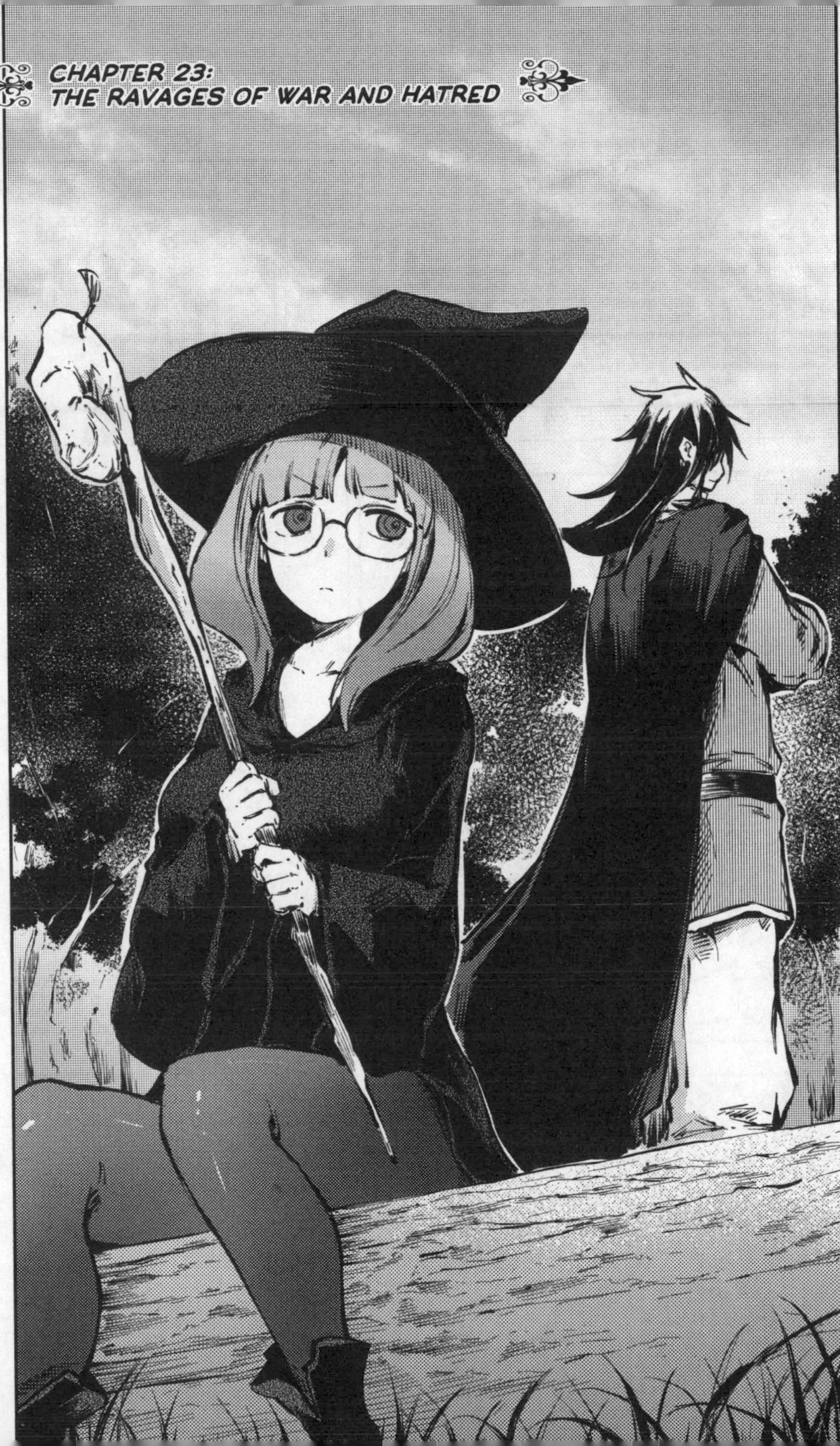

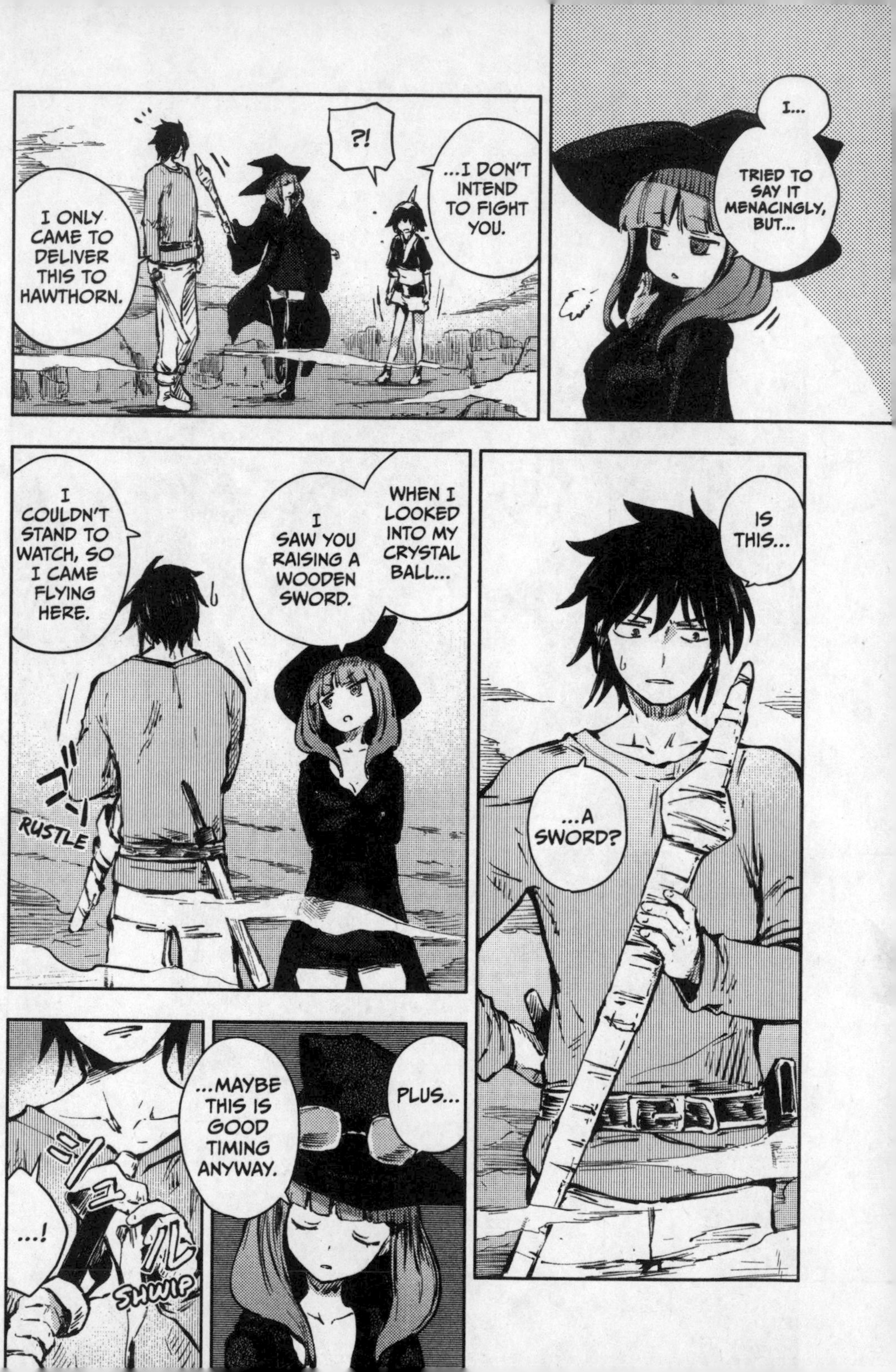
I...
TRIED TO SAY IT MENACINGLY, BUT...
...I DON'T INTEND TO FIGHT YOU.
?!
I ONLY CAME TO DELIVER THIS TO HAWTHORN.
IS THIS...
...A SWORD?
WHEN I LOOKED INTO MY CRYSTAL BALL...
I SAW YOU RAISING A WOODEN SWORD.
I COULDN'T STAND TO WATCH, SO I CAME FLYING HERE.
RUSTLE
PLUS...
...MAYBE THIS IS GOOD TIMING ANYWAY.
...!
SHWIP

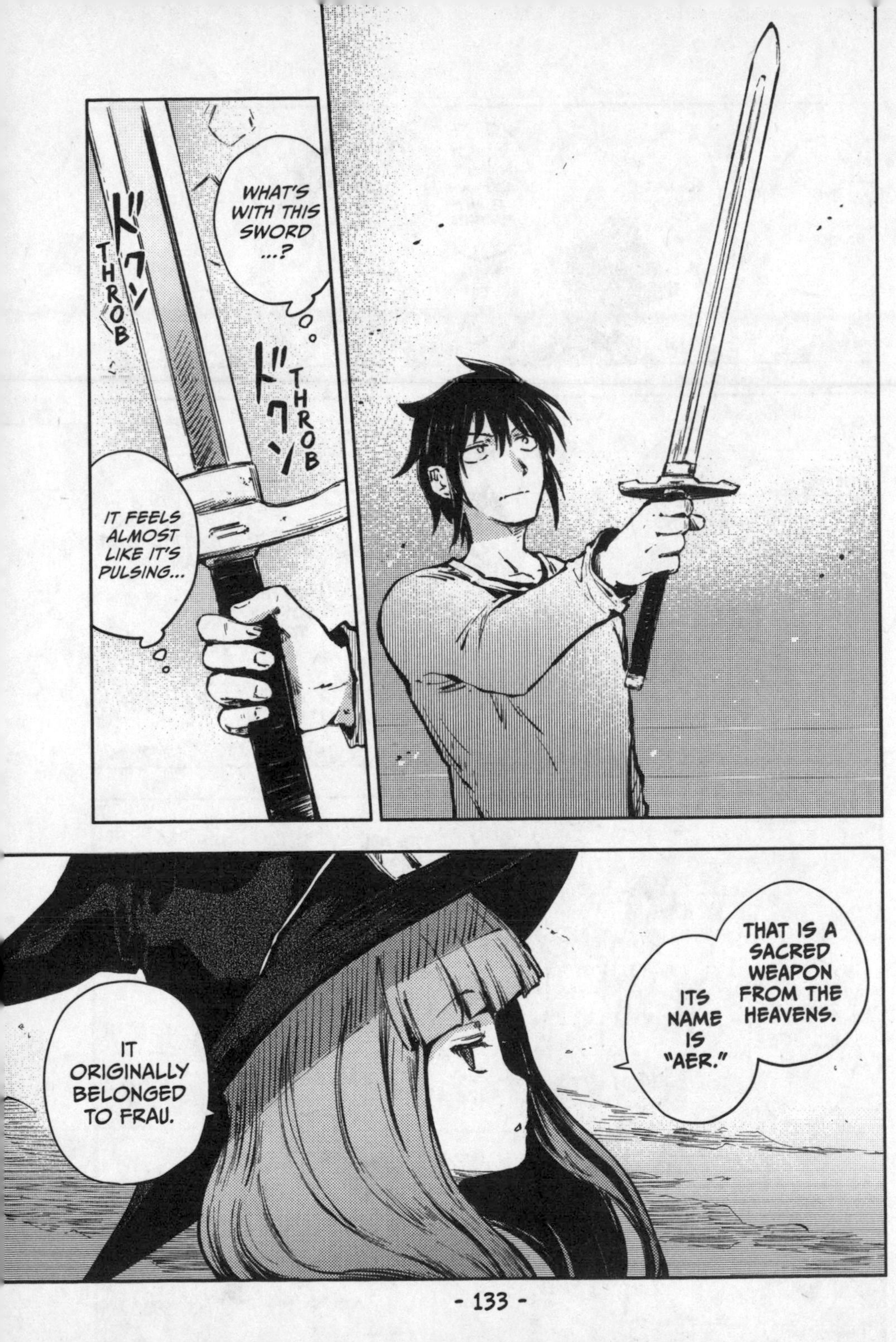
WHAT'S WITH THIS SWORD ...?
ドクン
THROB
ドクン
THROB
IT FEELS ALMOST LIKE IT'S PULSING...
THAT IS A SACRED WEAPON FROM THE HEAVENS.
ITS NAME IS "AER."
IT ORIGINALLY BELONGED TO FRAU.

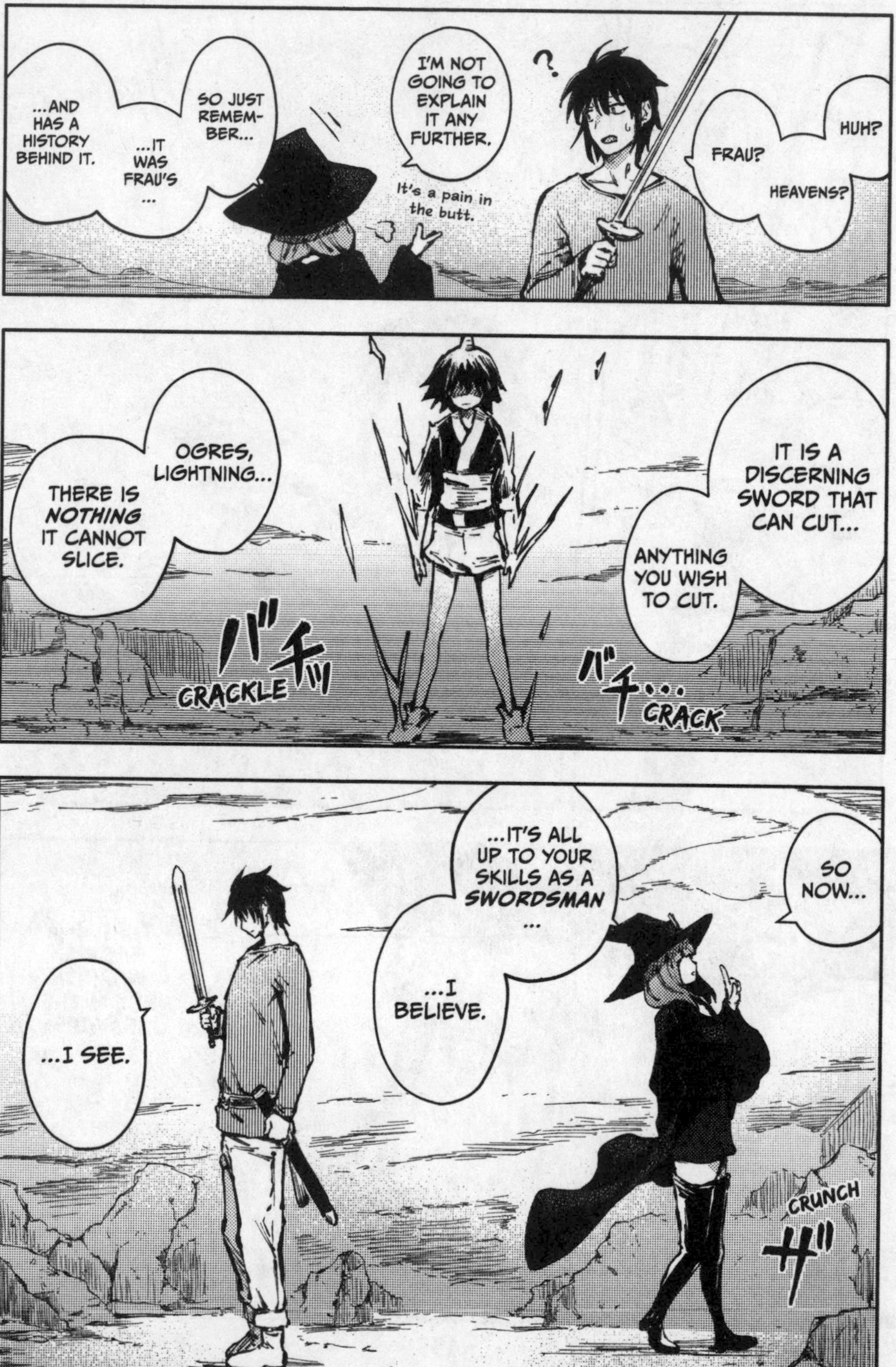
HUH? FRAU? HEAVENS?
?
I'M NOT GOING TO EXPLAIN IT ANY FURTHER.
It's a pain in the butt.
SO JUST REMEMBER...
...IT WAS FRAU'S ...
...AND HAS A HISTORY BEHIND IT.
IT IS A DISCERNING SWORD THAT CAN CUT...
ANYTHING YOU WISH TO CUT.
OGRES, LIGHTNING...
THERE IS NOTHING IT CANNOT SLICE.
バチ... CRACK
バチッ CRACKLE
SO NOW...
...IT'S ALL UP TO YOUR SKILLS AS A SWORDSMAN ...
...I BELIEVE.
ザッ CRUNCH
...I SEE.

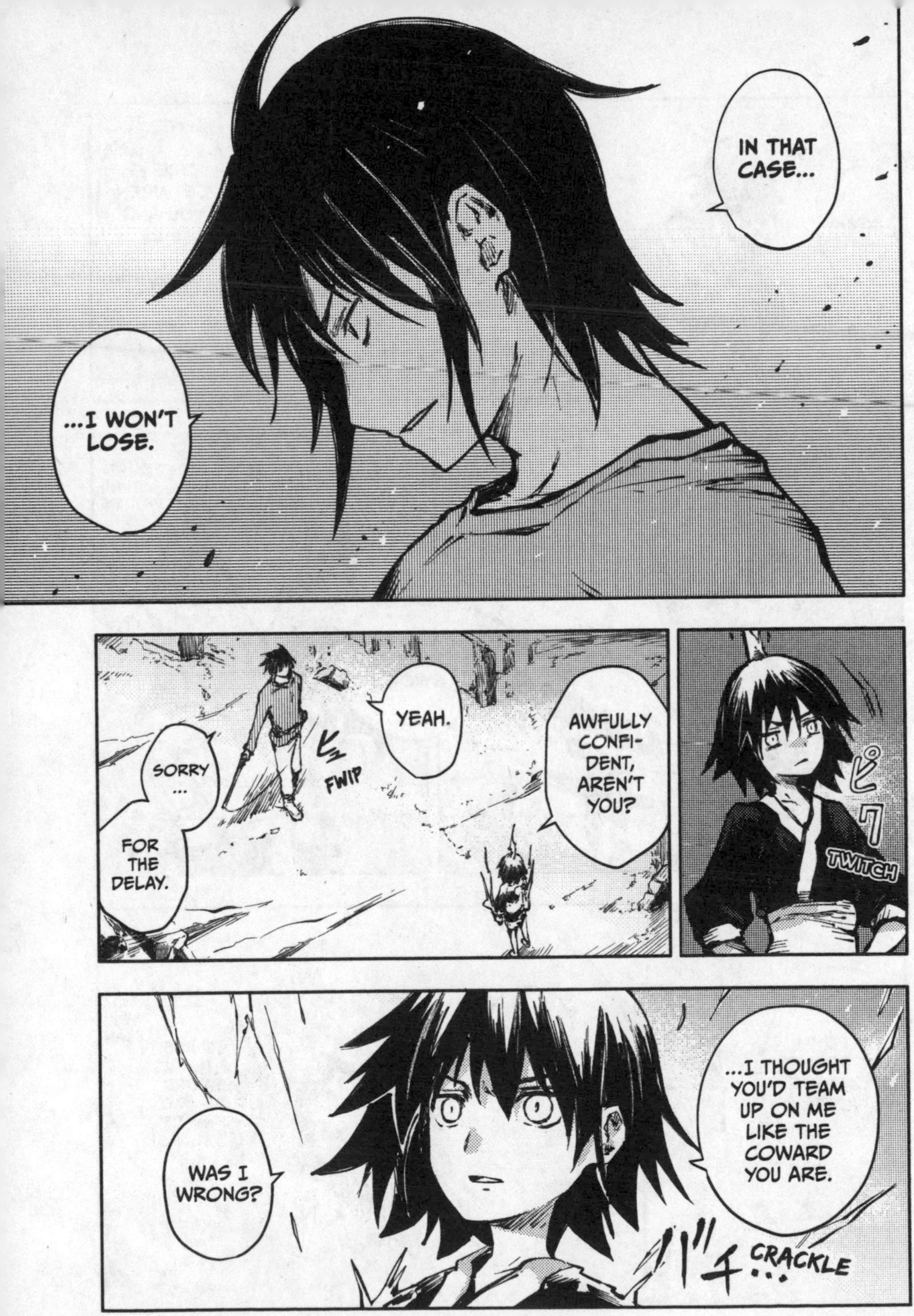
IN THAT CASE...
...I WON'T LOSE.
TWITCH
AWFULLY CONFI-DENT, AREN'T YOU?
YEAH.
FWIP
SORRY... FOR THE DELAY.
...I THOUGHT YOU'D TEAM UP ON ME LIKE THE COWARD YOU ARE.
CRACKLE...
WAS I WRONG?

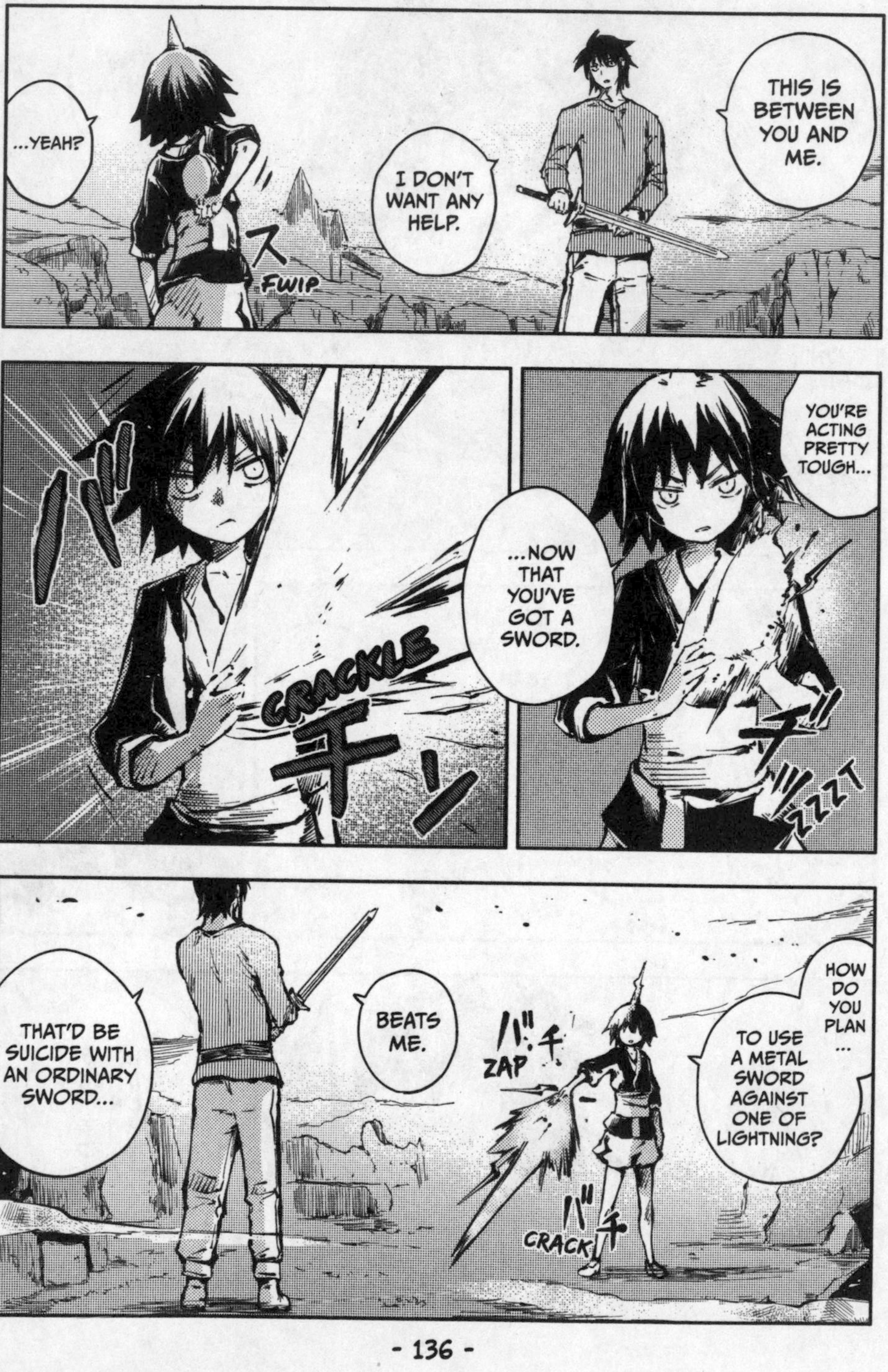

THIS IS BETWEEN YOU AND ME.
I DON'T WANT ANY HELP.
ス
FWIP
...YEAH?
YOU'RE ACTING PRETTY TOUGH...
...NOW THAT YOU'VE GOT A SWORD.
ZZZZT
CRACKLE
チン
HOW DO YOU PLAN ...
TO USE A METAL SWORD AGAINST ONE OF LIGHTNING?
バチ
ZAP
バチ
CRACK
BEATS ME.
THAT'D BE SUICIDE WITH AN ORDINARY SWORD...

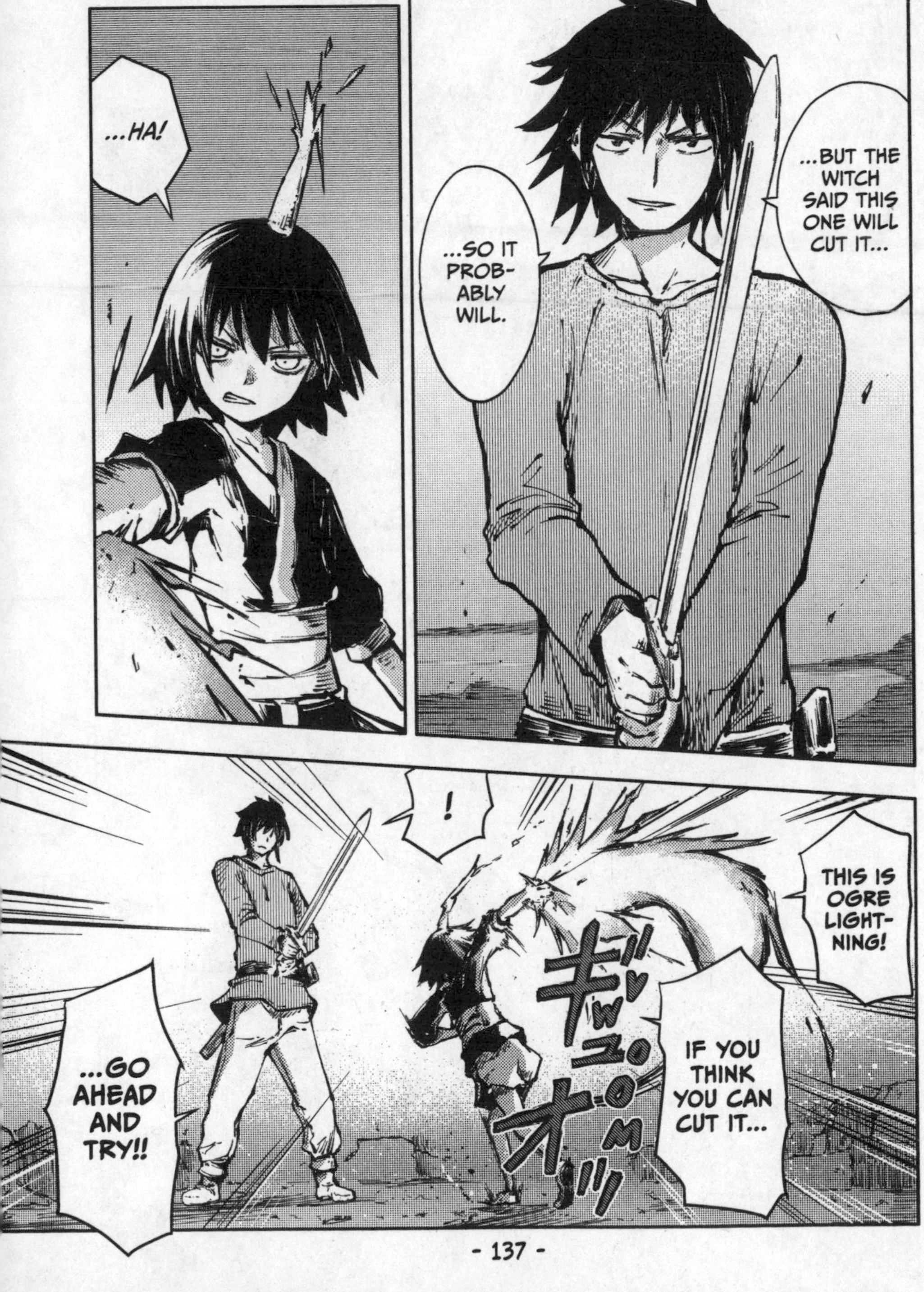
...BUT THE WITCH SAID THIS ONE WILL CUT IT...
...SO IT PROBABLY WILL.
...HA!
THIS IS OGRE LIGHTNING!
!
IF YOU THINK YOU CAN CUT IT...
...GO AHEAD AND TRY!!

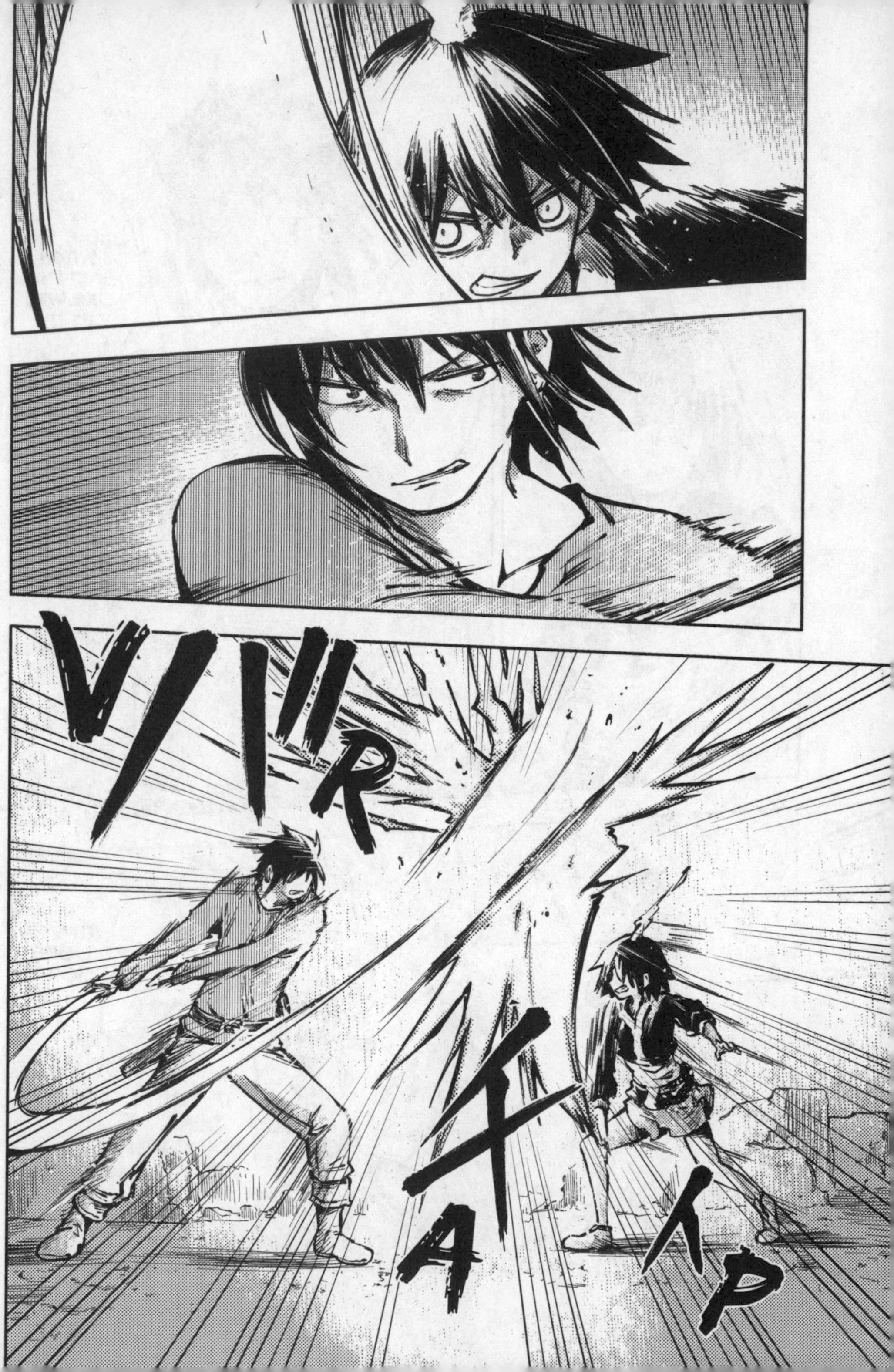

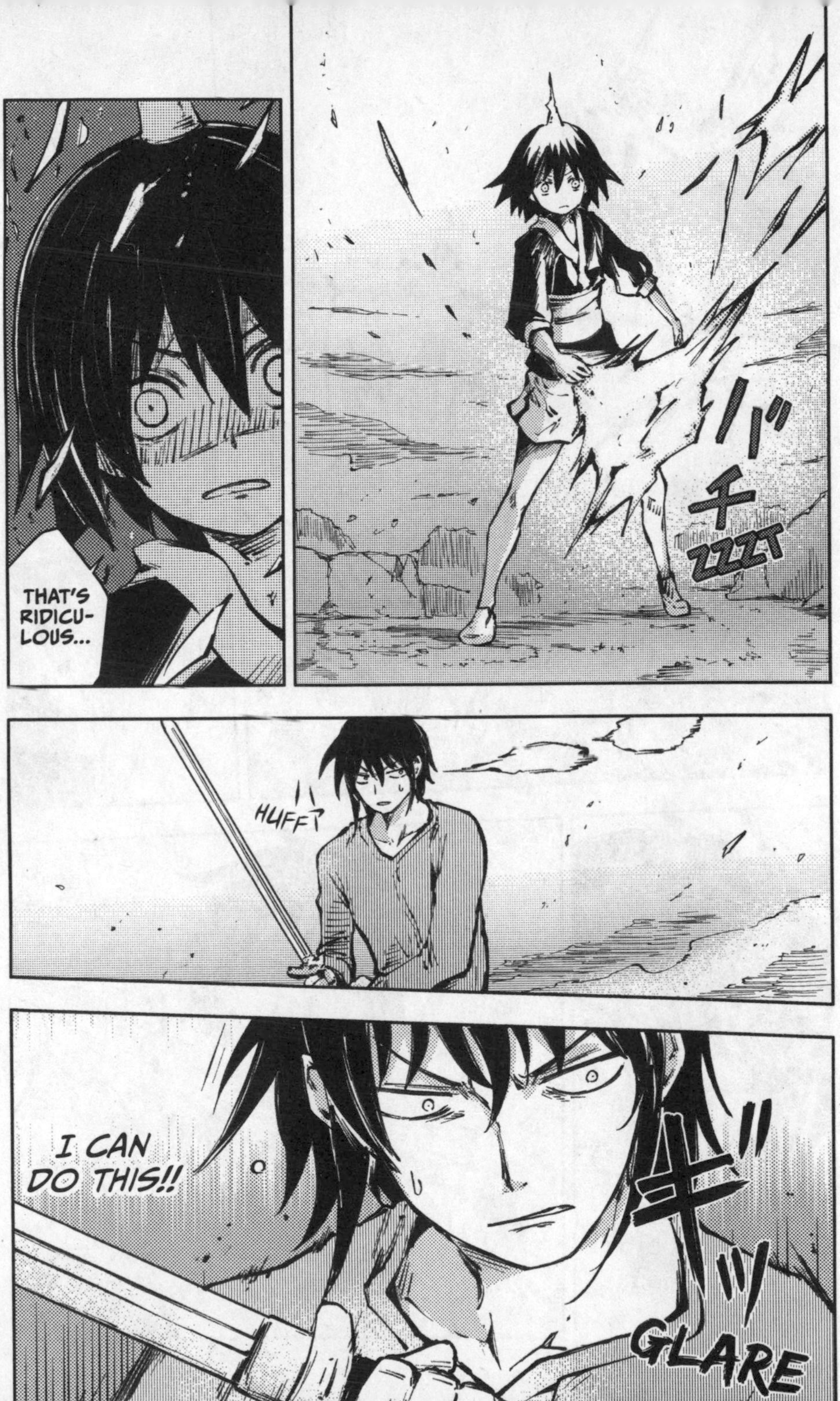
バチ
ZZZT
THAT'S RIDICULOUS...
HUFF
I CAN DO THIS!!
ギッ
GLARE

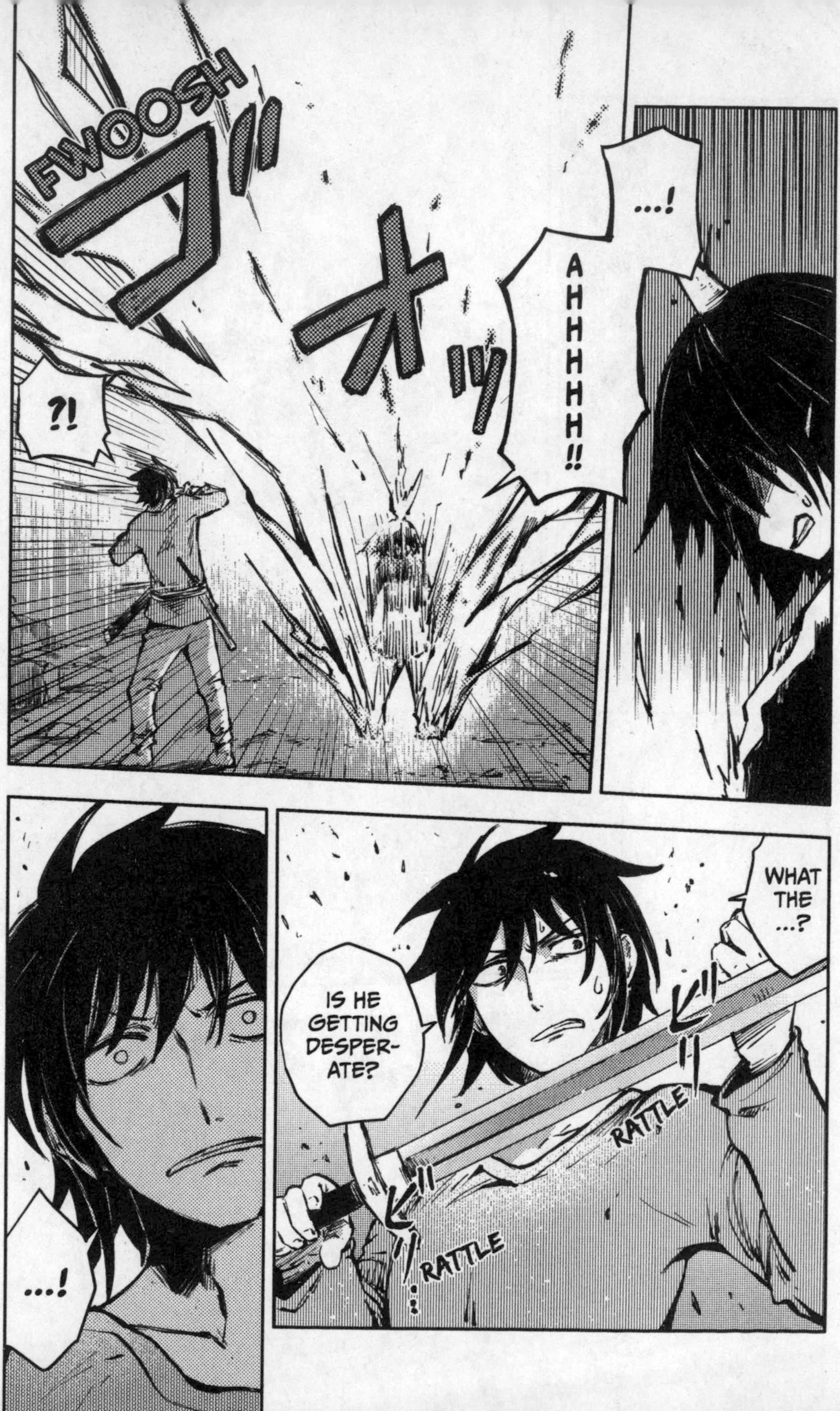
...!
AHHHHHH!!
FWOOSH
?!
WHAT THE ...?
IS HE GETTING DESPERATE?
RATTLE
RATTLE
...!

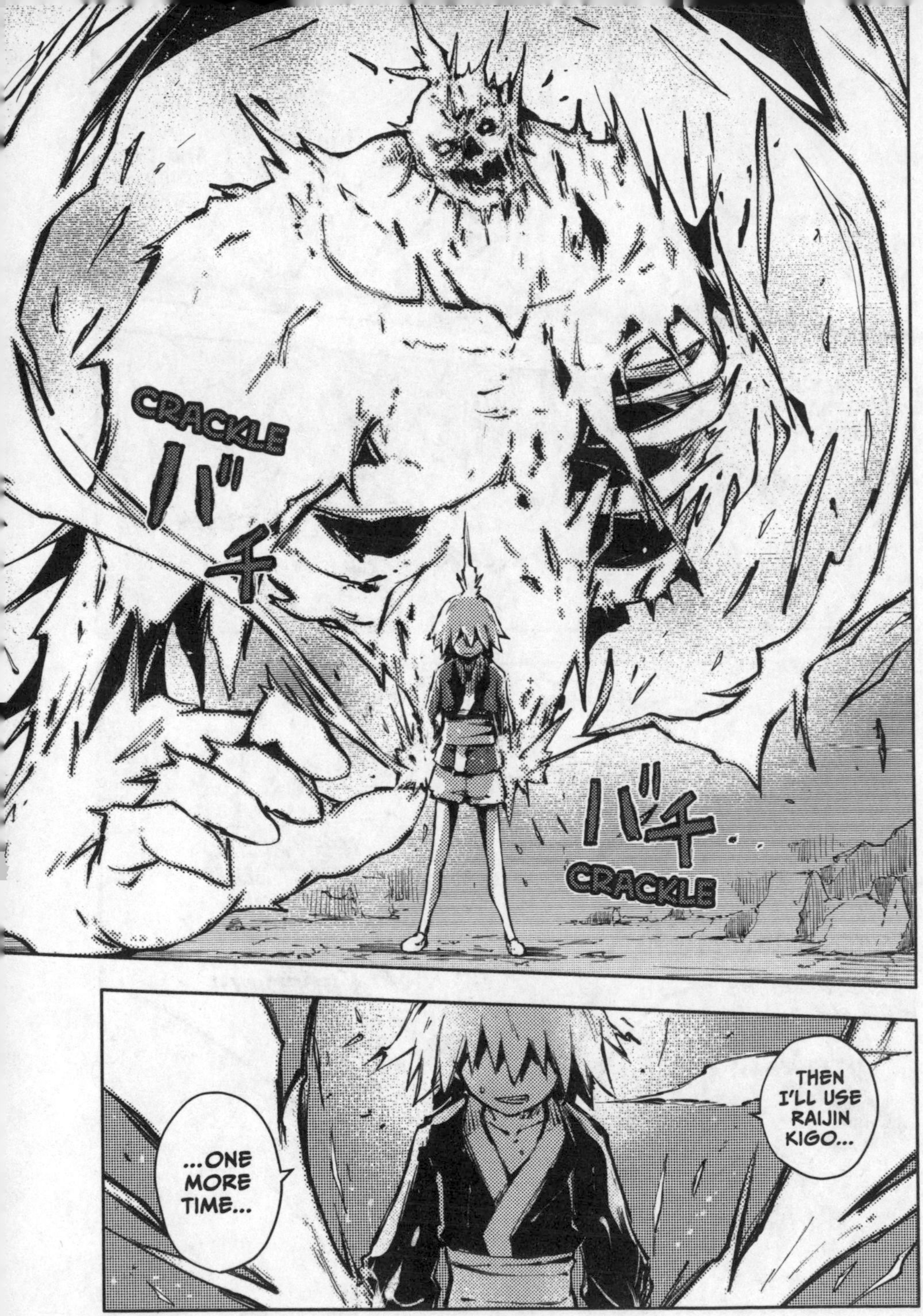
CRACKLE
バチ
バチ
CRACKLE
THEN I'LL USE RAIJIN KIGO...
...ONE MORE TIME...

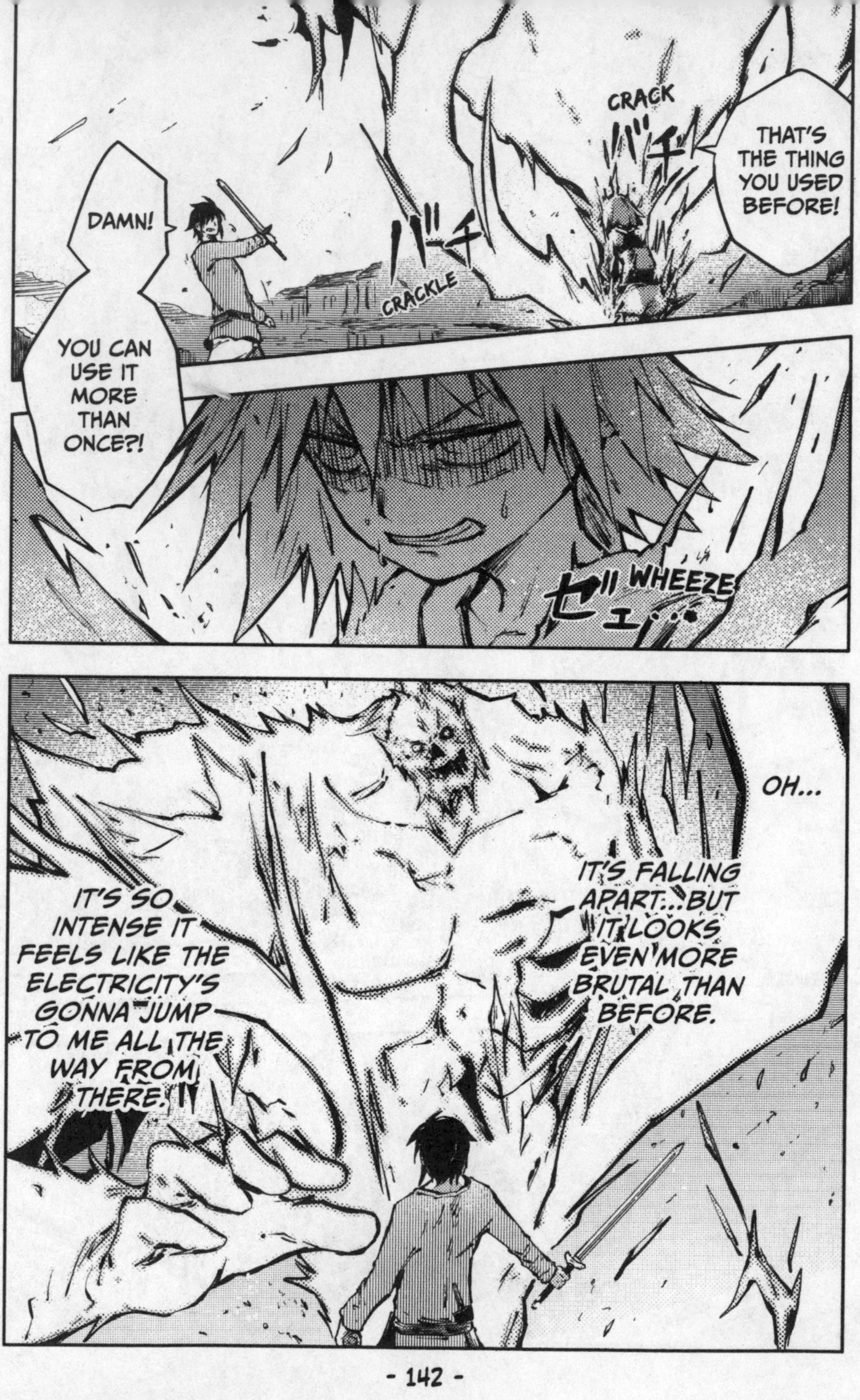
THAT'S THE THING YOU USED BEFORE!
CRACK
CRACKLE
DAMN!
YOU CAN USE IT MORE THAN ONCE?!
WHEEZE
OH...
IT'S FALLING APART... BUT IT LOOKS EVEN MORE BRUTAL THAN BEFORE.
IT'S SO INTENSE IT FEELS LIKE THE ELECTRICITY'S GONNA JUMP TO ME ALL THE WAY FROM THERE.

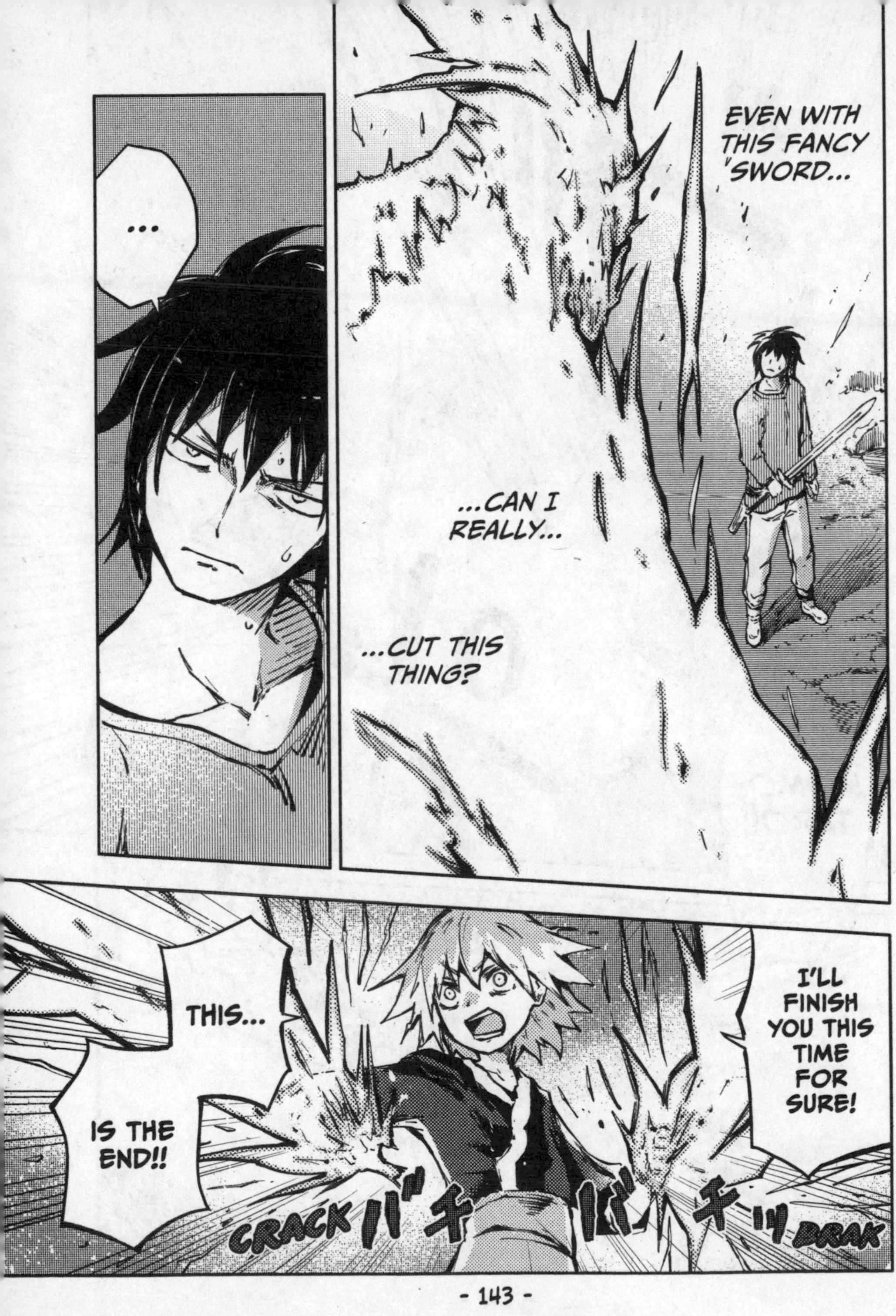
EVEN WITH THIS FANCY SWORD...
...CAN I REALLY...
...CUT THIS THING?
...
I'LL FINISH YOU THIS TIME FOR SURE!
THIS...
IS THE END!!
BRAK
バチッ
CRACK
バチ

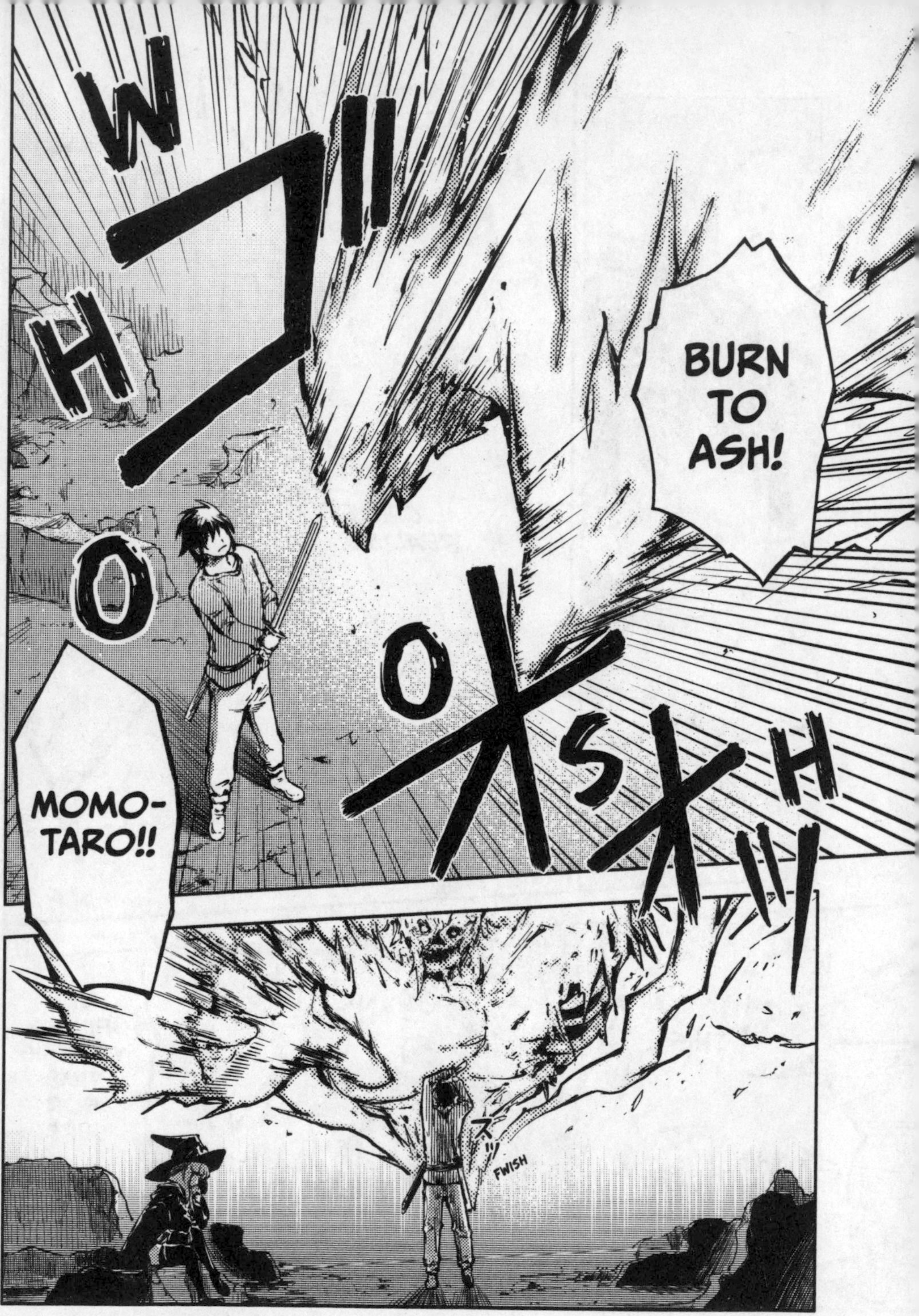
BURN TO ASH!
WHOOOSH
MOMO-TARO!!
FWISH

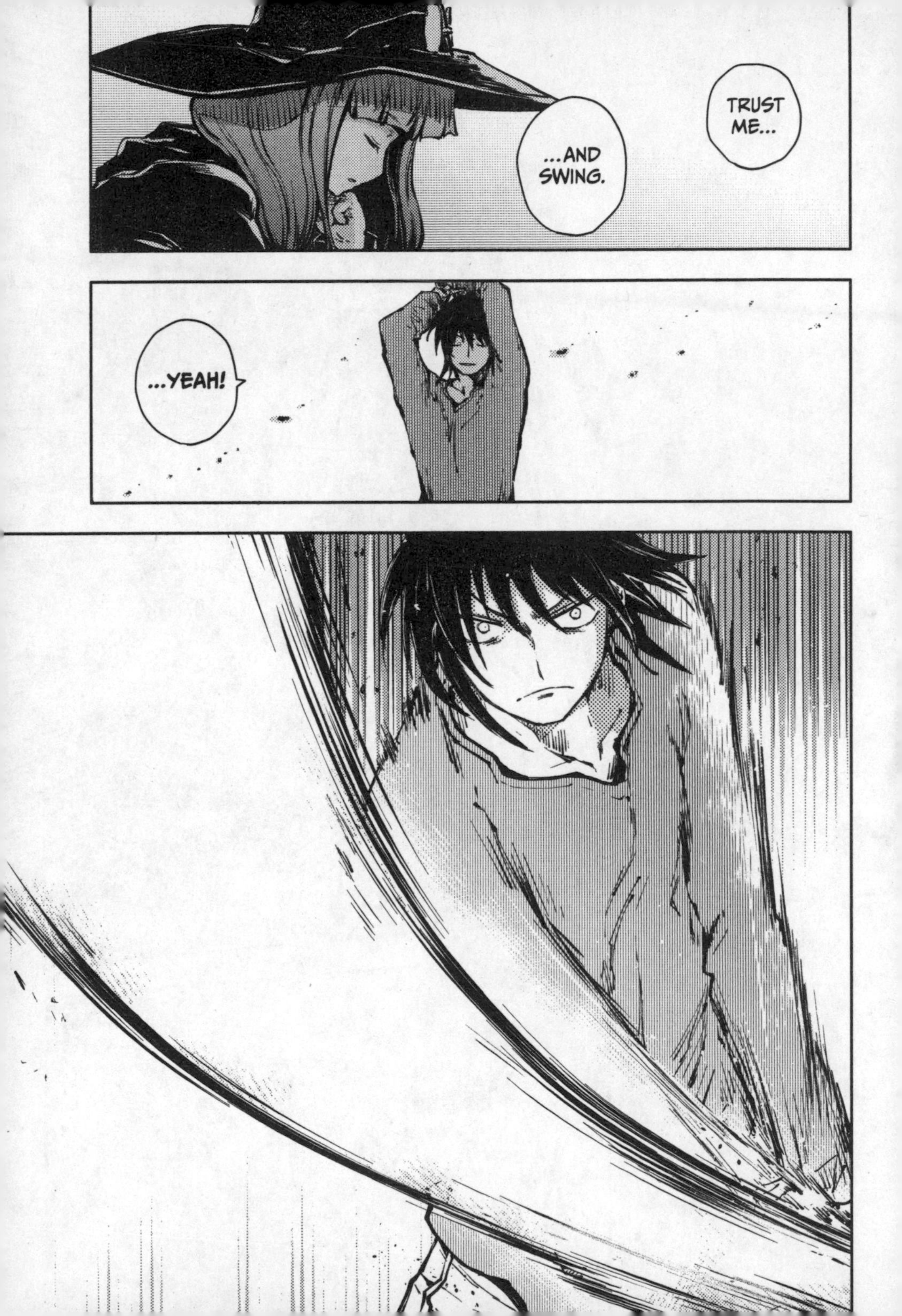
TRUST ME...
...AND SWING.
...YEAH!

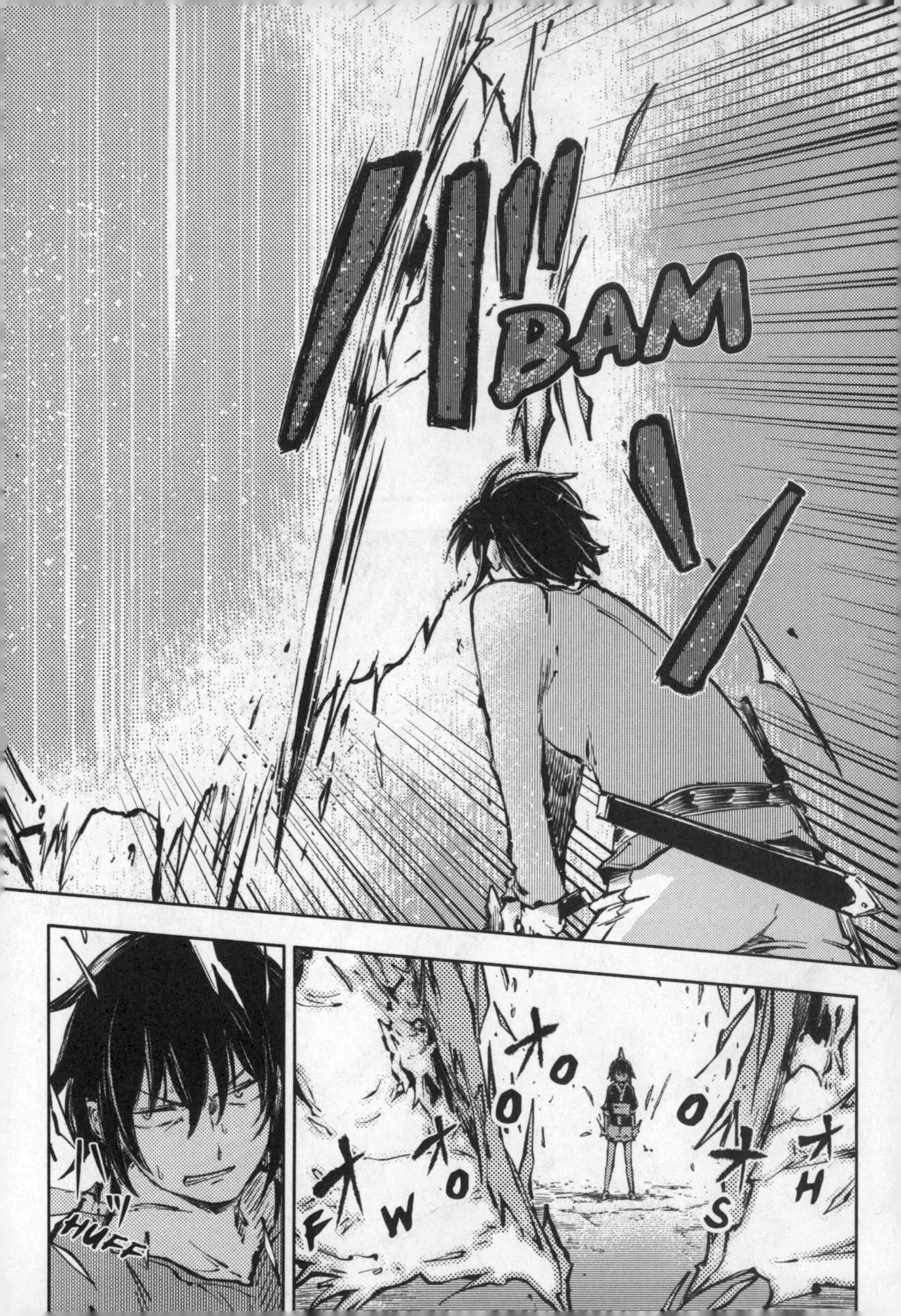
BAM
FWOOOOSH
HUFF

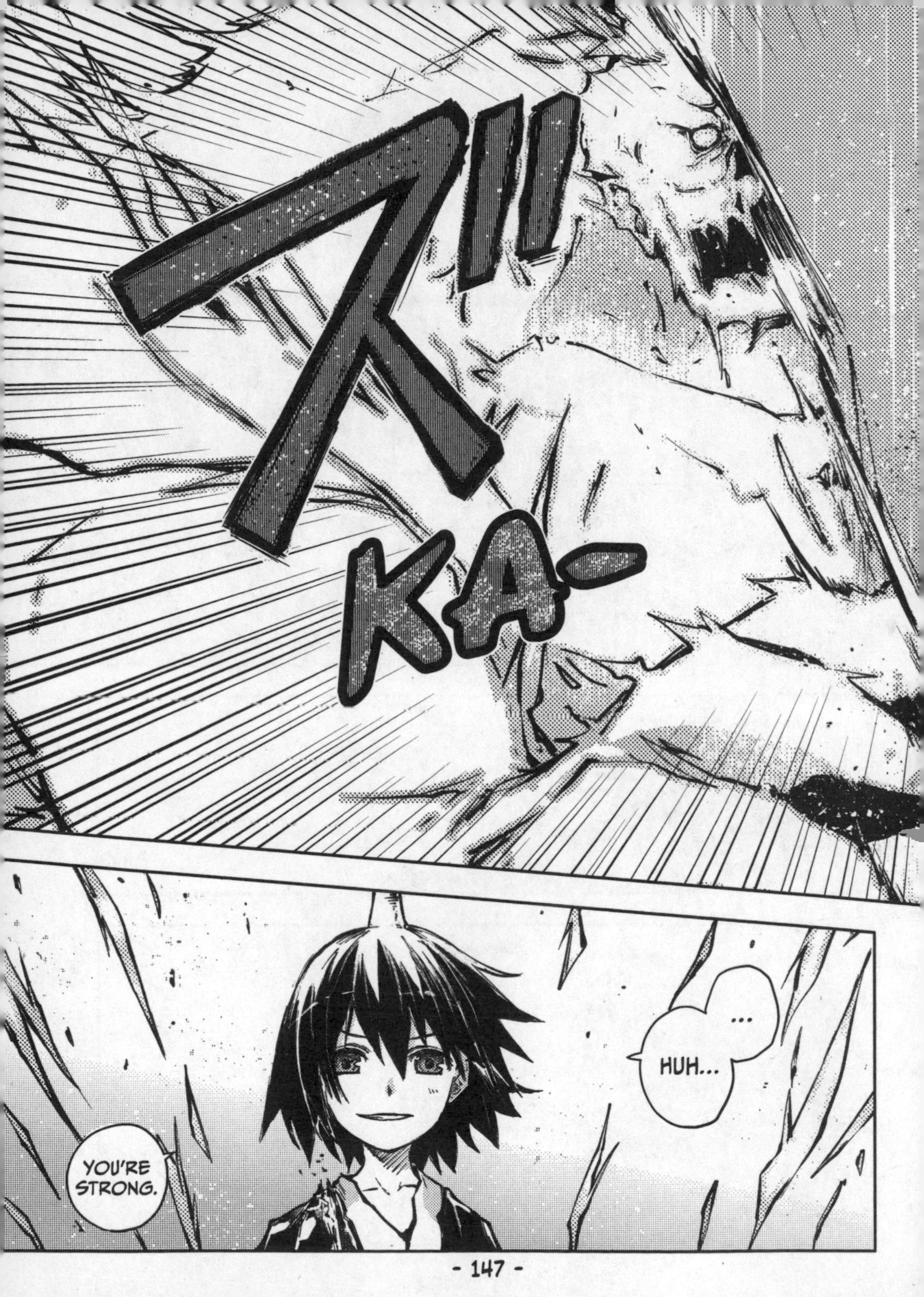
ズ
KA-
... HUH...
YOU'RE STRONG.

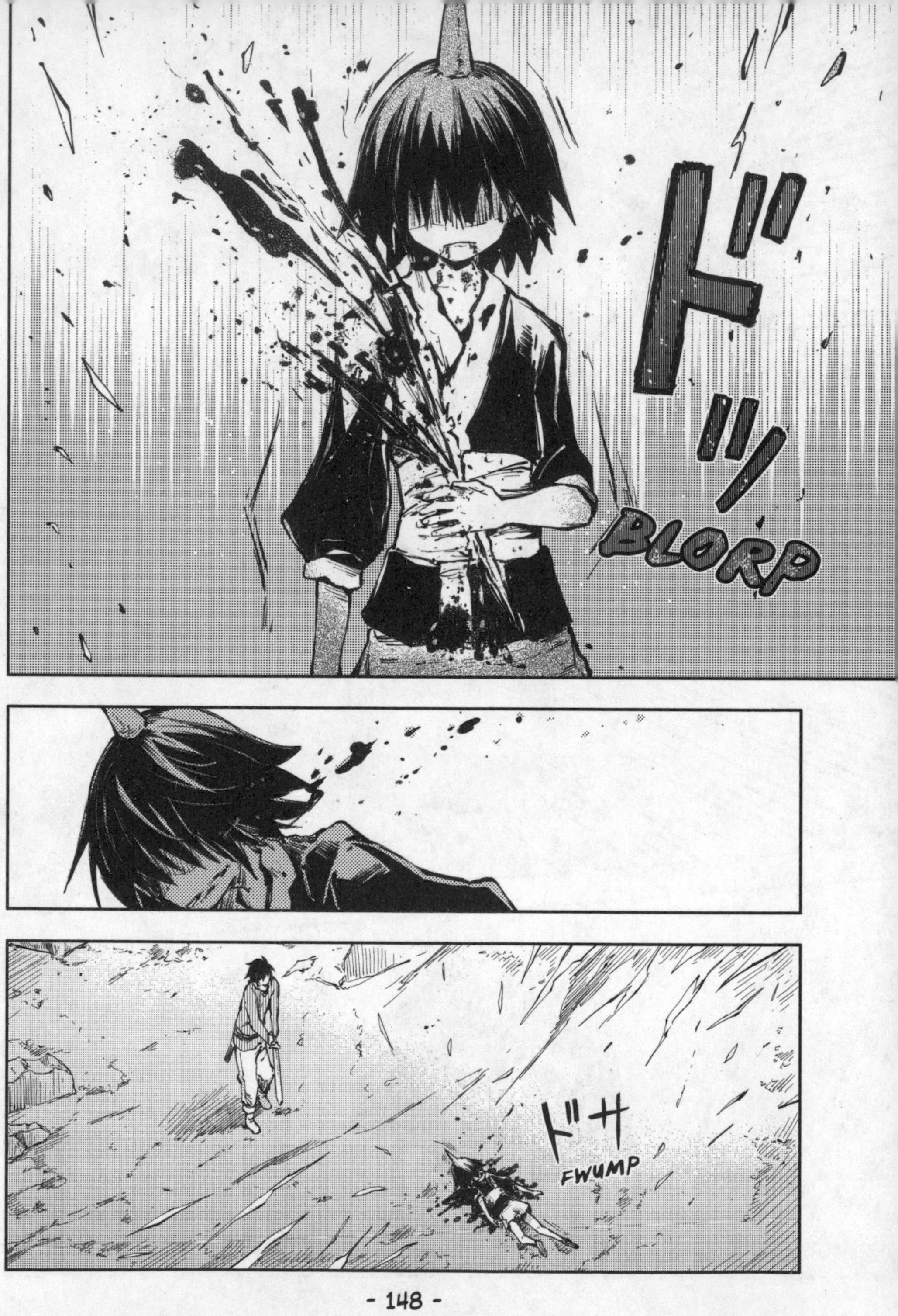
ドドッ
BLORP
ドサ
FWUMP

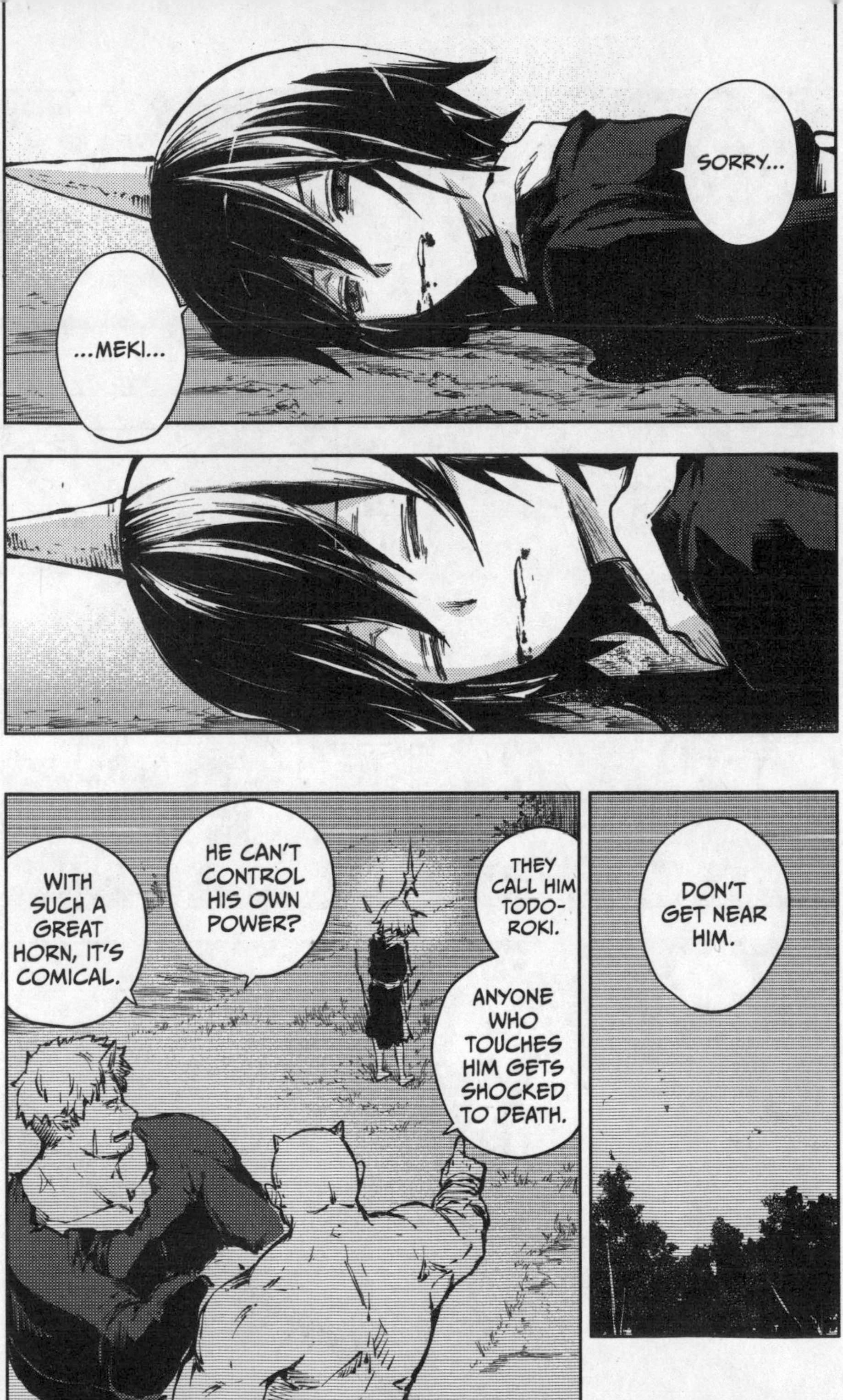
SORRY...
...MEKI...
DON'T GET NEAR HIM.
THEY CALL HIM TODO-ROKI.
ANYONE WHO TOUCHES HIM GETS SHOCKED TO DEATH.
HE CAN'T CONTROL HIS OWN POWER?
WITH SUCH A GREAT HORN, IT'S COMICAL.

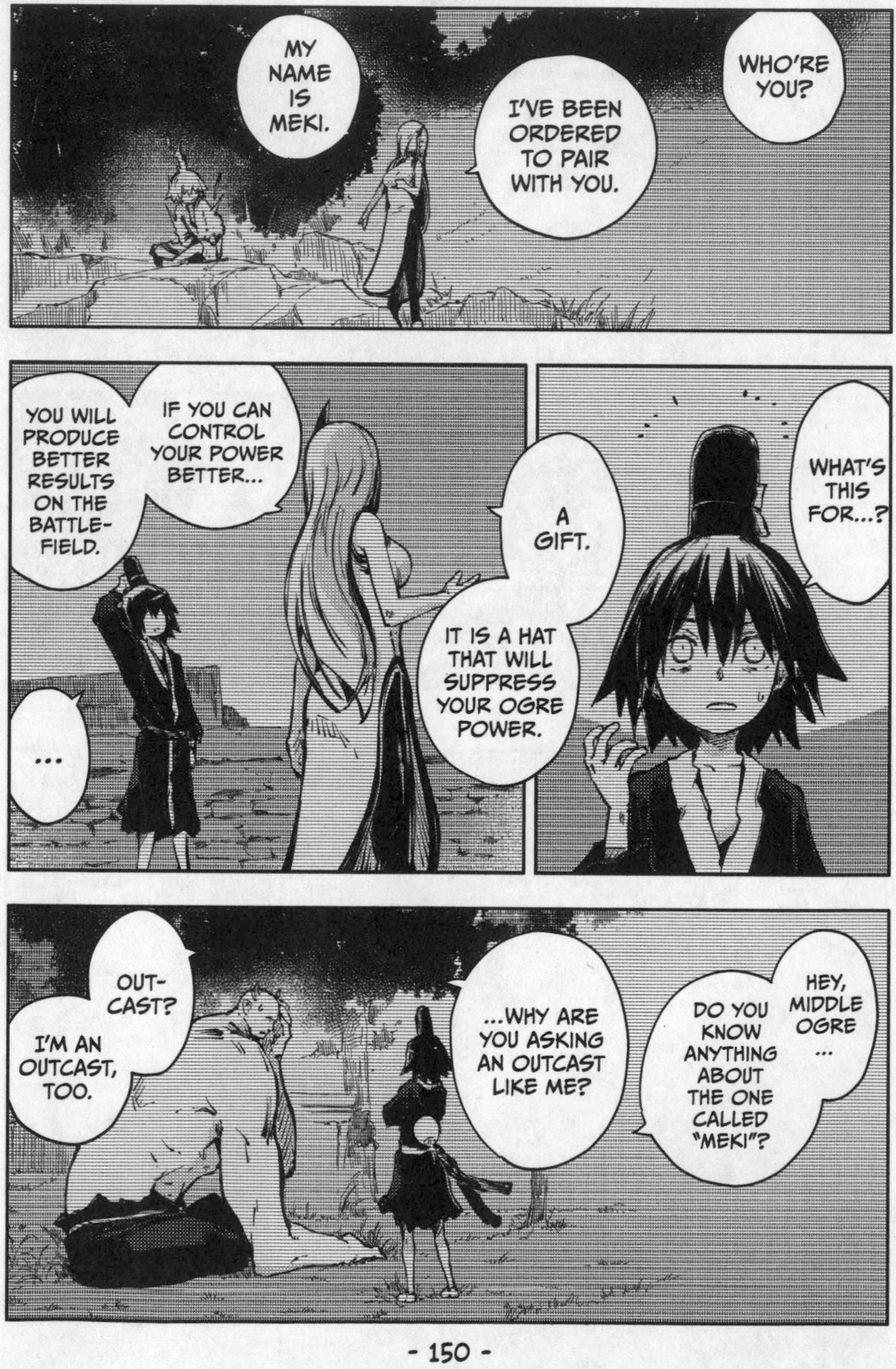
WHO'RE YOU?
MY NAME IS MEKI.
I'VE BEEN ORDERED TO PAIR WITH YOU.
WHAT'S THIS FOR...?
A GIFT.
IT IS A HAT THAT WILL SUPPRESS YOUR OGRE POWER.
IF YOU CAN CONTROL YOUR POWER BETTER...
YOU WILL PRODUCE BETTER RESULTS ON THE BATTLE-FIELD.
...
HEY, MIDDLE OGRE...
DO YOU KNOW ANYTHING ABOUT THE ONE CALLED "MEKI"?
...WHY ARE YOU ASKING AN OUTCAST LIKE ME?
OUT-CAST?
I'M AN OUTCAST, TOO.

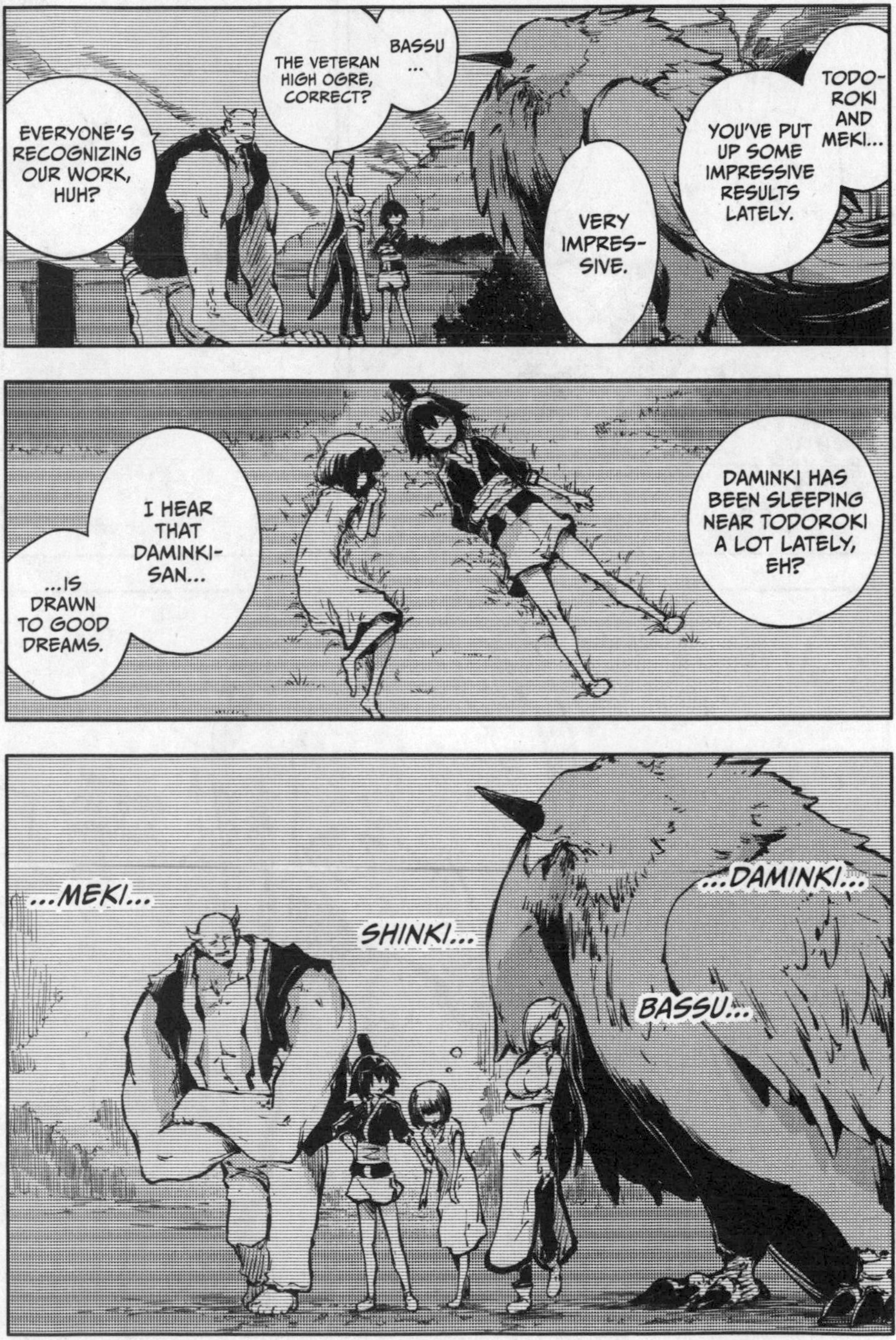
TODOROKI AND MEKI...
YOU'VE PUT UP SOME IMPRESSIVE RESULTS LATELY.
VERY IMPRESSIVE.
BASSU ...
THE VETERAN HIGH OGRE, CORRECT?
EVERYONE'S RECOGNIZING OUR WORK, HUH?
DAMINKI HAS BEEN SLEEPING NEAR TODOROKI A LOT LATELY, EH?
I HEAR THAT DAMINKI-SAN...
...IS DRAWN TO GOOD DREAMS.
...DAMINKI...
BASSU...
SHINKI...
...MEKI...

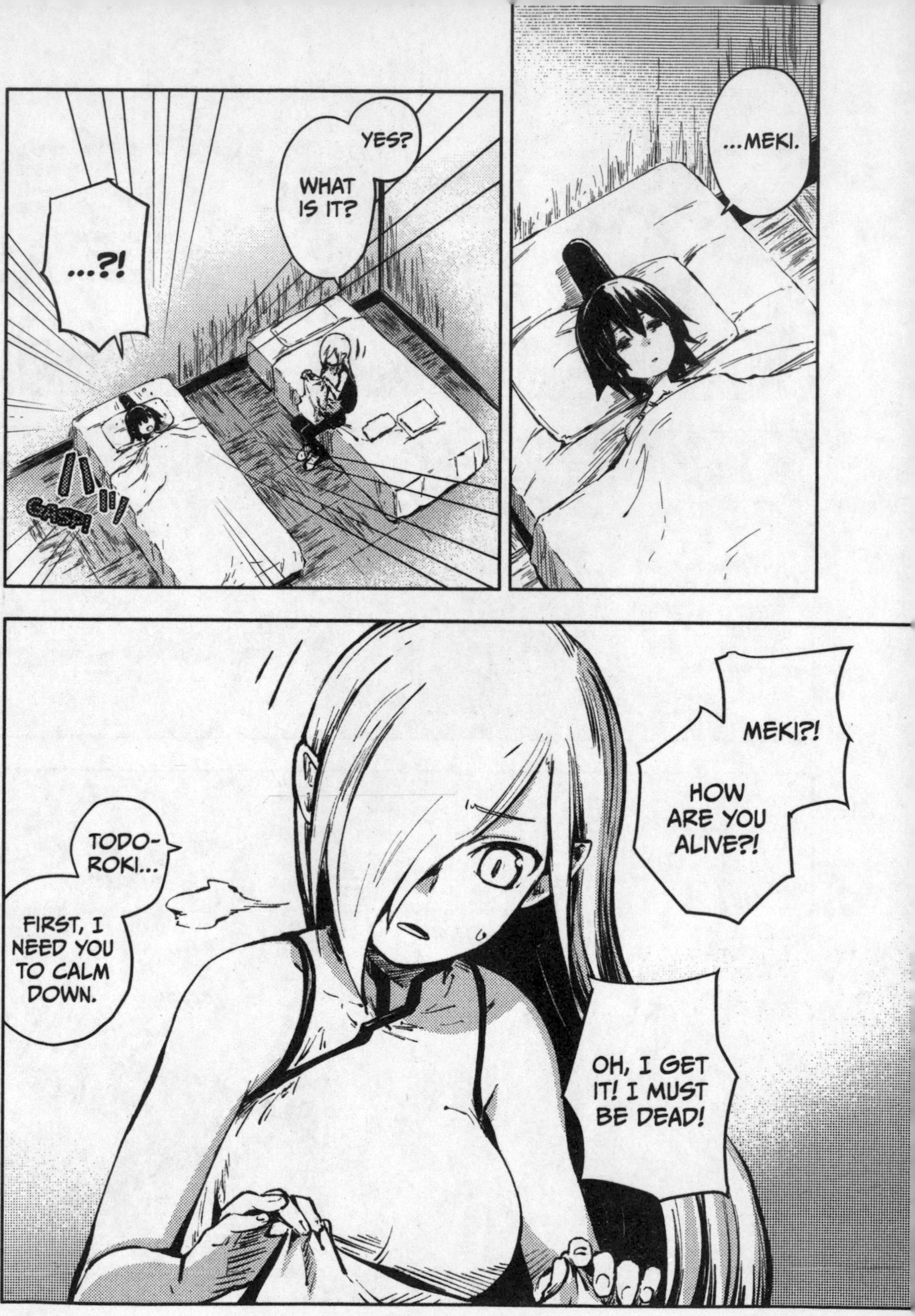
...MEKI.
YES?
WHAT IS IT?
...?!
GASP!
MEKI?!
HOW ARE YOU ALIVE?!
OH, I GET IT! I MUST BE DEAD!
TODO-ROKI...
FIRST, I NEED YOU TO CALM DOWN.

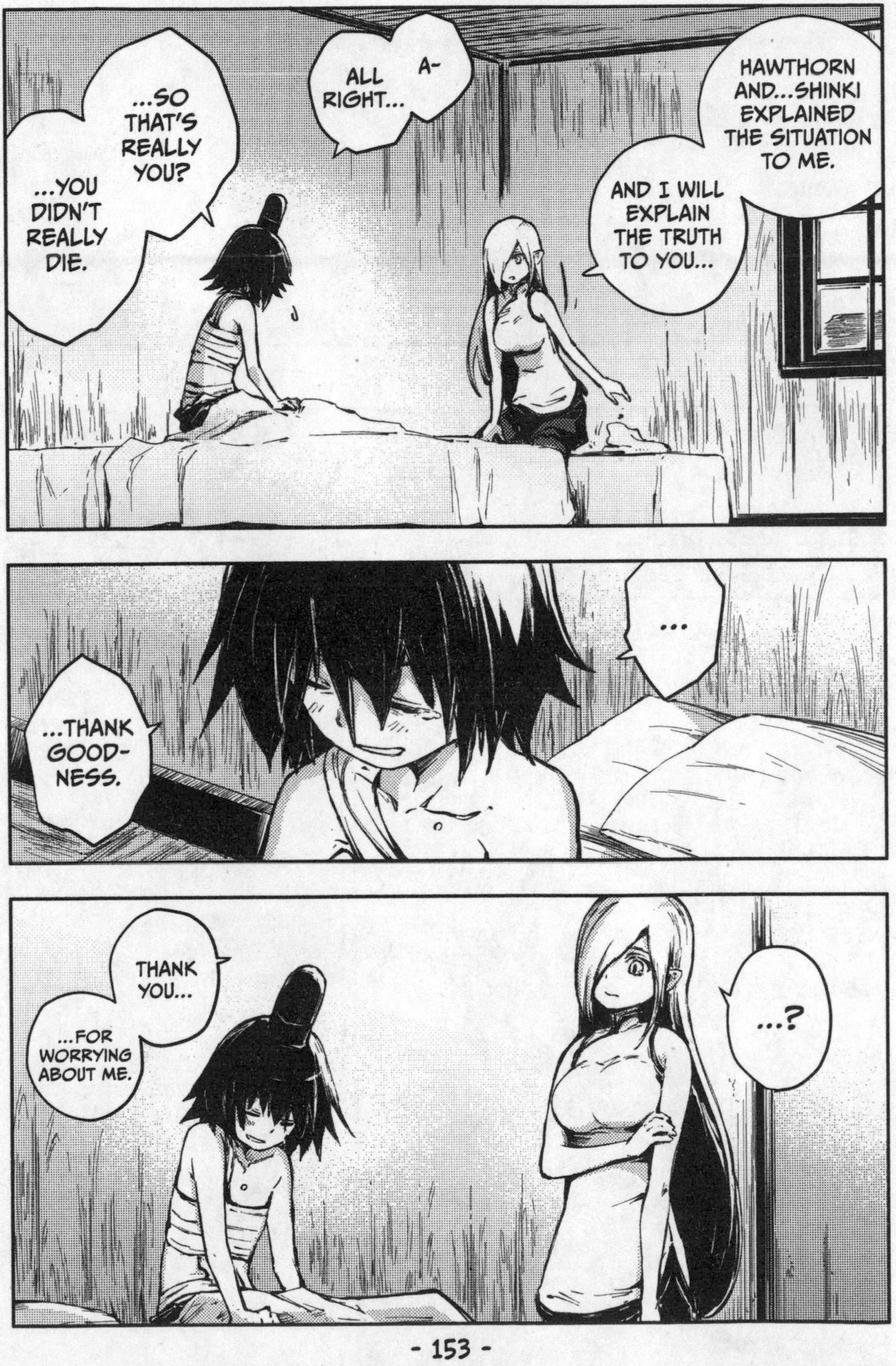
HAWTHORN AND...SHINKI EXPLAINED THE SITUATION TO ME.
AND I WILL EXPLAIN THE TRUTH TO YOU...
A- ALL RIGHT...
...SO THAT'S REALLY YOU?
...YOU DIDN'T REALLY DIE.
...
...THANK GOODNESS.
...?
THANK YOU...
...FOR WORRYING ABOUT ME.

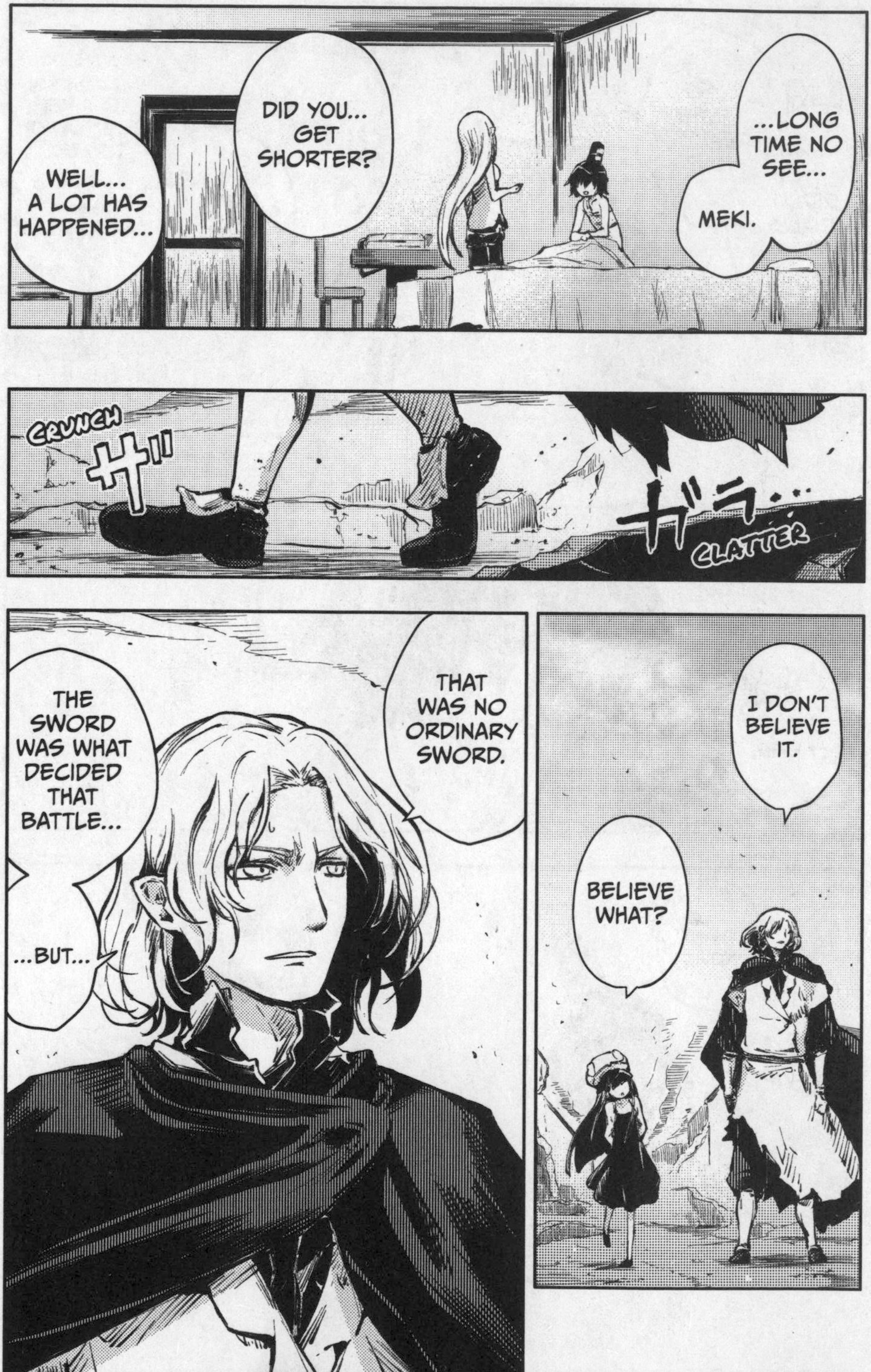
...LONG TIME NO SEE...
MEKI.
DID YOU... GET SHORTER?
WELL... A LOT HAS HAPPENED...
ガラ
CLATTER
ザリ
CRUNCH
I DON'T BELIEVE IT.
BELIEVE WHAT?
THAT WAS NO ORDINARY SWORD.
THE SWORD WAS WHAT DECIDED THAT BATTLE...
...BUT...

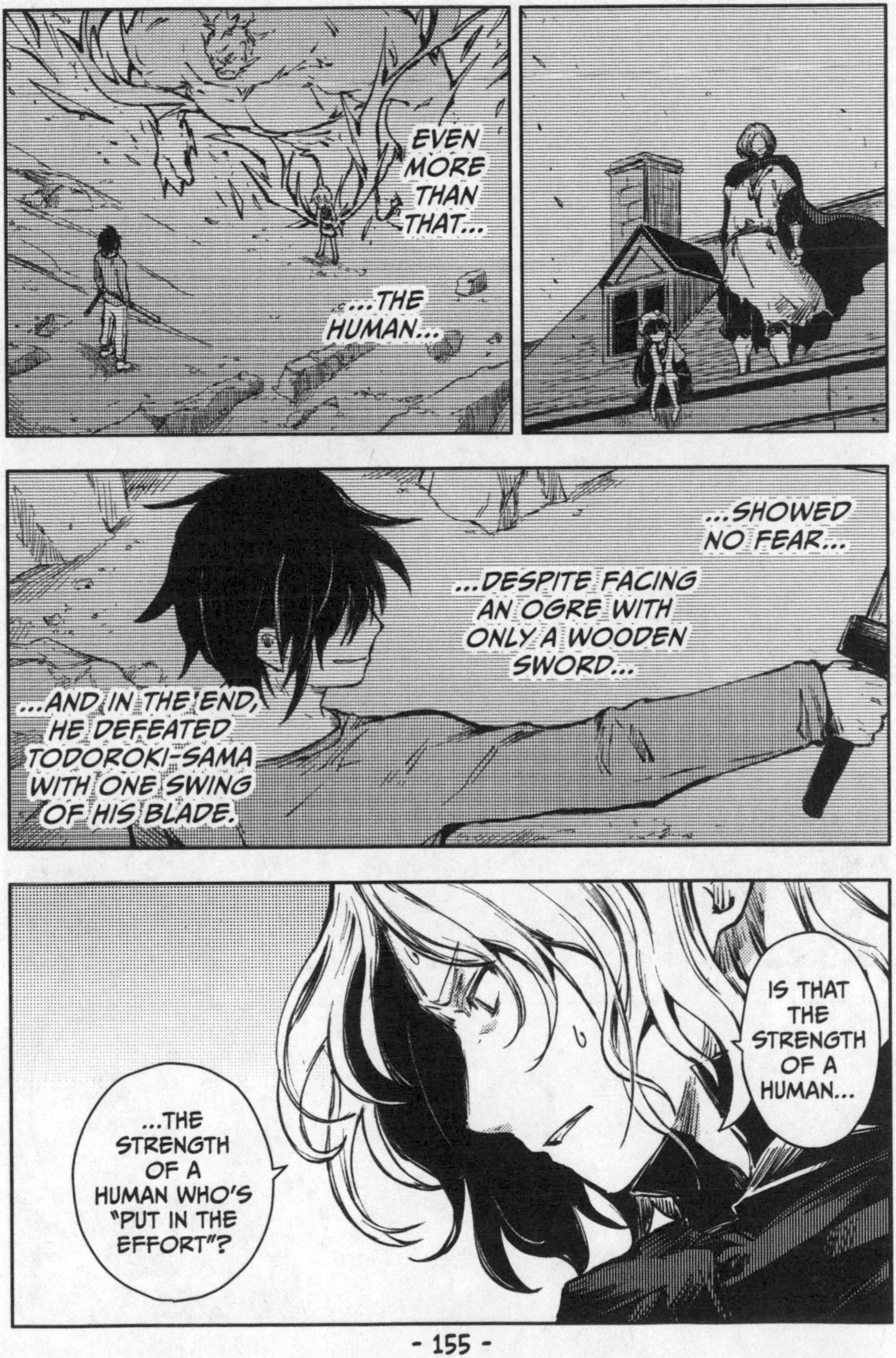
EVEN MORE THAN THAT...
...THE HUMAN...
...SHOWED NO FEAR...
...DESPITE FACING AN OGRE WITH ONLY A WOODEN SWORD...
...AND IN THE END, HE DEFEATED TODOROKI-SAMA WITH ONE SWING OF HIS BLADE.
IS THAT THE STRENGTH OF A HUMAN...
...THE STRENGTH OF A HUMAN WHO'S "PUT IN THE EFFORT"?

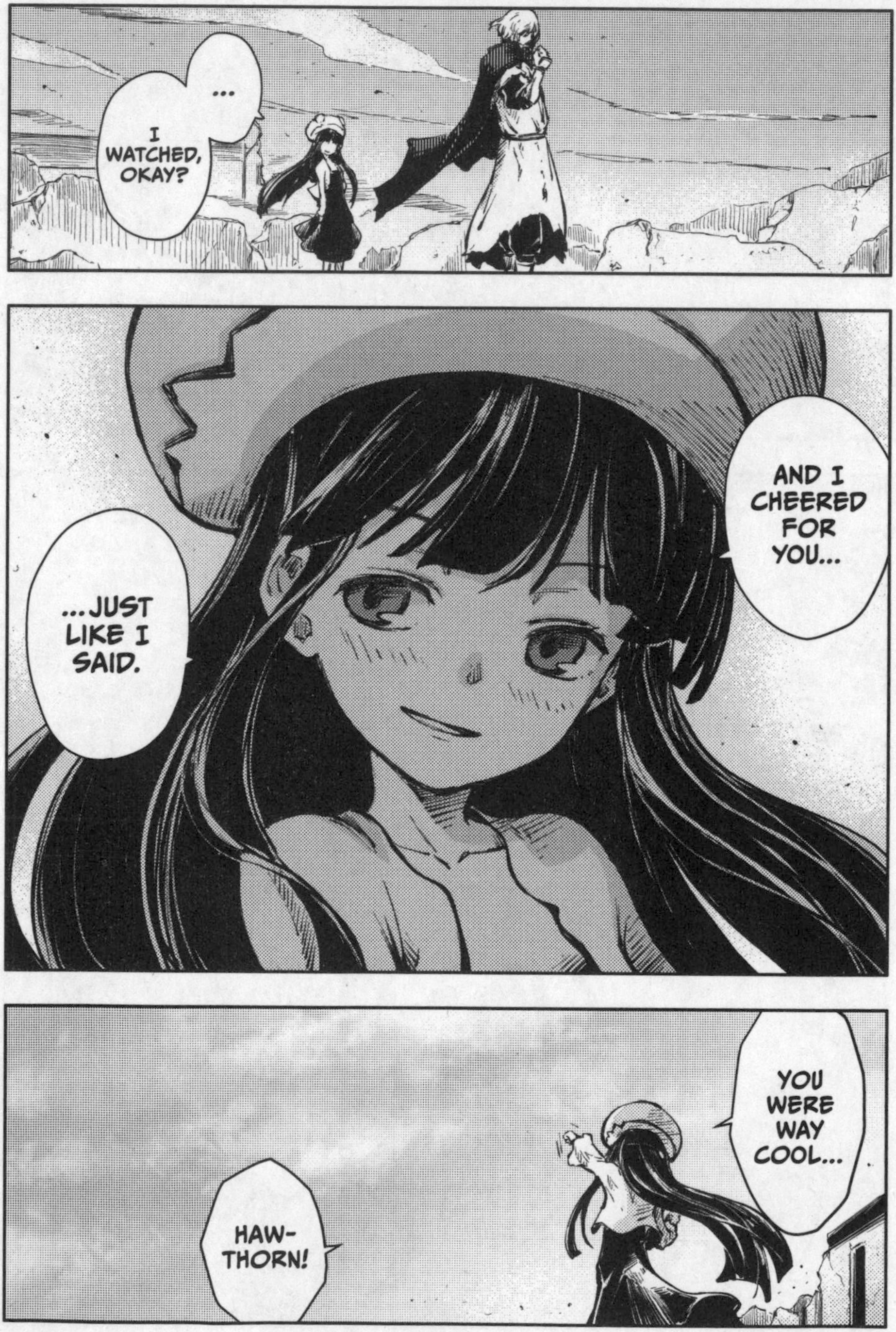
...
I WATCHED, OKAY?
AND I CHEERED FOR YOU...
...JUST LIKE I SAID.
YOU WERE WAY COOL...
HAW-THORN!

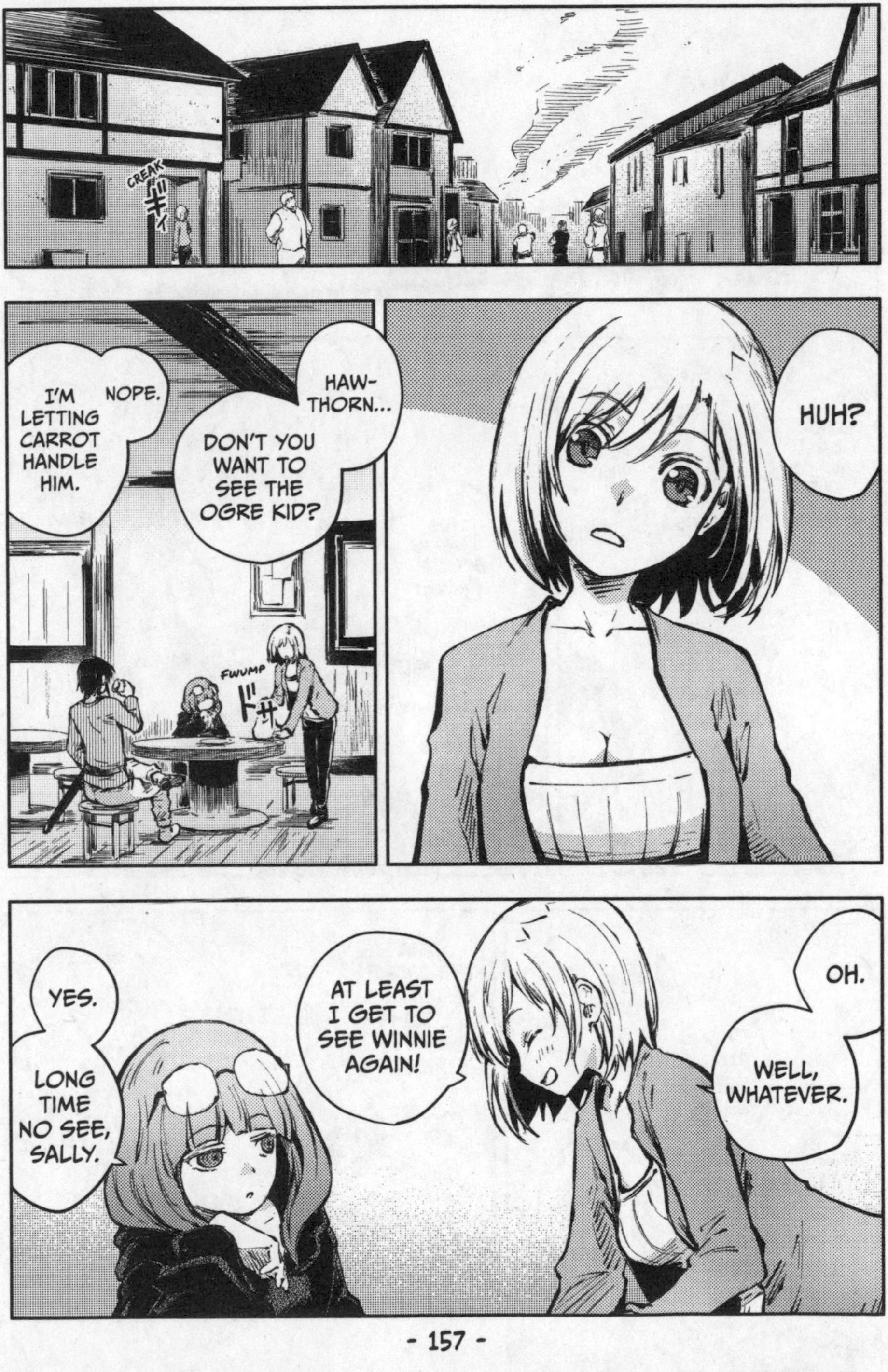
CREAK
ギィ
HUH?
HAW-THORN...
DON'T YOU WANT TO SEE THE OGRE KID?
NOPE.
I'M LETTING CARROT HANDLE HIM.
FWUMP
ドサ
OH.
WELL, WHATEVER.
AT LEAST I GET TO SEE WINNIE AGAIN!
YES.
LONG TIME NO SEE, SALLY.

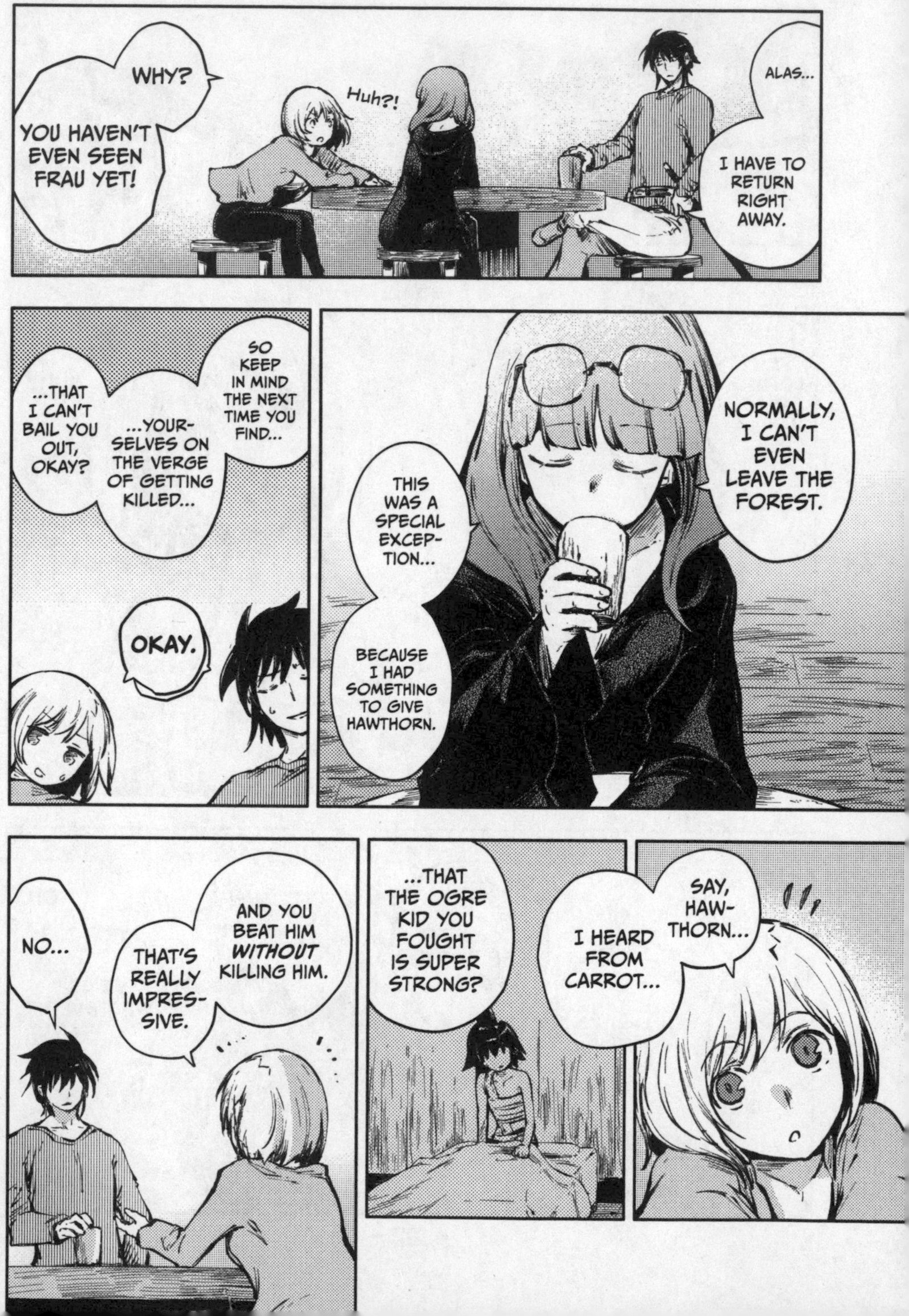
ALAS...
I HAVE TO RETURN RIGHT AWAY.
Huh?!
WHY?
YOU HAVEN'T EVEN SEEN FRAU YET!
NORMALLY, I CAN'T EVEN LEAVE THE FOREST.
THIS WAS A SPECIAL EXCEPTION...
BECAUSE I HAD SOMETHING TO GIVE HAWTHORN.
SO KEEP IN MIND THE NEXT TIME YOU FIND...
...YOURSELVES ON THE VERGE OF GETTING KILLED...
...THAT I CAN'T BAIL YOU OUT, OKAY?
OKAY.
SAY, HAWTHORN...
I HEARD FROM CARROT...
...THAT THE OGRE KID YOU FOUGHT IS SUPER STRONG?
AND YOU BEAT HIM *WITHOUT* KILLING HIM.
THAT'S REALLY IMPRESSIVE.
NO...

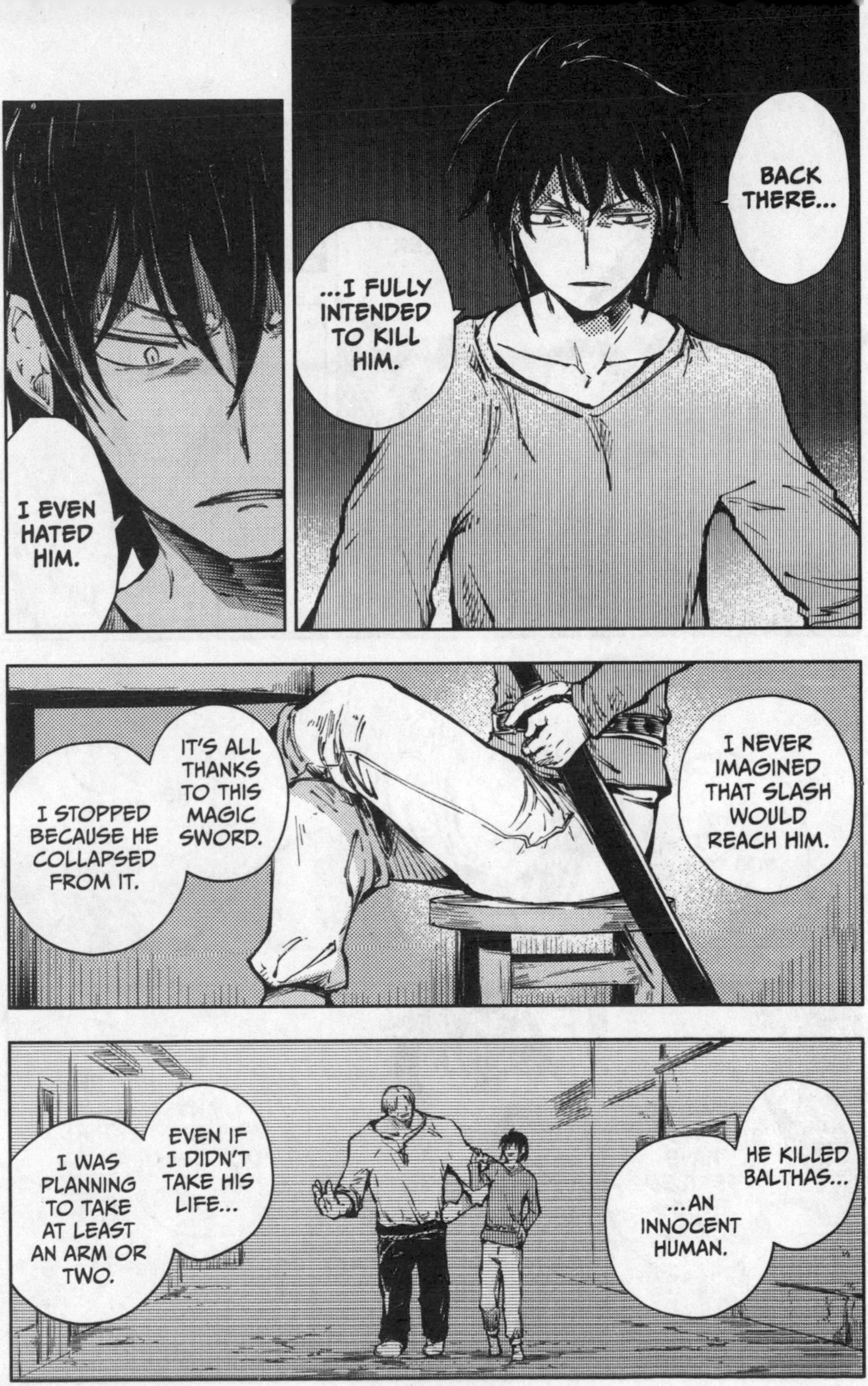
BACK THERE...
...I FULLY INTENDED TO KILL HIM.
I EVEN HATED HIM.
I NEVER IMAGINED THAT SLASH WOULD REACH HIM.
IT'S ALL THANKS TO THIS MAGIC SWORD.
I STOPPED BECAUSE HE COLLAPSED FROM IT.
HE KILLED BALTHAS...
...AN INNOCENT HUMAN.
EVEN IF I DIDN'T TAKE HIS LIFE...
I WAS PLANNING TO TAKE AT LEAST AN ARM OR TWO.

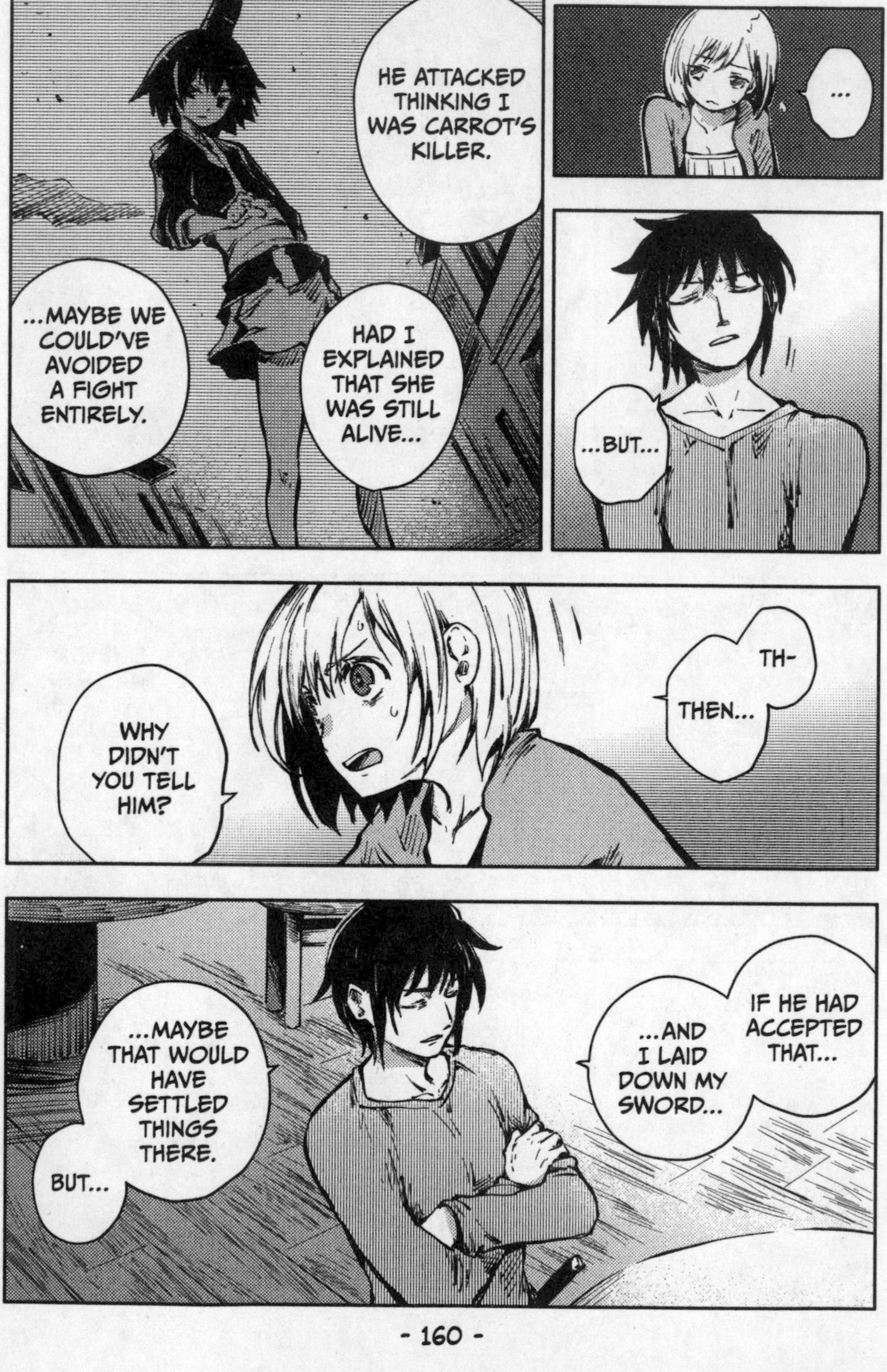
...
...BUT...
HE ATTACKED THINKING I WAS CARROT'S KILLER.
HAD I EXPLAINED THAT SHE WAS STILL ALIVE...
...MAYBE WE COULD'VE AVOIDED A FIGHT ENTIRELY.
TH- THEN...
WHY DIDN'T YOU TELL HIM?
IF HE HAD ACCEPTED THAT...
...AND I LAID DOWN MY SWORD...
...MAYBE THAT WOULD HAVE SETTLED THINGS THERE.
BUT...

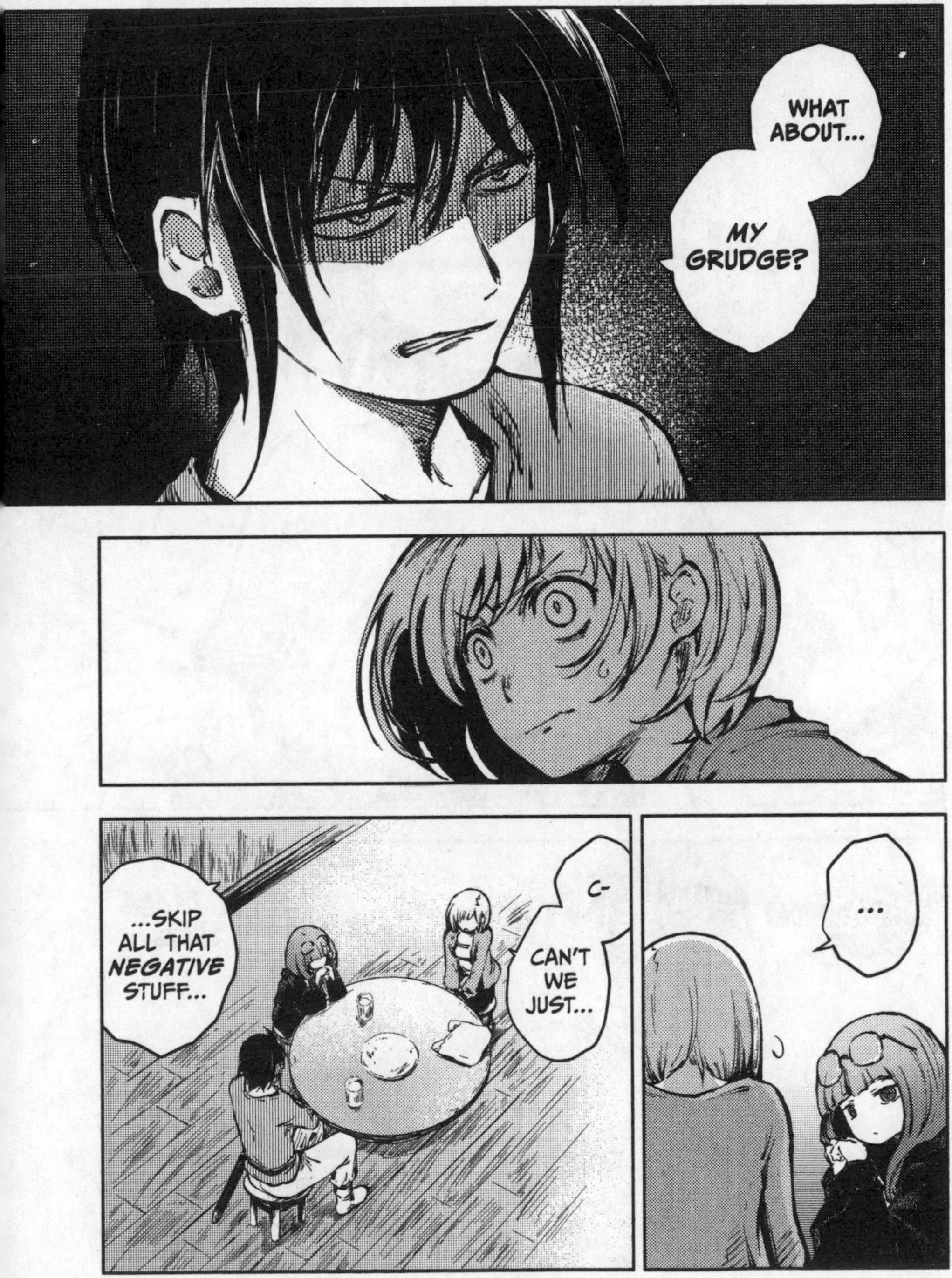
WHAT ABOUT...
MY GRUDGE?
...
C- CAN'T WE JUST...
...SKIP ALL THAT NEGATIVE STUFF...

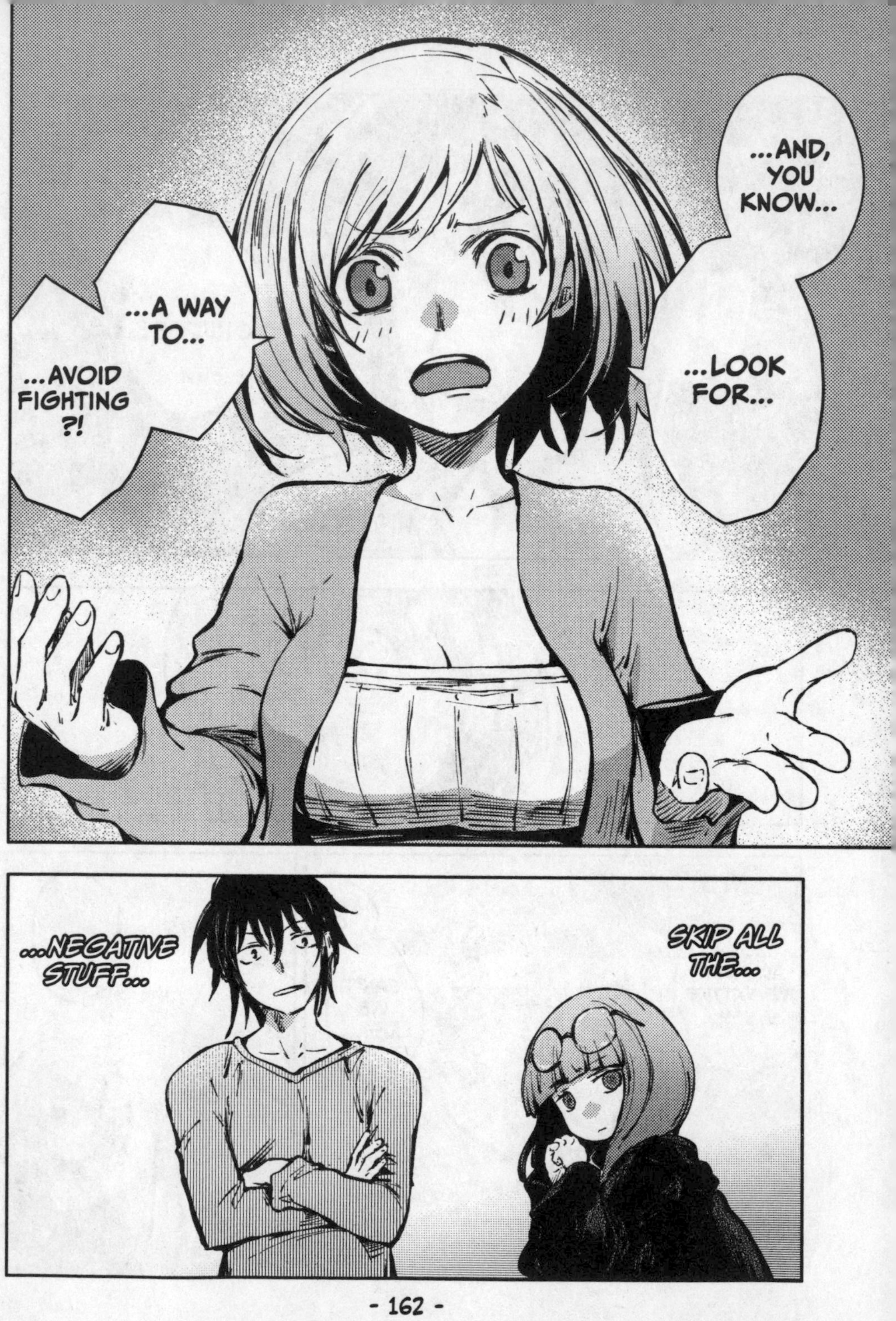
...AND, YOU KNOW...
...LOOK FOR...
...A WAY TO...
...AVOID FIGHTING?!
SKIP ALL THE...
...NEGATIVE STUFF...

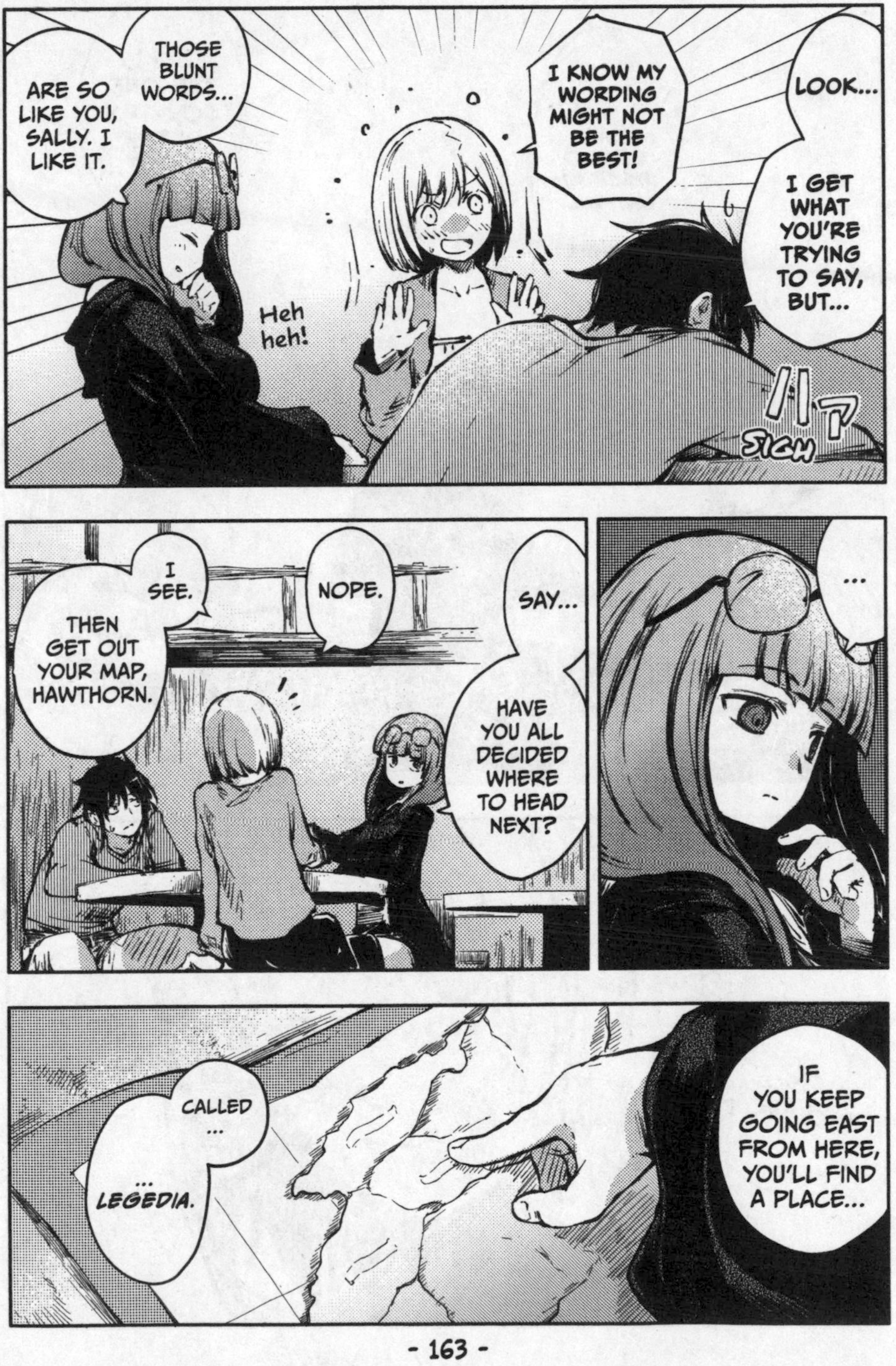
LOOK...
I GET WHAT YOU'RE TRYING TO SAY, BUT...
ハア
SIGH
I KNOW MY WORDING MIGHT NOT BE THE BEST!
THOSE BLUNT WORDS...
ARE SO LIKE YOU, SALLY. I LIKE IT.
Heh heh!
...
SAY...
HAVE YOU ALL DECIDED WHERE TO HEAD NEXT?
NOPE.
I SEE.
THEN GET OUT YOUR MAP, HAWTHORN.
IF YOU KEEP GOING EAST FROM HERE, YOU'LL FIND A PLACE...
CALLED...
...LEGEDIA.

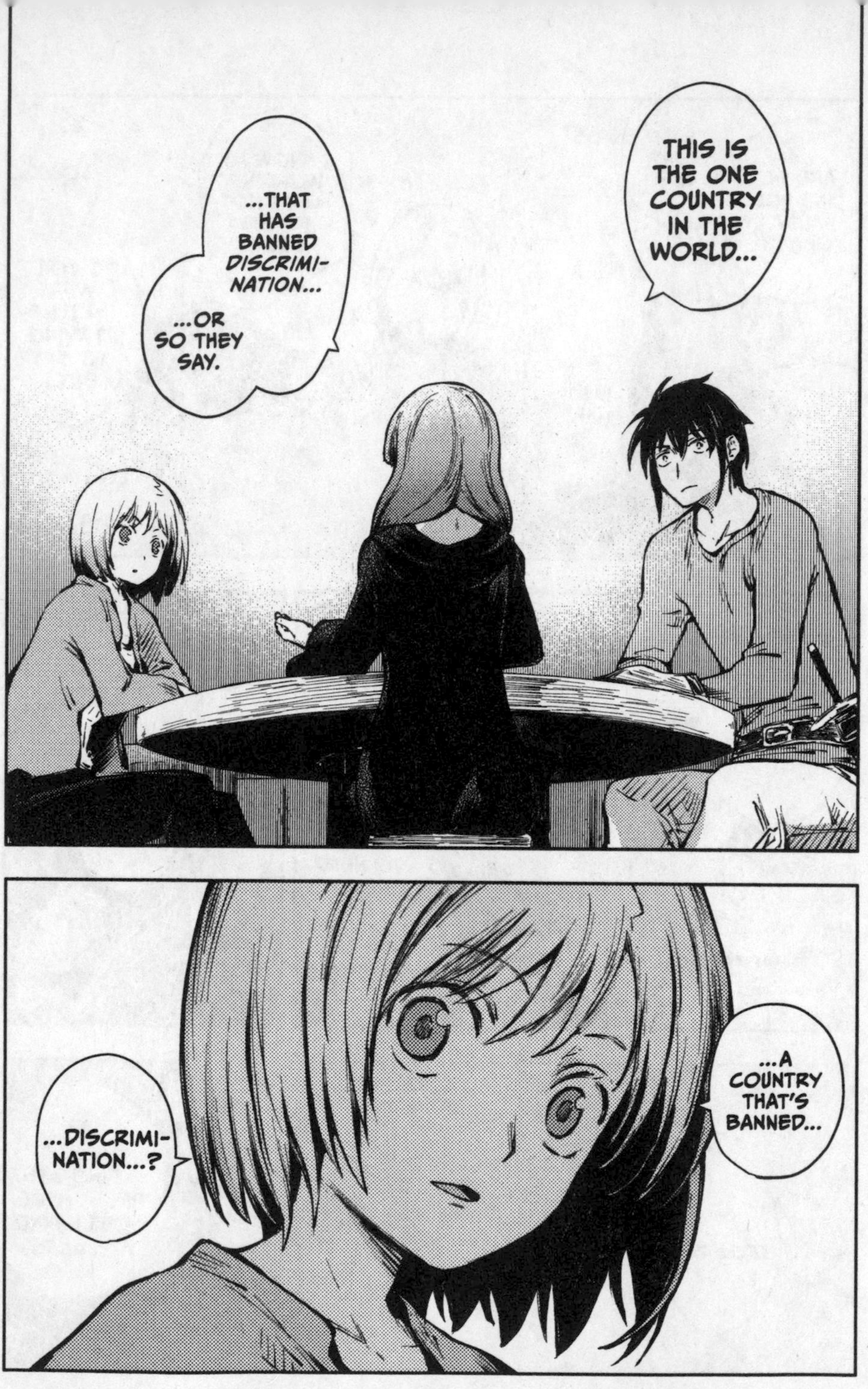
THIS IS THE ONE COUNTRY IN THE WORLD...
...THAT HAS BANNED DISCRIMINATION...
...OR SO THEY SAY.
...A COUNTRY THAT'S BANNED...
...DISCRIMINATION...?

CONTINUED IN VOLUME 7

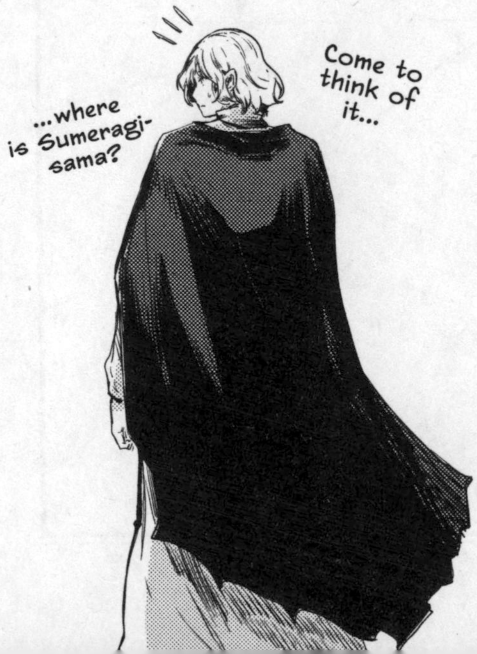
Come to think of it...
...where is Sumeragi-sama?

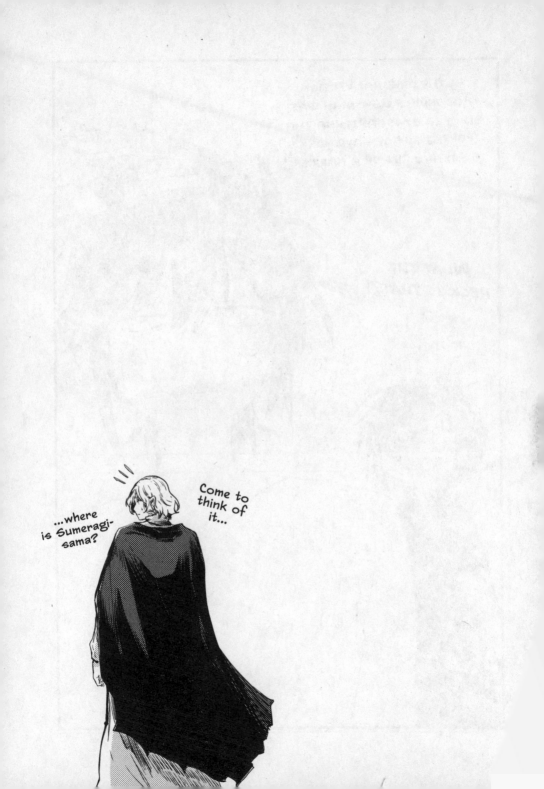

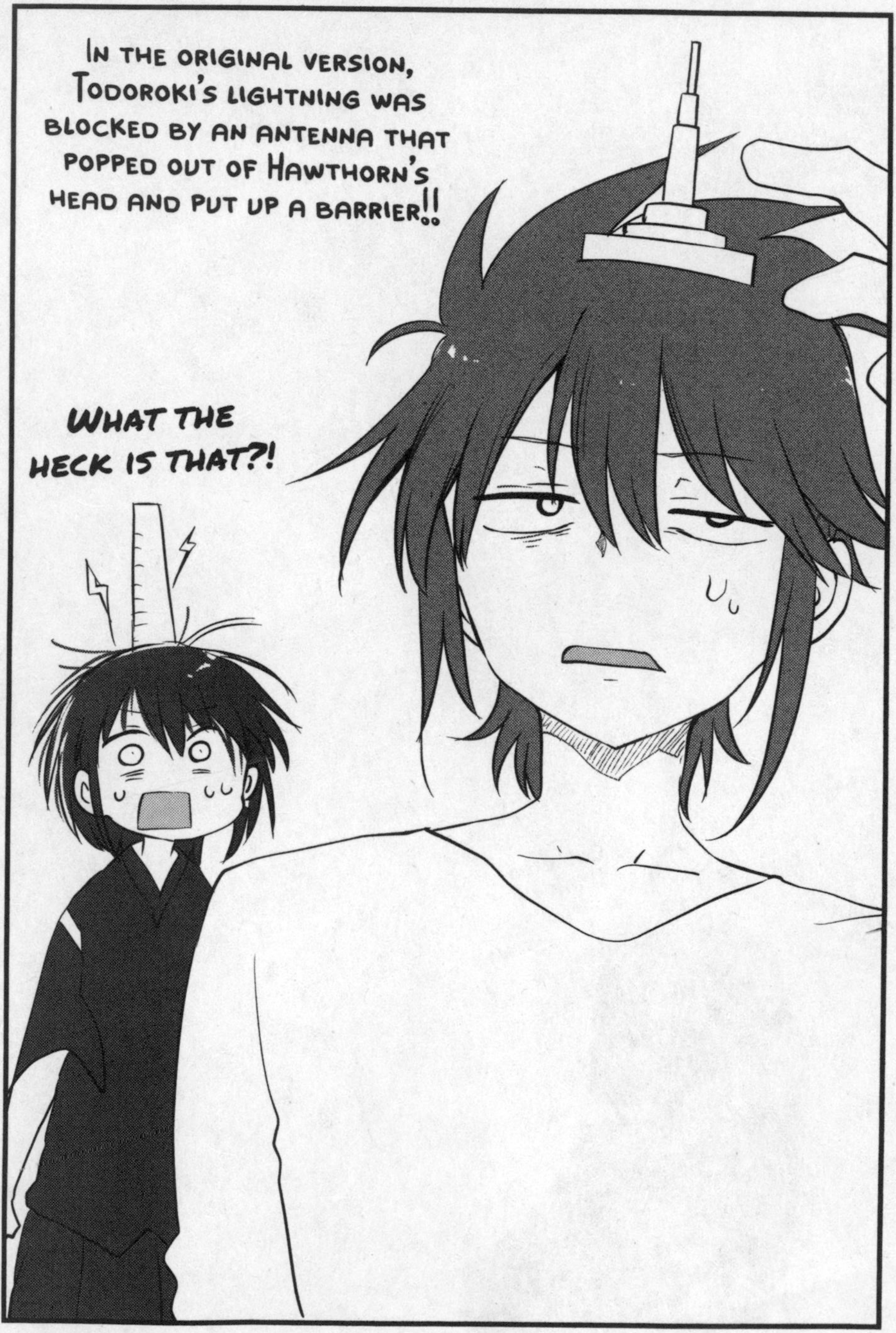
In the original version, Todoroki's lightning was blocked by an antenna that popped out of Hawthorn's head and put up a barrier!!
What the heck is that?!

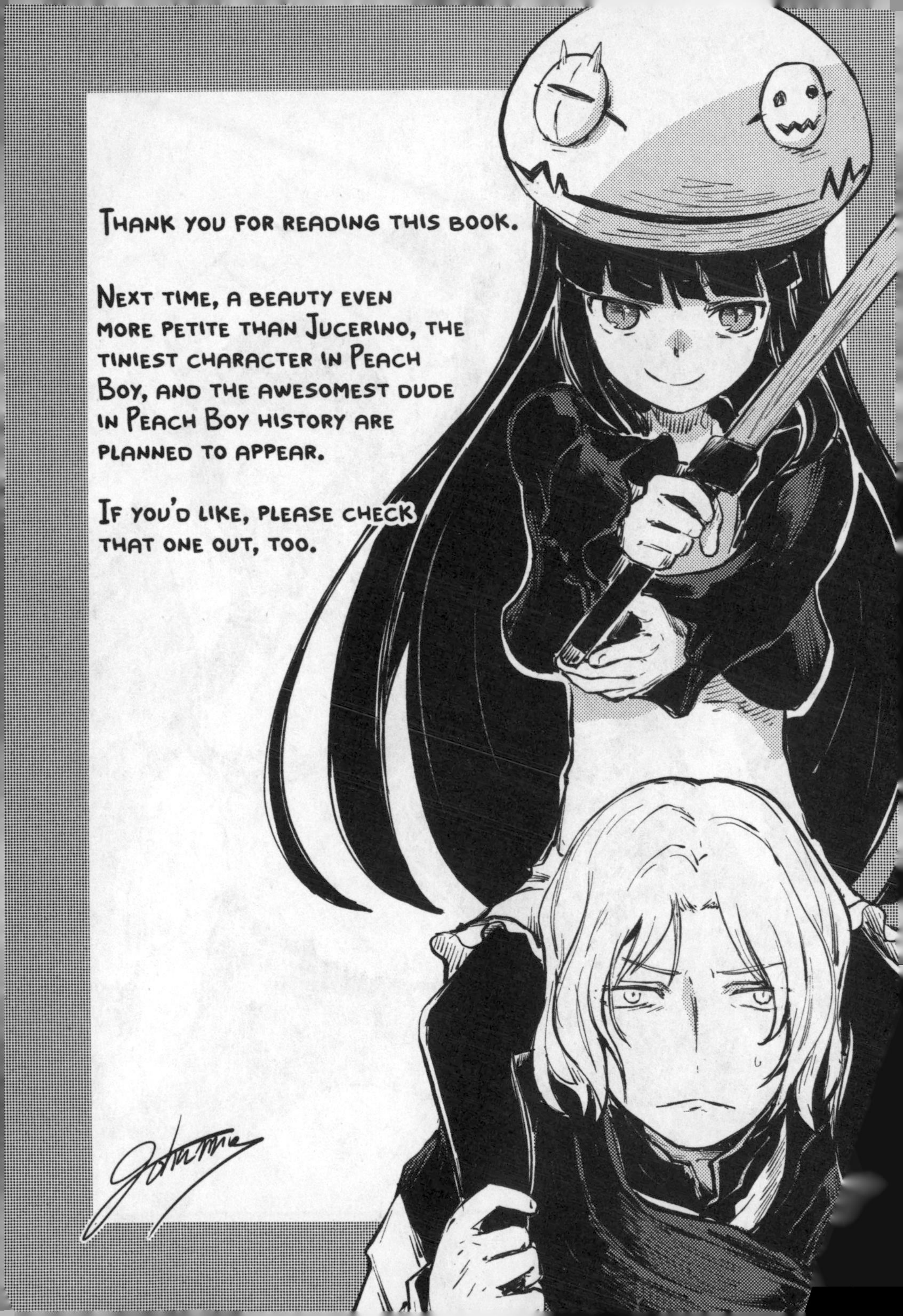
THANK YOU FOR READING THIS BOOK.
NEXT TIME, A BEAUTY EVEN MORE PETITE THAN JUCERINO, THE TINIEST CHARACTER IN PEACH BOY, AND THE AWESOMEST DUDE IN PEACH BOY HISTORY ARE PLANNED TO APPEAR.
IF YOU'D LIKE, PLEASE CHECK THAT ONE OUT, TOO.

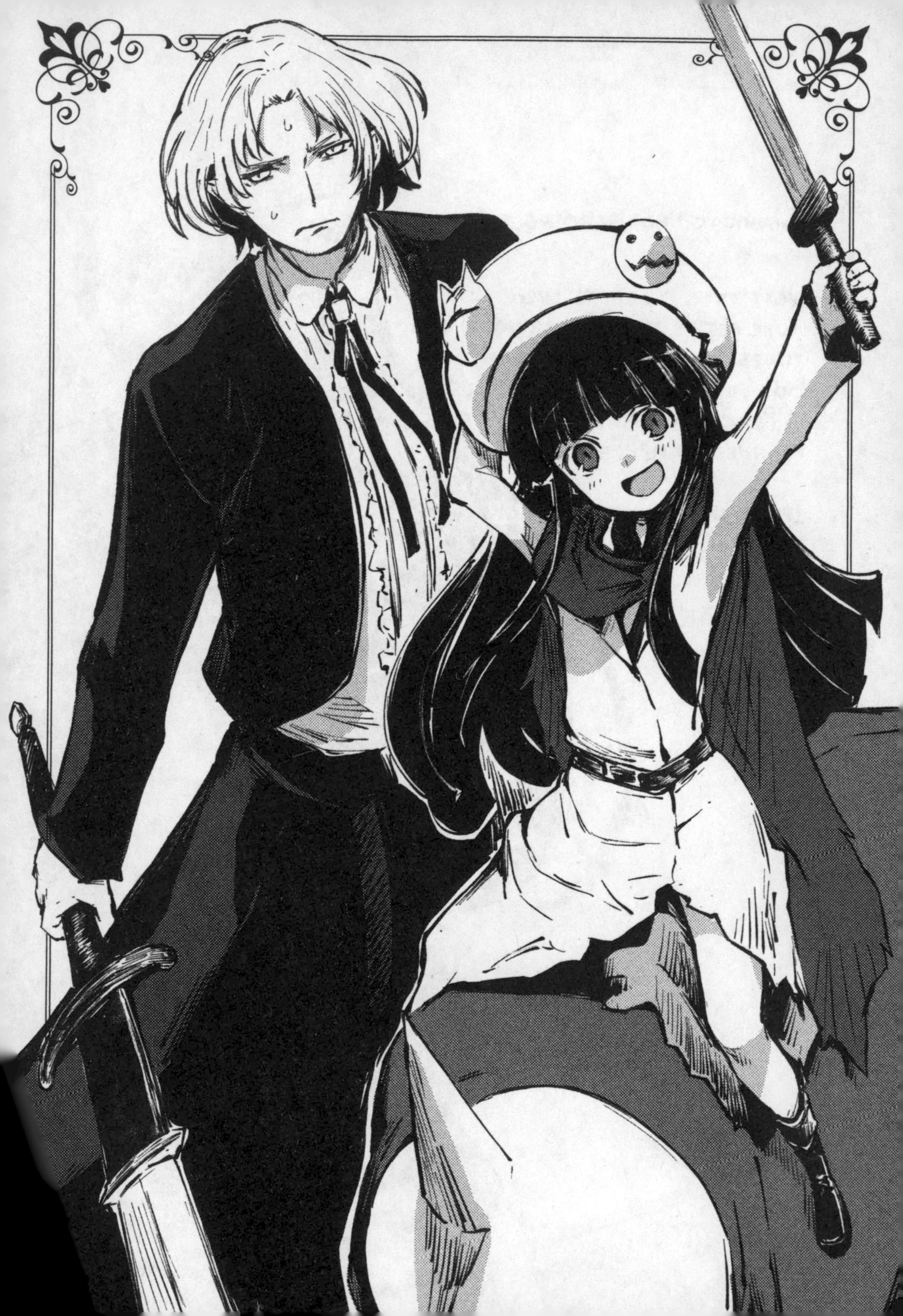

The afterlife sure is rambunctious...
Such a nuisance.

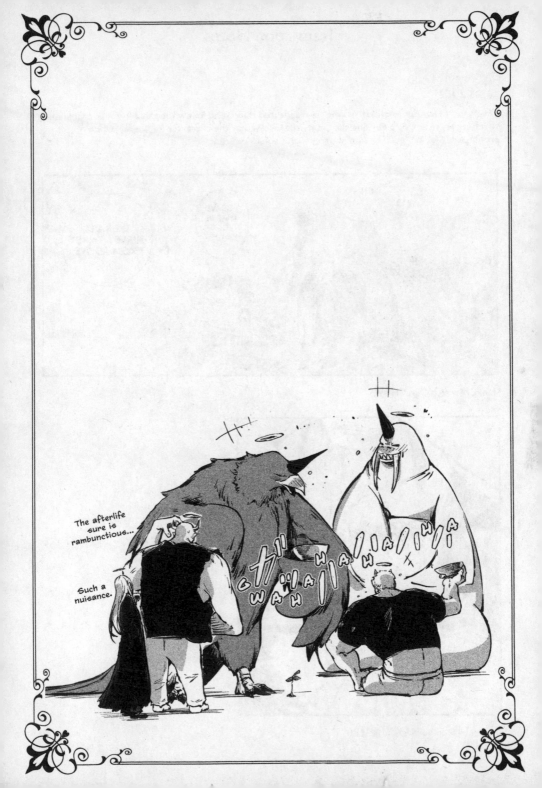

Translation Notes

Ogre names, pages 20, 21

The names of the humanoid ogres who have appeared thus far all follow the same formula: a Chinese character representing a defining characteristic, followed by the character for "ogre," which is pronounced "ki" or "gi." The named ogres in this volume were…

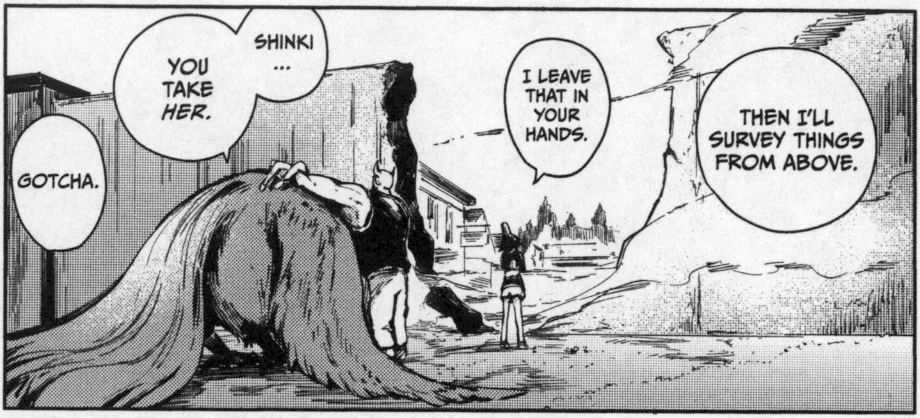

THEN I'LL SURVEY THINGS FROM ABOVE.
I LEAVE THAT IN YOUR HANDS.
SHINKI …
YOU TAKE *HER*.
GOTCHA.

Shinki: "Stretch Ogre" (**伸鬼**)

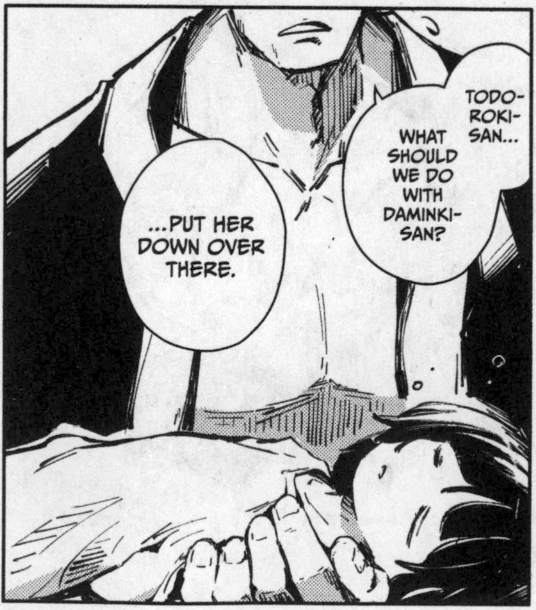

TODOROKI-SAN…
WHAT SHOULD WE DO WITH DAMINKI-SAN?
…PUT HER DOWN OVER THERE.

Daminki: "Slumber Ogre" (**惰眠鬼**)

PEACH BOY RIVERSIDE

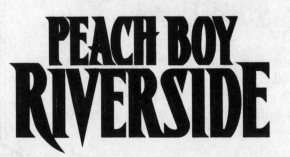

Young characters and steampunk setting, like *Howl's Moving Castle* and *Battle Angel Alita*

Beyond the Clouds © 2018 Nicke / Ki-oon

A boy with a talent for machines and a mysterious girl whose wings he's fixed will take you beyond the clouds! In the tradition of the high-flying, resonant adventure stories of Studio Ghibli comes a gorgeous tale about the longing of young hearts for adventure and friendship!

SAINT ☆ YOUNG MEN

A LONG AWAITED ARRIVAL IN PREMIUM 2-IN-1 HARDCOVER

After centuries of hard work, Jesus and Buddha take a break from their
heavenly duties to relax among the people of Japan, and their adventures in this
lighthearted buddy comedy are sure to bring mirth and merriment to all!

"Brilliant…the physical comedy
and facial expressions will
make you literally LOL."
—Sam Humphries
(host of *DC Daily*;
writer, *Green Lanterns,*
Legendary Star-Lord)

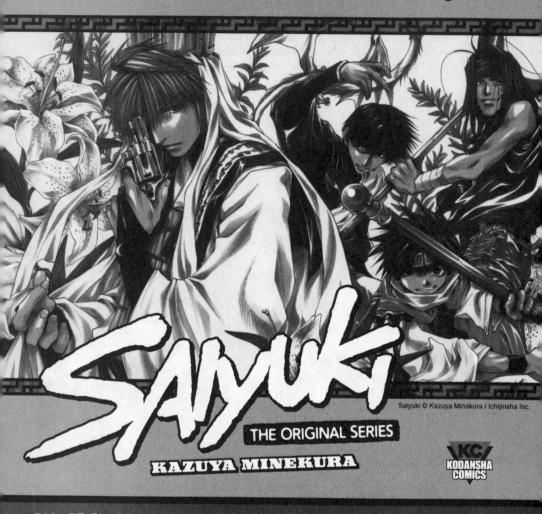

A Kodansha Comics Trade Paperback Original
Peach Boy Riverside 6 copyright © 2019 Coolkyousinnjya/Johanne
English translation copyright © 2022 Coolkyousinnjya/Johanne

Published in the United States by Kodansha Comics, an imprint of Kodansha USA Publishing, LLC, New York.

Publication rights for this English edition arranged through Kodansha Ltd., Tokyo.

First published in Japan in 2019 by Kodansha Ltd., Tokyo.

ISBN 978-1-64651-344-4

Original cover design by Tadashi Hisamochi (hive&co.,ltd.)

Printed in the United States of America.

www.kodansha.us

1st Printing
Translation: Steven LeCroy
Lettering: Andrew Copeland
Additional Lettering: Belynda Ungurath
Editing: Thalia Sutton, Maggie Le
YKS Services LLC/SKY Japan, Inc.
Kodansha Comics edition cover design by Matthew Akuginow
Kodansha Comics edition logo design by Adam Del Re

Publisher: Kiichiro Sugawara

Director of publishing services: Ben Applegate
Associate director of publishing operations: Stephen Pakula
Publishing services managing editors: Alanna Ruse, Madison Salters
Production managers: Emi Lotto, Angela Zurlo
Logo and character art ©Kodansha USA Publishing, LLC